THE HOME OF MEANING

The Hermeneutics of the Subject of Paul Ricoeur

John W. Van Den Hengel S.C.J.

UNIVERSITY
PRESS OF
AMERICA

Copyright © 1982 by

University Press of America, Inc.

P.O. Box 19101, Washington, D.C. 20036

Library of Congress Cataloging in Publication Data

Van Den Hengel, John W., 1939-
    The home of meaning.

    Thesis (doctoral)--Katholieke Universiteit of Nijmegen.
    Bibliography: p.
    Includes index.
    1. Ricoeur, Paul. 2. Subject (Philosophy)--History--
20th century. 3. Hermeneutics--History--20th century.
I. Title.
B2430.R554V36 1982   194   82-40204
ISBN 0-8191-2602-0
ISBN 0-8191-2603-9 (pbk.)

TABLE OF CONTENTS

Introduction.

> "The metaphor of the home is really 'a metaphor for metaphor: expropriation, being-away-from-home, but still in a home but in someone's home, a place of self-recovery, self-recognition, self-mustering, self-resemblance: it is itself. This philosophical metaphor as a detour in (or in view of) the reappropriation, the second coming, the self-presence of the idea in its light. A metaphorical journey from the Platonic eidos to the Hegelian Idea' "
>
> From: J. Derrida, "La mythologie blanche" in: P. Ricoeur, The Rule of Metaphor, p.289.

The conscious emergence of the human being as subject is central to the thrust of Western history. From Thomas Aquinas and the Nominalists through Leonardo da Vinci's discovery of perspective in painting and the exuberant celebration of humanism during the Renaissance period to Levi-Strauss' programme of the 'dissolution of man',[1] and Michel Foucault's sobering slogan of the death of the human subject in our time, the issue of human subjectivity has been dominant. Even though the 'haemorrhage of subjectivity' (Jean Beaufret) seems characteristic of our age, the concept of subjectivity holds modernity together to such an extent that it may be called the depth-movement of our time. Hegel attested to it in his famous aphorism, "substance is subject." And history subsequent to Hegel, while eschewing his mode of being as absolutist and idealistic, has not ceased to identify the truth and freedom of being with subjectivity.

This book, presented as a doctoral dissertation to the Katholieke Universiteit of Nijmegen, will examine Paul Ricoeur's position on the human subject. A number of reasons can be brought forward to justify the choice of this French philosopher. Few among contemporary philosophers listen as avidly to the mainstream of modern philosophy as Paul Ricoeur does. As a historian of philosophy he is acutely aware not only of the contribution the 'classical' philosophers have made to the shape of the world of our existence, but also of the contribution contemporary schools of philosophy are making. Indeed his philosophy takes the form of a history of philosophy. He reads existence and being through the texts of the great shapers of modern self-consciousness. To engage the philosophy of Paul Ricoeur is to insert oneself into the complex history of Western thought and to be enticed into a reading of that history from a perspective of hermeneutical phenomenology - a position that Ricoeur embraces even as an historian of philosophy - with a horizon open to positions that are, in reality, counterpositions. Accordingly,

---

1. La pensée sauvage, Paris, Plon, 1962, p.326-327.

the issue of human subjectivity offers itself as one of the central themes of Ricoeur's philosophy.

But secondly, it is specifically Ricoeur's own grounding in the phenomenology of Husserl and the subsequent expansion of this phenomenology into the area of hermeneutics that justifies our choice of Ricoeur. The philosophy of Husserl was not the original philosophical position of Ricoeur. His earliest influence was the thought of Gabriel Marcel. He was attracted to Marcel's approach to the mystery of being. Ricoeur's introduction to the 'existentialism' of Gabriel Marcel in 1934 coincided with the emergence of the existentialist movement in France. The French search for a 'concrete' philosophy in the 1930's provoked a revival of the works of Kierkegaard and introduced the works of Karl Jaspers[2] and the existentially interpreted Sein und Zeit of Heidegger into France. Ricoeur, however, was somewhat disenchanted with existentialism's lack of method. The search for a more disciplined thinking brought Ricoeur into contact with the works of Edmund Husserl, whose phenomenology was introduced into France at about the same time as existentialism.[3]

Husserl's phenomenology which is rooted in the movement of thought leading from Descartes by way of Kant, Hegel, and Fichte is the foremost contemporary statement of the transcendental subject. It is a philosophy that excludes the ontological question of being. Instead of asking the question of being, it seeks to relate the regions of reality such as things, animals, people, to the subjective processes of consciousness. In so doing it makes explicit that the appearance (phenomenon) of things is conditioned by the structures of human subjectivity. For that reason the subject is transcendental: the condition for the appearance of things.

---

2. Ricoeur made his own contribution to the existentialist movement when, as a prisoner of war during World War II, he collaborated with Mikel Defrenne on a commentary of Karl Jaspers entitled, Karl Jaspers et la philosophie de l'existence (préface by K. Jaspers, Paris, Seuil, 1947). After the war, while teaching the history of philosophy at the Collège Cévenol in Strasbourg, he wrote a book comparing Gabriel Marcel and Karl Jaspers (Gabriel Marcel et Karl Jaspers. Philosophie du mystère et philosophie du paradoxe. Paris, Temps présent, 1948). In the comparison Ricoeur is clearly more drawn to Marcel's mystery than to Jasper's paradox.

3. Ricoeur played a significant role in introducing Husserl's phenomenology to France. He is recognized as France's foremost interpreter of Husserl (See. H. Spiegelberg, The Phenomenological Movement, The Hague, Martinus Nijhoff, 1960, Vol.II, p.563-564). He translated and introduced Husserl's Ideen I (Idées directrices pour une phénoménologie (Bibliothèque de philosophie) Paris, Gallimard, 1950. Ricoeur's lengthy introduction is found from p. xi to xxxix). A collection of his articles on Husserl was translated and published in Husserl. An Analysis of His Phenomenology (Studies in Phenomenology and Existential Philosophy) translation and introduction by E.G. Ballard and L.E. Embree, Evanston, Northwestern University Press, 1967.

Despite Ricoeur's reservation and adaptations[4] Husserl's phenomenology has become the foundation to which he has anchored his philosophy. Ricoeur's positioning of the human subject takes its point of departure from Edmund Husserl's meditation on the transcendental subject. Ricoeur's radical critique of the transcendental subject remains incomprehensible unless one takes into account that he regards Husserl as the contemporary representative of the Cartesian heritage. Despite the fateful challenge of Structuralism or Semiology to phenomenology and the subsequent fading away of the subject in French philosophy into a silent presence, Ricoeur has not ceased to break that silence. His philosophy constantly reverts to its starting point in order to overcome it by redrawing the landscape of the human subject for our time.

But there is a third, more decisive, reason for turning to Ricoeur. Although Ricoeur's initial position was influenced by Husserl, his reading of the psychoanalytical theory of Sigmund Freud and of the works of Marx and Nietzsche - the philosophers of suspicion - and the sudden surfacing of Semiology in France forced him to radically rethink the Husserlian and Cartesian relationship between the subject and consciousness. Freud, Marx and Nietzsche propose that the subject's consciousness of him/herself is a false consciousness. Existence and thinking, according to these thinkers, do not enjoy an immediate presence to one another. This dissociation of the subject and consciousness - the subject is other than the immediate consciousness of him/herself - means in reality that the subject is not as primary and available a datum as Descartes' cogito suggests. The dissociation of subject and consciousness becomes, therefore, a dispossession and a dislocation of the subject. But, while such a painful breakdown of the subject's image of itself as a Promethean subject, could easily lead to nihilism, the disjointing of the subject and consciousness does not necessarily mean the death of the subject. Freud sought the relocation of the subject in a therapy of consciousness. Ricoeur, for his part, undertakes a prolonged study of the wounded subject in an effort to heal and recuperate the subject in our time.

To understand his effort, one must locate Ricoeur's philosophy within the horizon of France's philosophical trends because the latter frame his scope. Ricoeur belongs to the generation of French philosophers who received their philosophical schooling during the 1930's - one of the

---

4.   One needs to constantly qualify Ricoeur's phenomenology with labels such as existentialist or hermeneutical. In his effort to avoid the idealism of Husserl Ricoeur wishes to exercise phenomenology only as a methodical option. Whenever possible or necessary, he forces the phenomenological position to be confronted with non- or even anti-phenomenological counterpositions. For an analysis of Ricoeur's philosophical style see the very informative work of D. Ihde, Hermeneutic Phenomenology. The Philosophy of Paul Ricoeur, Evanston, Northwestern University Press, 1971.

watersheds of French philosophy.[5] Ricoeur's unique position is best examplified by his own masterful reading of the history of this century's French philosophy.[6] He perceives two trends in the early part of this century on the thorny issue of the subject's place in the world. Philosophers such as Lachelier, Lagneau, Alain and Brunschvicg, who were influenced by neo-Kantianism, gave a response that determined the subject's place in the world mainly on the basis of the activity of the intellect. Ricoeur calls the movement intellectualist.[7] The intellectualist trend believed that the power of the intellect and wisdom would secure the betterment of society. It instigated, for that reason, a broad reflection on the intellectual achievements of science and morality. The members of this movement superseded the narrow neo-Kantian epistemological concern by concentrating instead upon the activity of the spirit through which the achievements of science and morality were thought to come into being. In their analysis of the act of judgment as the core activity of the spirit they hoped to express not only the subject's proper identity but also to promote his/her well-being. Human life was said to be promoted by a proper attention to the intellectual heritage and to understanding and wisdom.

But his pre-World War II type of philosophy could not exorcise the destructive forces that threatened and almost destroyed Western civilization in this century. In France the intellectualist trend co-existed with another trend which, for want of a better term, Ricoeur calls interiorist.[8] The interiorist trend asked a new question about the human subject. It looked for a source or the ground of the subject as it surfaces in feelings, thoughts and aspirations. But in Bergson's philosophy the interiorist trend refuses or fails to link up with the intellectualist trend and almost, therefore, sinks into irrationalism.

---

5.   Vincent Descombes' history of French philosophy says that the period between 1930 and 1945 was dominated by the three H's: Hegel, Husserl and Heidegger. All three are present in Ricoeur's philosophy with a preponderant presence of Husserl. Heidegger had not yet exerted much influence upon Ricoeur. The Heidegger that was being propagated in France was the existentially interpreted Heidegger of Sein und Zeit. Ricoeur's work also attests to the shift in perspective that took place between 1945 and 1960 when the three masters of suspicion, Marx, Nietzsche, and Freud dominated philosophical discourse. After 1960 semiology held centre-stage. See Modern French Philosophy, Cambridge, Cambridge University Press, 1980.

6.   See Ricoeur's "L'humanité de l'homme. Contribution de la philosophie française contemporaine" in Studium Generale 15, 1962, p.309-323.

7.   Idem, p.310.

8.   Idem, p.313.

xii

In a similar vein post-war Existentialism's search for human existence is fundamentally anti-intellectualist. Schooled in Hegel's analysis of the negative dimensions of life such as struggle, conflict, and contradiction, existentialist philosophers sought to incorporate the tragic dimension of existence that had become so tangible in the first half of this century in their philosophy. But the failure to mediate between intellectualism and interiority, between judgment and life, between truth and existence, remained the weakness of Existentialism.

In Ricoeur's opinion Jean Nabert was the only French philosopher who succeeded in mediating these antithetical trends. Nabert did not dissociate truth and existence. Existence, according to Nabert, is a journey of meaning that is guided by an original act whose meaning humans seek to recuperate without ever succeeding in doing so. On the one hand, by positing an origin that is an act and not a consciousness or a judgment, Nabert stands on the side of interiority; on the other hand, by arguing that the originary act exteriorizes itself in signs and hence becomes subject to analysis, Nabert counters the irrationalism that threatened the philosophy of life and existentialism. Nabert's humanism accentuated the human desire to be and its mission - and its failure - to live up to this affirmation and desire at the root of human existence.

Ricoeur was greatly influenced by Nabert's view of existence and being as the act of becoming and as the process of freedom. In seeking to be faithful to Nabert's achievement, he veers away from the theory of perception that dominates Husserl's phenomenology and seeks instead to bend the Husserlian intentionality analysis into a tool for investigating the structures and activity of the will. As a result, Ricoeur's phenomenology is not first of all a phenomenology of perception but a philosophy of the will which makes use of Husserl's intentionality analysis and the époché. The recovery and healing of the subject is not achieved by an intellectual or theoretical activity but through a healing of the will and of freedom. It takes place in a practical philosophy. This priority of praxis over theory remains a hallmark of Ricoeur's philosophy.[9] To seek for a new basis of humanism in the will is not to say, however, that the will has an immediate access to the root of being and of existence. The dictum that one must first lose oneself before one finds oneself prevails. The will too must undergo a despoliation similar to that of consciousness in order for the subject to be truly healed.

In the context of this philosophy of the will Ricoeur proposes that the fullest recovery of the subject lies in what he calls a 'poetics of the

---

9. Despite the numerous detours into more theoretical areas such as his analysis of the theory of discourse and the theory of the text and related matters, they remain detours. The practical dimension of his philosophy laid out in his earliest works has not been discarded. Ricoeur's philosophy remains a philosophy of the will and of freedom.

will', [10] in a radical origin of the 'I will'. This poetics of the will encompasses two basic dimensions which more than any others reveal the originality of Ricoeur's ontology of subjectivity. They are the relationship between freedom and evil and the relationship between freedom and transcendence. If Ricoeur laid the groundwork for a dialectic of freedom and nature in the first volume of his La philosophie de la volonté,[11] in the two-volume second part of this Philosophie de la volonté I. L'homme faillible[12] and II. La symbolique du mal[13] he began his engrossing study of the relationship between freedom and evil. In the experience of evil, he insists, the subject experiences his/her freedom both in the discovery of a freedom that could and should be other than it is (the dream of innocence amidst a guilty existence) and in the recognition that human freedom is a freedom in bondage. But this discovery would be groundless, according to Ricoeur, without an affirmation of transcendence. The self whose freedom is weighted down and made powerless by sin is a self that can be healed. Ricoeur proposes that the healing of the broken freedom of the subject, i.e., the recovery of the subject, is the gift of Transcendence, of God.

Accordingly the dislocation of the subject is not only a cognitive process but equally a cultural, historical event that encounters us as the drama of evil and sin. But this practical dispossession, Ricoeur maintains, is only comprehensible in the face of a more original situation that speaks to us either of innocence or of a healing of our freedom. Ricoeur views this positing of an eschaton of freedom as the final measure of the subject. The subject's effort to be source of him/herself and of his/her freedom is disrupted most radically by Transcendence. Ricoeur insists that for freedom to be healed, freedom must live as a gifted freedom.

Ricoeur refuses, therefore, to accept the Sartrean nothingness or void in answer to the contemporary failure of freedom and to the demons of our time. By taking up again the Judaeo-Christian tradition of the symbols and myths of evil and redemption, he injects a dimension of hope into humanism.

That certainly is the ultimate reason for choosing Ricoeur in our analysis of the present state of the human subject. His poetics of the will proposes to be a conjuring up of the world as created.[14] This injection of

---

10. The philosophical project which is to lead up to his "poetics of the will" was announced in his doctoral dissertation, La philosophie de la volonté. I. Le volontaire et l'involontaire (Philosophie de l'esprit) Paris, Aubier, 1950, p. 30. To date this project has not yet been completed, although the basic contours of such a 'poetics' have begun to emerge.

11. Op. cit.

12. (Philosophie de l'esprit) Paris, Aubier, 1960.

13. (Philosophie de l'esprit) Paris, Aubier, 1960.

14. La philosophie de la volonté. I. Le volontaire et l'involontaire, op. cit., p.30.

the Name of God and of Jesus of Nazareth into a schema of hope is worth examining in a time, characterized by L. Althusser, as a time of anti-humanism.

This third reason is also the major reason Ricoeur's treatment of the recovery of the subject is of interest not only to the philosopher but also to the theologian. The issue of Christian faith is never far removed from his works. He was raised in the Protestant faith and even before he started his philosophical studies he had received a less than tasty dose of Karl Barth's theology. As H. Spiegelberg reports, Ricoeur was at first repelled by the Barthian _Krisis_ theology.[15] But that distaste did not seem to affect his conviction that a philosopher may not shunt aside his insertion in a faith tradition. Gabriel Marcel, in whose thought, Ricoeur admits, he first found himself set him an example.[16] Marcel did not hide his Christian convictions in his philosophy. Moreover, Ricoeur was very active in the movement of 'Christianisme social' and belonged and still belongs to the circle of friends of Emmanuel Mounier, the great Christian personalist.[17] The Christian faith and its articulation in the text of the Bible have been for him sources that give rise to thinking. Thus, for example, in his philosophy of the subject the Pauline teaching of the justification by faith is the highest expression of the recovery of the subject as gift and creation.

In recent years Ricoeur's philosophy has generated a considerable interest among theologians, particularly in North America.[18] This is due partly because of his sensitive reading of the symbols and myths of evil and salvation, partly also because of his proposal for a theological hermeneutics as an extension - or more accurately, an inversion - of his philosophical hermeneutics.

But, despite the warm reception theologians have given Ricoeur's philosophy because of his treatment of issues close to their heart, it would be wrong to qualify Ricoeur as a theologian. He insists that he is a

---

15. Op. cit., p.569.

16. P. Ricoeur, "My Relation to the History of Philosophy" in The Iliff Review 35, 1978, p.6.

17. See Ricoeur's "Une philosophie personaliste" (E. Mounier) in Esprit 18, 1950, p. 860-887.

18. Ricoeur's hermeneutics of the sacred text and his analysis of the confession of evil have attracted the attention of a number of theologians. See for instance B. McDermott, "The Theology of Original Sin: Recent Developments" in Th.St., 38, 1977, p. 478-512; G. Vandervelde, Original Sin. Two Major Trends in Contemporary Roman Catholic Reinterpretations, Amsterdam, Ropodi, 1975; J. Boonen, "Erfzonde of mysterie van het kwaad" in Collationes 72, 1976, p. 289-311. Ricoeur's influence on North-American theologians is most in evidence in the Chicago Cluster, and among such theologians as David Tracy, David Pellauer, Mary Gerhart, and J.D. Crossan.

philosopher, and that he reads existence as a believing philosopher. Only on a few occasions does Ricoeur step across the boundary between philosophy and proclamation.[19] But those occasions are clearly intended transgressions which do not jeopardize his standing as a philosopher.

Nor does Ricoeur's philosophy make philosophy into a new _ancilla_ of theology. The relationship between theology and philosophy is more complex. It can be approached from the perspective of content and form.

On the level of content it can be maintained that both a theology of justification and a poetics of the will seek one and the same healing of the subject. Ricoeur's poetics of the will and a theology of justification derive their thrust from the same source, namely, the biblical text. Moreover, the underlying interest of both is contiguous. The interest of a poetics of the will is practical and emancipatory. It seeks the liberation of the subject in transcendence or the sacred. The interest of a theology of justification which proclaims the God who justifies us in Christ Jesus is also practical and emancipatory. It proclaims salvation and freedom despite sin and death. This unity of the ultimate ground out of which one lives and out of which one reflects as a theologian and as a believing philosopher may be maintained without papering over the equally radical discontinuity that persists between the two. For theology reflects on the proclamation of its faith in a Saviour God as the hope of human existence, while a philosophical approach to this ground of existence can do no more than examine the reasonableness of the claims of the hope of the subject. But a philosophical hope is a hope without recourse. Ricoeur himself can ultimately do no more than search out a philosophical approximation of a hope for which there is no answering proclamation of a God who sets free our freedom. In itself this is, of course, a considerable achievement - and of interest to fundamental theology - but it serves as a warning not to confuse the lines

---

19. See for example, "The Logic of Jesus: the Logic of God" in Anglican Theological Review 62, 1980, p. 37-41; and "La logique de Jésus: Romains 5" in Et.théol. et rel., 55, 1980, p.420-425. Ricoeur's selection of proclamation as his basic theological paradigm is clearly inspired by the Reformed tradition. He rejects a theological paradigm, whose objective it is to manifest, to make epiphanous, charging with J. Moltmann that such a model is more Greek than Hebrew. See his "Manifestation et proclamation" in Le Sacré. Études et recherches. Actes du colloque organisé par le centre international d'études humanistes et par l'institut d'études philosophiques de Rome, edited by E. Castelli, Paris, Aubier, 1974, p.57-76. The model based on religion as epiphany corresponds more closely to the Roman Catholic paradigm of theology. This confirms the adherence of Ricoeur to the Reformed tradition in which he was brought up and his continued reservations about the Roman Catholic tradition. In one of his earlier reflections he stated with all due nuances that Catholic theology proposes a reason that precedes faith. See his "Le renouvellement du problème de la philosophie chrétienne par les philosophies de l'existence" in Le problème de la philosophie chrétienne (Les problèmes de la pensée chrétienne) edited by J. Boisset, Paris, P.U.F. 1949, p.48.

between philosophy and theology.

On the level of form the continuity and discontinuity between theology and philosophy are equally delicate. Although Ricoeur's grounding philosophy remains phenomenology, his interaction with the philosophies of language and with the philosophies of suspicion shift his phenomenology towards a hermeneutical phenomenology. It is on the level of hermeneutics that philosophy and theology encounter one another. Thus we can ask, to what extent a theological hermeneutics of the biblical text follows the form of a philosophical hermeneutics of the same text. Both a theological and a philosophical hermeneutics share an interest in a generalized theory of discourse which examines the properties of identification and predication, sense and reference, structural analysis, and the capacity of language to enunciate being. Both hermeneutical styles struggle with the issue of explanation and understanding, and of distanciation and appropriation. A theological hermeneutics cannot bypass a general theory of hermeneutics which Ricoeur defines as "an inquiry about the art of understanding involved in the interpretation of texts."[20]

Yet despite this similarity, theological hermeneutics is not just one hermeneutics alongside other hermeneutical enterprises. The intense concentration of theological hermeneutics upon the Name of God that draws all the biblical texts to itself gives a unique and privileged position to theological hermeneutics withdrawing it from the aegis of philosophical hermeneutics. God's Name re-organizes the whole field in such a manner that the general hermeneutics becomes an organon of the theological.[21] Although this inversion of the relationship of theological and philosophical hermeneutics operates under a unique organizing principle, it does not remove the theological hermeneutics from a general philosophy of language and of hermeneutics.

This interlacing of form and content has also determined the form and content of my analysis of Ricoeur. Although I seek to determine the outcome of the human subject in the philosophy of Paul Ricoeur in the face of the proclamations of the death of the subject, I can only do so by retracing the long route which Ricoeur is constrained to take to back up his contention of a recovery of the human subject. The route of Ricoeur - and as a consequence it might appear also to be so of this book - seems interminable. That is perhaps the ultimate drawback of Ricoeur's approach. The process of a hermeneutical phenomenology is without outcome because it operates with a Kantian limit-concept or with an indefinite postponement of the ultimate recovery of the subject. This could well leave it open to the charge that it weighs itself down with an impossible aim, because a never-ending journey to the promised land of the subject could ultimately lead

---

20. "Philosophical Hermeneutics and Theological Hermeneutics" in Studies in Religion/Sciences religieuses 5, 1975, p.16.

21. Idem p.17.

nowhere. But before we examine the charge we must map the territory through which Ricoeur leads us in this never-to-be-completed journey.

The route to be covered is complex because it also involves an amount of backtracking and rerouting. In Chapter One there is a sketch of the grounding position of Husserlian phenomenology and the perceived need to move from a transcendental subjectivity of phenomenology towards a new transcendental in the form of language. Since the destabilizers of phenomenology were the Freudian psychoanalysis of the unconscious and Structuralism, their deconstruction will be briefly introduced. Chapter Two begins the arduous journey of the reconstruction of the subject by means of the theory of discourse and the text. It is, however, in part a detour because the theory of discourse and the text are part of the process whereby the subject is dispossessed before it can be found again. The theory of discourse and the theory of the text provide the structure or form which, according to Ricoeur, a new philosophy of the subject must recognize.

Chapter Three begins to explore the reference of the language of discourse and the language of the text. This world of the text is probed by means of an examination of the uniquely creative language of the metaphor and its ability to reach into the realm of the inexpressible. Since the home of the subject is located in this realm, the power of the poetic and the role of the imagination are introduced.

Chapter Four takes account of the methodological repercussions of the previous chapters. If meaning and the subject must be sought in what is prior to language and sees the light of day in symbolic and poetic language, their emergence will be a hermeneutical exercise. This calls for a presentation of the larger tradition of contemporary hermeneutics indelibly stamped by the contributions of Friedrich Schleiermacher, Wilhelm Dilthey, Martin Heidegger and Hans-Georg Gadamer. Ricoeur's own hermeneutical style incorporates the intentions of that hermeneutical tradition and resolves some of its more critical impasses.

Chapter Five and Chapter Six extend the examination of the ontology which hermeneutics explores. Chapter Five proposes the temporal dimension of meaning and of the subject by an examination of the symbol, the myth and the fictional and historical narrative. Chapter Six shows that there is also an ethical dimension to the recovery of the subject. Ricoeur's ontology is not to be limited to the level of perception but must be extended to the realm of praxis.

Chapter Seven applies the phenomenological dictum that all understanding is in the final analysis self-understanding. It examines the process of appropriation of the world of the text to which the hermeneutical exercise leads.

The final two chapters present Ricoeur's philosophy of religion as a hermeneutics of hope. If transcendence extends true subjectivity to us, a hermeneutics of the sacred text of the bible is the avenue open to the realization of our true freedom. Keeping in mind that the final text of the poetics of the will has not as yet been written, we follow Ricoeur's own delicate extension of the Kantian philosophy of religion within the bounds of reason to his proposal of a subjectivity that is the gift of a God who justified us in Christ Jesus.[22]

The genre of interpretation that this work presents can best be described as a sympathetic reading of Ricoeur. It does not pretend to judge Ricoeur's work from some higher perspective nor to locate him critically among this contemporaries. In sympathy with the aim and the execution of the aim, I have read Ricoeur in order to understand him. And it is this understanding of his text that I here propose. In organizing the massive material of Ricoeur's writings, I have relied almost exclusively upon the writings of what might be called the second phase that began after his work on Freud.[23] The material prior to 1965 has been incorporated to the extent that it has a bearing upon his linguistic philosophy of the second phase. The shift between the first and second stages of Ricoeur's philosophy was not radical. It was largely a methodological shift. It did not affect his basic aim of producing a philosophy of the will. This work attests to the continuity and traces the extensive detour that Ricoeur had to undertake in order to realize his original project.

The difficulty one faces in a reading of Ricoeur's philosophy is compounded by the fact that Ricoeur has written relatively few books. Outside of the books written during the early part of his philosophical career,[24] all other works are either compilations of articles or the result of lectures or seminars.[25] The articles and lectures found elsewhere were

---

22. The basic structure of the more philosophical part of my analysis is suggested by Ricoeur himself in a number of articles. In the article "Philosophical Hermeneutics and Theological Hermeneutics" op. cit. Ricoeur draws the parallels between a philosophical hermeneutics and a theological hermeneutics by drawing on the four characteristics of a general hermeneutics. These are (1) the theory of discourse and of the text, (2) the text as production (composition, genre, style), (3) the world of the text as the object of hermeneutics, (4) the appropriation of the world of the text: to understand oneself before the text. Similarly, the outline of this book summarizes the first two categories in Chapter Two, the third category (the world of the text) in Chapter Three to Chapter Six, and the final category in Chapter Seven. The same outline of a general hermeneutics is given in Interpretation Theory: Discourse and the Surplus of Meaning, Fort Worth, The Texas Christian University Press, 1976.

23. De l'interprétation. Essai sur Freud (L'ordre philosophique) Paris, Seuil, 1965.

24. Gabriel Marcel et Karl Jaspers; Philosophie du mystère et philosophie du paradoxe, op. cit. and the first two parts of his Philosophie de la volonté, op. cit.

25. Thus, for example, De l'interprétation. Essai sur Freud, (op. cit.) grew out of the Terry Lectures which Ricoeur gave at Yale University in

generated by specific occasions to which Ricoeur was invited to contribute. As he himself acknowledges, this type of occasional writing hardly permits one to provide a genetic construct of his philosophical project.[22]

I have called my reading of Ricoeur a sympathetic reading. It is not a critically analytic reading precisely because all the building blocks of a poetics of the will are not yet in place. Two points, however, must be made. First of all, it is of some importance to note Ricoeur's specific way of being a philosopher of history. His articles and lectures often take the method of an architectonic reading of a number of authors in which each author contributes to the total structure by the questions they resolve but also leave unanswered. It is a philosophical method dear to existentialist phenomenology. Although Ricoeur's approach is not as negative as, for example, Merleau-Ponty's so that it could be characterized as a 'neither-nor' philosophy (it is neither this nor that), he constructs his case with positions and counterpositions. The challenge of counterpositions affects his own position to such an extent that a solution 'between the two' is proposed. For Ricoeur this is part of his struggle against Hegelian absolutism. Ricoeur is after a finite synthesis: a synthesis that is never complete and ever precarious because of the possibility of further erosion by subsequent positions. A critical examination of Ricoeur's reading of these authors is hardly possible in the context of this work, and, except for his more extensive analysis of such authors as Sigmund Freud, hardly fruitful. Of greater significance is how his reading of these authors stimulates the construction of his own view of existence and being. The other authors are not proof texts but rather historical moments into which Ricoeur inserts himself for the sake of understanding and self-understanding.

Secondly, this work is not meant to be a critique of the total project. It is true that one could contest the approach both of phenomenology and hermeneutics. Has Ricoeur avoided the pitfall of the absolute subject of phenomenology through the diversion of the hermeneutics of the subject? Is his return to the Aristotelian concept of being - being is said in many ways - sufficiently sensitive to the contemporary concern for identity and difference? Does his proposal of the subject as gift sufficiently counteract and resolve the critique of the subject of other thinkers? Does his project succeed? I have not attempted to answer these questions. These are matters of philosophical concern. As a theologian I have chosen to listen to a philosopher who as a philosopher has listened to the texts of faith. His attentiveness and the manner of his reading of the texts of faith for the sake of human liberation are of themselves worth interpreting in a continuous text.

1961. Le conflit des interprétations (Essais d'herméneutique (L'ordre philosophique) Paris, Seuil, 1969) is a compilation of articles written in the 1960's or given as conferences during that time. La métaphore vive (L'ordre philosophie) Paris, Seuil, 1975) grew out of a seminar given at the University of Toronto in 1971.

To avoid an excessive number of footnotes I have chosen to insert references into the text itself. By numbering the books and articles of Ricoeur chronologically and indicating the texts used in each chapter at the beginning of the chapter, I have reduced the number of footnotes and permitted the reader to perceive at which stage of Ricoeur's philosophy a particular text was written.

CHAPTER ONE: THE CARTESIAN HERITAGE.

Bibliography.

12.	Gabriel Marcel et Karl Jaspers. Philosophie du mystère et philosophie du paradoxe (1948).
53.	"Méthodes et tâches d'une phénoménologie de la volonté" (1952).
76.	"Étude sur les méditations Cartésiennes de Husserl" (1954).
108.	"Phénoménologie existentielle" (1957).
153.	La symbolique du mal (1960).
185.	"L'acte et le signe selon Jean Nabert" (1962).
186.	"L'humanité de l'homme" (1962).
190.	"Préface" in J. Nabert, Éléments pour une éthique (1962).
191.	"Herméneutique et réflexion" (1962).
214.	"Technique et nontechnique dans l'interprétation" (1964).
216.	"Le symbolisme et l'explication structurale" (1964).
227.	De l'interprétation. Essai sur Freud (1965).
228.	"La psychanalyse et le mouvement de la culture contemporaine" (1965).
229.	"Existence et herméneutique" (1965).
243.	"Le conscient et l'inconscient" (1966).
246.	"Une interprétation philosophique de Freud" (1966).
263.	Husserl. An Analysis of His Phenomenology (1967).
264.	"Philosophy of Will and Action" (1967).
275.	"La structure, le mot, l'événement" (1967).
278.	"New Developments in Phenomenology in France: The Phenomenology of Language" (1967).
283.	Entretiens Paul Ricoeur - Gabriel Marcel (1968).
320.	Le conflit des interprétations (1969).
345.	"Problèmes actuels de l'interprétation" (1970).
371.	"From Existentialism to the Philosophy of Language" (1971).
374.	"Cours sur l'herméneutique" (1971).
375.	"The Problem of the Will and Philosophical Discourse" (1971).
378.	"Signe et sens" (1972).
386.	"Herméneutique et critique des idéologies" (1973).
392.	Tragic Wisdom and Beyond (1973).
398.	"Phénoménologie et herméneutique" (1974).
399.	"Hegel aujourd'hui" (1974).
420.	"Gabriel Marcel et la phénoménologie" (1976).
426.	"Entre Gabriel Marcel et Jean Wahl" (1976).
438.	"Herméneutique et l'idée de révélation" (1977).
451.	"My Relation to the History of Philosophy" (1978).
475.	"Herméneutique et sémiotique" (1980).

The isolation of the human subject from its environment and its emergence in the loneliness of doubt and in the clarity of its self-assertion found its first celebrated meditation in the philosophy of René Descartes. Descartes' methodical doubt and the search for a new certainty placed the

1

subject and the problem of subjectivity at the center of the modern philosophical project. For Ricoeur, the Cartesian cogito is the starting point of modern philosophy which has not yet been surpassed. And in a number of ways, he insists, this historical moment is not to be overcome. For him the Cartesian cogito is an indelible moment in the history of the emergence of being (375:285-286). And yet he also recognizes that a new relationship to the subject must be instituted in our time. This problematic pursues Ricoeur in all his writings.[1] In his earliest writings - he admits until his La symbolique du mal (153) - he had not yet liberated himself from the unique hold that Descartes' cogito has had upon Western consciousness and praxis (438:27). With La symbolique du mal and more consciously with De l'interprétation. Essai sur Freud (227) the hold is broken and Ricoeur begins the struggle against the vanity of the Cartesian heritage in earnest. It is this struggle of Ricoeur that we wish to record.[2]

Descartes' cogito, or, more to the point, his dubito was intended to be the first, indubitable truth of the I am. Descartes said of this truth that it was a conscious experience, and that its consciousness provided immediate certainty of the truth of the cogito. That it is a truth and a certainty can hardly be doubted. But, as Ricoeur says of it,

> (It) is a truth as vain as it is invincible... It is a truth which posits itself, and as such it can be neither verified nor deduced. It posits at once a being and an act, an existence and an operation of thought: I am, I think; to exist for me, is to think; I exist insofar as I think (320(229):17).

As a first truth this is an empty truth. It presupposes that the certainty of the cogito is also the truth of my consciousness. It also presupposes, therefore, that I am in immediate and certain possession of my consciousness. Existence is the thought and the consciousness of my existence. The I am is a truth, however, that posits itself. It is immediately and intuitively reflective. The I am follows ineluctably from the I think. This self-positing of the I am is reflection.

---

1. Cf. A. Lavers, "Man, Meaning and Subject. A Current Reappraisal" in J. Brit. Soc. Phenomenol. 1, 1970, p.44-49; J. Lacroix, "Un philosophe du sens: P. Ricoeur" in Panorama de la philosophie française contemporaine, Paris, Presses Universitaires de France, 1966.

2. For a more detailed analysis of the early stages of Paul Ricoeur's philosophical itinerary see especially the very helpful work of D. Ihde, Hermeneutic Phenomenology. The Philosophy of Paul Ricoeur. Evanston, Northwestern University Press, 1971. See also D. Vansina, "Schets, orientatie en betekenis van Paul Ricoeurs wijsgerige onderneming" in Tijdschr. Filos. 25, 1963, p.109-178 (Summary p.178-182); D. Rasmussen, Mythic-Symbolic Language and Philosophical Anthropology. A Constructive

Now, it cannot be doubted that the cogito provides a certain evidence about the ego of the cogito. But one can hardly call this evidence and certainty a truth that can function as the starting-point of philosophy. The cogito gives no more than, what Kant would call, an apperception of myself and my acts. As Malebranche realized, this apperception is only a feeling and not an idea. I feel that I exist and that I think; I form no idea about the I of that existence and thinking. Kant recognized that such a feeling, this apperception, of the ego can accompany all my representations, but that does not mean that I have arrived at self-knowledge. In other words, reflection is not intuitive. The I that I feel is not an I that I know intuitively (320(191):329).

Whatever our present reservations, it is the Cartesian cogito that set the groundwork for the subjective tradition of Continental European philosophy. With Kant, in particular, the self-knowledge of the ego that accompanies all my representations is subjected to the critique of reason. The reflection, which in Descartes' philosophy is still intuitive, Kant draws into his epistemological concern. He elaborated the a priori structures of human knowledge upon which he founded the objectivity of the representations.

A. THE PHENOMENOLOGICAL OPTION.

While Descartes' privileged access to existence is the cogito, thinking, Husserl and the phenomenological tradition does not ask the question of existence and being except by way of a consideration of perception. While Descartes supposed that there is an immediate and intuitive access to existence, phenomenology inserts its famous époché between being and the subject. It acknowledges the validity of Kant's critique of the availability of the object in itself (Ding-an-sich) and insists that the question to ask is how reality relates to the subjective processes of consciousness. As a consequence the issue of being becomes the issue of its being-for-me.

That is also Ricoeur's initial position. Unlike the French phenomenologist Merleau-Ponty who referred mainly to the later Husserl, Ricoeur based himself on a reading of the early Husserl, the Husserl of Ideen I and Ideen II and of the Cartesian Meditations (320(229):17;398:224). Ricoeur justifies his own procedure by arguing that there is no radical break but rather a fundamental continuity between the early and later Husserl (263(54):115).[3] The early works of Husserl expressed the basic response of phenomenology to the issue of the subject in a more radical fashion than his

Interpretation of the Thought of Paul Ricoeur, The Hague, Nijhoff, 1971, p.24-111; P. Bourgeois, Extension of Ricoeur's Hermeneutic, The Hague, Nijhoff, 1975, p.10-127; R. Bergeron, La vocation de la liberté dans la philosophie de Paul Ricoeur, Montréal, Les éditions Bellarmin, Freiburg, Éditions universitaires, 1974, p.17-116.

3.   Cf. H. Spiegelberg, op. cit., p.564.

later writings. Ricoeur, at any rate, saw in Husserl's philosophy a radicalization of the Cartesian cogito, in which the theme of the cogito is transformed into a science and becomes the ground of all science.

Let us briefly examine how Ricoeur interprets Husserl's philosophy of the subject which he has assumed rather curiously as a point of departure that he consistently seeks to dislodge. Husserl's phenomenology is grounded in the transcendental subject to the point that it is in fact an egology. In the words of Ricoeur,

> This is a philosophy where being not only never gives the force of reality to the object, but above all never founds the reality of the ego itself. Thus, as an egology it is a cogito without a "res cogitans". (263(76):84)

The ultimate foundation of Husserl's philosophy is not reality or being. They recede behind a fog that so obscures them that they never re-appear except in the faintest outline. The real foundation is the ego, the subject. For that reason, Husserl's ego is an originary ego, a transcendental ego.

Husserl does not go so far, however, as to admit to the coincidence of the subject's consciousness and this world for me. In his Crisis he gives this world in me the name of Lebenswelt. In his Cartesian Meditations, the originary ego, if not identified with consciousness, is found at least within the realm of experience. And as an experience the cogito can be probed. What Husserl was after in his transcendental phenomenology is an elaboration of this experience toward the structure of the cogito. Reality is reduced to its performance in the ego.

Husserl's egology cut itself off from ontology by way of the époché. The methodological procedure of the époché is never cancelled to re-open the ontological thrust. While Descartes has grounded the ego in a higher reality, namely, the veracity of God and retained an ontological strain by positing the ego cogitans as an ens creatum, Husserl has no such recourse. In an egology without an ontology, the only measure of objectivity can lie in intersubjectivity inasmuch as the other is another I. Although meaning's source remains the subject, because of the apodictic evidence of the cogito, the link with the Other as another I is to guarantee its objectivity (263(76):90).

But what sort of a subject is promoted by this type of egology of transcendental phenomenology?

1. The ego is the final justification of all objectivity. The ego is the quest for the ultimate foundation of human knowledge and activity. It is the foundation that is autonomous and without presupposition. For Husserl this foundation lies in the field of experience; it has a certain relationship to the order of perception - of seeing. It is not a speculative construction, but the foundational ego is an Erfahrungsfeld. And whatever procedures might be used to uncover the structure of this Erfahrungsfeld such as the

transcendental époché, or the imaginative variations of my own life, the cogito remains in the sight of an experience (398:224-225).

2. This foundational ego is an idealistic ego. For Husserl, according to Ricoeur, the height of intuition, the place where intuition is most complete, is subjectivity. Subjectivity is not doubtful. In consequence, every transcendence is said to be doubtful while only immanence is indubitable (398:225). Since transcendence comes only in sketches or profiles, one can easily be deceived. But immanence does not operate with profiles, but allows a coincidence of reflection with what is lived. This subjectivity is not the empirical consciousness that can be investigated by psychology, but a transcendental subject, available only to philosophy (398:226). For Ricoeur, this is the core of Husserl's idealism.

3. This work of reflection, whereby I become conscious of myself, also has ethical implications, for it is an act that is immediately responsible for itself. The ethical dimension is immediately bound up with the foundational act (398:226-227).

4. The subject does not have an ontological depth. The subject is perceived as self-positing and as responsible to itself. This subject without an ontology is grounded only in itself and its act. The only equivalent to an ontology during this phase of Husserl's philosophy is his consideration of the Other in the establishment of intersubjective truth.

The significance of Husserl's phenomenology lies in the shift from the Cartesian cogito with its unmediated access to the subject to the insertion of the distinction between the world in-itself and the world for-me. He sought to bridge this non-coincidence of the 'in-itself' and the 'for-me' by a philosophy of perception. Because he insists on the pre-eminence of the 'for-me' of reality, perception is placed at the center. And although phenomenology is not prepared to state that the world is as I perceive it to be, yet it cannot escape the conclusion that all perception is perspectival. Nor can it avoid stumbling over the necessary conclusion that truth's origin is but all too human and relative. Perception is limited by the perspective that the solipsist "I" can give it. The "I" is then the real source, the final foundation, of the truth of existence.

From the beginning Ricoeur was cautious about replacing Descartes' cogito with Husserl's percipio and about the repercussions the replacement would have on the question of the human subject. He saw it as a dangerous reassertion of the absolute and self-constituting subject. In his Philosophie de la volonté I. Le volontaire et l'involontaire (29) he undertook, therefore, to transform Husserl's phenomenology of perception into a phenomenology of the will.[4] He used Husserl's intentionality analysis

---

4. The fact that Ricoeur dedicated this work to Gabriel Marcel is instructive. Ricoeur's utilization of Husserl is basically a methodological decision. In Le volontaire et l'involontaire a number of existentialist themes recur.

(consciousness is a consciousness of...) and applied it to the will: the will as deciding, acting, and consenting. He transferred the époché from the realm of perception, where it had reduced the question of being to the meaning of being, and applied it to the structure of the will. As applied to the will the époché abstracted the essential structures of the will from the taint of irrational evil and from the power of super-rational transcendence.[5] In this eidetic phenomenology the structures of the will show themselves to be not the result of the cogito but of an active participation in a prereflective existence. The cogito does not rule here; in fact, one may conclude that willing is dialectically determined by what precedes it and limits it, viz. nature. Subjectivity emerges as fundamentally bipolar. It is not the absolute source, but it makes the real a subjective real.

The incorporation of a number of existentialist themes, that are reminiscent of Gabriel Marcel, made Ricoeur recognize the need to break down the theory of the absolutist subject even further. This theme becomes more pronounced in the second part of his Philosophie de la volonté: Finitude et culpabilité, especially in volume II: La symbolique du mal (153) and in De l'interprétation (227). Here the dispossessing of the subject as the source of meaning becomes a dominant theme.

B. DECONSTRUCTION OF CONSCIOUSNESS AS THE HOME OF MEANING.

Ricoeur's major objection to the transcendental constitution of the subject is that it posits an immediate and intuitive consciousness of the self. For Ricoeur such an immediate and intuitive self-possession is not available. Reflection, he says, is not an intuition (320(191):327). "The home of meaning is not consciousness but something other than consciousness" (227:55). This is a conviction that colours Ricoeur's work throughout. The subject is not constitutive of meaning, because the subject is not to be identified with consciousness. For him that was the "infirmity of Descartes' Cogito" (436:27) (264:32). In other words, the 'I am' must not be identified with the 'I think'. To pierce the secret of the subject, one may not rely on intuition or on immediacy.

1. The decentering of the subject: Marx, Nietzsche, Freud.

Even though Husserl was also aware that the supremacy of consciousness must be critiqued and, therefore, as a consequence introduced the notion of Lebenswelt as the prereflected, Ricoeur recognizes that Husserl's phenomenology cannot accompany the failure of consciousness all the way (320(243):102). For Ricoeur this deconstruction of the subject as consciousness was accomplished by the three philosophers, whom Ricoeur calls the philosophers of suspicion, Marx, Nietzsche, and Freud. The three

---

5. The validity of this transfer is disputed by D. Vansina, "Schets, orientatie en betekenis van Paul Ricoeur's wijsgerige onderneming" in Tijdschrift voor filosofie 25, 1963, p.109-178, esp. p.112-119.

philosophers contested, each in their own manner, the primacy of consciousness by placing the principle of reality elsewhere. There is an equal recognition in each of these philosophers that the unmasking of the false and dissimulating cogito requires an arduous labour. The breach of the vanity of the subject will only come through struggle and conflict, just as historically Copernicus' demotion of the subject from the centre-stage of the universe, or Darwin's insertion of the subject within the great evolution of life was received with great opposition. The shattering of the vanity of the subject is a painful process. But Nietzsche, Marx, and Freud also realized that the shattering of the vanity of the subject is not a shattering of the subject.

Of the three philosophers Ricoeur has written extensively only about Freud. We propose to follow the lead that Freud gave to Ricoeur in his meditation on the subject and to leave aside the infrequent references to Marx and Nietzsche.[6] It was through a reading of Freud that Ricoeur deepened his awareness of the transcendental illusion.

Freud's psychoanalytic theory reverses the phenomenological movement. In his discovery of the 'topography' and the 'economy' of the unconscious, Freud had shown that the self and consciousness are at odds with each other and even wage a struggle to keep their distance. This Freudian unconscious is a dimension of subjectivity.[7] It is not conscious subjectivity but preconscious. And although seeking to come to language, the unconscious is only latent language (227:453). The place where this latent language discloses itself and where the key to an understanding of the unconscious is handed over is the dream. The dream brings to the surface what is prior to consciousness in the subject. By opening up this 'region' prior to consciousness, the dream gives entry to something that expresses

----

6. Ricoeur came to undertake a study of Freud apparently through his interest in the power of symbolic expression. Having studied the symbolism of evil and the power of sacred symbolism to gather meaning, he also wanted to investigate the oneiric dimension of the symbol. In studying Freud's dream interpretation, he became conscious of the power of the symbol not only to reveal but also to hide and to dissimulate: hence a conflict of interpretation. But before one can come to the more hermeneutical dimension of Freud, one can see in Freud first of all the thinker who dislodged the subject from the central position on consciousness.

7. It must be said that Husserl, too, did not identify the subject as totally self-constituting. However, he was incapable of going beyond considering the unconscious as the unreflected or as implicit consciousness. He could not give a realism to the unconscious in the way that Freud could. It is because of this failure that Freud offers a serious critique of the phenomenological presumption (320(243):101-102).

the subject more than the subject expresses it.[8] This 'region' becomes the puzzle of consciousness because it appears to express a more primordial self than the conscious subject.

The dream, as we know it in our waking hours, is not the language of consciousness. The dream, which has become a text in our recollection, can be called a mixed discourse (320(246):160). The dream-text is a mixture of meaning and desire, or, more accurately, the effect of desire upon meaning. Meaning and force interact here as a mixed discourse, it seeks to fuse into a semantics of desire both the force and desire that lie at the origin of our being (conflict, repression, and cathexis of the dream-text) and meaning (the language dimension of the dream). Two characteristics of this semantics of desire ought to be highlighted.

First, the dream-text is the language-expression of opaque desire. The desire and the effort to be does not express itself in an univocal language but in the ambiguity of multi-meaning language. A semantics of desire employs the strategy of metaphorical language. Just as in metaphorical language, the strategy of dream language is to forge an entry into the subsurface world of pre-linguistic desire. The desire and effort to be are given only in the ambiguity of the dream-text. But if the desire and effort to be, which constitutes our existence, is given only in ambiguous language, they are not directly available to human consciousness. Our only access to the primordial desire is by way of the interpretation of the ambiguous mixed discourse of the dream-text. Only an interpretation of the semantics of desire which turns to the psychic representations of desire in language can reveal the interaction (320(246):168). According to Ricoeur, the problem is that the psychic representatives are neither biological nor semantic. "It is delegated by the instincts only in their derivatives while gaining access to language only by the twisted combinations of object cathexis which precede verbal representation" (320(246):169). Reflection is not intuition but interpretation. This is Freud's first contribution.

Freud's second contribution was his discovery that the mixed discourse of the dream-text has been tampered with. The interpretation of the dream-text is hampered not only by the type of metaphorical language of the dream-text but even more so by the attempt of the text to dissimulate, disguise or dissemble the desire and effort to be. According to Freud, neither the subject nor the object are as they present themselves in the dream-text. Both clothe themselves in a variety of disguises or

---

8. Freud in discussing the unconscious used the spatial metaphor of topography. But the unconscious is, of course, not a region. Its reality must not be given existence outside of the hermeneutical process, outside of its representations. To predicate meaning to the unconscious leads to a naive realism (320(243):107-108). To predicate meaning to the unconscious would lead to the assertion that the unconscious is conscious. It is only in interlocution through the interpretations of the signs that come from the narrated dream that the unconscious attains reality.

psychological displacements.   Thus, the object is not the object of consciousness but it must be sought in the economy of the instincts as a 'mere variable of the aim of the instinct' (227:424).   The genesis of the object lies not in consciousness but with the genesis of love and hate (227:425).   The same holds true for the subject.   Also the subject is a variable of the aim of the instinct (Ichtrieb).   Instead of being the last bastion of certitude, the subject, according to Freud, is itself an object of desire.   It is not what it thinks it is.   Far from being the subject of the Cogito, the ego is the desired object. The ego is the aim of the instinct.

For Ricoeur, this narcissism is the heart of the false cogito. Narcissism is the original form of desire, the child, the archaism, to which we always return. But it hides itself in the disguise of many other objects of desire with which the subject as object can be substituted.

Narcissism itself, in its primary form, is always hidden behind its innumerable symptoms (perversion, the schizophrenic's loss of interest, the omnipotence of thought on the part of primitives and children, the withdrawal into sleep, the selling of the ego in hypochodria); one has the impression that if it were possible to pinpoint the nucleus of this Versagung, this withdrawal of the ego that shuns and refuses the risk of loving, one would have the key to many fantasy formations in which arises which might be called an egotistic archaism (227:446).

This means for Ricoeur that Freud effectively destroyed two basic tenets of phenomenology: neither the object nor the subject are what they appear in their immediacy. As Ricoeur remarks,

To raise this discovery to the reflective level is to make the dispossession of the subject of consciousness coequal with the dispossession ... of the intended object (227:425).

Of Ricoeur's painstaking and often difficult analysis of Freud, I wish to retain three points.

a. The humiliation of the ego.

If one must relinquish immediate consciousness because it is a false consciousness, one must also break with the narcissism that resists this despoliation of the conscious subject. I must make myself homeless of the false illusion (227:422), and I must attack the masked enemy of my narcissism (227:427). The ego - more precisely the libido of the ego - must be humiliated.   The unveiling, therefore, of the topography of the unconscious or the process whereby the Id becomes ego is a struggle, a work. Every analysis is a struggle against resistence (320(214):179). It is the "wounding of our self-love" (227:428). Hence a hermeneutical praxis must be reminded of the ascesis or the arduous path of the unveiling. The process of becoming conscious, the process of the recuperation of the subject, is

9

itself a process of negation and of the painful loss of the master subject (320(228):151-152). It is a recentering of oneself in another home. "It finds itself by losing itself" (320(228):153).

b. The archaeology of the subject.

This painful unveiling and the breakdown of our narcissism is at the same time a becoming conscious of our effort and desire to be. If there is a "displacement of the birthplace of meaning" (227:422), it is not a discountenancing of consciousness. If the home of meaning lies not in consciousness but elsewhere, it becomes the task of consciousness to go in search of its home, in order to liberate the subject so that it might become conscious of its home of meaning (320(228):150). According to Ricoeur, as we shall see, this task pertains to reflection. Like Freud, Ricoeur proposes a recapture of consciousness in reflection by means of an arduous interpretative process, always keeping in mind that our consciousness will never attain the level of the instincts themselves but only their psychic representatives (227:434). The movement of the displacement of immediate consciousness towards the recapturing of consciousness at the point where it rejoins the authentic Cogito Ricoeur labels archaeology (227:439). According to Ricoeur, for reflection, psychoanalysis is an archaeology of the subject. This backward movement toward the subject is not a secret return to a self-constituting subject. The conscious subject remains wounded. It is "a Cogito that posits itself but does not possess itself; a Cogito that sees its original truth only in and through the avowal of the inadequacy, illusion, and lying of actual consciousness" (227:439).

Freud's road to freedom, as Ricoeur perceives it, seeks a twofold outlet. Ricoeur calls them the ability to speak and the ability to love. At the end of the route to the arché of the subject is not a new domination of life by speech but a being set free to speak 'without end', i.e. to discourse (320(214):193). Ricoeur recognizes in this not a domination of the desire and the effort to be but a "new orientation for his desire, a new power to live" or, a re-education of desire (320(214):194). Desire requires a governance in order that one can regain a capacity to enjoy.

This archaeology of the subject points to a Cogito that does not possess itself but which is rooted in an anterior, namely, the unsurpassable character of desire. The Cogito is secondary to the sum. It is rooted in existence itself which, according to Freud, is to be understood as desire and effort (227:458). It is this desire and effort that accompany all my exteriorizations. It is indestructible. It is irretrievable. This archaism is pre-linguistic: "the unnameable at the root of speech" (227:454). It is a substratum that strives toward language but which can itself never be named fully. The route back towards the substratum of desire as desire brings us to the lower limits of language. It becomes intelligible only in its derivatives at the borderline of language (227:454). Freud, in other words, leads us constantly back to the beginning, but the beginning never becomes transparent. It keeps beckoning us and its accompaniment to our existence never ceases. The infantile is like a fate whose necessity must become unmasked in order that we may become mature.

10

c. The intersubjectivity of becoming-conscious.

Another dimension of the process of becoming conscious in Freud's psychoanalysis is the intersubjective dimension of the process. For Ricoeur this is of considerable importance because of his own position concerning the intersubjective dimension of truth. The work of psychoanalysis is a hermeneutical technique that calls for the mediation of another consciousness: the analyst's. Because of the blockage of consciousness in its resistance to reality the analyst must guide the painful process towards the <u>arché</u>. Only the interlocution of the analyst and the analysand working through the signs emerging out of the mute chaos of our desire can break the resistance to the truth of the self (227:456). In fact, it is only through the analyst that I have an unconscious. The effort at dispossession is for that reason not into a void but into another person, into a witness-consciousness (320(243):107).

Having brought Freud's theory of the unconscious within dialectical range of phenomenology, Ricoeur has at once both decentered and re-oriented reflection.[9] The archaeology of the subject and its regression of consciousness towards the lower limit of the language of desire has deflected a reflection that considers consciousness as primary and radicalized it by making consciousness its task.

> The arduous self-knowledge that phenomenology goes on to articulate clearly shows that the first truth is also the last truth known; though the Cogito is the starting point, there is no end to reaching the starting point; you do not start from it, you proceed to it; the whole of phenomenology is a movement toward the starting point (227:377).

But this radicalization forced on phenomenology by Freud calls for a re-interpretation of phenomenology that transcends the antithesis of

---

9. Ricoeur's reading of Freud has been severely criticized. See, for instance, A. de Waelens, "La force du langage et le langage de la force", in Revue philosophique de Louvain 63, 1965, p.591-612; M. Tort, "De l'interprétation ou la machine herméneutique", in Les Temps Modernes 21, 1966, p.1461-1493 and p.1629-1652. Both A. de Waelens and M. Tort, although with unequal intensity, find fault with the distinction that Ricoeur has made between an analytic reading of Freud and the philosophical interpretation. De Waelens' more sympathetic reading says that Ricoeur buried the historical Freud under his dialectical blanket. M. Tort's sharp critique enters into the debate by insisting that every reading of an author is of necessity an interpretation. This invalidates the distinction between an analytic and an interpretative reading which Ricoeur applies to Freud. See also M. Robert, "Remarque sur l'exégèse de Freud", in Les Temps Modernes 20, 1965, p.664-681, and J. Laplanche, "Interpréter (avec) Freud" in L'Arc 34, 1968, p.37-46.

Husserl and Freud. As a philosophy of the subject phenomenology must abjure its status as a transcendental philosophy of consciousness.[10]

2. The subject and the process of becoming conscious.

But Freud's decentering of consciousness by means of the unconscious does not express the full extent of the displacement of the subject. Freud had probed the 'region' prior to consciousness, bringing us to the point of the emerging of desire, showing it to be the archaic form of the human. He had shown the character of life and of desire to be both unsurpassable and unintelligible. But, according to Ricoeur, one cannot remain at this abstract level of an archaeology of the subject.

If the subject is to attain its true being, it is not enough for it to discover the inadequacy of its self-awareness, or even to discover the power of desire that posits it in existence. The subject must also discover that the process of "becoming conscious", through which it appropriates the meaning of its existence as desire and effort, does not belong to it. The subject must mediate self-consciousness through spirit or mind, that is, through the figures that give a telos to this "becoming conscious" (227:459).

His meditation on Freud, which coincided in point of time with the immence interest that French philosophers showed in the 1960's in the 'masters of suspicion', does not mean that Ricoeur joined the massive desertion of the phenomenological scene. Freud, in particular, was thought to have effectively destroyed the foundations of phenomenology. The sovereign subject is declared dead and buried in the unconscious. Ricoeur refuses to abandon ship. In the quote above he forges a link between his interpretation of the psychoanalytic theory and phenomenological theory in its earliest from: Hegel's Phänomenologie des Geistes. The latter differs

---

10. By applying Husserl's phenomenology to the will in Le volontaire et l'involontaire, Ricoeur implies that the structures of the will can be obtained by an immediate reflection. He obtains the eidetic structures of the will by resorting to an époché of both the issue of evil and transcendence. Consequently, the will assumes the same function as consciousness on the level of perception. The will becomes the source of meaning. In the face of evil, it takes on full responsibility because it alone is the origin of evil. When in La symbolique du mal he is confronted with a confession of an evil of which I am not the source, but which nevertheless adheres to me, Ricoeur is forced to reconsider his point of departure. However, Patrick Bourgeois (Extension of Ricoeur's Hermeneutic, op. cit.) has shown rather convincingly that implicit in the position of Le volontaire et l'involontaire, one finds the hermeneutical thrust of Ricoeur's later works. But he needed his interpretation of Freud to bring to the surface the full impact of the notion of the involontary as analogous to the Freudian conscious.

radically from Husserlian phenomenology, but its insistence on identifying substance with subject through a process of consciousness indicates a similarity despite a difference.

According to Ricoeur the phenomenology of mind or spirit is an inversion of Freud's psychoanalytic theory (227:461). While Freud's theory of becoming conscious is a backward movement towards the archaism of desire, Hegel's philosophy of the spirit is a proleptic process homologous to the regression of the archaeology. By dialectically relating Freud's archaeology with Hegel's teleology, Ricoeur preserves the birthright of phenomenology, but the latter would, like Jacob, henceforth walk with a limp.

Because Hegel's meditation on mind or spirit has a bearing on the issue of subjectivity, we must briefly indicate how Ricoeur works out the dialectic between Hegel and Freud.[11]

Hegel recognized that the movement of consciousness to self-consciousness is a dialectical movement. For that reason his 'phenomenology' is not of consciousness but of the movement of the figures, categories and symbols that guide the movement of consciousness toward a synthesis of consciousness with self-consciousness. In other words, like Freud, Hegel allows that consciousness does not coincide with itself. The subject is not master over meaning. The home of meaning lies in the spirit. The spirit is for Hegel the dialectic of the figures that mediate the meaning and the process of self-consciousness. Consciousness itself can be called a movement. It is the movement in which the dialectic of the figures is appropriated. Consciousness is the movement of meaning. But the movement is not born through consciousness, but it is formed in it. Consciousness is the 'internalization of this movement' (227:463). It recaptures the spirit that dwells in it.

a. The Progressive movement of consciousness.

The form of the dialectic of the figures of the spirit is progressive. The figure receives its meaning from the subsequent figure

---

11. For Ricoeur's presentation of Hegel, see (227:459-472;320(191):322-326;320(243):108-120;320(246):160-176;399). Ricoeur's relationship to other philosophers and to the history of philosophy is unique. He shows a deep respect for his fellow explorers of the issue of human existence. One might be tempted to call him a scavenger of the history of human thought. He forges a path through history as the pathway of humanity's search for truth. He reads human existence constantly through the text of his fellow philosophers. His philosophy is consistently a history of philosophy. See his "My Relation to the History of Philosophy" (451). See also M. Philibert, Paul Ricoeur ou la liberté selon l'espérance. Présentation, choix de textes. (Philosophes de tous les temps, 72) Paris, Seghers, 1971, p.5-40.

(227:464). The meaning of consciousness for that reason cannot be found in itself. Its truth lies ahead in the next form or figure. Accordingly the truth of consciousness lies latent in consciousness and can only be made to appear through a subsequent meaning, which reveals the truth of the previous meaning. It is the spirit which informs consciousness as its movement that makes explicit what previously was implicit. For Hegel consciousness does manifest the being of the world but without reflection (227:464). The exegesis of consciousness would disclose a world of the progression of "all spheres of meaning that a given consciousness must encounter and appropriate in order to reflect itself as a self, a human, adult, conscious self" (227:463). Consciousness is proleptic; it prefigures its goal but unreflectedly.

b. Content of the movement of consciousness.

What we might term the truth or real movement of consciousness Hegel labelled Geist, spirit. As Ricoeur says, for Hegel "spirit is the truth of life, a truth which is not yet aware of itself in the emergence of desire, but which becomes self-reflective in the life process of becoming conscious" (227:465). That non-coincidence of consciousness with its self, i.e., its truth, is life's restlessness (Unruhigkeit). The restlessness of life, the tension of consciousness and its truth, at first makes that truth the not-self in order that in its otherness I can make it self. Because this is homologous to Freud let us explain this process in greater detail.

Self-consciousness according to Hegel manifests itself as desire. Human desire is human inasmuch as it desires the desire of another. It is addressed to another's desire and for that reason it is a desire that reaches out to language. The desire is not intelligible until consciousness reaches beyond itself in addressing another human. It is only in the positing of itself as desire that reflection becomes possible (227:466). There is no intelligibility proper to desire as such. In its reaching out to things desire dissolves or negates the otherness of things and of the world and finds itself in the other. Humans do so particularly in their desire for the desire of another consciousness. In the desire for recognition by another the desire is both object (that is, the other) and self-consciousness. In other words "desire is desire only if life manifests itself as another desire" (227:467). One does not derive it from oneself; it can only be mediated in and through the desire of another. The desire of another is a new moment that makes the unknown of desire in me manifest.

For Hegel the movement of consciousness is an infinite movement. Each figure takes one beyond the present limit and towards another in a never-ending progression. The self's struggle to be at one with consciousness is an infinite struggle. What it desires is itself as totally transparent communication. But its very openness, its infinity, reveals at the same time that the movement has a substrate that is never surpassed and is indestructible. Life and desire that are at the source of this movement, are a source to which one constantly returns. What life and desire pursue as other is in fact the mediation of life and desire itself. Life

14

and desire are the "substance constantly negated, but also constantly retained and re-affirmed" (227:471).

Hegel summed up this movement in the saying: "The substance is subject" (399:338-339). This aphorism states that the movement of consciousness proceeds from a substance that lacks consciousness to its negation or contradiction whereby it becomes conscious and can begin to reflect so that a mediation of the contradiction can take place. Hegel perceived his philosophy to be the point of highest mediation of the history of philosophy. It brought to reflection 'le fond non maîtrisable', the substance of life and desire (386:37). "That which is passes into that which it is not and from this passage is born the taking hold of the consciousness of being through itself" (399:339 my translation). The increase in subjectivity, in other words, goes hand in hand with an increase in reflection and meaning. Subjectivity is granted us in and through the great variety of experiences that have shaped a cultural heritage.

C. REFLECTION AS INTERPRETATION.

There is another interlocutor in addition to Freud and Hegel whose influence on the transformation of Ricoeur's phenomenology ought to be recorded. Freud and Hegel had dislodged the immediacy of consciousness. Consciousness and subjectivity are not immediately available. As the title of Ricoeur's series of lectures on Freud, De l'interprétation (227), intimates, the return of the subject is mediated by interpretation. This other interlocutor, Jean Nabert, whose premature death Ricoeur mourns on a number of occasions, was not a phenomenologist but a practical philosopher.[12] His philosophy was not a philosophy of consciousness but a reflective philosophy whose aim was to appropriate in praxis an originary dynamism which grounds human existence and with which the conscious, practical self does not coincide. This movement of the appropriation of one's primary affirmation - the 'yes' of existence - is a reflective movement that is neither direct nor immediate. According to

---

12. Despite the repeated expressions of his indebtedness to Jean Nabert (cf.   e.g.,186:321-322;320(191):328-329;320(246):169-170;190:5-16;320(259)) it is surprizing that in Ricoeur's account of his philosophical itinerary, "From Existentialism to the Philosophy of Language", (371:14-18), the name of Jean Nabert is not mentioned at all. However, in two accounts of the history of philosophy, both of which clearly reflect Ricoeur's reading of that history toward his own position, Nabert holds a place of honour (cf.451:8;186:321-322).   J. Nabert published three books: L'Expérience intérieure de la liberté, Paris, P.U.F., 1924; Eléments pour une éthique, Paris, P.U.F., 1943; and Essai sur le mal, Paris, P.U.F., 1955. Another book bearing Nabert's name, Le désir de Dieu (Paris, Aubier, 1966) was reconstructed from his notes by Ricoeur and some others. Ricoeur wrote a preface to this book as well as to Eléments pour une éthique. It is to Jean Nabert that Ricoeur dedicated his La symbolique du mal.

Ricoeur's estimation, Jean Nabert succeeded in linking this original desire to be and the signs in which that desire is expressed.

While Freud and Hegel had effectively made a return to an unadulterated phenomenology impossible, Jean Nabert's reflective philosophy offered a well-ordered retreat from the embarrassing linkage of the subject and consciousness. After the destruction of the direct, intuitive apprehension of the self by the self, Nabert comes to the rescue on a number of fronts. We shall mention four.

1. Nabert's ethical philosophy does not operate on the narrow epistemological and psychological base of either Kant or Freud. Ricoeur finds in Nabert a practical philosophy, that, unlike Kant's, is not dependent upon the structure of theoretical reason. In the signs of the desire to be, Nabert seeks to recapture or to re-appropriate the primordial source of human existence. He promotes an ethics that in its itinerary seeks to appropriate in an ever fuller fashion an act that is ever prior and never given, which he calls the primary or originary affirmation (320(246):169-170). This primary affirmation is the source of the self. For Nabert, this primary affirmation reveals two dimensions of existence. First of all, it is an act, an affirmation, that institutes consciousness and, therefore, surpasses consciousness. But this act also manifests in the feeling of fault, failure and solitude that there is a lack of being, or better, a lack of identity with the originary act. As a consequence, Nabert perceives the task of philosophy as an ethical task of appropriating that form from which it is separated: the originary or primary affirmation (cf.320(185):219). The ethical reflection that Nabert proposes is fundamentally a mediated reflection. It takes the longer route that seeks to re-appropriate the self by way of the interpretation of the signs in which the desire to be - the primary affirmation - is inscribed.

2. In this process of interpretation Nabert also asserts that there is a direct relationship between the understanding of the signs of the inscription of the desire to be and self-understanding. Accordingly, all understanding becomes self-understanding. To arrive at self-understanding one must pass through the signs in which the self inscribes itself.

3. With the establishment of a primordial act of human existence in the primary affirmation, Nabert reintroduced an ontological motif into reflective thought. Husserl's egology was without an ontology. The theme of the primary affirmation offers a concrete ontology which Ricoeur along with Marcel sought without requiring the acceptance of the direct ontology of Heidegger (451:8). For Ricoeur, Nabert's indirect approach by way of the sign corrects the excessively lofty ontological approach of Heidegger.[13]

4. In the retracing of the trajectory of Ricoeur's phenomenology of the subject, the most significant contribution of Nabert is his thesis on

---

13. See below, p.102-105.

the relationship between the act of the primary affirmation and the sign. At issue is the following. Between the act of existence and the signs in which this act is represented there exists a relationship that is often overlooked. Frequently, the primary act is subordinated to the sign and the sign is given an objectivity that does not at all reflect the relationship to the primary act. The representation or sign becomes then the primary datum and function. As the first known it becomes the only known (320(185):212). But once the bond between the sign or representation and the primary act is restored, the sign or representation takes on a different texture. It becomes secondary to the primary act. It takes on a mediating function. It is not itself the aim of understanding, but must be understood as a sign of the act that gave rise to it (320(185):214). But, in a view in which the sign is only a tracing of the act, the sign becomes a symbol of the natural desire (320(185):221). The sign becomes an issue then not so much of knowledge as of the imagination. To quote Ricoeur's text, "The phenomenon is the manifestation, in a 'graspable expression', 'of an inner operation, which can assure itself as to what it is only by forcing itself toward this expression'" (320(185):221).

The phenomenon, representation, or sign, then, is the expression of the self, but the self in its objectification. Self-possession by way of this objectification is not immediate nor ever complete. According to Ricoeur, "We never produce the total act that we gather up and project in the ideal of an absolute choice; we must endlessly appropriate what we are through the mediations of the multiple expressions of our desire to be" (320(185):222). This reflection as interpretation needs to be made more precise, however. Through Nabert, Ricoeur is well on the way towards a hermeneutics. But Nabert's reflective philosophy has not yet tackled the question of language. With the question of language we arrive at the most recent stage of Ricoeur's itinerary.[14]

---

14. The real urgency for the introduction of language as the mediation must be sought in the fact that for both Nabert and Ricoeur the source and the origin of meaning, the originary act, cannot be grasped by pure reflection. From Husserl Ricoeur had already borrowed the idea that that to which all consciousness and all expressions of meaning tend does not have to be attained or fulfilled. The object of intentionality, in other words, does not have to be present, in order for consciousness to be a consciousness of... The language of intentionality can consequently be an empty language which seeks fulfillment without attaining it. For Ricoeur, therefore, both the Ursprung and the telos of meaning manifest themselves in ambiguity and in a metaphorical tension that is without surcease. Cf. P. Bourgeois, "Hermeneutics of Symbols and Philosophical Reflection: Paul Ricoeur" in Phil. Today 15, 1971, p.232-235. See also: Patrick Bourgeois, "Paul Ricoeur's Hermeneutical Phenomenology" in Phil. Today 16, 972, p.20-27, esp. p.24; P. Gisel, "Paul Ricoeur: Discourse between Speech and Language" in Phil. Today 21, 1977, p.446-456; D. Charles, "Dire, entendre, parler. L'herméneutique et le langage selon P. Ricoeur" in Algemeen Nederlands Tijdschrift voor Wijsbegeerte 68, 1976, p.74-98; P. Bourgeois, "From

D. LANGUAGE AND MEANING.

Ricoeur's move toward language and a hermeneutical phenomenology began with his La symbolique du mal.[15] The symbolism in which humanity expresses its contact and contamination with evil which this work examined threw Ricoeur into the midst of the problem of language. Evil resists a direct description and expression of itself and tends toward the symbolic, mythical and narrative expression (451:9). The ambiguity and the extravagance of the symbolic language in which evil is expressed in cultures demands an interpretative process of this double-meaning, ambiguous language. In La symbolique du mal and in his subsequent work on Freud, De l'interprétation. Essai sur Freud, Ricoeur defines hermeneutics and symbolism in terms of each other (371:88). Symbolism makes use of indirect language and, therefore, involves the art of decipherment of hermeneutics. Accordingly, at this phase of Ricoeur's philosophical development, hermeneutics unscrambles indirect meanings.

But at this stage the study of language was still peripheral to Ricoeur's concerns. The question of evil and guilt in the context of a philosophy of the will still predominated. The reflection upon language was indirect. The external occasion that made the implicit concern with language an explicit one was the sudden prominence on the philosophical scene in France of Structural Linguistics or Semiotics. Also his interest in religious language was whetted by the theologies of Ebeling and Fuchs of the Post-Bultmannian School (371:88).

What is at stake here? Beyond Nabert's preoccupation with the sign what is novel in Ricoeur's presentation? The home of meaning, we said, is not consciousness but something prior to consciousness. In his probing of the primary act that lies prior to consciousness, Nabert had insisted that this primary act does not release itself except through the signs and monuments in which that act is inscribed. With the advent of the strong linguistic currents, Ricoeur recognizes that the mediation of the primary act is a linguistic mediation. If Nabert linked meaning with the sign, Ricoeur, in the period subsequent to De l'interprétation, focussed upon the sign in terms of language and sought to relate meaning and language.

In his contribution "Signe et sens" (378) Ricoeur provides an illuminating perspective of the relationship between meaning and language. In a few bold strokes he describes the history of that relationship as a constant shifting back and forth of accents. At certain moments in the

---

Hermeneutics of Symbols to the Interpretation of Texts" in Studies in the Philosophy of Paul Ricoeur, ed. by Charles E. Reagan, Athens, Ohio, Ohio University Press, 1979, p.84-95.

15. See also P. Kemp, "Phänomenologie und Hermeneutik in der Philosophie Paul Ricoeurs" in Z. Theol. Kirche 67, 1970, p.335-347.

history of thought the accent fell upon the sign while at others the accent was placed upon the meaning. Either the sign is the sole support of meaning or the meaning pertains to an idea that is captured by thought to which convention attaches a certain word (378:1011). Ricoeur argues accordingly that Husserl's transcendental phenomenology follows the idealistic perspective where meaning is not attached to the sign but is objective and ideal, distinct from mental contents and, therefore, from linguistic signs.[16] The contribution of Structural Linguistics, on the other hand, represents the modern reversal of the relationship of meaning and language of transcendental phenomenology. It makes meaning once again subservient to language (378:1012).

The founding father of French Structural Linguistics is the Swiss linguist, Ferdinand de Saussure (1857-1913).[17] His presentation of the science of language represents a profound challenge to the phenomenological position. The semiotic challenge affects the major theses of phenomenology regarding meaning, the subject as the bearer of meaning, and the transcendental reduction whereby every question of being is reduced to the question of the meaning of being. The near identification of being with meaning which, in the final analysis, leads to the conclusion that being is no more than what human experience has brought to expression is severely 'deconstructed'. Is it not an assumption of phenomenology, semiology asks, that being can only be 'for me' or a vécu, a lived experience? To break this supposed naiveté of phenomenology, semiology proposes a radically incompatible series of propositions. As represented by the following four theses, semiology succeeded in considerably undermining the credibility and viability of the phenomenological movement in France.[18] Ricoeur took up the challenge in

---

16.   This view must not be radicalized because a certain relationship between meaning and signs is accepted by Husserl.

17.   See his Cours de linguistique générale, Paris, Payot, 1971 (1916). De Saussure was not alone in his discovery. He perfected the theories of Jan Baudoin de Courtenai and of Kruszewski. Cf. P. Ricoeur, "Langage (Philosophie)" in Encyclopaedia Universalis, IX, Paris, Encyclopaedia Universalis France, 1979, p.771. De Saussure did not employ the word 'structure'. Instead he used the word 'system'. The words 'structure' and 'structuralism' were coined at the First International Congress of Linguists at The Hague in 1928. Cf. "Structure - Word -Event", in Philosophy Today 12, 1968, p.116.

18.   Ricoeur's description of Saussurean linguistics varies little. The theses presented here are derived mainly from Interpretation Theory: Discourse and the Surplus of Meaning, (Four Essays Comprising the Centennial Lectures Delivered at Texas Christian University 27-30 November, 1973), Fort Worth, The Texas Christian University Press, 1976, p.3-4.   For a more extensive treatment of the history of modern linguistics,see 475:229-242.   The postulates were formulated by Louis

characteristic fashion. He allowed some of the basic tenets of semiology, but withstood the almost unbearable academic pressure to fall in line with the prevailing philosophy. He remained a phenomenologist, albeit a 'deconstructed' one.

1. The postulates of semiotics.

a. Structural linguistics distinguishes between language as langue and language as parole (speech). The linguistics of de Saussure broke radically with the study of language of the 19th century, where the emphasis was on the historical roots of language and upon the evolution of the classical Indo-European languages (216:83). De Saussure set himself to study the code or set of codes that form the structure of the system of the various languages of the human community. By doing so, he discovered two aspects of language: language as a code or a lexical system, which studies in a semi-algebraic manner the combinations and oppositions of the component elements or units (phonemes, lexemes, morphemes and syntagma) of language (langue), and language as the activity of speaking subjects who intend to say something to someone about something (parole). De Saussure was particularly interested in language as langue. He has in fact little to say about language as parole. Linguistics has become primarily a linguistics of langue, that is, of the lexical system, and only derivatively of the parole.

The core unit, studied by linguistics, is the sign or the sign system. The linguistic sign does not unite a 'thing' and a 'name', but it is a phenomenon which relates and opposes a signifier (a sound, a written pattern, a gesture...called signifiant in French)[19] and a signified (signifié). The signified is not a thing or an object outside of language but merely the differential values in the lexical system. At first, de Saussure explained these correlative terms as a relationship between the acoustic image of a word and its corresponding concept derived from linguistic community. In his later works this was considered too psychological and sociological an explanation. Yet, what must be retained is the correlation of the signifier and the signified. The signified remains within the bounds of language, because for linguistics the question of meaning cannot be detached from the intra-linguistic sign. Meaning results from the correlation of the signifier and the signified in the sign. No entity of the system has a meaning of its

---

Hjelmslev of the linguistic school of Copenhagen in his Prolegomena to a Theory of Language (1943).

19. By extension, the signifier includes also the written pattern and the gesture. It was the linguistic Circle of Prague (founded in 1926 at the initiative of V. Mathesius) which first recognized language as a functional system. The Circle is specifically known for its structural treatment of phonology. Phonology excludes from language the objective physiological factors to emphasize the phonemes and their interrelationships (cf.345:771;473:231).

own. The sign-units relate to other signs purely by their oppositions and differences. Just as a sound can be defined only in relation to other sounds so a meaning is only a difference in a lexical system. A sign has meaning only by its place in the whole lexical system. In a system of signs we must not look for the proper existence of a word. The sign has no other existence than in the lexicon where it is defined by the opposition to other words (374:10).

b.   The distinction between _langue_ and _parole_ gives rise to another important distinction. _Langue_ and _parole_ operate in a different framework of time. Linguistics distinguishes sharply between the synchronie of the system of signs and the diachronie of discourse. _Langue_ deals with the differences and the oppositions of the signs within the system of language at any given moment. It leaves aside any consideration of the process of the change of meaning in language. The system of signs is a-historical while discourse incorporates the changes of meaning that characterize a living language. Linguistics gives priority to the synchronic system. It subordinates the historical process and the diachronic changes of meaning to the system underlying the changes. For linguistics a change of meaning is understood as two distinct states of a word.

c.   The most far-reaching consequence of synchronic linguistics is its relationship to reality. The units of language are enclosed in a finite set of discrete entities of the system. In other words the lexical system is to be considered finite. It contains only a limited number of phonemes, lexemes, morphemes and syntagma.[20] This closure of the system must be expanded to include the thesis that all the relations between these units remain immanent to the system. For linguistics, _langue_ is a self-sufficient system of inner relationships. As we said above, the signified does not refer to reality or to a thing. It is the counterpart of the signifier. The consequence of this is that this language has no outside. The words of a dictionary refer only to other words in the dictionary. The system is closed in on itself. As de Saussure expresses it, "Language is not a substance but a form" (275:117). A sign is defined in itself as a purely internal or immediate difference. The reference to reality is blocked by the imprisonment of the sign within the system.

d.   The fourth thesis resumes the other three. For linguistics language has become, as Hjelmslev describes it, "an autonomous entity of internal dependencies, in a word, a structure" (320(278):250). It is a closed system of signs, existing only for itself. With no outside, language is not a mediation of reality, but a circumscribable entity that is self-enclosed. As a consequence, language becomes a homogeneous object of science because of the closure of the system.

---

20.   Thus, for example, the English language has 44 or 45 phonemes, and the Oxford Dictionary contains some 45,000 words.

2. Language without a subject.

The critique of Ricoeur of a language with only an inside takes a familiar route. Instead of juxtaposing Saussurean linguistics with phenomenology, he investigates the possibility of a dialectic between linguistics and phenomenology. He chooses to examine the basic distinctions between langue and parole, synchronie and diachronie, closed and open system of linguistics in the light of the phenomenological theories of meaning, of the subject, and the phenomenological reduction (cf.320(278):251). He accepts the necessity of the semiotic challenge to the question of the subject and to consciousness. The transcendental reduction of Husserl's phenomenology which made consciousness absolutely primordial by reducing the question of being to the question of the meaning of being for consciousness, is deeply affected by this acceptance.

Consciousness, buffeted already by Freud's unconscious and further reduced by semiotics, cannot retain its primordial transcendental position. As Ricoeur says, "In the eyes of structuralism, this absolute privilege is the absolute prejudice of phenomenology" (320(278):257). Phenomenology had attempted to work out the difference between the human being and nature by reducing nature to the consciousness of that nature. Ricoeur now perceives that this reduction of nature to the consciousness of nature is too direct and immediate. He realizes that the subject does not emerge that easily and almost intuitively from the nature that surrounds it. Consciousness is not the transcendental, the condition of the possibility of meaning. In the challenge of semiotics Ricoeur opts to take the route that Merleau-Ponty had already taken before him.[21] He designates language as the new transcendental, that is, as the primordial difference between the human being and nature. What differentiates humans is perceived to be their capacity to relate to the real by signifying it through language (320(278):258).

But at the same time he realizes that the challenge of semiology must itself be challenged. A language that is closed in upon itself, a language without an outside, and a language without a subject cannot be incorporated within a phenomenology of the subject. It does not relate to the real because it signifies only differences. For this reason Ricoeur does not want to fall into the trap of canonizing Structuralism as the sole philosophy of language. Ricoeur will seek to broaden the structuralist theory of language into a theory of discourse that will try to overcome the shortcomings of a theory of signs and open up the philosophy of language to the concerns of phenomenology regarding the human subject.

The repercussions of this 'deconstruction' of phenomenology's prejudice will occupy us in the next chapters. Ricoeur's conversion to a linguistic-style phenomenology is a lengthy process.

---

21. The philosophy of Merleau-Ponty devolves more from the later Husserl. Ricoeur faults Merleau-Ponty, however, for moving too quickly to a phenomenology of speech. He insists that only after having listened to Structural Linguistics is it possible to construct an adequate phenomenology of speech.

CHAPTER TWO: <u>THE THEORY OF THE TEXT.</u>

Bibliography.

275.   "La structure, le mot, l'événement" (1967).
278.   "New Developments in Phenomenology in France: The Phenomenology of Language" (1967).
320.   Le conflict des interprétations (1969).
332.   Les incidences théologiques des recherches actuelles concernant le langage (1969).
337.   "Qu'est-ce qu'un texte? Expliquer et comprendre" (1970).
355.   "Langage (Philosophie)" (1971).
360.   "Esquisse de conclusion" (1971).
362.   "Evénement et sens dans le discours" (1971).
363.   "Le conflit: signe de contradiction ou d'unité" (1971).
365.   "Préface" in O. Reboul, Kant et le problème du mal (1971).
370.   "The Model of the Text: Meaningful Action Considered as a Text" (1971).
373.   "Sémantique de l'action" (1971).
374.   "Cours sur l'herméneutique" (1971).
376.   "Discours et communication: la communication problèmatique" (1971).
377.   "Ontologie" (1972).
378.   "Signe et sens" (1972).
379.   "Remarques sur la communication de Karl Löwith" (1972).
387.   "Creativity in Language, Word, Polysemy, Metaphor" (1973).
388.   "The Task of Hermeneutics" (1973).
409.   "Phenomenology of Freedom" (1975).
411.   "Biblical Hermeneutics" (1975).
413.   "Objectivation et aliénation dans l'expérience historique" (1975).
417.   La métaphore vive (1975).
423.   Interpretation Theory (1976).
458.   "Philosophie et langage" (1978).
459.   "Introduction" in H. Agiesay e.a., Le temps et les philosophies (1978).
475.   "Herméneutique et sémiotique" (1980).

With the new transcendental in Ricoeur's philosophy being language, what happens to the two other basic notions of phenomenology, meaning and the subject? How do meaning and the subject relate to a transcendental language? Phenomenology as a theory of generalized language (320(278):258) will not let go of the subject as easily and radically as structuralism. The new linkage of language and meaning cannot take place at the expense of the subject. And for Ricoeur the subject will remain dead as long as meaning remains indistinguishable from the signified of the sign. That extinction is not a mirage. Within the Structuralist schools one can detect two enlargements of the thesis of meaning which if successful would reinforce such a death. The first enlargement, inspired by C.S. Peirce, seeks to make all of existence subject to a science of signs, called semiotics. It would include not only linguistic signs but all other

23

structuralizable dimensions of human life such as rituals, clothing, architecture, social etiquette, economic exchange. Its presupposition is that all realms of life are structured homologously to the laws of the sign. The second extension of the thesis of meaning by Structuralists involves language itself. It hypothesizes that the laws that apply to the larger units of language such as the sentence, the story, the poem, and the essay are homologous to the laws of the sign. That would imprison meaning completely within the sign and would effectively spell the end of the subject (Cf. 378:1013). The success of the hypothesis of Structuralism in its analysis of the larger units of language can serve as a warning not to dismiss their thesis too lightly. But for Ricoeur the linguistics of Structuralism retains its validity and cannot be removed through some type of dialectic with another philosophy of language. The linguistics of langue is a genuine cultural acquisition.

What Ricoeur questions, however, is Structuralism's exclusive linkage of meaning and the sign by Structuralism. Is meaning solely to be linked to the sign or is there something else in language to which meaning can be attached? De Saussure had distinguished another linguistic level in the parole but he had hardly investigated the question of meaning on the level of speech. Is there also a signifier and signified that are irreducible to the relationship of the signifier and the signified in the sign? This is Ricoeur's conviction which we must now investigate.

One can distinguish three phases in Ricoeur's investigation. It must start with an examination of the theory of parole, or, in Ricoeur's terms, a theory of discourse. Then, this theory of discourse must undertake to study the changes that discourse undergoes when oral discourse becomes written discourse. Finally, the theory of written discourse must be expanded to include the composed and stylized discourse of the text. This chapter will examine mainly the logical contours of the theory of discourse. Subsequent chapters will search out the ontological and religious dimensions.

A. THE THEORY OF DISCOURSE.

Two basic criticisms characterize Ricoeur's evaluation of Saussurean Structuralism (275:118). The first criticism concerns de Saussure's methodical exclusion of the capacity of language to say something about something to someone. Language is not closed off in a universe of signs, but intends to mediate reality. The second criticism which will be the concern of the next chapter is that Structuralism cannot account for the creation or the innovation of meaning. Language possesses a creative power and a symbolic function which a structural, synchronic linguistics cannot account for except as a passage from one state of the system of signs to another (416:119-125).

For Ricoeur the theory of discourse has two sources. From the French sanskritist E. Beneveniste[1] he derived a theory of discourse based not

_____

1. In his article "Philosophie et langage", art. cit., p.455, Ricoeur acknowledges his "dette immense" to Benveniste for both his Le Conflit des

on the linguistics of the sign but on the linguistics of the sentence. From English-language philosophy and from Frege and Husserl he took over the reflections on the logic of meaning and of reference. We shall look at each in turn.

1. The linguistics of discourse.

a. Semiotics and semantics.

Benveniste's theory of discourse starts where de Saussure left off: the residual concept of parole.[2] For de Saussure parole was an execution of the free combination of language by individuals, unrestricted by the laws of langue. Benveniste, however, holds that parole also has a structure which is as rigorous as the structure of langue, but irreducible to it. To express this trait of parole, Benveniste replaces the Saussurean term parole with discours (discourse). His theory of discourse makes, therefore, a distinction between two functionings of language, each dependent upon a specific unit of language, but irreducible to one another. The semiotic function of language is based on the unit of the sign, while the semantic function of language is based on the unit of the sentence.[3]

Interprétations and La métaphore vive. Ricoeur draws mostly from Benveniste's Problèmes de Linguistique Générale, Paris, Gallimard, 1966 and "La forme et le sens dans le langage", in La Langage II, Actes des xiiie Congrès des Sociétés de Philosophie de Langue Française, Neuchâtel, Baconnière, 1967, p.29-40.

2. The discussion of the linguistic theory of E. Benveniste by Ricoeur differs little in the great number of articles in which he turns to him. Because of Ricoeur's primarily methodological concern the texts are brief. My presentation is derived from the following texts: "Événement et sens", (362), p.15-22; Cours sur l'herméneutique, (374), p.13-16; Langage (Philosophie), (355:772); "Discours et communication", (376:27-30); Signe et sens, (378), p.1013; "Creativity in Language: Word, Polysemy, Metaphor", (387), p.121-123; La métaphore vive, (410), p.88-100; Interpretation Theory: Discourse and the Surplus of Meaning, (423), p.6-22; "Philosophie et langage", (458), p.453-458. According to Ricoeur, the phenomenology of Husserl does not possess adequate tools to cope with linguistics without a subject (275:121). That is the reason for Ricoeur turning elsewhere. The linguistics of Benveniste provides the tool. But also Benveniste's theory needs to be complemented. Ricoeur will do so by turning to three other approaches to language; namely, (1) the theory of propositions of the English language analytic philosophy derived from the works of G. Frege, L. Wittgenstein, and B. Russell, (2) the theory of speech-acts of J.L. Austin and J. Searle, and (3) the theory of intention of P. Grice. Wherever possible, Ricoeur will link these theories with the work of E. Benveniste and E. Husserl.

3. The distinction between semiotics and semantics goes back to the earliest works of Benveniste but the terminology is of a later date.

What repercussion does this new unit of language have upon the question of meaning? It is Benveniste's theory that the communicative dimension of language must be given priority over the code. In other words the emphasis is displaced from semiotics to semantics. Hence, meaning is also dislodged from the sign to the sentence. Although the sentence is composed of signs it is not itself a sign. It is irreducible to the sign and constitutes the highest order of language. The question of meaning shifts, therefore, towards the sentence and away from the signified of the sign.

The sign's function is to be distinctive from other signs. A sign is defined by its difference from and opposition to other signs within the lexical system. It has no intrinsic or immanent definition. It is sufficient for a sign to exist in opposition to other signs that delimit its position in language. In other words, the sign is defined by its form. For a sign to have meaning it must achieve distinctiveness in relationship to other signs. The major trait of the sign is difference (457:456).

The function of the sentence, on the other hand, is synthetic. It seeks the integration of the lower units into a composition that makes it irreducible to its component units. With the sentence, a boundary is crossed into a new domain: the domain where things are said by someone to another. The life of human discourse in action is portrayed by the limitless variety of human synthetic compositions. The sign has only a 'form'; it is the sentence which has meaning.

By linking meaning with discourse, meaning also assumes a temporal dimension. An act of discourse is an event that takes place between people. Benveniste calls it an instance de discours, an occurrence of discourse. As an event it appears and it disappears. As an event, discourse has an actual existence. On the other hand, the sign and the system of signs is a-temporal. It has only a virtual existence (408:456).

The event of discourse is founded upon the unique operation of the sentence, namely, predication. By means of predication discourse has the unique ability to say something about something. To it alone can be attributed the giving of meaning to an occurrence of discourse. We must return below to the place that Ordinary Language Philosophy gives to predication. Predication has little in common with the signified of semiotics. Whereas the signified of the sign remains within language, it cannot be transferred to another language. The signified remains unique in its difference and opposition and, hence, is not translatable. The meaning of a sentence in its predication is eminently translatable into another language (378:1013).

b. The dialectic of event and meaning.

What has been described above as the occurrence of discourse can be formulated by what Ricoeur calls the dialectic of event and meaning (416:70). What he means by this is that the evanescent event of speech somehow does not disappear but is captured and repeatable. Discourse is the singular event whereby the linguistic signs of language are combined in such a unique fashion that something occurs between two speakers. It is not just that the material aspect, the words, of the discourse can be repeated, but also the event. Its character of event does not derive however from the signs. Discourse actualizes language and gives it existence.

But how can meaning capture the event? An event as an event is incommunicable. It is fleeting and transitory. Ricoeur calls the event a monad (365:33). It is individual, unique, unrepeatable, and hence incommunicable.

And yet, and this is the enigma of discourse, the event-character does not pass into oblivion. The event can be repeated and recognized as the same. The sublation of the event of speech into something enduring is called the meaning of discourse. The event is rescued in its meaning. Hence, the aphorism that discourse occurs as an event but is to be understood as meaning (417:70). For Ricoeur this sublation of the event in meaning is the foundation of communication (374:30).

But what is this enduring something of discourse? For Benveniste meaning is constituted by the sentence, more specifically, by the predicative power of the sentence. The meaning of the sentence, however, no longer is confined to opposition and difference of the signs of the sentence but has broken the bonds of language to penetrate something beyond language. Language has become mediation.

2. Philosophical semantics.

Philosophical semantics has gained its greatest impulse from the work of English philosophers. Their theory of meaning devolved from the attempts to reformulate ordinary language according to the maxims of artificial, scientific language. The originators were Whitehead and Russell and Wittgenstein (at the time of his Tractatus) and Carnap. The hold of logical and mathematical language upon ordinary language was shed in the second phase of Ordinary Language Philosophy, mainly through the influence of Ryle, Wittgenstein (at the time of his Philosophical Investigations), J.L. Austin and P.F. Strawson. The reflections on meaning by this School have been immense and impressive. Because their contribution to the question of meaning has also influenced Ricoeur we must examine their position.

a. Potential and actual meaning.

A debate about meaning similar to the debate in France about the linkage of meaning to the sign or to discourse surfaced in England. The debate centred on whether meaning should be attached to the word or to the sentence. But if the debate is similar, it is also radically dissimilar. English language philosophy knows no equivalent of the Structuralist signe.[4] It

---

4.   The English language Ordinary-Language Philosophy has largely ignored the semiotic and semantic linguistics. Its emphasis is upon the performance of ordinary language, to the exclusion of artificial language. For Ricoeur's critique of this philosophy cf. 365:775-776.

speaks of the word. And there is no direct link between the signe and the word. In discourse the signe becomes a word (mot) (417:125). The formal Structuralists speak of signe, lexeme, phoneme, because they abstract from any use in discourse and refer only to a code. It is for that reason that a word, as a unit of discourse, that contributes to an outside of language, must be distinguished clearly from the sign (365:58-60). In discourse a word is a noun or a verb or an adjective and not merely a lexical difference.

That raises the issue anew whether in this new context meaning attaches itself primarily to the word or to the sentence? Or, to state it in other words, is meaning an issue of predication (i.e., a function of the sentence) or an issue of denomination (i.e., a function of the word)?

What is the thesis of denomination? It postulates that a certain name is attached properly to a thing, so that a word is said to have a proper meaning. The proper meaning is opposed to an improper meaning or a figurative meaning that also may be attached to the word. It maintains, therefore, that essentially one name belongs to a thing. There is a fundamental link between this name and this thing. Meaning consists then in the proper naming of a thing. It is the position of nominalism (417:45). According to Ricoeur the art of rhetoric deteriorated into a senseless word-game precisely because of the "tyranny of the word" (417:45) in the struggle for meaning. From the high art of persuasion in the areas of human public life in Greece, rhetoric declined first to a theory of style and finally to a theory of tropes, i.e., to word-focussed figures of speech. Its bond with philosophy was broken and rhetoric became the archivist of the figures of speech (417:7-13). Because every other meaning attached to the word outside of its so-called essential denomination was called improper, its effect could only be declared stylistic or figurative. The aim of seeking another word can only be to please, or in the worst case, to seduce.

English language philosophy rejects such a nominalism. Ryle emphasized that words have meaning only to the extent that they are used. A word has no proper meaning. According to a dictum of Wittgenstein, "The meaning of a word is its use in the language" (417:128).[5] Words have a use precisely in the sentence so that their meaning is derived from the sentence or from the discourse situation. If a word has a meaning, it is because of its use in discourse. English Language Philosophy tends toward the total subordination of the meaning of words to the over-all meaning of the sentence (378:1014).

But does this mean that the meaning of the sentence so dominates that the word in fact dissolves into the sentence? Are words meaningul only in and through the context of discourse, as I.A. Richards maintains in The Philosophy of Rhetoric?[6] He argues that the meaning of a

---

5.   Wittgenstein's dictum is found in his Philosophical Investigations, New York, MacMillan, 1953, par. 43.

6.   London, Oxford University Press, 1936 (1971).

sentence is due, not to the meaning of words, but to the interanimation of words in a sentence. It is the interanimation of words in a sentence, according to Richards, that allow us to stabilize or to guess the meaning of individual words (417:79).

Ricoeur finds that such a contextual theory of meaning goes too far in denying a proper identity to words. He seeks to forge a different link between the semantics of the sentence and a possible semantics of the word. He accepts that there is an interplay of meaning between the sentence and the word. As such he recognizes with Richards the contextual functioning of the word. The word receives the 'imprint' of predication (417:125). But this contextual functioning of a word does not lead to the dissipation of the meaning of the word. A word does possess a semantic autonomy. This is evidenced by the fact that the operation of naming in certain areas exists independently of predication. The very existence of dictionaries indicates that the game of naming is not meaningless (417:11-112). But it is not the most important language game. That is played out in the realm of discourse at the level of predication. At the level of the word, Ricoeur holds, the context sits right within the perimeter of the word. The various acceptances of a word are so many 'contextual classes', that is, so many usages of words in different contexts. The use in a sentence, then, is more determinative of the meaning of a word than the denominative function (417:128).

For that reason the isolated word has only a potential meaning. The word is a series of possible meanings in a variety of possible contexts (417:129). A word has only a semantic potential or kernel, but it is not real or actual. The word has an actual meaning only in a sentence. Only a sentence can induce the passage from the potential to the actual meaning of a word. In a sentence, the meaning of the totality reverts to and inhabits the word, allowing it to refer to a specified object. Hence a difference exists between the meaning of a sentence and the meaning of a word. Wittgenstein called the meaning of a sentence a 'state of affairs', while the meaning of a word he called an 'object' (417:129).[7]

The meaning of discourse issues, therefore, from the interplay between the word and the sentence. The word brings to the sentence the variety of contexts in which it has functioned, and which Ricoeur calls its 'semantic capital' (417:130). It is this multiplicity, this semantic capital, that the sentence manages and sorts out to actualize meaning in a certain manner. A word is, therefore, identifiable not merely in the context of a sentence. It possesses a proper identity, which allows us to use it again and again as the same word, but in a different context. But its proper framework is provided by the sentence.

---

7. Cf. also "Discours et communication: La communication problèmatique" art. cit., p.56.

b. Predication and identification.

Ordinary Language Philosophy defines the sentence logically by its functions.[8] Reducing the sentence to its bare essentials, it has two basic functions: identification and predication.[9] The dictum, 'meaning is use' becomes operational, according to Strawson, in the interrelationship of identification and predication.

The identifying function of the sentence bears on the subject of a proposition. Every proposition identifies the 'bodies' or 'persons' about which something is said. These are the logically proper subject of the proposition. The subject is individual and specifies as closely as possible that about which something is said. Each proposition clearly identifies the singular existents that are the subject of a statement.

The predicative function links the logically proper subject with universal qualities or classes or actions or relations. Because they are universal they are predicable to a series of subjects. The sentence interlinks this universal predicate with a logically proper subject. The function of predication and identification are interrelated to the point that, in discourse, a predicate logically presupposes the subject and the subject presupposes the predicate.

Now it is to the identifying function of language that the reality of existence must be attached. What is identified is said to exist. In other words, according to Strawson, the logically proper subjects are potential existents. Here, language attaches itself to things. Predicates, on the other hand, are not potential existents. The predicate deals with universal qualities and actions and as such does not exist.[10]

---

8. The main contributor is P.F. Strawson in his work Individuals. An Essay in Descriptive Metaphysics, London, Methuen, 1959, part II. Cf. La métaphore vive, (416), p.92-95.

9. The suggestion that Benveniste considered only the predicative function essential and not the identifying function is refuted by Ricoeur in La métaphore vive, (417), p.94-95. The predicate by itself can hardly be the sole determinant of the sentence. The sentence as a whole carries the particular application of a generic predicate.

10. It is John Searle in his Speech Acts (Cambridge University Press, 1969) who identified the ontological trait of the identifying function. If the subject is the bearer of existence, it must be remembered that, by itself, it has only a potential, virtual existence. The subject must become actualized in a full proposition. Ricoeur sees in this the modern solution to the question that plagued the Medievals, when they asked whether universals existed (378:1011).

c. The 'force' of the sentence.

Ordinary Language Philosophy proposes also another dimension of the semantics of discourse. It is what is called the 'force' of the sentence. Acts of discourse do things with words. They state; they order; they wish; they promise. The propositional content packs an additional punch. This theory of the acts of discourse was first proposed by J.L. Austin in his theory of Speech-Act.[11] Ricoeur adopts this theory to advance a deepening of the question of meaning through the power of words to do something in the very saying. Language according to Austin is performative. When someone says, "Jane, I take you as my wife", language is given a thrust that gives 'force' to the statement. Austin recognized three levels where that force is operative.

The first performative level Austin calls the locutionary act. The locutionary act involves that which is said in each instance. It is language at its logical level. Searle in his Speech-Acts[12] calls it the propositional act. The locutionary act is the basic act of discourse, where someone states what is the case. Every statement, even a mere observation, is a performative act.

The second performative level Austin calls the illocutionary act. Certain propositions do something in the very saying (hence, illocutionary). Besides possessing the properties of a proposition, discourse cannot predicate or refer without doing so in an assertive or commanding fashion. In the stating, promising, or commanding, language breaks through its boundaries to an outside through the force that lies in the statement. What I say is said with the force of a promise or of an order (417:72-73). For the Philosophy of Mind the illocutionary act is the act of total discourse. This philosophy examines and charts, therefore, the verbs for their performative factor.[13] Each class of verbs has its own type of language game with its own internal rules. The Philosophy of Mind seeks to uncover these rules and apply them to the acts of discourse. The illocutionary act of what one does in saying has certain other marks whereby it embeds itself in language.

---

11.   How to Do Things with Words? (Oxford Conferences), Oxford, The Clarendon Press, 1962. Ordinary Language Philosophy credits its origin to Wittgenstein's Philosophical Investigations, with its famous aphorism, "Meaning is use". Ricoeur perceives this movement as a protest against any Platonic idealization of meaning (378:1013-1014), as well as against the attempt by Russell and Whitehead (Principia mathematica) to reduce language to the rules of symbolic logic (373), p.29.

12.   An Essay In the Philosophy of Language, Cambridge, Cambridge University Press, 1969. John Searle, a pupil of J.L. Austin, brought more system into the variety of the acts of discourse as analysed by Austin.

13.   Austin lists at least five classes of performatives: the verdictives, the exercitives, the promissives, the comportamentatives, and the expositives.

These marks are certain grammatical and lexical devices such as verb-moods (subjunctive, imperative, optative...), the exclamation mark, and the question mark. These marks allow for the identification of the force of the proposition (365:40-41). Moreover, for the Philosophy of Mind predication and reference are meaningful only in an illocutionary act. It is the illocutionary act that is the speech-act proper (362:47).

The third performative level Austin calls the perlocutionary act. The perlocutionary act is what the speaker achieves by saying. The speech-act can also lead to effects, to acts, that take place because of a wish, a promise or a persuasion. Thus, for instance, a threat can induce fear. Discourse can become a stimulus effecting certain results in the hearer. The perlocutionary act is the act that is least embedded in linguistic traces (365:44; 423:14).[14]

3. The dialectic of sense and reference.

We have already noted a number of times that Ricoeur's theory of discourse is built upon the common experience of speech as a saying of something about something to someone. This saying of something about something is expressed in linguistic philosophy by sense and reference. The discussion of the dialectical pair of sense and reference was introduced into philosophy by Gottlob Frege in his famous article, "Über Sinn und Bedeutung".[15] The distinction validates itself in the proposition where a differentiation can be made between what is said (sense) and that of which it is said (reference).

In semiotics, the question of reference is automatically excluded. The sign constituted by the signifier and the signified remains within the confines of language. Signs refer only to other signs within the system in their difference or opposition.[16] The contribution of Frege lies

---

14. Ricoeur has no difficulty in incorporating the theory of speech acts into a theory of discourse. The theory of speech acts provides a more encompassing model of discourse than the French linguistic theory. Moreover, it clearly concretizes the phenomenological model. The speech acts are hierarchically ordered in such a fashion that the locutionary act founds the illocutionary act and the illocutionary act founds the perlocutionary act. This permits the distinctions of semiotics and semantics to be introduced into the analysis of speech acts.

15. Zeitschrift für Philosophie und philosophische Kritik, 100 (1892). Ricoeur accepts the translation in English of the title by Peter Geach as most appropriate. Geach translates "Sinn" as "sense" and "Bedeutung" as "reference". (423:19).

16. The 'signified' of semiotics is not to be confused with the 'intended' of Benveniste or with the concept of intentionality of Husserlian phenomenology. The signified is the counterpart of the sign but it does not reach beyond language. Benveniste's intended and Husserl's fulfilment

32

precisely in his situating of sense. In singular fashion, he showed that sense must not be identified with psychological meaning. He divorced sense from subjectivity and affirmed that sense does not exist in nature or in the spirit. And yet sense is objective. That is, sense is ideally objective. It is not a representation that varies with each subject, but informs identically in a multitude of psychic events.

Reference, on the other hand, adds to sense the grasp towards reality. There is in discourse a breaking through the barriers of the sign system in a creative process that gives form to the human mind - the German word Bildung expresses it well - and to the world. What this reference takes into account is the vast field of reality outside of language that is brought near and overcome in language. Reference, then, relates language to the world.[17]

Again, it is not the word but the sentence in use that gives access to reference. As Strawson says, "to refer is what a sentence does in a certain situation and according to a certain use."[18] The reality referred to by the speaker does not escape the structure of the sense. The speech-event even in its reality-reference is structured by its intertwining of subject and predicate. The ideal structure of sense forms the basic reference (423:20).

It is this ontological thrust of reference that has the most far-reaching consequences for a theory of discourse. The language of reference says something, not only about things, but also about the ontological condition of our being in the world. That world is not language itself. But language brings the world of our experience into focus. It is our experience, our feeling of participation in reality, that is brought to language. If the identifying function of the sentence presupposes existence, as we saw, this

---

(remplissement) of the ideal empty aim (la visée vide) corresponds to Frege's Bedeutung. See also 475:119-120.

17. In linguistics, a clear distinction must be maintained between the predicate and the reference. To predicate is not to attribute existence. This function pertains to the identifying function within a proposition. Things are singular identities while concepts are predicatives. The latter sorts objects into a class, a quality, a relation or an action. They are universals and as such they do not exist and have no need to exist in order to have meaning. "Beautiful" as a qualitative predicate 'refers' to nothing in reality. The anchoring of language in reality is achieved by its reference and not by its predication. Predication is an intra-linguistic device, operative as a semiotic sign except that the frame within which it is operative is not the lexical code as code but as a word within a sentence. In his discussion of this question, Ricoeur relies on the analysis of John Searle's Speech-Acts. Cf. 374:53-55.

18. P.F. Strawson, "On Referring", Mind, 59 (1950), quoted by Ricoeur in Interpretation Theory, (423), p.20.

identification of singular things as existent has significance only if these singular things are rooted in an even more originary experience of being in the world. Ricoeur holds that it is this originary rootedness, this ontological condition, that moves to expression in language: "It is because there is first something to say, because we have an experience to bring to language, that conversely, language is not only directed towards ideal meanings but also refers to what is" (423:21).

For Ricoeur, the dialectic of sense and reference is such that it becomes the fundamental rule of the theory of language as discourse (423:21). It founds the dialectic of event and meaning; even semiotics must pay prior tribute to the capacity of language to refer. For Ricoeur, discourse's dialectic of sense and reference provides the foundation for linguistics.

4. The subject in the logic of meaning.

Has the subject, so central to phenomenology, disappeared in the dialectic of sense and meaning and of sense and reference? Are subject and meaning still the correlatives of phenomenology? We indicated above that this correlation was definitively broken. But is there no place for the subject in a theory of discourse? Ricoeur denies that the subject is totally absent but admits at the same time that, "This subject might not be me or who I think I am; in any case, the question 'Who is speaking?' has a sense at this level, even if it must remain a question without an answer" (320(278):254).

For the philosophy of language the subject surfaces again in the phenomenon of reference. Reference is dialectical in the sense that it refers both to a 'world' and to a speaker. It refers to the speaker by a number of grammatical procedures which linguists call shifters (423:13). These shifters are personal pronouns, certain verb forms, proper nouns, verb tenses, demonstrative pronouns, etc., that refer to the world of the speaker. The personal pronoun 'I', for instance, is a self-referent of the sentence. It is an asemic reality, having no meaning by itself. Its sole function is to refer the discourse to the one who is speaking. Shifters in fact indicate a different reality in each speech-event. Similarly the verb-tense is an auto-referent. Grammatically, the tenses constitute different systems, but they must be seen as anchored in the present tense. The present tense is auto-designative because it is the very moment of the utterance of the discourse. It is the temporal qualifier of discourse. Also the adverbs of space and time, 'here' and 'now', and the demonstrative, 'this' and 'that' function as an auto-reference.

The significance of this auto-referential character of discourse may not appear at first glance. But, in a discussion of the meaning, a distinction must be made between the meaning of the speaker and the meaning of the proposition. The meaning of the proposition we have identified formally as the intertwining of the twofold functions of identification and predication. This meaning of the proposition may not be identified with the meaning of the speaker. What I say is not necessarily identical with what I intend to say. In other words, one must not identify the meaning of a proposition with the psychic meaning of the speaker. As a matter of fact, for Ricoeur the psychic dimension is an incommunicable dimension of life (365:48). If the proposition expresses the utterer's meaning it is not a psychic meaning but rather a noetic or intentional meaning. The psychic is, by definition, the non-intentional part of life. The psychic is 'life's solitude' because it cannot be communicated (365:48). The meaning of the speaker does not control the meaning of the proposition. But that prohibition against identifying the speaker and the meaning does not mean that the speaker must be excluded altogether. The speaker is part of the text. The speaker is part of the semantics of the text. The utterer's meaning has found its inscription in the text itself. One does not have to look beyond or behind what is said in order to uncover the meaning of the speaker but one must look for it within what is said (423:13, see also 417:75).

B. WRITTEN DISCOURSE.

Thus far no distinction has been made between oral and written discourse. What happens, however, to the question of meaning and the subject when oral discourse becomes written discourse? For Ricoeur this shift to writing is highly significant, since he calls writing the complete measure of discourse (423:25).

It is Ricoeur's thesis that written discourse is grounded in oral discourse but that it obtains a new type of objectivity which oral discourse does not possess (370:546). In this, he differs both from the Romanticist hermeneutics and from Jacques Derrida. Romanticist hermeneutics does not distinguish sufficiently between oral discourse and written discourse. It takes oral discourse and the type of understanding and interpretation that flows from orality as its paradigm (370:546). The two are thought to be the same. On the other hand, Jacques Derrida's distinction of the written and spoken word is judged as too radical (362:18).[19] For Derrida writing is not founded on the spoken language but writing is the direct source of the traits of language.

Although oral discourse is not always at the origin of writing, e.g., in literature where human thought is immediately committed to inscription (423:28-29), a text is a discourse about something addressed to an audience. However, a written text is not merely a transcription of oral discourse. Rather, it is a direct inscription of discourse. Technically speaking, a text is a substitution of oral discourse, not an appendix. Or, as Ricoeur says, "One writes precisely because one does not speak" (337:136). With the introduction of writing, a decisive shift takes place. Speech is preserved and snatched from forgetfulness. The exchange of the viva vox for the linguistic marks has brought with it a series of political, economic

---

19.   Cf. his following works: La voix et le phénomène, Paris, Presses Universitaires de France, 1967: L'écriture et la différence, Paris, Seuil, 1967; De la grammatologie, Paris, Ed. de minuit, 1967.

and juridical repercussions that have extended not only the range of communication but also the power of communication within the human linguistic community (423:28).

The exteriorization and objectification that the graphic inscription permits has been considered at several periods in history as a grave threat to our humanity. To understand that threat, but also the response that Ricoeur gives to it, allows us to understand Ricoeur's own plea for a culture of the written text.

The warning against writing is found as early as in Plato's Phaedrus (423:38-39). The exteriority of writing, he thought, would destroy the immediacy that hearing and authentic meaning bring to the human community. Writing is not a real remedy against forgetfulness because it remains external. It does not possess the flexibility of discourse to respond to the questioner and to the circumstance. It is, therefore, a threat to wisdom and to education. Writing promotes forgetfulness, or, as J.J. Rousseau said later, it encourages distance and division within the human community (423:39).

The issue raised by Plato's Phaedrus is the issue that might be raised against all of modernity. It is the challenge that the massive objectification of reality in all its forms addresses to humanity's desire for immediacy. Ricoeur's response to Plato's plea against writing equally reveals his basic response to the current critique of objectification.

The objectivation that writing brings about, according to Plato, is comparable to the objectivation of the eikon, a painting. To Plato, an eikon is a weakened representation, a mere shadow, of reality. As a shadow, it is only an impression, a vague outline. Ricoeur's theory of art rejects such a view. Building on a theory of François Dagognet concerning painting, he holds that painting - and in a similar fashion, writing - is not an attempt to duplicate reality but to augment the real.[20] François Dagognet conceives the strategy of painting to be that of contracting and miniaturizing reality. But in the very abbreviation of the time-space dimension, it enlarges our vision of reality. The painter, like the writer, works with an 'optic' alphabet: two-dimensionality, centering, the use of colour pigments and contrasts. These are his materials with which he writes "a new text of reality" (423:41). As Ricoeur comments, "Painting for the Dutch masters was neither the reproduction nor the production of the universe, but its metamorphosis" (423:41). Instead of being only an aide-de-mémoire of the real thing, the eikon opens up a reality that is more real than the ordinary real.

This iconic property of written characters is perhaps not clearly evident in the Western phonetic alphabet. Western culture, more than other cultures, has used sound or dialogue as the basis for inscription. But the

---

20. The text referred to by Ricoeur is Dagognet's Ecriture et Iconographie, Paris, Vrin, 1973.

phonetic inscription, as well as the pictogram, but even more clearly the ideogram, which directly inscribes thought-meanings, also reveals a novelty in reality. We could point to the space-structure of the linguistic marks, the ordering of the linguistic marks in a linear fashion, the spacing of the linguistic marks in a specific form, etc. These characteristics proper to writing - whether in a phonetic alphabet or in an ideogram - bring writing to a form that is analogous to painting and its more obvious capacity to refocus reality.

The capacity of writing to redescribe reality is focal to Ricoeur's hermeneutics of the text.[21] But it achieves this redescription by means of the transformations that oral discourse undergoes when it becomes inscribed. It is this transformation that needs to be specified. Ricoeur indicates four areas in which writing changes the relationships operative in speech.

1. Fixation of discourse.

In a first approximation of the problem of writing, one is tempted to view writing as a graphic inscription of oral discourse. This would assign to writing the same properties as to orality. This is, however, not the case. It is obvious that the written text even as a transcription of an original speech event is not the speech event itself. The speech event is a temporal event. It takes place in the present. It is evanescent, dying with the passing sound. Writing cannot save that event. The event fades, to be survived only by its sense. In its attempt to rescue the event, writing fixes the sense with the alphabetical, lexical and syntactical inscription. Hence, the temporality of the event is replaced by the spaciality of the inscription. Writing accentuates what in oral discourse itself is fixed or objectified; namely, the sense of discourse. In fact, writing is activated precisely by the type of objectivation that takes place when in discourse the event is suppressed in the sense. It is not the saying-event of speaking but the 'said' that is conserved in the sense but more decisively in writing. By applying to our discussion the traits of communicability, we can say that "what we write is the noema of the speaking" (370:532).

The first characteristic of writing, then, is its fixation of discourse. For Ricoeur, the link with discourse is not obliterated in the written text. The condition of the possibility of writing lies in the structure that precedes any split between oral and written discourse. Discourse itself is already a form of exteriorization. Writing is the material support or exterior mark of that exteriorization. If discourse becomes exterior in propositions, writing engraves those propositions. Ricoeur's example says it well: "I say: it is day-break. But when the day is over that which was designated, opined, or meant in my saying, remains as the said. That is why it can be written" (413:35). Before anything can be written, it is presupposed that it can be said.

---

21. The redescription of reality will be taken up again in Chapter Three. See below p.79-83.

But once the substitution from oral to written discourse has taken place, the written text becomes a system of signs all its own. According to Ricoeur, what was virtually, inchoatively manifest in the living word becomes apparent in writing. The accentuation of the sense has in writing become full-fledged to the point that the written combinations of the sign-system are no longer reducible to the oral. Graphism gives to signs a substance similar to the phonic substance of signs. But in graphics the signs are more objectified, and hence alienated, than in phonics. This accentuation of the sense in the icon of writing has a number of other consequences that affect Ricoeur's relating of language and meaning. These we will now examine.

2. The autonomy from the speaker: the author.

The radicalization of the alienation of discourse in writing is most apparent in the disjunction of the written text from the immediate presence of the speaker of the spoken discourse. In writing, the speaker has become the author and assumes a different relationship to his/her discourse than in speech.

In the spoken discourse, there is an overlapping of the subjective intention of the speaker (Paul Grice's 'utterer's meaning') and the verbal meaning of the proposition (Paul Grice's 'utterance meaning'). The speaker intends to say what s/he means. The amount of self-effacement - Ricoeur says that a speaker dies a little in his/her speaking for the benefit of what is said - remains within limits in speech. In the written text, the speaker's immediacy is dissolved and what remains is the text and its meaning. The text becomes autonomous. It becomes an object of reading and no longer of listening.

Having broken away from the immediacy of the speaker, the text achieves a freedom to roam beyond the historical, psychological and sociological confines that impose themselves upon the speaker-hearer situation. With the speaker absent, the emphasis falls upon the text and what it says, rather than what the author intended to say.

This leads to a further spiritualization of the sense. It has achieved a higher form of alienation of the meaning because the psycho-physical presence of the author ceases to concretize the meaning in the temporal, spatial circumstances of the author. But since the author is not there to guide the understanding of what s/he says, the text falls under the protection of interpretation. For Ricoeur, the interpretation is required because of the weakness of discourse in the absence of the author. But here he insists upon two caveats (423:30). Interpretation must be guarded against two excesses.

The first excess is called the fallacy of the absolute text. It would maintain that the author and the author's intention are entirely excluded from the process of interpretation. The text is the thing. This 'fallacy of the hypothesized text' replaced an earlier view which Ricoeur (following W.K. Wimsatt)[22] calls the 'intentional fallacy'. This is the thesis of Romanticist hermeneutics. It held that the author's intention is the source to be approximated in any valid interpretation.

Ricoeur maintains an intermediate position. Because of the auto-designative traces in the text itself, the author is not totally absent from the text. The author's meaning must therefore not be sought outside of the text - as Romanticist hermeneutics does - but as the property of the text. The author's unavailability for guidance leaves the reader only with the verbal meaning in which the psychic intention has found its exteriorization. Ricoeur appears to call for a dialectical relationship between the author's meaning and the verbal meaning. For him these are dependent upon each other (423:30).[23]

3. Autonomy from the listener.

The 'interlocutor' is constitutive for oral discourse. When I speak, I speak with and to a 'you'. The second person is present to the speaker. Because of the fixation of discourse in the autonomous text with the author absent, the listener/reader is also released from the here and now situation and becomes public property. Ricoeur calls this trait "the most exemplary achievement of discourse in writing" (360:28). The written discourse as an autonomous text is addressed to an audience that the text itself creates. Here, discourse attains a potential universality. Its public is potentially all who can read.[24] That, in fact, social factors limit the audience and create distinctions and classes is not due to the text itself.

However, the text and its public cannot be totally divorced. The significance and the importance of a text are derived from the dialectic between the text and its audience. If a text is written for a public, it is the public's response to the text that determines its acceptance and its role in

---

22.   See W.K. Wimsatt and M. Beardsley, The Verbal Icon, Lexington, University of Kentucky Press, 1954.

23.   This is further evidence of Ricoeur's anti-psychologizing attitude. It may be questioned, however, whether the verbal traces of the author's intention could not be clarified further by extra-textual research. Are the frequent auditory references in James Joyce's Finnegan's Wake not more comprehensible when the critic knows that Joyce wrote Finnegan's Wake when he was almost completely blind? The critic's knowledge that Joyce's heightened hearing because of his blindness has become accentuated in the text, is an extra-textual aid to the interpretation of the auditory traces. Furthermore, will not the resolve of the critic to continue the effort of interpreting the extreme complex references of Finnegan's Wake be strengthened if s/he knows that Joyce spent seventeen years composing the work and completed it only shortly before his death?

24.   In this section, and in the following, Ricoeur draws upon the work of H.G. Gadamer, Wahrheit und Methode, Tübingen, J.C.B. Mohr, 1960.

the human community (423:31). Furthermore, it is the acclaim granted a text that equally determines its survival. A text, for that reason, can break open the dialogal situation not only in the present but also to new circumstances beyond its time. This semantic autonomy of the text from the contemporaneous readers in different cultural and historical constructs opens up the text to a greater variety of readings. This also suggests that the reader enjoys a new type of autonomy vis-à-vis the text. The text can be read in a variety of ways and a critical hermeneutics will be forced to determine how it elaborates the dialectical relationship of the right of the reader and the right of the text. "Where dialogue ends, hermeneutics begins" (423:32).

4. Autonomy from ostensive reference.

Finally, the reference of discourse is affected by the shift from the dialogal situation to the written disourse. In oral discourse a common situation (Gadamer's Umwelt) is created by the speakers so that the reference locks into that situation. The speaker can point out the reference physically by gestures, or linguistically by such speech indicators as, for example, the demonstratives.

But once again the semantic autonomy of the text breaks apart this immediacy of the dialogal situation. What happens to the 'this', 'here', and 'now' of the two speakers? The ostensive reference is unmoored and set adrift. Ricoeur calls it "the suspension of ostensive or demonstrative reference" (376(377):1014). But the suspension is not an abolition of reference. Instead of giving entry to the Umwelt of the author, the written text enlarges the Umwelt into a world. This world is not the sum of the presences of the Umwelt, but, one might say, the horizon of presences (374:36). This is the world of the text. It reflects that the human being can be unbound from a situation and be released to inhabit a world beyond his/her immediate Umwelt. This world, Ricoeur contends, is "the ensemble of references opened up by the text" (370:535).

The references of the text are no longer ostensive references. Writing has the power to open up a 'world' in which we can dwell that is not bound by our immediate situation. "To understand a text is at the same time to light up our own situation, or, if you will, to interpolate among the predicates of our situation all the significations which make a Welt of our Umwelt" (370:536). Once again, the text spiritualizes. It suspends the immediate materiality to open up another vision of reality, or, to use Heidegger's phrase, a new dimension of our being-in-the-world. In his Sein und Zeit, Heidegger had already indicated that what is first understood in discourse is not another person but a project. That project is an outline of a new being-in-the-world (370:536). It is the destiny of writing in its autonomy to project that world.[25]

---

25. For a more detailed discussion of the world of the text see below p.118.

In unmooring the discourse from an immediate situation and turning it towards the origin of our being-in-the-world, the written text gravitates towards that body of texts that opens up the world of possibilities, the world of our project. Together these texts form the world of literature, a world, in which "words become words for their own sake" (337:139). Because of the importance of this project for hermeneutics, I will return to Ricoeur's analysis of this later.

With the conversion of oral discourse into writing, the question of meaning as well as the fate of the speaking subject undergoes a radical shift. The fixation of meaning in the fixation of discourse allows it to be identified again and again. The objectivation of the original event of discourse in the durable form of writing permits meaning to be stored in archives and to be transmitted in a written tradition. Meaning takes on a different temporal dimension because, in its fixation, it can be inserted somewhere in humanity's history. Moreover, the speaking subject or the author is available only in his or her noetic presence and not in his or her psychic presence. The author is absent except through the indices of the text itself. But it is the bonding of meaning to reference that is most affected by this conversion. To Ricoeur this shift from the ostensive reference towards the 'world' of meaning is so central that we shall reserve its discussion until the next chapter.

C. THE TEXT.

Ricoeur's theory of discourse, as we have examined it in the two previous paragraphs, is applicable equally to individual sentences and to a sequence of sentences. In shifting the quest for meaning and the subject to the area of written discourse, he had accepted the wager that the process of objectification that writing had introduced was not a harmful but a necessary process. But the focussing of the quest is not just upon any writing or any random sequence of sentences. If we ask, from which writings do we seek to recover meaning, Ricoeur would point to the written discourse as text. On a formal level, for Ricoeur the mediation of meaning must be sought in the text.[26]

1. Three categories of the text.

At its most general level, a text is a particular sequence of sentences which in their configuration form a totality that is irreducible to the individual sentences. One can study the text like a literary critic who deals with completed texts and composes a taxonomy of texts. Ricoeur, however, is concerned less with the finished product than with the process through which the text comes into being. His approach focusses on the production of the text. For him the text is a work of discourse. The text is

---

26. For the centrality of the notion of the text in Ricoeur's philosophy see D. Pellauer, "The Significance of the Text in Paul Ricoeur's Hermeneutical Theory" in Studies in the Philosophy of Paul Ricoeur, op. cit., p.98-114.

the production of a particular, ordered, sequence of sentences: it is an oeuvre, a work (370:94). Ricoeur insists that a text is only a text when it is considered from the perspective of production (417:219). Beside the trait of the inscription of discourse the text carries the trait of work (423:33).

Let us look briefly at the three criteria of the text as Ricoeur proposes them.

a. Composition.

The text is, first of all, a work of composition or 'disposition'.[27] It consists of a unique arrangement or configuration of a sequence of sentences. Its uniqueness makes the totality of the text to be irreducible to the sum of the individual sentences. The text is, for that reason, usually longer than a sentence. The composition of the totality is subject to closure. Every composition is a finite, closed whole (417:219).

b. Literary genre.

Literary genres are the generative devices that preside over the production of discourse (423:33). Every text is produced as a type of discourse. These generative devices can be compared, as Ricoeur does, to the code that underlies the structure of the sentence. Literary genres, one might say, codify the composition of the text. The genre varies according to the type of composition. Whereas in literary criticism the genres are perceived as taxonomic devices to categorize literary works, Ricoeur perceives the genres as rules of craftsmanship (379:135). Genres, such as narratives, essays, novels, poems, are not mere classifications; they are generative devices, applied to language. From discourse is fashioned a poem, a novel, an essay, a parable.

Accordingly, the text is a work of discourse that is recognizable in the forms. The recognition of the forms can proffer a decisive aid to interpretion of the text. This is so because the genres carry traits that have become traditional. The use of these traditional genres to encode a new message facilitates the interpretation because it unites the novel with the established. Because of the encodement in an established form, the message is not as easily distorted. Moreover, the form safeguards the message from dissolution after the loss of the original Sitz im Leben. In the encodement of the genre, it allows the message to find a new reference (411:71).

---

27. Ricoeur accepts a similarity between composition and the ancient rhetorical term 'dispositio', or Aristotle's 'taxis'. Aristotle divided rhetoric into three parts: taxis, that is, the composition of the discourse of persuasion, heuresis, that is, the invention of arguments which precedes the taxis, and lexis, a word which could perhaps best be rendered by the word diction. Lexis follows upon taxis. Cf. "Philosophy and Religious Language", Journal of Religion, 54 (1974), p.74.

c. **Style.**

The third and most important trait of the production of a text is style. Every work of discourse is a production that is both individual and unique. It is style that makes a text this poem or novel and the work of this poet. Ricoeur elaborates the theme of style through the work of Gilles-Gaston Granger.[28] His philosophy of praxis develops style not as a fact of the text but as a process and production within a social context. Style is a praxis of the organization of language in a given social configuration. But as a praxis its primary function is the practical determination of the individual. What Granger means by this is that all work, including the aesthetic creation, is an attempt at shaping individuality. Work tends to recuperate, to bring into focus, the individual as this individual. Consequently, Granger defines a philosophy of style as a "modality of the integration of the individual in a concrete process which is work and which is present of necessity in all the forms of praxis" (374:39, my translation).[29]

But the structuring of style also fulfills another function. In a text the structuring is inserted in a singular situation, in an individual praxis. But by inserting this structuring into this individual, unique situation the author releases that situation from its singularity, in much the same way that a predicate in a sentence releases the individuality of the subject. The situation cannot be understood in its singularity. Through the insertion of the structure, the situation is opened for understanding. The aesthetic style creates the conditions of this insertion of structure in singular situations.

This praxis of style assigns style not to the realm of facts, but to the realm of significations. Style produces singularities, but it does so at the point where structures touch the singularities of a lived situation. In that fashion style becomes a production of meaning despite the fact that as a work it creates the individual at the same time. Style continues to bear an individual signature. Style, as a philosophical discipline, is a meditation on human work (374:40).

This philosophy of style affects the previous analysis of discourse at three points: (1) the relationship of event and meaning, (2) the notion of author, and (3) the notion of reference.

In a philosophy of style the event of discourse has its parallel in the event of a production of a text. When we speak of a literary event, we generally refer to the publication of a literary work. The publication is in fact a mode of production, because in publishing a literary work one structures a situation by means of language. It is historical because

---

28.   Essai d'une philosophie de style, Paris, A. Colin, 1968.

29.   "Modalité d'intégration de l'individuel dans un processus concret qui est travail et qui se présente nécessairement dans toutes les formes de la pratique."

language in and through a literary work enters into the history of works or, more precisely, into "a history of the events of the production of works" (374:41). A literary work is an event precisely in its structuring of a situation. It is through style that this event-making survives. The praxis of style inscribes this structuring of a situation into the materiality of language (374:42).

Within this perspective the author becomes the actor or agent of style. It is the author who discovers the situation and structures it. He or she is the craftsman of language. Through style a new perspective is placed upon the relationship of author and text. The author is to be correlated with the process of individuality of work (374:43). The author is the artisan of a specific work of discourse, which, because of its style, now bears his or her signature. The text points back to its author. For that reason, the category of author is a category of interpretation of the text. Through the text as work the author must be correlated to the text. The author is individualized precisely in his or her production of a singular, individual work. But the presence of the author in the work is not the psychological presence but the stylistic presence. The name of the author is the name of the style. It is through the style that the author becomes a category of interpretation and not as a psychic presence behind the work. Plato's style, for example, is unique. But even though its uniqueness is not recognizable except through comparison with another author's style, Plato's uniqueness is part of the text and to be interpreted from the text (388:21).

A third area to be affected by style is the notion of reference. By applying the category of work to the reference of the text one may give the impression that the text becomes even more closed off from reality. But if it closes off the text from one dimension of reality, Ricoeur suggests, that is only the condition of the possibility of opening up another dimension of reality. For Ricoeur, the reference of a text in a practical philosophy of style accentuates even more strongly the capacity of the text to open up the world of the text. In the written text, it was stated above,[30] the ostensive reference is abolished to make way for the world of the text. The work of reference is precisely this fashioning of the world of the text. Nowhere is this more apparent - as we shall see in greater detail in the next chapter - than in the poetic text. No literary creation appears more structured than poetic language. By fusing sense and sound, the poet fashions a particular identity. The poem is pure poiesis, a new fashioning of reality by interlacing sense and sound (374:50).

2. Meaning and the structural analysis of narrative texts.

The approach of Ricoeur to the text is rather unique. In fact he proposes two correlated approaches which are extensions of the dialectic of meaning in the theory of discourse. Just as in the theory of discourse he maintains that there is a semiotics of meaning and a semantics of meaning, so too in the text he distinguishes between form and content (411:30). The

---

30.   Cf. above p.38-39.

question of meaning raises its head again in a manner similar to the way that Structuralism and the philosophy of language raised it earlier. Can a closure similar to the closure of signs in semiotics be imposed upon the text? Can meaning remain immanent to the text so that the text is without an outside?

The success of the schools of Structuralism imposes itself here. These schools have extrapolated the hypothesis of the theory of the sign of semiology to apply also to the larger units of language, postulating an homology of structure of the larger units to the smallest units. It has been most successfully and most widely applied to the narrative genre. Because of its effectiveness it cannot be dismissed. It must be incorporated within a comprehensive theory of meaning. In other words, the same works can be considered both as extensions of the theory of the sign and as extensions of the theory of discourse. The two theories of meaning that confront themselves here correspond to two attitudes before the text. The attitude of explanation covers the semiological treatment. It suggests that meaning is immanent to the text. The attitude of understanding covers the semantic treatment. For Ricoeur, as we shall see in greater detail below, these two attitudes have become inseparable today and are required for any contemporary recuperation of meaning.[31]

a. Meaning as the deep structure of the narrative.

Ricoeur's sources for the structural analysis of narratives have been on the one side the Russian formalist of the folktale, V. Propp,[32] and on the other side the French-language structuralists A-J. Greimas,[33] R. Barthes,[34] Cl. Brémont,[35] and Cl. Lévi-Strauss.[36] Ricoeur does not

---

31. Ricoeur has not worked out any text with the methods of structuralism. He has continuously relied on the work of others. Cf. "Sur l'exégèse de Genèse 1, 1-2, 4a", in Exégèse et herméneutique (Parole de Dieu), Paris, Seuil, 1971, p.67-84, and "Biblical Hermeneutics", Semeia, 13 (1975), p.29-148.

32. Morphology of the Folktale, Austin, University of Texas Press, second rev. ed., 1968.

33. Ricoeur acknowledges a degree of philosophical affinity to A. Greimas. Chapter Five of La métaphore vive is dedicated to Greimas. Greimas is best known for his work Sémantique structurale, Paris, Larousse, 1966.

34. Cf. Barthes' "Introduction à l'analyse structurale des récits", Communications, 8 (1966), p.1-27.

35. Cf. Cl. Brémond, "Le message narratif" in Communications 4 (1964), p.4-32, and "La logique des possibles narratifs" in Communications 8 (1966), p.69-76.

36. Structural Anthropology, New York, Doubleday.

provide an extensive analysis of their findings, because his interest lies more in the underlying thesis of Structuralism. I will present these here to the extent that they affect Ricoeur's theory of meaning.

(1) Vladimir Propp.

The Russian Formalists of the School of V. Propp set the tone with their study of the Russian folktale. In his analysis of Propp's work, Ricoeur finds three principles that have become generally acceptable to all Structuralists of the narrative. We present these common principles first and then the points of divergence.

1. It was Propp's intention to discover a descriptive model of the Russian folktale to uncover the unity in the multiplicity of the variations of the folktale. In order to discover this unity, he postulated that units larger than a sentence are composed according to the same laws as units that compose the sentence. Hence, a structural homology is said to exist between a text and a sentence (332:67).

2. The diachronic aspects of the story are subordinated to the synchronic, structural level of the story. A structural analysis searches primarily for the depth-structure of a story, and only secondarily for questions relating to the genesis or history of the story. The latter only enters into the analysis to the extent that they are determined by the formal structure (411:39).

3. In a text one can apply a twofold law of operation, called the syntagmatic and the paradigmatic. The paradigmatic law governs the operation of the distribution and the segmentation of the units and of their classification. The syntagmatic law governs the operation of the integration of the units. In the language of Benveniste, the two operations are called 'form' and 'sense'. The operations are completely immanent to the text. The sense of text is the internal integration of the units and the sub-units. It is the sense of the story that is the object of structural analysis (332:67). For that reason in structural analysis, on the one hand an attempt is made to provide an exhaustive description of all the constituent parts of the story. These are placed in a series of general classifications which offer the constants of the story. On the other hand, the syntagmatic task of integration seeks to discern the interrelation of these constants. This is the depth-structure of a text. It is the depth-structure that is the source of the meaning of a text. To understand a story is, therefore, not simply to follow a sequence (the 'and then...') of the story, but the structural constants and their interrelationship or distribution.

Up to this point structuralists generally agree. To the three positions of V. Propp we must add the following points, to which less general agreement is given. The differences apply principally to the third thesis.

According to Propp, the constant of a story is provided by the functions in the story and not by the characters of the story. The functions are fundamental and constitutive of the story, because by the functions are meant the actions of a character that are essential for the unfolding of a plot (411:40). The number of functions is limited and finite. In fact, according to Propp, the number of functions is limited to thirty-one. He arrived at this limited number by stripping the great variety of actions of a character of its various modalities, so that only a defined number of processes were left. It is this limited number of processes that function as the constants that support the great variety of actions.

To this central position of Propp two subsidiary postulates must be added.

1. According to Propp, the functions follow a specific sequence (411:41). In a story, there is a logic of narration in which particular functions will always relate to other functions in terms of a prior and a posterior. The succession of the functions is always identical. The story first proceeds from a description of an initial situation to the description of a lack either in the form of an internal lack (poverty) or an external lack (brought about through mischief, such as kidnapping, robbery, murder). Second in the succession of functions is the quest by a hero-seeker or hero-victim. And the final moment of the succession is the resolution or reintegration. The composition of a story must follow this process. The only freedom in the story lies in the expansion or omission of functions at a particular stage of the story but not in the order. It is the type of freedom exhibited in the story that differentiates the folktales from one another.

This point becomes accentuated if we remember that Propp postulated that, underlying the great variety of the Russian folktales, there is a single story: the Russian folktale.[37] This means, according to Lévi-Strauss, that Propp must distinguish the functions from the original story. The original story is the deep structure or the form of the folktale, while the functions are the structure.[38] The one story is ruled by the specific order of the functions. That is why all folktales are only variations of this one story and why it cannot deviate from the order of the original folktale (411:44-45).

2. The characters of the story, which are delineated by the spheres of action, are the actors. Propp identified seven characters: the villain, the donor, the helper, the sought-for person, the dispatcher, the hero, and the false hero. A sphere of action may pertain to one character or to several, and one character can be engaged in more than one sphere of action. It is the relationship of the character and the function that is essential to the story. The attributes of the character, such as features, name, and locale, are considered variants and for that reason, secondary to the story (411:45).

---

37. Propp's source of the Russian folktale, Afanas 'ev, had accumulated one hundred such tales.

38. Cf. "Biblical Hermeneutics", Semeia, 13 (1975), p.45.

(2) The French-language Structuralists of the Narrative.

Algirdas Julien Greimas and Roland Barthes parted ways with Propp on the question of the functions and the sequence of functions. They considered Propp's structure of functions to be too rigid. Instead, they built up the structure of the story upon the basis of the spheres of action. This meant an inversion of the order of Propp, for whom the constants were provided by the functions and the sequence of the functions. Greimas, in particular, sought the constants of the story in the interrelationship of the characters and the spheres of action. Using Lucien Tesnière's work, Greimas discovered that every sentence is a drama involving three syntactic components. These are the processes (that is, the classes of verbs), the actors (called 'actants'), and the circumstances (called 'circumstants').

Instead of accepting Propp's seven character-types, which Propp had derived from the inventory of the Russian folktales, Greimas sought to discover, in a more a priori fashion, the matrix of 'actants'. This he found by applying Jakobson's theory of binary opposites to the 'actants'. This led him to six roles: lord versus sought person, dispatcher versus addressee, and helper versus opponent.

This position affects Propp's thesis of the sequential structure of the folktale. Greimas holds that what rules the story is an actantial logic. The quest of the story follows a schema of human action "in which (a) an object of desire, aimed at by a subject (b) is situated, as object of communication, between a 'destinateur' (dispatcher) and a 'destinatoire' (the one who benefits from the action of the hero), and (c) is either 'helped' or 'harmed' by the desire of other beings" (411:47). The sequence of the story, Greimas maintains, is not as rigid as Propp would have it. Instead of an unchangeable sequence, Greimas applies a binary principle. Units of a story unfold within an alternative, for example, injunction versus acceptance, or confrontation versus success. These pairs form a depth-structure of the story, or, in the words of Greimas, a 'semic basis' (411:48). At this semic level, the structure is achronical. The temporal order of the sequence is dissipated. But, for Greimas, this does not mean that the surface structure, the semantic level, is totally encompassed by the semic basis. Greimas retains a diachronicity of the story as a residue to the semic basis. The comparison of the achronic deep structure with the diachronic surface structure, that remains as a residue in any semic analysis, enlarges the dramatic quality of the story.

For Ricoeur, this diachronic residue becomes central to his attempt to link this Structuralist approach to a more hermeneutical one. In fact, he suggests that it must be the goal of structural analysis to single out the diachronic kernel. This diachronic kernel constitutes the depth-semantics of the story. Greimas does not take that step because his concern lies in uncovering the actantial model of the text, i.e., its semic basis. For Ricoeur, however, this opening towards the diachronicity of a narrative, released by the structure of the story, provides the possibility of a twofold analysis of the narrative: an achronical structural analysis and a diachronic interpretation. As he suggests, it is the narrative itself that mediates the two interpretations (411:60).

Claude Lévi-Strauss' analysis of the mythic narrative follows a somewhat different route from Greimas (411:51-54).[39] He, too, drops the sequential order of the functions as the constant of the narrative. But he takes the additional step of depriving the narrative of all chronological and, therefore, narrative, characteristics. The story as a narrative sequence is only the surface that reveals a depth-structure. Lévi-Strauss sacrifices the narrative completely to a code. For Lévi-Strauss as for Roland Barthes "the message is the mere quotation of its underlying codes".[40]

Lévi-Strauss proposes, therefore, a radical application of the principles of semiotics, outlined by de Saussure, not just to the linguistic signs but also to texts. Mythic texts, accordingly, are composed of units that exhibit properties similar to the phonemes and morphemes of semiotics. The mythic units (Lévi-Strauss characteristically calls these units 'mythemes') can be subjected to the semiotic rules of linguistics. In the same way that phonemes are not concrete sounds, mythemes are not messages but oppositive differences or interplays of relationships. The meaning of the myth lies in the arrangement of the mythemes. Thus, for example, in his analysis of the Oedipus Rex myth, Lévi-Strauss discovered four packets of relationships (mythemes): the over-esteemed parental relation (e.g. Oedipus marries his mother), the under-esteemed parental relation (e.g. Oedipus kills his father), the negation of human autochthony (e.g. Oedipus kills the Sphinx), and the persistence of human autochthony (e.g. Oedipus has a swollen foot). These packets, he says, are interrelated. "The overrating of blood relations is to the underrating of blood relations as the attempt to escape autochthony is to the impossibility to succeed in it."[41] Instead of its narrative structure, the myth displays an achronical logical structure that interrelates its component units in such a fashion that the underlying contradictions are superceded into a harmony (332:39).

Ricoeur's evaluation of this analysis of Lévi-Strauss is quite harsh. When language is no longer discourse, when the referential function of a narrative is abolished, linguistic analysis - particularly when elevated to

---

39. Cf. his Anthropologie structurale (Paris), Plon, 1958, and La pensée sauvage, (Paris), Plon, (1963, c1962)).

40. This statement is derived from Roland Barthes' "L'analyse structurale du récit. A propos d'Actes X-XI", Recherches de Sciences Religieuses, 58 (1970). Cf. "Biblical Hermeneutics", art. cit., p.51. For a further discussion of the structuralism of R. Barthes see "Biblical Hermeneutics", art. cit., p.71-72, and Les incidences théologiques de recherches actuelles concernant le langage, (Paris), Institut d'Études oecuméniques, (1968), (ronéotypé).

41. Anthropologie structurale, (Paris), Plon, 1958. Cf. "Biblical Hermeneutics" Semeia, 13 (1975), p.54.

a philosophy - becomes ideological (411:51). At the point where narrative remains only intra-textual, the meaning and the sense coincide. Ricoeur applies to this structuralism the same critique that he passed over de Saussure's linguistics.[42] Without its referential function, the literary form of narrative becomes a 'mirror-game' (411:62), that reflects nothing but "language alone, the adventure of language, the advent of which keeps being celebrated".[43]

b. Ricoeur's evaluation of the Structuralist Method.

Despite the validity and even the necessity of the method of structuralism, Ricoeur refuses to isolate method from content to such an extent that the structure exists for its own sake at the expense of the reference. For Ricoeur, every text, beside having a sense, must also possess a reference. Structure must move for process. The necessity to go beyond sense to reference lies, according to Ricoeur, within the narrative text itself. He accepts from Greimas that a text contains a residue, which demands another kind of interpretation. This interpretation would respect the "movement of transcendence of the text beyond itself" (411:63). Ricoeur insists that it must be possible to return from the deep structures to the surface structures, that is, to language as discourse or as communication (411:65).[44]

This warning, however, does not remove the possibility and, at times, the necessity, of a structural analysis of texts. For Ricoeur, the possibility of such an analysis lies first of all in the gap between form and content. On the level of the form, the possibility of a structural analysis is accentuated by Ricoeur's own consideration of the form as a structuration. Textual discourse is structured according to certain modalities. These modes or genres, as the work of discourse, or as the specific fashioning of the text, enhance the possibility of a structural approach to the text. The form imposed upon the matter of language can be 'decoded' because the

---

42.   See p.22 of Chapter One.

43.   The quote regarding the celebration of language for its own sake comes from R. Barthes, "Introduction à l'analyse structurale des récits", Communications, 8, 1966, p.27. See "Biblical Hermeneutics", Semeia, 13, 1975, p.51.

44.   From his earliest writings on the merits and demerits of structuralism, Ricoeur has held that a structural analysis is both indispensible and subordinate to the process of communication.   In "Symbolique et temporalité" he writes, "Structuralism's raison d'être would then be to rebuild this full understanding, but only after having first stripped it, objectified it , and replaced it with structural understanding.   Thus mediated by the structural form, the semantic base would become accessible to an understanding which, although more indirect, would be more certain."   See "Structure and Hermeneutics", in The Conflict of Interpretations. Essays in Hermeneutics, (320), p.37.

discourse was first of all 'encoded'. That is why Ricoeur can write, "A structural approach is not only possible, it is necessary, to the extent that the codification at work belongs to the production of discourse as a poem, or as a narrative, an essay, etc." (411:68-69). This trait of disclosure indicates rather precisely how far Ricoeur will go along the structuralist path. The codification, or the literary genre, that is at work in discourse as a text, is not the message itself, but "a means to produce similar messages" (411:69, emphasis mine). It is a generative code to produce a discourse, and the function of discourse is to say.

The function of structural analysis is to aid in the decoding of the message. When it stops at the code itself and identifies the message with the code, it fails to understand that the code is only a means of the production of discourse. The code is not the discourse itself.

It is the task of hermeneutics to identify the individual discourse (the "message") through the modes of discourse (the "codes") which generate it as a work of discourse. In other words, it is the task of hermeneutics to use the dialectics of discourse and work, or performance and competence, as a mediation at the service not of the code, but of the message (411:70).

A structural analysis proves itself when it permits a better understanding of the message than a first surface reading. It becomes ideological when it refuses to go beyond the text and falls into the "for-the-sake-of-the-code" fallacy (411:69).[45]

Ricoeur is careful to preserve the function of structural analysis in the quest for meaning. But the quest for meaning through the use of this analysis must remain within a dialectical relationship with the capacity of the text to break beyond the boundaries of the language of the text to an outside of the text. It is this world of the text that we must now examine because it introduces another dimension of meaning, of which language is only the mediation, namely, the ontological dimension of the Being-in-the-world.

---

45. It is against the power of the structuralist ideology that Ricoeur addresses some of his strongest words. In "Structure, Word, Event", he rails against the "more or less terroristic prohibitions" that structuralists impose. Cf. The Conflict of Interpretations, (320), p.90.

CHAPTER THREE: THE WORLD OF THE TEXT.

Bibliography.

82.	Platon et Aristote (1954).
152.	L'homme faillible (1960).
153.	La symbolique du mal (1960).
157.	"L'antinomie de la réalité humaine et le problème de l'anthropologie philosophique" (1960).
186.	"L'humanité de l'homme" (1962).
220.	"Le langage de la foi" (1964).
228.	"La psychanalyse et le mouvement de la culture contemporaine" (1965).
247.	"Le problème de double-sens comme problème herméneutique et comme problème sémantique" (1966).
277.	"Urbanisation et sécularisation" (1967).
278.	"New Developments in Phenomenology in France: The Phenomenology of Language" (1967).
289.	"Philosophie et communication" (1968).
290.	"Aliénation" (1968).
320.	Le conflit des interprétations (1969).
321.	"Philosophie et langage" (1969).
328.	"La paternité: du fantasme au symbole" (1969).
355.	"Langage (Philosophie)" (1971).
370.	"The Model of the Text: Meaningful Action Considered as a Text" (1971).
373.	"Sémantique de l'action" (1971).
376.	"Discours et communication: La communication problèmatique" (1971).
387.	"Creativity in Language. Word. Polysemy. Metaphor" (1973).
408.	"Puissance de la parole: science et poésie" (1975).
411.	"Biblical Hermeneutics" (1975).
413.	"Objectivation et aliénation dans l'expérience historique" (1975).
417.	La métaphore vive (1975).
423.	Interpretation Theory (1976).
424.	"L'imagination dans le discours et dans l'action" (1976).
475.	"Herméneutique et sémiotique" (1980).

We have arrived at the point where we can begin to "pour language back into the universe" (328:148). We have seen that, according to Ricoeur, there is a twofold drive to meaning in language. The first is the drive to ideal meanings that is examined by an immanent study of language. The second is the drive to what is, to an outside reality. With Frege, Ricoeur maintains that it is the mind's drive to truth that forces us to advance beyond the ideal meaning - beyond sense - to reference (423:21). The drive to go beyond sense to a reference lies not within the structure but in the subject's intentionality and ultimately in the very being of the subject. This is what Ricoeur has identified as the "ontological vehemence" (417:21).

The immanent structure does not manifest the bond of language with the outside. But language in use makes explicit the awesome capacity of language to reveal the ontological condition of being in the world. And thus, after having examined linguistic meaning at the logical and semiotic level in the previous chapter, we must take Ricoeur's theory of discourse and the text one step further and relate it to reality or to an ontology. For Ricoeur this relationship to reality, as we saw above, is made by way of Frege's notion of reference. It is this power of reference of language towards an ontology of language that we wish to examine in this chapter.

A. FROM THE REFERENCE OF LANGUAGE TO AN ONTOLOGY OF LANGUAGE.

What we have accomplished thus far is to establish a linkage between language and meaning on a twofold level. We have also considered the linkage between discourse and reference. All discourse, we saw, is saying something about something to someone. But what is the relationship between the reference and existence? When we say something about something, we presuppose after all that what we refer to exists.

On the logical level we indicated that for Ricoeur the function of referring to reality lay with the asymetrical relationship between the identifying and predicative functions of a proposition. He placed the ontological commitment with the function of identification. But the ontological commitment of identification is insufficient to resolve the difficulties raised by the identifications found in fictive writings or in the theatre. According to Ricoeur, linguistic philosophy does not have the resources to adequately explain the distinction between fictive and 'true' identifications (373:99).

But if the logical functions of identification and predication cannot explain the linkage between reference and existence, we cannot turn to the speaker to release us from the impasse. In the theory of speech-act of Austin and Searle the illocutionary force of a sentence ('I assert that...' 'I believe that...' 'I state that...') affirms that for the speaker something is, but what is asserted or believed may not necessarily be the case. Moreover, the illocutionary force was said to pervade the act of discourse, and the speaker's presence was in the force of the proposition. In other words, the ontological commitment is not derived from the speaker.

But that state of affairs brings us to a totally different constellation of things. If the ontological does not come from the logical functions nor from the speaker, it must come from the object. And that has a number of repercussions. It inverts the perspective. It draws the point of gravity away from language and the speaker of language towards something that lies outside of language. Not language, but reality takes over the focal position. A question of Ricoeur sums up this perspective quite accurately, "What must be the structure of reality for signs to appear which represent and designate it" (321:282, my translation)? Having been pushed into a central position, language cannot become the first and last reality (321:291).

It is that through which we refer to reality, but it is not the sole reality. From the perspective of reality, language is clearly secondary. Ricoeur's aphorism expresses it well, "Language only captures the foam on the surface of life" (423:63).

A linguistic philosophy must cede here to a phenomenology of language which is better endowed to provide access to ontology. For Ricoeur, the French phenomenological tradition which, more than any other tradition, tried to combine the phenomenological method with the problem of existence, shows a rare capacity to bring forward the ontological dimension of language. For Ricoeur himself, it meant, that he could assume once again the ontological concern of Gabriel Marcel and link it with a concern of Husserl (278:9). Like Marcel, Ricoeur's concern is the mystery of existence as it surrounds us and encompasses us. Marcel had not linked being and the phenomenon, or being and language as Ricoeur attempts to do, but rather being and existence. For him, it was existence that opened up the realm of mystery. And existence revealed itself in the interpersonal relationships of which the theatre provided the most adequate witness (373:101). This concern for existence serves as a backdrop to Ricoeur's own concern for language and phenomenology. Marcel's relationship of existence and being was too close for Ricoeur; Husserl's phenomenological reduction and the intermediation of language, for which phenomenology gives space, were for Ricoeur more adequate means to arrive at a contemporary perception of existence.

Husserl's phenomenology was transcendental before being existential. In essence this means that phenomenology comes upon the scene by means of a reduction which transforms the question of being into a question of the meaning of being. The relationship to existence is intercepted by the reduction in order to permit our relationship to existence to appear. And by making it appear, the reduction shows humanity to be other than nature. The function of phenomenology becomes precisely to disclose our bond with reality. We relate to reality by signifying it (320(278):258). For phenomenology the fact that language refers to reality can only mean that we are already turned towards reality and linked with reality. For it language is a mediation and an expression of that bond with reality (373:100). In other words, in the movement toward existence, toward what lies at the origin, language is not the aim of the movement but the privileged medium (321:282;325:282). Language is not primary but secondary. Because Ricoeur searches for the meaning of something in order to arrive at the being of something, language returns to a central position, for as Ricoeur says, "With the search for the original, the question of meaning becomes a total one" (278:10;285:10). The question of language belongs to this environment of meaning as its most significant mediation.

The position of language is paradoxical, therefore. It is by means of language that we apprehend what lies before language or at the origin of language. We attend to language but at the same time we acknowledge that language is not primary. It is only a secondary expression of our apprehension of reality. This suggests that there is meaning before there is language. But Ricoeur is careful not to be drawn into idealism. He stipulates therefore, "Language thus appears not only as a mediator between man and the world, but more precisely as a shifter (échangeur) between two exigencies, an exigency of logicity which gives it a telos, and an exigency of foundation in the prepredicative which gives it an archê" (355:776). But how can one transfer from reference, which is a fact of language, to reality which is outside of language?

In his last works Husserl provides some hints about the operation whereby language returns to the experience that lies prior to language. Husserl calls the world of experience prior to language, Lebenswelt. This Lebenswelt is a reality that is not immediately available. For him it comes into sight in the operation of language. As a matter of fact, it is as much something that happens in language as something that happens to language. For Husserl it is an operation of language in reverse. Language is sent back by means of what Husserl calls the Rückfrage to its origin. The Rückfrage proposes that language itself designates what within it enables it to exist as language. The Rückfrage, however, does not operate on the level of semantics. Rather, it is a transcendental quest. It seeks to designate the conditions of the possibility of the whole symbolic function (355:776).

But the route from reference to reality and back to language again is best expressed for Ricoeur in the phenomenology of perception of Merleau-Ponty, who succeeded in bridging several Heideggerean themes with Husserl's phenomenology.[1] Merleau-Ponty made an express point of linking the Lebenswelt with language. For him language flowed out of the Lebenswelt. In Le visible et l'invisible he writes, "This is an act of creation called for and engendered by the Lebenswelt as operant, latent historicity, extending that Lebenswelt and bearing witness to it"[2] (475:252).   The Lebenswelt is like a power for Merleau-Ponty. It is an act cutting a swath before it by means of language. Language articulates and opens up the Lebenswelt.   The link between the reference of language to the extra-linguistic reality is therefore not direct but indirect. The Lebenswelt that lies before the verbal and logical world always remains anterior.   The Rückfrage is never ending: it is never given. It is made available only in the operation of language that bears witness to it (321:284-286).

For Ricoeur too, language is not the first reality. Language manifests what lies prior to it. In language what lies prior to it receives a name and achieves an identity (277:95). As Ricoeur writes in the article "Volonté",

Experience is articulated in a discourse from which philosophy extracts its logic. It is philosophy's task then to indicate that this

---

1.   The works to which Ricoeur refers are Le visible et l'invisible, Paris, Gallimard, 1963; Signes, Paris, Gallimard, 1960; L'oeil et l'esprit, Paris, Gallimard, 1964.

2.   Op. cit., p.228.

logic is not a formal, empty structure, but the logic of being itself, in the final analysis, the discourse of experience (385:946, my translation).[3]

For Ricoeur what lies prior to language is not a mute or thingified reality, as Sartre perceived it (278:9). It is not merely an expérience vécu, but an experience that is a dynamic act, surrounded by language. It adheres to discourse (247:68). And it is ultimately brought to the surface in the movement of language (186:55-56).[4] But it will have to be a language that has spoken us more than we have spoken it.

B. THE TEXT AND METAPHORICAL LANGUAGE.

Not every language, however, is equally capable of bringing the Lebenswelt to the surface. Neither scientific language nor the language of description are devoid of ontological import, but they operate on a level of knowledge which attempts to manipulate and control language. It seems less capable of bringing us in touch with a language that is discontinuous with the human project, a language that creates us rather than a language that we create (320(278):258). For Ricoeur, as it is for Heidegger, that symbolic function of language is reserved to the poets.

It is significant that Ricoeur undertook his earliest studies of semiotics and semantics to get a better grasp of language in its highest form and its greatest density, namely, the symbol.[5] Here we return to the wager that he made in La symbolique du mal that "I shall have a better understanding of man and the bond between the being of man and the being of all beings if I follow the indication of symbolic thought" (153:355). In this chapter we shall follow that indication of symbolic thought, for there one may hope to manifest the real power of language (220:16).

---

3. "L'expérience est articulée par un discours, dont la philosophie extrait la logique, pour montrer ensuite que cette logique n'est pas une structure formelle et vide, mais bien la logique de l'être, c'est-à-dire finallement le discours de l'expérience."

4. For Ricoeur, experience is a dialectical moment of human consciousness. The dialectical poles comprise the cognitive process on the one hand and the object of knowledge on the other. While knowledge reaches out to the object, consciousness turns it back to the self. Experience is the result of this dialectical movement (395:105-106).

5. See, for example, "Structure et herméneutique" and "Le problème de double-sens, comme problème herméneutique et comme problème sémantique" in Le conflit des interprétations, op. cit., p.31-63, and p.64-79.

1. The metaphor: the poetic text in miniature.

But where do we have access to this power of language, so that we can perceive the operation of poetic language at the level of the text? Together with a number of literary critics, Ricoeur does not think it necessary to turn to a lengthy poem, novel or essay to exemplify the symbolic function of language. The properties and characteristics of the symbolic function of language are found in all its intensity in the jewel of language, called the metaphor. Monroe Beardsley has called the metaphor a poem in miniature (417:93-94).[6] The metaphor possesses a structure that is homogeneous to the basic structure of literary works. For that reason the metaphor has become in Ricoeur's later works "the touchstone of the cognitive value of literary works" (423:45).

It is for that reason that in the later works of Paul Ricoeur there is a shift away from symbols and myths which he had studied in his earlier works such as La symbolique du mal (153) and De l'interprétation. Essai sur Freud. (227) These studies, as he acknowledges in his later works, were not, properly speaking, linguistic studies. In the linguistic phase of his philosophy Ricoeur recognizes that the symbol has both a verbal and a non-verbal dimension. The non-verbal dimension becomes evident, however, only in the verbal. But of greatest significance for Ricoeur is the fact that a semantic analysis of the verbal dimension of the symbol reveals it to have the same structure as the metaphor. A theory of the metaphor provides the linguistic framework for a semantic approach to the symbol (423:45-46).

If we exhaustively trace Ricoeur's theory of metaphor in this Chapter, it is precisely to permit a perception of the power of the poetic text to say out our being. Meaning for Ricoeur has become concentrated in the power of the poetic text to bring the ground of our existence to us in language.[7] A study of the semantics of the metaphor can bring this power to vision.[7]

Historically, the metaphor was first wrestled with in the art of rhetoric. Aristotle, for instance, placed the metaphor under the heading of lexis.[8] This places the metaphor alongside the letter, the syllable, the conjunction, the noun and the verb, as that part of speech that classifies the changes in meaning in the use of words (417:14). Consequently, the

---

6.   Aesthetics, New York, Harcourt, Brace and World, 1958.

7.   For a review of Ricoeur's theory of metaphor see G. Vincent, " 'La metaphore vive' de P. Ricoeur" in Rev. Hist. Philos. relig. 56, 1976, p.567-582. See also M. Gerhart, "La métaphore vive" in Religious Studies Review 2, 1976, p.23-30.

8.   Lexis is difficult to translate. Ricoeur provides the following synonyms, derived from a variety of translations of Aristotle's works: discours, élocution, style, diction. Lexis concerns the area of the use of words in language expressions. Cf. La métaphore vive, (417:19, footnote 4).

metaphor became classified in Western tradition as a trope, concerned with the transfer of the meaning of nouns or names. By retaining it only on the level of the word and not of the sentence, Western tradition left the metaphor on the level of denomination. Thus, in Aristotle's Poetics (1457b 6-9) the metaphor is defined as "giving the thing a name that belongs to something else; the transference being either from genus to species, or from species to genus, or from species to species, or on grounds of analogy" (see 417:13).

Ricoeur's theory of metaphor is one lengthy contestation of this reduction of the metaphor to denomination. Not only does he blame the death of rhetoric in the 19th century on this reduction of the metaphor to the tyranny of the word, but also our blindness to the symbolic function. The function of the metaphor became twofold. It received as its first task to express an idea or an experience which did not as yet have a name in the lexical code. This filling of the semantic lacuna took place by means of a name, derived from the current stock of words, and applying that name to the new object or person. This filling of the semantic lacuna is known as catechresis. The second task of the metaphor, when left at the level of denomination, is the decorative one. In these cases the object has a proper name but a metaphor replaces or substitutes the proper name with a figurative one for the sake of pleasing, or, in the case of the decrepid rhetoric, of seducing the audience. Ricoeur contests this theory of metaphor precisely because it presupposes that a name properly and essentially belongs to a thing and is not primarily a function of the sentence. In both instances the figurative word makes no cognitive contribution to the subject at hand (411:76;421:48). For Ricoeur, the production and the change of meaning is a predicative function and not a denominative function. He proposes, therefore, a semantic approach to the metaphor based not on the semantics of the word but on the semantics of the sentence. He places the metaphor between the sentence and the word, between predication and denomination (417:125). It is this new theory of metaphor that we must explore here.

2. The semantic theory of the metaphor.

The new semantics of the metaphor, based on a theory of discourse, is endebted to The Philosophy of Rhetoric of I.A. Richards.[9] He pioneered the renewed study of rhetoric as a study of verbal understanding and misunderstanding. His new rhetoric does not explicitly develop a semantics of the sentence, but it presupposes one. Filling out the terrain which Richards had cleared, are the works of other authors who are more explicitly semantic. Ricoeur has turned to Max Black[10] (see 417:107-

---

9.   Op. cit.

10.   "Metaphor", in Models and Metaphors, Ithica, Cornell University Press, 1962, Chapter Three.

116;302-310), Colin Turbayne[11] (see 416:316-320), and Philip Wheelwright[12] (417:316-320) to complete the contours of a semantics of metaphor.

According to Richards the metaphorical pervades our language. All language expresses the attempt to grasp the relations between things that hitherto had not been perceived. Metaphor is a specific manner of interrelating two thoughts of different things in a simple expression or word, e.g., "blue angelus" or "green night". The meaning of the expression or of the word results from the interaction of two thoughts. A metaphor holds these thoughts together in tension with one another without dissolving the one into the other. A metaphor, therefore, is not a mere transfer of words but an interaction between thoughts. But not every pair of thoughts which come together in a simple expression is a metaphor. Only those which express one thought by means of the features of the other is properly a metaphor. Richards calls the underlying idea, the 'tenor', while that idea by whose features the first idea is apprehended he calls the 'vehicle' (417:80). For Richards, a metaphor calls for the coincidence of both the tenor and the vehicle. It is their interaction, which makes the metaphor (417:81). Their interaction founds the structure of the metaphorical statement.

Max Black's logical grammar[13] of the metaphor is able to bring more precision to the vehicle-tenor relationship Richards had proposed. Black focusses more directly than Richards did upon not just any two ideas but upon two features in the sentence that interact, one of which is taken literally while the other is taken metaphorically. Black insists, that, although the whole statement constitutes the metaphor, it is one word in that statement which makes it a metaphorical statement. In the statement, "The chairman plowed through the discussion", it is the word 'plowed', which is taken metaphorically, while the rest of the sentence is taken literally.

Black calls the metaphorical word the 'focus', the rest of the sentence he calls the 'frame' (cf. see 417:85). The focus falls upon a particular word precisely because of its interaction with the frame, which consists of the rest of the sentence. A metaphor is the interaction of some words that are taken metaphorically with the rest of the sentence, which is taken non-metaphorically (417:84).

How does this interaction function? In two ways. First of all, the 'frame' or context acts upon the 'focus'. Let us use, as Ricoeur does, the example of Black, "Man is a wolf". To call man a wolf is to evoke in the

---

11.   The Myth of Metaphors, Yale University Press, 1962.

12.   The Burning Fountain, Bloomington, Indiana University Press, 1968, rev.ed.

13.   Ricoeur questions whether Max Black's approach can properly be called a logical grammar. The possibility of translating a metaphor into another language sets the metaphor free from its particular grammatical form. Cf. La métaphore vive, (417:89).

focus, wolf, a series of opinions and preconceptions, which a linguistic community associates with the word 'wolf'. These opinions and preconceptions, which Black calls the "system of associated commonplaces",[14] attach themselves to the literal meaning of the word 'wolf'. The 'frame' not only evokes this system of associated commonplaces, but screens or filters out some of the details and emphasizes others. Secondly, the focus also acts on the frame. The metaphor 'wolf' "organizes our view of man" (417:87). It gives an 'insight'; it informs by having the wolf-metaphor - the subsidiary subject - applied to the principal subject. In its own fashion, the application of the metaphor "selects, emphasizes, suppresses, and organizes features of the principal subject" (Black, op. cit. p.44-45; see 417:89).

Ricoeur finds a suggestion in Black, that, if better exploited, would have allowed Black to extend the creative activity of the metaphor. Black refers not only to the system of associated commonplaces, but also to "specially constructed systems of implications" (Black, op. cit. p.43; see 417:88). The system of associated commonplaces, as attached to words, limits, according to Ricoeur, the work of the metaphorical interaction to already established connotations. Consequently, it is hardly creative of new meaning. In this sense, Ricoeur calls the metaphor, "Man is a wolf" merely trivial (417:88). But, by adding specially constructed implications, Black opens up possibilities of truly innovative metaphors. It is this creative activity, leading to novel meaning, which Ricoeur seeks out specifically.

Monroe Beardsley's critical literary theory of metaphor brings Ricoeur one step closer to an apprehension of the innovative, creative character of the metaphor (417:90-100). We select two points from Beardsley's analysis. First of all, Beardsley points out that the strategy of metaphorical discourse in the creation of meaning is that of logical absurdity. The interaction within the metaphorical discourse, he maintains, involves a coincidence in one statement of a primary level and a secondary level of meaning at the same time. Their interaction produces a logical absurdity if accepted only on the primary level of meaning. The absurdity forces the liberation of a second level of meaning without destroying the first. The logical absurdity indicates that in a metaphor there exists a fundamental incompatibility. The characteristics of the primary meaning of the 'modifier', which is Beardsley's equivalent to Black's 'focus' or Richards' 'tenor', is incompatible with the characteristics of the primary meaning of the 'subject' (Beardsley's equivalent of 'frame' and 'vehicle'). Because of the conflictual tension between the primary meanings, the reader is forced to draw upon the secondary meanings in order to make meaningful the logical absurdity at the primary level.

---

14. Because the associated commonplaces are non-lexical implications of words, Ricoeur hesitates to call Black's theory semantic. The associated commonplaces of words are properly speaking psychological connotations of words. Cf. La métaphore vive, (417:89-90) (E). Once again, Ricoeur attempts to tread around a psychological interpretation in the direction of a semantic interpretation.

A second contribution of Beardsley is built upon the first. The activity of resolving the logical absurdity at the primary level belongs to the reader. The reader has to search among the range of connotations of the modifier in order to make the absurd statement meaningful. The emergence of new meaning is the very work of the hearer or reader in the act of hearing and reading. What is most striking in Beardsley's theory of metaphor is that it is not an event which takes place between two terms but between two interpretations of the statement. One reading takes place at the primary level of meaning, which is logically absurd. This is followed by a second reading, which leads to a meaningful resolution of the absurdity.

But Beardsley is not yet able to account adequately for the level of innovation in the metaphor. Like Black, who spoke of the associated commonplaces, Beardsley's connotations, which are linguistic, and not psychological as Black's commonplaces are, hardly go beyond the present storehouse of meanings. Beardsley attempts to circumvent this by speaking of connotations, which "wait, so to speak, lurking in the nature of things, for actualization - wait to be captured by the word... as part of its meaning in some future context"[15] (cf. see 417:97). But an already existing connotation is not truly novel. Like Black, who spoke of the specially constructed systems, Beardsley admits that the interaction transforms both the subject and the modifier to such an extent that, through it, a new event in language takes place. The first time a poet describes virginity as the 'enamel of the soul', a property of enamel was brought to language that had not been expressed before.

The question raised here, namely, where does that previously unexpressed property come from, is not adequately answered by Beardsley. The notion of meaning, now expanded to include secondary meanings, is still within the range of the present perimeter of language. Only the notion of the properties of a thing that have not as yet found expression in language can help us forward. The properties are not yet linguistic. It is the metaphor which transforms them into a sense, i.e., brings them to language. If such be the case, one must speak of a true semantic innovation. The property, which had no previous status in language, and which was not part of the designation or connotation of the word, achieves a place in language by means of the metaphor.

Ricoeur concludes from the work of Richards, Black, and Beardsley that a metaphorical attribution is the work of a network of interactions, which makes a certain context a unique context (417:127). The interaction of these several intersecting semantic fields is a semantic event. The semantic event is brought about by what Ricoeur aptly calls the metaphorical twist (417:127). The metaphor is the embodiment of the event of interaction. The interaction event is given durability and repeatability in a specific linguistic construction. The metaphor is then both event and meaning. It is an event that means and a meaning created by language (417:99). The metaphor exists only in this context.

---

15. Beardsley, op. cit., p.300.

We will hold in reserve, for the moment, the question of the reference of the metaphorical statement. First we must carefully examine how Ricoeur envisages the semantic status of the word in the metaphorical statement and in the process of the work of resemblance.

3. The metaphor and the semantics of the word.

The interaction theory of metaphor incorporates the theory of the reciprocal interplay between the word and the sentence discussed above. If the initiative of meaning lies with the sentence, meaning discovers itself sedimented in the word. Thus if the word is the "institutionalization of previous contextual values" (417:130), our quest for the production process of novel meaning cannot bypass an examination of the metaphorical word.

We saw above that Ricoeur rejected the essential linking of a name with a thing. He maintains that in natural languages, as opposed to artificial languages, it is a distinctive trait of the word that it has more than one meaning. In technical terms, words in common speech are polysemic. Polysemy is a key characteristic of the word and essential to the understanding of the symbolic function of language.[16]

a. The polysemy of words.

Stephen Ullmann[17] defined polysemy as the phenomenon according to which a name has more than one 'sense'. Polysemy refers to the vagueness and lack of precise identification of most of the words of our language. They have no definite frontiers. Words in living language have an open texture. Polysemy indicates that words can have more than one 'sense', but it also suggests that words have a cumulative power. They can draw new meanings within their sphere, without, at the same time, losing the old meanings (417:127).[18] Words can invade each other's territory.

---

16. The polysemy of natural languages is an indispensable feature of language. It is demanded by the principle of economy because otherwise the lexicon would be infinite. It is also demanded by the rule of communication. Without polysemy every experience would demand a proper designation which would cripple communication. See also "Puissance de la parole: science et poésie", (403:159-170).

17. Stephen Ullmann's three successive versions of semantics are found in his The Principle of Semantics, Glasgow, Glasgow University Publication, 1951; Précis de sémantique française, Berne, A. Francke, 1952; Semantics. An Introduction to the Science of Meaning. Oxford, Blackwell, 1962, 1967. Ricoeur uses Ullmann's analysis as an example of a Post-Saussurean linguistics with its major emphasis upon the word. We borrow here Ricoeur's analysis of Ullmann's notion of polysemy.

18. This also means that words are not to be defined solely by their differences and their oppositions to one another.

Opposed to polysemy is synonomy: the same 'sense' for several names.[19]

Because of the open texture of words and the vagueness of the semantic boundaries, words can acquire new meanings. It is this cumulative character of words that opens language to innovation. Corresponding to the infinite variations of the use of language in its capacity to say, there is the flexibility of words to respond to contexts in the gathering of new meaning. It is to this cumulative power of the word that we must attach the notion of the metaphor.

b. The metaphorical enrichment.

The metaphor implies all the present acceptations of a word plus one. This novel meaning is the one that, in the collision of interpretations, rescues the statement from being self-contradictory, and, therefore, meaningless. The metaphor has as task to establish meaning, where at the primary level there is only self-contradiction. With reference to this, Jean Cohen maintains that statements are governed by a code of pertinence. Where such a code of pertinence is abused, such as in poetic messages or metaphors, a syntactically correct sentence may be absurd literally, that is, semantically impertinent, or incorrect, with respect to meaning. In these instances, the predicate is not pertinent in relation to the subject. It failed the law of semantic pertinence, which stipulates which type of combinations are intelligible (417:151-152). In the very establishment of this semantic pertinence out of the impertinence at the literal level, the metaphorical word plays a focal role. The metaphorical word is the reduction of the impertinence. The operation of meaning of the two colliding interpretations condenses itself, or becomes crystalized in the word. In other words, the metaphor occurs between the word and the sentence, between denomination and predication (417:130-131). However, in contradistinction to the normal interchange of word and sentence, the metaphorical word is not a potential meaning. It establishes meaning. Metaphorical meaning comes from nowhere. It emerges out of the interplay (see 370:104). A metaphor is a change of meaning, or more exactly, to use Aristotle's word, an epiphora, a transfer of meaning.

Thus, corresponding to the new pertinence at the predicative level, there is also a transfer of meaning, a change of meaning at the lexical

---

19. Artificial languages, on the other hand, require univocity: one name for one sense. Context matters little because a name is to retain its sense in whatever context it is used. Scientific language functions as a corrective of ordinary language. Its goal to define reality relies on a precision in language that excludes all ambiguity. The pressure of scientific language upon the other language games seeks to exclude ambiguity in language. This had led to the rationalization of the language-games. The attempt to apply this rationalization universally by Leibniz, Russell (at least in his Principia mathematica) and Wittgenstein (in his Tractatus logico-philosophicus) failed because it faltered in all language games that had to account for its context.

level. Besides the semantic innovation at the level of the sentence, there is equally a change at the level of the word. This latter change describes the impact of the interaction upon the lexical code (417:157). We can say that the intersection of semantic fields jerks or twists the word in a certain direction. A new meaning is twisted out of a word - Ricoeur calls it a "labour of meaning" (411:78) - in order that a statement may make sense, whereas a literal interpretation is absurd (417:99).

The open texture of the word is the condition for the acquisition of new meaning. But novel meaning is primarily a predicative creation. A metaphor is not derived, therefore, from the polysemic character of words. But it is in constant movement toward polysemy. At a certain moment the metaphor ceases to be the tension of two interpretations. At that moment the metaphorical word assumes a standard linguistic identity. As a metaphor, it has died. As a new lexical entity, it enters into the dictionary and becomes an enrichment of the polysemy of words (417:170).

The semantic enrichment is not confined, however, only to the lexical level. It must be extended to include innovation and enrichment on the level of the sentence and beyond the sentence to the text. The polysemic character of words has a corresponding trait on the level of sentence and the text. While normally it is the task of the sentence to reduce the polysemy of the word by means of the identifying and predicative functions of the sentence, not all textual compositions seek to reduce the polysemy. In certain cases instead of screening out polysemic contexts, discourse promotes and encourages more than one interpretation. On the level of the sentence and the text Ricoeur calls this coincidence of more than one semantic value ambiguity.[20] Ambiguity at the level of discourse is what polysemy is at the level of the word (376:62). In scientific discourse ambiguous discourse is anathema and assiduously excluded. In ordinary language too, homology is the ideal. But there are modes of discourse where ambiguity is the work of discourse, the work of its style.[21] The literary work is such a mode of discourse. Ambiguity is one of its criteria (376:63).

---

20. By proposing an ambiguity that is a constructed, intended ambiguity, Ricoeur parts ways with Husserl. Husserl's phenomenology is not hermeneutical, because he excluded the intentional ambiguity in his search for univocal meaning. But the parting of ways is only partial. Ricoeur introduces ambiguity within the framework of Husserl's theory of signification. It is one further example of Ricoeur's non-idealistic use of Husserl's philosophy. See 320(228):15.

21. This is not the first time that the notion of ambiguity arises in Ricoeur's hermeneutical phenomenology. In La symbolique du mal, ambiguity had been linked with equivocal expression. But the ambiguity of expression is almost immediately linked to the ambiguity of the experience itself. Experience is said to be available mediately rather than immediately. It is made available indirectly by means of language. Language expressions thematize these pre-linguistic experiences. Ricoeur postulates that this pre-linguistic experience is a "blind experience" that is

In the case of literary works Ricoeur points to two criteria in order that the characteristic of ambiguity may apply. The first condition is that the ambiguity be truly intended and hence is a constructed ambiguity. The second condition is that the intended ambiguity evinces as its aim to say a reality that could not have been said with a homological, descriptive, or didactic discourse (376:63).

Let us examine these two conditions in more detail.

(a) Ricoeur turns to Monroe Beardsley's semantic analysis of literary works to exemplify the first condition of intended ambiguity.[22] Although ambiguity is a criterion of the literary work as a whole, Beardsley examines it principally at the level of the sentence on the presupposition that the sentence is homogeneous in structure to the literary work as a whole. According to Beardsley, just as a sentence has a sense and reference, so does a literary work. The sense of the work is its verbal design. Its reference is the world of the work, i.e., the projection by means of the work of discourse of a possible, inhabitable world (417:91-93). Ricoeur makes grateful use of this thesis of homogeneity.

Now, in a sentence there is operative a signification at two levels. A sentence, first of all, states something to be such and such. That is its primary signification. But, in that very statement, there is also a suggestion of something else. The sentence may imply in the very statement why the statement was made, or why a certain decision was reached, or why a certain action was undertaken. This is its secondary signification. To varying degrees, every sentence has both a primary, explicit, signification and a secondary, suggested, implicit, signification. The explicit signification Beardsley calls denotation, i.e., that which is designated. The implicit signification he calls connotation. In ordinary discourse, but even more stringently in scientific discourse, there is a control exercised over the connotations. In literature, especially in the poem, this control is lifted, so that both the primary and the secondary levels of meaning operate at the same time. The intended ambiguity, because it is intended, becomes in fact multiple meaning: both the primary and the secondary significations are intended.

Beardsley's approach provides Ricoeur with an avenue to examine the multiple meanings, manifested in literary works. Being freed

---

"embedded in the matrix of emotion, fear, anguish" (op. cit., p.7). Emotions push this experience to the surface in discourse when it reveals the experience to be clothed in the ambiguity and equivocity of a "multiplicity of meanings" (idem, p.9). The semantic approach, which Ricoeur favours in La métaphore vive, is more reserved in the establishment of the nexus between language and pre-linguistic experience. Only after the detour of the semantics of double-meaning language does Ricoeur return to the ontological question.

22.   Idem.

from directly examining the poem, the essay, or the prose fiction to detail the functioning of multiple meaning, Beardsley has turned to the sentence-type, in which this intended ambiguity is operative. And this again is the metaphor. The metaphor -for Beardsley and for Ricoeur - becomes the test-case of ambiguous discourse. An analysis of its sense and reference can serve as model for the analysis of works of discourse, such as the poem, where a discussion of the semantics of multiple-meaning discourse might not be as directly accessible. This is the avenue which Ricoeur has chosen and which we must pursue in the next paragraphs.

(b) The aim of calculated ambiguity must differ from the aim of discourse that seeks to reduce the polysemy of words and the ambiguity of discourse. If sentences describe a 'state of affairs' and words designate 'objects', intended ambiguity must suspend this description, this primary signification, and call for a new mode of reference. Beardsley proposes that this suspension of the primary signification and the novel reference takes place through the liberating presence of the secondary levels of significations (376:65; 417:94-95).

4. The ground of the metaphor: resemblance.

In the preceding sections it was argued that Ricoeur advanced a theory of metaphor in which, through a clash of semantic fields, a leap in meaning or a semantic innovation was brought about. Ricoeur grounds this semantic innovation upon resemblance. To do so, however, he must undertake to loosen the bond that existed in classical rhetoric between resemblance and the metaphor as a trope. In a tropological approach to metaphor, the metaphorical activity consists only of a substitution of terms. It precludes novelty of meaning because the figurative meaning of a word merely replaces the literal meaning, which could have been used in its stead. In classical rhetoric the basis for the substitution of the figurative for the literal was their underlying resemblance. Ricoeur undertakes, therefore, to dissolve the exclusiveness of the bond between substitution and resemblance and will insist on a semantic theory of metaphor, in which resemblance will still be the ground (417:173).

Ricoeur, therefore, takes the question of resemblance and generalizes its meaning so that it applies not only to the substitution theory of metaphor, i.e., metaphor at the level of the sign and word[23] but also to the interaction theory of metaphor. The semantic theory of metaphor of Richards, Black and Beardsley largely ignored the grounds for the shifts of meaning from a literal to a figurative sense (417:188-191). With Beardsley in particular, the issue had become logical absurdity in the clash of two meanings, which forced one to pass from a plane of primary meaning to a new meaning. But the question remains whether an aptness or suitability exists between the primary and the novel meaning. According to Beardsley,

---

23. This is the approach of R. Jakobson in his "Two Aspects of Language and Two Types of Aphasic Disturbances", in Fundamentals of Language, The Hague, 1956.

there is no analogy that pre-exists the metaphor. The metaphor brings about the alliance between two fields. In that case, the resemblance would not be the cause, but the consequence, of the metaphor. But what, then, constitutes the metaphoricity of the metaphor?

For Ricoeur, it is resemblance. Resemblance is central to his explanation of the metaphorical process. The resemblance is not only fashioned by the metaphorical statement but it also "guides and produces this statement" (416:193). How? In the attribution of a predicate, the metaphor, in fashioning a "meaningful self-contradictory statement from a self-destructive self-contradictory statement" (Beardsley, see 417:194), brings near what previously was distant. But what is brought near must have, as Aristotle remarked, the 'virtue' of being 'appropriate' (Rhetoric 3:1404b3; see 417:194). The impertinent made pertinent cannot be too 'far-fetched'. It must be derived from 'kindred' material (Aristotle see 417:194).

But how is the distant proximated? Applying a suggestion of Ph. Wheelwright,[24] Ricoeur proposes that two processes take place. The first process is what unites or assimilates the contradictory ideas. Aristotle described it beautifully when he stated, "To metaphorize well is to see - to contemplate, to have the right eye for - the similar" (see 417:195). It is an intuitive moment of the genius, an apperception, a seeing, of the similar in the dissimilar. But his intuitive moment of the genius cannot be had without a discursive moment. There is no seeing of the similar in the dissimilar without at the same time a constructing of the similar in the dissimilar. The kinship between things is not perceivable through ordinary vision. It must be made to appear. The resemblance is a constructed resemblance as much as it is an intuitive glance. The predicate chooses and organizes certain aspects of the principal subject (417:195). The metaphorical expression of N. Goodman captures well both the glance and the discursive moment. Metaphor is the "reassignment of labels", but the figure of the reassignment is fashioned by "an affair between a predicate with a past and an object that yields while protesting" (see 417:196). The glance that sees the similar in the protesting dissimilar, is fashioned into a yielding object in the discursive moment.

The metaphor of N. Goodman equally captures the unrelenting tension in the living metaphor between the similar and the dissimilar. In a living metaphor the similar remains visible despite difference, in spite of the contradiction. The contradictory usage of a literal meaning remains intact, so that a metaphor retains the clash of the 'same' and the 'different' (417:196). The site of the clash of the 'same' and the 'different' in metaphor is resemblance. Therefore, Ricoeur applies to metaphor the concept of Gilbert Ryle who described metaphor as a planned 'category mistake', because a metaphor is an intentional speaking of one thing in the terms and idioms which apply to another thing that resembles it (417:197). A metaphor is a 'calculated error', bringing together two ideas previously thought incompatible (423:55).

---

24. <u>Metaphor and Reality</u>, Indiana University Press, 1962, 1968.

If metaphor is not merely intuited but also constructed, might it not be possible then to conceive the strategy at work in the metaphor, as Ricoeur proposes, to be the "obliterating (of) the logical and established frontiers of language, in order to bring to light new resemblances the previous classification kept us from seeing" (417:197)? Ricoeur sees in this relating of previously unrelated things the eruption of new possible meanings which previously had been ignored or forbidden (423:51).

At this point Ricoeur provides an enlightening hypothesis, which clarifies a position that appears to be an undercurrent to his whole study of creative language. He hypothesizes that the dynamic of thought, which brings resemblance to light, stands at the generative origin of all classifications, of all genera. This could mean that the metaphorical process, which, at the semantic level appears as a deviation, is homogeneous with the process at the root of all semantic fields including the literal meaning from which the figurative meaning deviates. Of this he says,

> "A family resemblance first brings individuals together before the rule of a logical class dominates them. Metaphor, a figure of speech, presents in an open fashion, by means of a conflict between identity and difference, the process that, in a covert manner, generates semantic grids by fusion of differences into identity" (417:198).

Metaphor, according to this view, would pertain to the heuristics of new semantic fields. The metaphor, by fusing differences does not operate wholly within the presently constituted order of language but creates a new order by creating rifts in the old. Assuming Gadamer's view that the metaphoric is at the origin of all logical thought, Ricoeur also postulates that the order of language is born in the same way that it changes (417:22). The resolution of the conflict of similarity and difference brings about new semantic fields. By creating new kinships, it discovers novel ways of bypassing the inadequacies of the conventional categories to express a new experience (386:109-110).

C. THE TEXT AND REFERENCE: THE 'WORLD' OF THE TEXT.

1. Poetic texts and the thesis of the suspension of reference.

Ricoeur notes a large degree of consensus regarding the non-referential character of poetic language among literary critics. Literary criticism postulates that, in literature, there is a suspension of the relationship between sense and reference. For some, this lack of reference is perceived primarily in the restricted literary genre of the poem. For others, this non-reference is extended to the whole field of literature. Ricoeur holds that there is a suspension of reference, but that that suspension applies only to a certain type of reference and not to all reference. To accentuate Ricoeur's position, I shall first present the anti-reference thesis of literary criticism, as Ricoeur summarizes it.[25]

The dominant thesis of literary criticism is that the production of literary discourse suspends the relationship of sense to reference and, consequently, of sense to 'reality' or truth. Literature accomplishes this suspension, it is claimed, by a sort of reversion of meaning. The poetic text, for example, does not seek an eruption beyond the text, but remains narcissistically within the confines of the text. The literary poetic text is said to resemble an icon, or sculpture-like thing, that is admired for its unique configuration of sense and sound (Jakobson 410:83). In Ricoeur's words

"Like sculpture, poetry converts language into matter, worked for its own sake. This solid object is not the representation of some thing, but an expression of itself" (417:224).

This interplay of sense and sound exhausts the force of the poem. It plays itself out solely within the confines of itself. The orientation of the poetic discourse is, therefore, not a centrifugal, i.e., an outward, movement, but a centripetal movement of words into a literary configuration (Northrop Frye). It is a language satisfied in itself (New Rhetoric of France), not denotative but only connotative (Le Guern).

The palpability of the signs, according to Jakobson, is affected by the recurrence of certain phonic figures in rhyme, alliteration, parallelism, repetition of similar or opposing sounds. The recurrence in poetry is a case of the principle of equivalence, which is operative in non-poetic language as a rule of the selection of more or less similar terms. Together with combination, selection is the fundamental mode of arranging verbal behaviour. In speaking, I choose among a series of existent names, which are more or less similar (for example, I choose among the following: child, youth, youngster, infant, kid, gamin) and among a series of verbs (such as, sleep, slumber, doze ...), which I combine into a continuous chain of speech. As Jakobson says, "The selection is produced on the basis of equivalence, of similarity and dissimilarity, synonymity and antinomy, while the combination, the construction of the sequence, relies on continuity"[26] (see 408:170). It is Jakobson's thesis that in poetry a transfer takes place. The principle of equivalence which pertains to the axis of selection, is

---

25. Ricoeur finds this position in the linguistic work of Roman Jakobson (La métaphore vive, 417:222-224), and in the "dominant current" of European and American literary criticism: Hester (417:225), Northrop Frye (417:225-226), Suzanne Langer (417:227), The New Rhetoric of e.g., Todorov (417:227), Jean Cohen (417:227-228), Le Groupe de Liège (417:228), and Le Guern (417 p.228).

26. Essais de linguistique générale, Paris, Ed. de Minuit, 1963, p.220.

projected, according to Jakobson, upon the axis of combination. In poetry the equivalence, which governs the selection of words on the basis of their similarity for ordinary language, is promoted to govern also the combination of words into a sequence. Similarity in poetry then governs not only selection but also combination. That is how sonic recurrences such as rhyme affect the meaning and create novel semantic parentages - Ricoeur uses the apt metaphor of 'semantic contamination' (408:170). Through the combination of similars, poetic meanings are mutually contaminated. They are displaced or transported (to translate Aristotle's epiphora) (408:170). Recurrent sounds lead then not only to a semantic proximation but also to semantic equivalence, creating a parallel meaning. Sound becomes an instigator of meaning (376:185).

Without rejecting this thesis of literary criticism, Ricoeur nevertheless wishes to strip it of the positivistic bias that underlies it. The function of the fusion of sense and sound in poetic discourse, if no longer referential, that is, object oriented, must be typified as emotional, that is, as only subjective. Ricoeur argues that by falling prey to this spirit of subject and object, the literary critics have fallen into the trap of positivism. Reference, then, appears only in scientific, descriptive language, while poetic language as 'feeling'-language (Cohen) or 'mood'-language (N. Frye), remains capsulated by its sense. Emotion, feeling, mood are purely subjective according to this view, i.e., they do not adhere to an object or to an outside. Feelings describe only the state of the subject (417:147-148).

2. Inverted reference.

To counter the positivistic threat of literary criticism, Ricoeur turns to some powerful suggestions of Nelson Goodman's theory of metaphor. Goodman makes a good case for a mode of referring that is more fundamental than the descriptive, didactic reference of scientific language (417:231-239).

Ricoeur insists that the reference of poetic language, if such there be, must be established within the very analysis of that poetic language. We have already established that, for Ricoeur, the meaning of a metaphorical statement emerges out of the impasse of a literal interpretation of the statement. The literal meaning breaks apart under the force of the clash of the tenor with the vehicle. The literal meaning's destruction is equally the loss of the reference of the literal meaning. As a matter of fact, the whole strategy of the metaphorical statement is directed to the abolition of this reference. But the abolition of the primary reference is only the negative side of the coin. We noted that the destruction of the literal meaning was the condition for the emergence of the metaphorical meaning. Does this emergence of the metaphorical meaning indicate in parallel fashion the emergence of a reference, which can be called analogously a metaphorical reference? Does the failed reference become the condition for a successful metaphorical reference?

This is Ricoeur's thesis (417:230;407:87). However, he wants to show how such a metaphorical reference works. He discovers a basis in the fact that the foundation of the metaphorical or of semantic innovation lies in resemblance, in the seeing of similars in dissimilars. Is this new seeing, by making proximate two previously remote meanings through a category mistake, a real seeing? The function of resemblance would indicate that the seeing is a case of 'seeing-as'. It is not a direct seeing but a sort of stereoscopic vision (417:231). Something new is perceived in the very blending of two dissimilars through a category mistake. This novel perception indicates in fact a new reference. But it is a reference that is different from a descriptive, didactic reference. This emergence of a new reference takes place in a manner parallel to the emergence of new meaning, of metaphorical meaning.

The contribution of Nelson Goodman lies precisely in his expansion of the theory of metaphor to the point where it clearly includes the metaphorical reference. N. Goodman's <u>Languages of Art</u>[27] approaches all symbolic operations such as music, painting, literature, dance and architecture from the perspective of their referential function. All these activities 'stand for' or 'refer to' the organization of the world. The symbolic systems of music and painting, etc. 'make' and 'remake' the world according to Goodman. They are part of the great work of creating and recreating the world.

Nelson distinguishes the function of linguistic symbols from artistic symbols by assigning to the former the function of description and to the latter the function of representation. The purpose of both symbolic operations must not be sought, however, at the emotive or affective level, but at the cognitive level. As he remarks, "Aesthetic excellence is a cognitive excellence" (see 417:232).

The metaphor stands as paradigm of this cognitive reference. What then is the truth of the metaphor? And, how does this metaphorical truth relate to literal truth? Goodman proposes to link the organizing and re-organizing talents of the symbolic operation of metaphor with the operation of denotation, which, at a primary level, is synonymous with reference. The denotation in metaphorical truth takes place through the transference of predicates or properties from one realm to another, e.g., the application of sound to colour.[28] Such a transference is a type of remaking, refashioning, organizing and re-organizing.

The application of a predicate, according to Goodman, can assume two orientations. It can first of all take the direction from the symbol to the thing. In this direction, one applies a predicate - Goodman's

---

27. <u>An Approach to a Theory of Symbols</u>, Indianapolis, The Bobbs-Merrill Co., 1968.

28. Goodman gave the chapter dealing with transference the apt title, "The Sounds of Pictures".

word is 'label' - to denote a thing. On the verbal level, to 'label' something is to describe something. On the non-verbal level, such as in painting, the 'label' represents something. The denotation, at this level, can be multiple, singular, or zero. That is, a 'label' can denote many things, one thing, or no thing (for example, a painting of a unicorn). What is denoted in this application of a symbol to a thing are objects and events. Goodman is careful to note that this representation is not an imitation or a copy of nature. For him, it is a denoting of nature in the sense that it remakes reality. Nature here becomes a product of art and discourse. In the direction of the application of a predicate to a thing, we are, however, still in the realm of the literal reference of a symbol without implying a metaphorical reference.

But a predicate can also go from the thing to the symbol. Here, a thing is presented as an example of a meaning or of a property that something or someone 'possess'. Goodman's word for this is 'sample', that is, the tailor's booklet of swatches of cloth. Since this type of use of a predicate takes place in a metaphor, this orientation from the thing to the symbol must be examined more carefully. Goodman demonstrates this use of the predicate with the example of a picture painted in dull grays and expressing great sadness. The painting of trees and cliffs does not, however, denote trees or cliffs by representing them. In fact, according to Goodman, the process reverses itself. The reference is not a denoting but a being-denoted. To say it another way: the predicate here does not denote but exemplifies. The picture possesses a certain property or quality: it is a dull gray picture. This does not mean, however, that the picture denotes that property of grayness. It is more accurate to say that the picture is denoted by the predicate 'gray'. In the gray picture, the label gray is like a sample. The picture, like the tailor's sample, possesses not only the quality gray, but it also 'stands for' something by means of the quality of gray.

This coincidence of a possession of a property and of a reference Goodman calls exemplification. When one exemplifies, one points to a property, which something possesses. But at the same time, one refers like the tailor's swatch to the properties of colour, weave, texture, and pattern and ultimately to the bolt of cloth. So the dull gray picture exemplifies. It possesses grayness, but it is denoted by the property gray to express sadness. Goodman calls the exemplification type of reference a reverse reference.

Through Goodman's analysis, Ricoeur finds the metaphor firmly implanted in the domain of reference. A metaphor for Goodman is a case of a 'possession', which is transferred from one realm to another. In other words, a metaphor is a type of exemplification. Its reference would be then an inverted reference. To return to the dull gray picture, we might say that the sadness that the picture expresses is a metaphor. The label sadness, drawn from familiar usage, is applied to a new object "that resists at first and then gives in" (417:235).[29] The property of sadness, by its being

29. Goodman's own turn of phrase is more colourful: "(it) is a matter of teaching an old word new tricks... Metaphor is an affair between a

assigned to the picture, becomes a possession of the picture not literally, but metaphorically or figuratively. The re-assignment of the label has a ring of truth to it. In the case of the picture, the metaphor 'sad' is more appropriate than the metaphor 'gay'. Literally false, metaphorically it is true because of the re-assignment of labels (417:235).

With reference implanted in the metaphor, we can return to the question of the truth of metaphor. Here again, Goodman provides some helpful hints. He suggests that the label 'sad' is not an isolated predicate but is derived from a schema, that is, from a group of labels, which operates in a particular realm. In the case of the 'sad' picture, that realm is the realm of feeling. It was said above that the transfer of predicates from one realm to another is a type of organizing and re-organizing reality. The transference of the predicate 'sad' from the realm of feeling to the visual realm of painting means at the same time the transporting of the whole schema of feeling into the visual realm. That emigration brings about a re-organizing of the adopted realm by means of the entire network of feeling. It is, therefore, not the label which forces the re-organization, but the schema, a whole group of labels (417:237).[30]

Let us summarize briefly what Riceour has gained from the analysis of N. Goodman.

(1) The metaphor has a referential function, albeit a reversed reference. Poetic discourse is no less deprived of reference than descriptive discourse.

(2) The sensa (the images, sounds, and feelings) which, we said above, adhered to the verbal meaning in metaphorical statements are, to interject Goodman's analysis, representations (not descriptions), which exemplify (possession and reference), and transfer possession. The transferred qualities are real. They belong to things, even if simultaneously they are feelings experienced by the reader or viewer.

(3) Metaphorical qualities or poetic qualities contribute in the shaping of the world. Their truth lies in their appropriateness (417:238).

---

predicate with a past and an object that yields while protesting". Op. cit., p.69.

30.   But, according to Goodman, the truth of the metaphor cannot be justified. Ricoeur says that this is due to Goodman's nominalism (417:236). The literal usage of a label is only justified by its usage, he maintains. He considers the same to be true of the metaphorical label. The only difference is that the metaphor is a label that has not yet been endorsed by usage. Metaphorical usage merely underlines or accentuates what already takes place in literal usage. The truth quality of the metaphor is described by Goodman in terms such as 'appropriate', 'fitting', 'evident', and 'satisfying'. This nominalism is not satisfactory to Ricoeur.

On two points Ricoeur will go beyond the notion of truth and reality, which Goodman opened up but could not complete. The first area of expansion is the examination of the activity of poetic discourse in the fashioning of the world. How does poetic discourse 're-describe' or 're-organize' the world? Nelson Goodman pointed out one way through his theory of transference. To Ricoeur, a theory of models appears a more appropriate avenue. The second area of expansion will be the area of metaphorical truth. Nelson Goodman's notion of appropriateness can be taken as a lead. Ricoeur maintains that one predicate is more appropriate than another because it is a truer manifestation of the 'way of being of things' (417:239). But how does semantic innovation "discover what it creates, and invent what it finds" (417:239, emphasis mine)?

3. The role of the imagination.

To perceive an identity between dissimilars is a type of 'seeing as'. This apperception is unlike a concept, because the dissimilars are not united into a genus, but they are resolved into an identity within the very differences (417:198). The metaphor, according to Ricoeur, intercepts such a movement towards a similar, which would unite the dissimilars under a common genus. Of this he says, "To contemplate the similar or the same... is to grasp the genus, but not yet as genus, to grasp the same in the difference, and not yet as above or beside the difference" (373:109). The difference only yields under protest. In other words, the work of resemblance operates within the differences without going as far as the unitive concept.

If the playing space of the concept is speculative thought, Ricoeur postulates that the work towards figurative meaning in the metaphor pertains to the imagination (417:199). The 'seeing as', thematized in the metaphor in a "figurative presentation" or "as an image depicting abstract relationships" (417:198), is the work of imagination. The figurative, or, to use an image of Paul Henle,[31] the icon, has its own level and its own order of discourse. It is the discourse of the imagination (417:302).

The theory of the imagination, according to Ricoeur, admits of two traits, both of which require clarification. Ricoeur maintains that the imagination has both a linguistic, semantic dimension and a pre-linguistic, sensible dimension.

a. The semantics of the imagination.

Ricoeur's philosophy of the imagination attempts to avoid the present impasse of this philosophy by inserting it in a semantic theory of the metaphor.[32] The stumbling block of the classical theory of imagination has

---

31. "Metaphor, in Language, Thought and Culture, Ann Arbor, University of Michigan Press, 1958, p.

32. With Mary Schaldenbrand I would assign a pivotal role to the imagination in the philosophy of Paul Ricoeur. As we shall see, the

been the abusive use of the term 'image'. Image was perceived either as a mental impression, or mental copy, of the real thing, or as the stuff which tailors our abstract ideas (424:211). It is perceived as a weakened, mental copy of reality. To avoid the impasse of the watered-down reality of the image, Ricoeur insists first of all that the imagination is a certain way of using language. It is only secondarily that he will turn to its non-linguistic dimension. For him, our images are spoken before they are seen, i.e., our images are not derived from perception but from language.

The prime source for such a theory of productive imagination is Kant's theory of the schema (see 424:214f;157:393-396;152:63f). The theory of the schema attempts to discover a mediation or synthesis in a philosophy of pure reason between understanding and sensibility. Or, to say it in other words, the theory of the schema seeks to mediate between the rules of expressibility and the conditions of appearance, between intellection and reception. It is suggested by Kant that the duality of mediation is overcome in the object itself, but that the unity is available to us only in an enigmatic transcendental imagination. Transcendental imagination bonds the two powers of understanding and sensibility, without ever being able to reflect that unity (152:64).

For Kant, the transcendental schematism is first of all a method or an act. With Kant, one could call it an art - a hidden art which mediates in us the intellectual and the sensible (160:395). It is not a content. But it is a method for giving an image to a concept, or a method for opening up meaning.[33] This productive imagination in Kant, Ricoeur says, is operative in language, specifically in metaphorical language. In metaphorical language, through the interplay of identity and difference, the imagination produces a semantic innovation by producing the figurative meaning (417:199). The figurative meaning, the image, is therefore first of all a work of discourse. The discourse is made to resonate, to vibrate, with the image according to the strategy of discourse, which is operative in metaphorical statements. Precisely in the clash of two interpretations the imagination mediates. Upon the ruins of a literal interpretation, the imagination mediates the emergence of a new meaning. As Ricoeur says, "The imagination is the apperception, the sudden glimpse, of a new predicative pertinence, that is, a way of constructing pertinence in the impertinence... To imagine is first of all to restructure the semantic fields"

---

imagination is the mediating function inthe probing of the possible and, in the final analysis, in the appropriation of an existence that is truly human. See her "Metaphoric Imagination: Kinship Through Conflict" in Studies in the Philosophy of Paul Ricoeur, op. cit., p.57-81. See also M. Gerhart, "Imagination and History in Ricoeur's Interpretation Theory" in Phil. Today 23, 1979, p.51-68.

33. In a suggestive turn of phrase, Ricoeur defines the human subject as a "power of anticipation of the realm of the object." "Philosophie, sentiment et poésie. La notion d'a priori selon Mikel Dufrenne", Esprit, 29(1961), p.512.

(424:212). The images are, for that reason, products of language. They are emergent meanings (417:199).

b. The non-linguistic dimension of the imagination.

But Ricoeur also points to another dimension of the imagination, which is non-verbal and sensible. The image is also quasi-visual, quasi-auditory, quasi-olfactory (416:199). This aspect of the image, which the semantic theory of the metaphor seems to have excluded, brings into play the non-verbal ability of the image to make-see, or to use Aristotle's expression, 'to set before the eyes'. An image is also figurative. Paul Henle calls the image 'iconical'.[34] This iconical character is a consequence of seeing one thing through the medium of another term. He calls it icon, following Charles Sanders Peirce, because the icon has the distinct ability to contain within it an internal duality that it overcomes at the same time (417:189).

It is ironic that, in his diligent effort to tame the metaphor within a semantic theory, Ricoeur arrives finally at a non-verbal image. However, he will not let the image escape language too easily.

His guide in this area is Marcus Hester's The Meaning of Poetic Metaphor.[35] Hester proposes that the imaginary is rooted in a semantic theory of metaphor (417:208). He exemplifies it in the usage of poetic metaphors. He subscribes to the theory of literary criticism which states that in poetic language there is a fusion of meaning and the senses. Poetic language, according to this theory, appears to seek out the sensible rather than exclude it, as conventional signs do. This fusion of meaning and the sensible condenses this poetic language into a sculpture-like object, which focusses full attention upon itself. Poetic language takes on the form of an icon, that forces one to look at it and not beyond it to an outside. Like a sculpture or an icon, poetic language becomes a contoured object.

Hester clarifies this fusion of language and the sensible in a theory of reading. In the reading of this sculpture-like language, as in every reading, something like a Husserlian époché takes place. There is a suspension of our ordinary stance in reality. But the suspension sets free at the same time all the resonances, reverberations and echoes, which the liberated data can evoke. To read is to suspend reality and to open oneself to the text (417:266). In the suspension of reality in the act of reading, the imagination breaks free in every direction, awakening previous experiences and dormant memories. In this manner, the imagination is directed to the adjacent sensorial fields. Imagination is a free play with possibilities, opening up the no-where of everyday reality.[36] It is free in

---

34. Op. cit., p.177.

35. The Hague, Mouton, 1967.

36. The 'no-where' of the imagination - Utopia - will be examined in Chapter Six. See below p.176-181.

77

that in it there is no commitment to the world of perception. It is the free space for new ideas, new values, new ways of being in the world (424:213-214). The diffusion of the "wave of evoked or aroused images" (417:210) is bound only by the fact that it takes place within 'poetic diction': "The poet is the artisan in language, generating and shaping images by the sole medium of language" (424:213). The free space within which the imagination can play has as its sole barrier the limits, which the utmost possibilities of language impose. If it is true that in reading, reality exterior to the verbal icon is suspended, it does not mean that this petrifaction freezes reality. The text 'lets see' despite the suspension of the ostensive reference. This is basically the openness of the text (417:210).

Because of the close interrelationship between meaning and image, Hester maintains that the images are not totally 'free' images. The images are controlled by meaning, i.e., language places limits or closure upon the images. Hence, the non-verbal dimension of imagination does not lead to unlimited associations of images. The image remains tied to meaning. This creates the dialectic between the verbal and the non-verbal. The verbal icon is perceived as a method of constructing images (417:211).

This relationship of the verbal and the non-verbal in poetic language is best explained by the notion of 'seeing as'. This 'seeing as' is exposed in the act of reading. In the act of reading, the 'vehicle' discloses itself to be like the 'tenor' but only from a certain perspective. The vehicle is 'seen as' the tenor. The sense and the image are held together by seeing the one as the other from one point of view. This point of view is the proper and appropriate sense of the metaphor. To 'see as' is to have this image. It is half-thought and half-experience. In the example, "time is a beggar", time is seen imagistically, or pictorially, or sensibly. Two things happen. One constructs, first of all, in a living metaphor what one 'sees as'. It is the mixture of thought and experience, which 'seeing as' holds together. But an amount of closure is imposed upon the act. Time is not beggar-like under all the aspects which a beggar denotes in a literal sense. As Ricoeur says, " 'Seeing as' orders the flux and governs iconic deployment" (459:213). But, secondly, this act, this construction, is also intuitive. Ricoeur says, "The image arises, occurs, and there is no rule to be learned for 'having images'. One sees, or one does not see" (417:213). 'Seeing as' is, therefore, both an experience and an act of understanding.

By way of Hester's analysis, Ricoeur comes to express 'seeing as' in reading as a joining of verbal meaning with the fullness of imagery. Seeing-as takes place in language. Its ground lies in resemblance - not a resemblance between two ideas - but the resemblance between a verbal meaning and the image. The resemblance is the result of the experience. It did not exist before. 'Seeing as' instituted the resemblance and not vice versa. At times, the resemblance fails, such as in forced or inconsistent metaphors. It succeeds in living metaphors (417:213). Bringing the Kantian schematism into play Ricoeur resumes:

Thus 'seeing as' quite precisely plays the role of the schema that unites the _empty_ concept and the _blind_ impression; thanks to its character as half thought and half experience, it joins the light of sense with the fullness of the image. In this way, the non-verbal and the verbal are firmly united at the core of the image-ing function of language (417:213).

For Ricoeur, this iconical interpretation of imagination, in which there is a fusion of sense and the imagination, is essential to the interaction theory of metaphor. The release of a new semantic pertinence takes place at the scene of the interaction of the vehicle and tenor, at the intuitive fusion of sense and the imaginary: "Metaphorical meeting as such feeds on the density of imagery released by the poem" (417:214).

It is obvious that at this point the relationship of the verbal to the non-verbal is such that the non-verbal must be given priority. The imagery may be set free by the verbal, but its very activity discloses the limits of language. We reach here what Ricoeur calls the 'frontier' of semantics (417:214). The region beyond is best secured by a phenomenology of imagination, "where the verbal is vassal to the non-verbal" (417:214). However, the region beyond the verbal is still serviced by the verbal. The image remains word-bound. In the words of Bachelard, whose phenomenology of imagination inspires Ricoeur here,[37] the image remains an 'aura surrounding speech' (417:214). Ricoeur sums up his thought by saying, "The poem gives birth to the image: the poetic image 'becomes a new being in our language, expressing us by making us what it expresses; in other words, it is at once a becoming of expression, and a becoming of our being'" (417:214-215). But this region of being needs to be explored at greater length in its proper place.

c. Reference as redescription of reality.

Taking his cue once again from Nelson Goodman, Ricoeur gives the following elaboration of the referential quality of the poetic and metaphorical expression as a power to give shape to reality. Once the conditioned perception of the world, the world of our manipulation, the world of our control, is jolted, our vision of things, Ricoeur suggests, is actually increased (424:215). Its language, although centripetal, breaks through to reality, even to the very origin of reality. The concerns of this language are not to describe reality, but to organize and even to re-organize reality.

In this paragraph, we will examine how Ricoeur presents this power of the metaphor to redescribe reality. In a following paragraph, the truth of that redescribed reality will be tested. We must bracket provisionally the discussion of the referent of poetic texts. Ricoeur,

---

37. La Poétique de l'espace, P.U.F., 1957; La Poétique de la rêverie, P.U.F., 1960.

following Heidegger, calls the referent the 'world' of the text, as we saw above.[38] The present paragraph deploys the strategy and the process of that language alone. The world of the text is displayed only in the strategy of the language of the text. The task of opening up that world, as the world of my possibilities, belongs to hermeneutics, which we will examine in the next chapter.

The relationship of metaphor to reality is described in terms of Max Black's theory of models[39] and of Mary Hesse's theory of metaphor as redescription.[40] A metaphor is said to have the same function in poetic language as a model has in scientific language. Now, in the sciences, a model has a heuristic function. It is a cognitive fictional device in the discovery of a scientific theory.

The scientific model referred to is not the scale model, used, for example, in an architectural presentation or in mapping. Nor is it the analogue model used to indicate structural rather than visual or sensible relationships. Rather, the model is known as a theoretical model operative in the logic of scientific discovery (417:241). The model attempts to represent one field of scientific endeavour in the terms and language of another, which is better known or organized. Clark Maxwell's representation of an electrical field in terms of an imaginary incompressible fluid is such a theoretical model. In other words, the model is not visual or sensible. The model cannot even be constructed. It is a heuristic device, an imaginary medium. Its properties are derived from language and the conventions of language. The model is fruitful, if one knows how to make use of the correlations, which apply between the domain that one seeks to understand and the domain 'described' in the model. Via the detour of the described model, the imagination perceives new relationships.

The achievement of the model is that it opens up a new domain through a familiar theory. Mary Hesse calls this theoretical opening up of the new domain both an explanation and a metaphorical redescription. It is an explanation because, by introducing new language, it describes the less accessible domain through a more accessible domain. In other words, the theoretical model of Maxwell does not function as if the electrical field has properties similar to the incompressible fluid, but as though it possesses these properties.

This does not mean that one may conclude to a theory of deduction between the two domains. The less accessible is not deduced

---

38. See above p.40-41 of Chapter Two.

39. "Models and Archetypes", in Models and Metaphors, op. cit., p.219-243. See La métaphore vive, (417:239-242).

40. "The Explanatory Function of Metaphor", in Logic, Methodology and Philosophy of Science, ed. by Bar-Hillel, Amsterdam, North-Holland, 1965.

from the more accessible domain. The rules of correspondence between the domains cannot rationally be set to function in a deductive manner. The description of the new domain through another is best called, according to Mary Hesse, a metaphorical re-description (see 417:242). The new domain is 'seen as' the model. The new domain itself is not described - that route is blocked. In having destroyed the descriptive power of language in the strategy of the metaphor, the metaphor puts one in touch with a deeper level of language: a language that opens reality at the level of what Husserl called the Lebenswelt, or of Heidegger's being-in-the-world (411:87).

Two repercussions for the theory of the text must be touched on here before proceeding to an analysis of the power of the metaphor to express things at their core.

(1) The metaphor, as analogous to the model, is not a simple one-liner but the extended metaphor, such as the tale, the allegory, or the poem. The referential character of the metaphor is bound up with the work of discourse, requiring composition, a literary form, and style. A work of discourse will bring into play not just an isolated metaphor but a metaphoric network. It is not one metaphor that projects a world, but the whole poem, as an expanded metaphor, which gives foundation to a "metaphoric universe as a network" (417:243-244).[41]

(2) Mary Hesse and Max Black both maintain that models have a heuristic function since they describe one region or field through another. This linkage between heuristic function and description is a harkening back, according to Ricoeur, to Aristotle's theory of tragedy as an imitation of nature.

Because of the importance of this detail for Ricoeur, we must introduce his analysis of Aristotle's concepts of mimêsis and muthos in tragic poetry (417:34-40).

For Aristotle, poetry, particularly in its highest form of the tragic poem, is defined as an "imitation (mimêsis) of human action" (Poetics 1448a1,29). The mimêsis of human action in tragedy has six parts, which we enumerate here for the sake of clarity: 1. the fable or the plot (muthos), 2. characters (êthê), 3. diction (lexis), 4. thought or theme (dianoia), 5. the spectacle (opsis), and 6. the melody (melopoia). The dominant factor of the tragic poem is the muthos, the plot or the fable. This trait is so central that Aristotle maintains that the imitation of human action (mimêsis) must be derived or pass through the fable or plot (muthos) and that the other parts all converge on the muthos. The muthos is achieved through three instrumental factors, the spectacle, the melody and the diction (lexis). Thought and character are seen as the natural causes of the action (416:36).

---

41. This point was also made by Nelson Goodman, who placed the 'figure' in a 'schema', which, in the case of a transfer of figures, allowed the transporting of the whole region of feeling into the visual realm.

The muthos brings to the tragic poem its character of order, organization and composition. The order of the muthos invades all the other factors. It shapes the spectacle. It gives coherence to the characters. It orders the sequence of thought and the arrangement of the verses. The creation of tragic poetry is, therefore, an ordering, an arranging, a bringing into coherence of human action. In what sense, then, is the muthos a real mimêsis, a real imitation, of human action?

To translate mimêsis by imitation is more apt to confuse than clarify. Aristotle's mimêsis is a far throw from the Platonic imitation. Plato's imitation covers all areas of existence, because all areas are considered to be imitations of an ideal model. All areas reflect well or poorly that which may be considered the principle of things. Aristotle's mimêsis exists only where there is a 'making'. Mimêsis is not a proximate or remote resemblance but a production. And production, as we saw above, is always of individuals. An 'imitation' is a making of one thing. Imitation is a form of process. This process or production of mimêsis is, however, the process of the formation of the six parts of the tragic poem from plot to spectacle. In other words, mimêsis is the process whereby, in the variety of poetic creations (epic poetry, tragedy, and comedy), the six traits of poetry combine to make what Aristotle called the "imitation of nobler actions" (see 417:38). Mimêsis is, therefore, a poiêsis, a making. It is a poiêsis, because it composes, structures, constructs the fable, plot, or muthos. This leads to the paradoxical situation where Aristotle's mimêsis composes and constructs the poem which it imitates (417:39). Mimêsis can hardly be called, then, a duplication of reality. It is closer to what Mary Hesse, in the theory of models, called a redescription of reality. And since mimêsis accomplishes this redescription by means of the muthos, the relationship between mimêsis and muthos in poiêsis resembles the relationship between heuristic fiction and redescription in the theory of models.

Now, a tension exists between the muthos and the mimêsis that resembles the tension between heuristic fiction and redescription. It is the tension, according to Ricoeur, between the submission to reality and creativity (417:39). To accentuate this tension one must recall that Aristotle's mimêsis, his redescription of human action, is one that ennobles, magnifies, and enhances human action. As Ricoeur says,

> Muthos is not just a rearrangement of human action into a more coherent form, but a structuring that elevates this action; thus mimêsis preserves and represents that which is human, not just in its essential features, but in a way that makes it greater and nobler. There is thus a double tension proper to mimêsis: on the one hand, the imitation is at once a portrayal of human reality and an original creation; on the other, it is faithful to things as they are and it depicts them as higher and greater than they are (417:40).

The metaphorical activity at the level of the whole composition lies in the description of the less accessible domain - human reality - by a more accessible domain - the fictitious tragic poem. This metaphorical activity is a trait of the muthos, the plot.[42] It is a fictional organization of human actions in a tragic poem, placing human action into the whole schema, or, to use Ricoeur's terminology, into the whole metaphoric network, of the tragic poem. "Tragedy teaches us to 'see' human life, 'as' that which the muthos displays" (417:245).

The truth of the reality of the muthos is attached, however, to mimêsis. The muthos must remain at the service of mimêsis, of redescription, which retains its reference to reality, even though it is metaphorical reality. The redescription of reality takes the long route of the muthos or the heuristic fiction.

Ricoeur extrapolates this relationship of muthos and mimêsis in tragic and lyric poetry. Using Northrop Frye's centripetal analysis of poetry, he argues that poetry produces a mood, attached to the poem itself. If the poem creates mood, cannot this mood be conceived as the reference of the poem? Does the mood in some sense not redescribe reality, not so that it is seen as another, but so that it is felt as another? Ricoeur insists that such is the case: "The feeling articulated by the poem is not less heuristic than the tragic tale" (417:245). In a lyric poem, we may speak of a creation of an affective fiction.

Once again the question of truth looms up. But for the moment let us retain that, for Ricoeur, feeling is not an emotional state of the subject. As he affirms in his L'homme faillible (152:122-202), feeling has an intentionality that attaches to things, persons and the world.[43] This implies that the mood says something about the being of things and not merely about the subject. Feeling is that which prefigures the reconciliation of subject and object.

d. The truth of metaphorical and poetic reference.

We must now turn to Ricoeur's approach to the issue of the truth

---

42. Muthos shares the metaphor with lexis. According to Aristotle, the metaphor pertains to two areas of life - to rhetoric and to poetry. What binds it to both is lexis, a word impossible to render accurately in English, but generally translated by diction. Lexis provides the language dimension to the ordering of thought in both rhetoric and poetry. Lexis is the coherence of thought in words, or more accurately, the ordering of thought in the process of coming into language. The function of lexis is, therefore, to exteriorize, to make explicit the internal order of the muthos. The language dimension of the metaphor pertains to the lexis with its task of interpreting in language the internal order of human action of muthos. Cf. La métaphore vive, (417:37).

43. To borrow a phrase of Mikel Dufrenne, "To feel is to experience a feeling as a property of the object, not as a state of my being." Cf. La métaphore vive, (417:227).

of redescription and of mood. The semantics of reference has deposited the metaphor and poetic texts at the threshold of the sphere of truth. The first aspect of the discussion is provided by the status and the function of the copula 'is' in a metaphorical statement (see 417:247-256; 411:88).

(1) The existential commitment of the copula 'is'.

In the metaphorical statement, "Old age is a withered flower", the copula 'is' is not merely relational; that is, it is not a mere predicative link between 'old age' and 'withered flower'. The 'is' also intends a reference. Through it, reality is redescribed: things are as said. What is meant here? The use of the verb 'to be' has not only a literal meaning but also a metaphorical meaning. Ricoeur introduces in the verb 'to be' the same tension as is found between the tenor and the vehicle or between two interpretations (literal and metaphorical), or between identity and difference. He proposes to show that, within the verb 'to be', there is expressed at the same time an 'is not' and an 'is'. The 'is' marks an existential judgment.

This is an interesting extension of the metaphorical into the copula. In the tension of the comparison of terms there is a rebound upon the verb 'to be'. According to Ricoeur, to understand how the existential function of the verb 'to be' is affected by the tension is to have access to the notion of metaphorical truth (417:248). For Ricoeur the 'is' does not indicate complete identity between the two terms. It is not truth as found in the mathematical sciences. The 'is' is a metaphorical 'is'. This metaphorical 'to be', Ricoeur suggests, puts us in touch with language at "a pre-scientific, ante-predicative level, where the very notions of fact, object, reality, and truth, as delimited by epistemology, are called into question (417:254).[44] Like Douglas Berggren, Ricoeur insists on the truth value of poetic assertions.[45] The lead comes from the poets themselves, who think that their assertions are true in a certain sense. That certain sense is that poetic or metaphorical truth is a tensional truth. Within the 'is' of the metaphorical statement lies the 'is not' of a literal interpretation. As Ricoeur says, "There is no other way to do justice to the notion of metaphorical truth than to include the critical incision of the (literal) 'is not' within the ontological vehemence of the (metaphorical) 'is'" (417:255). The simile, which is a weakened metaphor, expresses this grammatically by

---

44. In his very asking of the question of metaphorical truth, Ricoeur brings back into focus his early concern with the second naiveté, which can only be built upon the ruins of the Cartesian naiveté. The meaning that is 'radical', the meaning that touches the root of existence, can only emerge out of and upon the ruins of the bankruptcy of a literal, manipulative approach to reality. Here something other than the authoritative subject or poet speaks. Here something beyond the control of the poet comes to language.

45. "The Use and Abuse of Metaphor", Rev. of Metaphysics, 16(1962-1963), p.227-258.

stating, 'it is like', that is, 'it is' but simultaneously by only being 'like' it says also 'it is not'.

(2) Metaphorical discourse and speculative discourse.

The question of truth and being is held to be the reserve of speculative thought. It is necessary, therefore, to examine the relationship between the speculative and the metaphorical in order to investigate the ontology that is implied in metaphorical discourse. The question is not an easy one because it has dominated philosophy and theology for a long time.[46] In its modern dress L. Wittgenstein proposed in his earlier philosophy that the variety of language games are so radically disparate or heterogeneous that communication between, for instance, the speculative and the poetic is to be excluded. In classical philosophy this discontinuity between the poetic and philosophical discourse was first proposed by Aristotle in the Categories and the Metaphysics. On the other hand, Thomas Aquinas in his doctrine of the analogy of being discovered a principle of mediation between modes of discourse. Since this issue is of some importance both to Ricoeur and to the development of this work, let us examine the position of Aristotle and Aquinas before proposing Ricoeur's own solution.

In his philosophy of being Aristotle maintained that "being is said in many ways" (417:260). That is, being is not said univocally, but polyvalently.[47] But if being is said in many ways, one must wonder whether the meaning of being does not dissolve in equivocity. How can the breakdown of communication among the multiple meanings of being be avoided?

The position of Aristotle in the Categories and in the Metaphysics maintains the impossibility of finding a principle of mediation linking the multiple ways of saying being. If the Metaphysics asks the question, What is being? and answers that being is said in many ways, it is in

46. At issue here is the possibility of one language game to express all of reality. In De l'interprétation. Essai sur Freud, (227) Ricoeur raises the issue of the unity of human discourse: "How can language be put to such diverse uses as mathematics and myth, physics and art?" p.3. "The dismemberment of that discourse" (p.4) in the contemporary context requires a mediation. But, as he suggests there, "the problem of the unity of language cannot validly be posed until a fixed status has been assigned to a group of expressions that share the peculiarity of designating an indirect meaning in and through a direct meaning." (p.12). The entry into Freudian psychoanalytical discourse provided an opportunity not only to discover humanity as desire but also to exemplify the interanimation of the discourse of psychoanalysis and of hermeneutics in order to enrich phenomenology.

47. Plato and Aristotle's philosophy of being is worked out more extensively in Platon et Aristote. Être, Essence et Substance chez Platon et Aristote, (82).

the treatise on the Categories that Aristotle seeks to safeguard the plurivocity of being from irretrievable scattering. Aristotle refuses to follow the path of Plato, who held that the multiple meanings were held together by their participation in the éidos, the first form (see 417:261). Instead, he argues that being is not a genus, nor a mere equivocal word. In the Categories he proposes an order among the multiple meanings. The order is one of categories as they relate to a first term (ousia). The categories, such as action, passion, quantity, quality, other than the substance, can be predicated of the substance and can be ranged according to their distance from the substance. It is the task of philosophy to stand guard over the ordering of meaning according to the categories.

But what is the philosophical principle which oversees the series of meanings of the term 'to be'? Aristotle suggests,[48] that the organizing principle of being is analogy. The table of categories is said to be formed by adding to or subtracting from the meaning of 'is'. Hence, the varied modes of being are said to weaken as they progressively recede from a primordial essential predication towards a derived accidental predication. The relation one to another is said to be governed by analogy. But what sort of analogy is predicated? It is not an analogy, as J. Vuillemin says,[49] governing, "the relation of element to set" or "the relation of part to whole". He calls the analogy, as applied to the multiple meanings of being, an "intuitive given" (417:263), whose meaning shifts from inherence to proportion, from proportion to proportionality.

Aristotle, however, hesitated to call this reference to essential predication an analogy. At the same time, he denied that the multiple meanings converge into a system. And yet, despite this, he did admit to a single science of the multiple meanings of being.

Ricoeur interprets this hesitancy of Aristotle ultimately as an inability to order the many ways of saying being by means of analogy. The multivocity of being resists a univocal organizing principle. This has some interesting consequences. On the one hand, it confirms for Ricoeur the heterogeneity of the modes of discourse. That means that, fundamentally, the speculative discourse is irreducible to poetic discourse (417:265). On the other hand, the search since Aristotle for an organizing principle, which would unify the various discourses, but which ran into an aporie, reveals at least what Ricoeur calls a "semantic aim" (417:266). In other words, Ricoeur holds that the heterogeneity of discourse is tempered by a semantic aim - traditionally expressed in terms of analogy. The semantic aim implies at least a level of communicability between the various discourses. He invokes for his argument the conceptual labour, which has entered into the

---

48.   In La métaphore vive, Ricoeur is less quick to introduce the notion of analogy into Aristotle's philosophy of being inasmuch as being than he was in Platon et Aristote, (417:106).

49.   De la logique à la théologie. Cinq études sur Aristote, Paris, Flammarion, 1967, p.110. See La métaphore vive, (417:263).

into the search for a unity along the many meanings of being, rather than the transcendental solution that analogy was to provide (417:272). It might, therefore, be necessary to think of the non-generic (that is, non-scientific) bond of being in a way that bypasses analogy. It is significant how Ricoeur expresses this:

> But this step beyond analogy was possible only because analogy itself had been a step beyond metaphor. It will thus have proved decisive for thought that a segment of equivocalness was wrested once from poetry and incorporated into philosophical discourse, just at the time when philosophical discourse was forced to disengage itself from the sway of pure univocity (417:272).

In other words, Ricoeur here recalls the historic event in which speculative thought fought itself free from the domain of poetry. It is that victory which speculative thought now seeks to protect. Ricoeur goes so far as to say that the semantic aim of speculative thought is precisely the refusal of speculative thought to enter into a compromise with poetic discourse (417:277). But this defensive action of speculative thought did not prevent medieval theologians -especially Thomas Aquinas - from determining the point of intersection between poetic and speculative discourse more precisely. Analogy, which for Aristotle had been a tentative principle, becomes in medieval theology a generally accepted bonding principle of being. But particularly the acceptance and the usage of the analogia entis by Thomas Aquinas reveals both the semantic aim of the search and the point of intersection of the metaphorical and speculative discourse.

Theology, in its doctrine of creation, aggravates the need for a point at which the ways of saying being converge. As a communication of being, creation theology re-introduced the concept of participation, which Aristotle had explicitly rejected. And with participation, the spectre of metaphor is thrown right back into the midst of speculative thought. For Aquinas, in the relation of creature to Creator - "the bond of participation" (417:276) - the creative causality is made ontologically possible by analogy: "The most heterogeneous cause (God) must therefore remain analogous cause" (417:277). But the application of the notion of analogy to the area of theology demanded an ever greater refinement of the concept, bringing analogy, especially the analogy of proportionality, in close proximity to metaphor. Once again, the intention is to safeguard reality from the Scylla and Charybdis of univocity and the complete dislocation of equivocity.

Only in the Summa Theologiae, where he asks whether names predicated of God are said principally of creatures (1^a, q.13, art.6), does Aquinas indicate a point of intersection for discourse. He says there that names essentially predicated of God, such as goodness and wisdom, apply primarily to God, and through Him, to creatures. At this level, which we can call the level of the thing, analogy applies. However, on the level of signification - at the level of the imposition of a name - Aquinas says, one must begin with what is best known to us as creatures. Here the process can only be called metaphorical.[50] Ricoeur concludes from this that an intersecting of discourses takes place here: the discourse of the order of being descending from God to creatures and the discourse on the level of signification ascending from creatures to God. In the intersecting, "the speculative verticalizes metaphor, while the poetic dresses speculative analogy in iconic garb" (417:279). Thus, the word 'wise' is applied to God analogously without leading to a univocal application of that word to God and human beings because the signification presents different features in both. In human beings, the perfections are distinct, and wise 'circumscribes' and 'comprehends'. In God, 'wise' does not 'circumscribe' nor does it 'comprehend', because wisdom is essentially God and wise exceeds the signification of the name. The excess of meaning of 'wise' in God does not prevent it, however, from signifying, but it does not create distinctions in God. Name and signification break apart here, just as in metaphorical statements, in which an unusual attribution can be applied to a word. In their predication of 'wise', analogical and metaphorical discourse remain distinct, although they intersect. The analogical rests on the predication of transcendental terms, while the metaphorical is founded on the predication of meanings that are not divested of their material content.

If the analogia entis reveals only the semantic aim, without itself being capable of mediating the interanimation of discourse, are there other mediations which might accomplish the task?

Ricoeur bypasses as seductive but not earth-shaking (417:291) the position of J. Derrida, which takes up the Heideggerean assertion that "the metaphorical exists only inside the metaphysical" (see 417:282).[51] Derrida's search for the point of intersection takes him away from the stated intentions of the modes of discourse, but, following the philosophies of suspicion, he turns to the level of the unconscious presuppositions of the discourses (417:280). Derrida's search leads to an investigation of the unsaid of the metaphor, i.e., the dead metaphor.[52] Concept, he maintains, is the 'raising'[53] of the dead metaphor. In other words, underlying the concept, there is a dead metaphor that has been 'raised'. Hence the slogan, the metaphorical exists only inside the metaphysical. The task of thinkers, according to Derrida, is to unmask the metaphorical that underlies all reality and to show that all reality shares the circularity of the metaphorical. All discourse according to this vision is condemned to remain in the terrifying void of circular metaphoricity.

---

50.   In the same article, Aquinas had already indicated that this type of metaphorical attribution places the discourse about God at the level of signification close to poetic discourse.

51.   Der Satz vom Grund, Pfüllingen, Neske, 1957, p.89.

52.   "Mythologie blanche (La métaphore dans le texte philosophique)", Poétique, 5(1971), p.1-52.

53.   "Relève" (raising) is Derrida's translation of Hegel's Aufhebung.

But, according to Ricoeur, this degree of fusion of the metaphorical and the metaphysical overlooks one thing. The transgression in metaphors from the literal to the figurative, and the transgression in metaphysics from the visible to the invisible world, may appear as one and the same transgression. But that does not necessarily fuse the two discourses. The metaphorical transgression, as Hegel saw already, is a transfer from one region to the next, from the literal to the figurative. It brings the whole network of intersignifications with it into the new region. This operation is, however, quite distinct from the metaphysical operation. The metaphysical transgression from the visible to the invisible is a true Aufhebung, a true sublation or 'raising'. It creates as Ricoeur says, "a proper sense in the spiritual order out of an improper sense coming from the sensible order" (417:292). In other words, it is an inverse operation to the metaphorical: it does not transport the whole realm of the intersignifications of the sensible into the concept, but the metaphysical 'suppresses' it only to preserve it at a proper level in a conceptual expression. Thus, 'insight' is philosophical because we no longer hear 'sight' in it. As Derrida remarks the 'seeing' has worn away into thought to the point that "the meaning aimed at through these figures is an essence rigorously independent of that which carries it over' (see 417:293).[54]

It is this insight that guides Ricoeur to his position that "the act of positing the concept proceeds dialectically from metaphor" (459:293, emphasis mine), i.e., that the relationship between metaphorical discourse and philosophical discourse is dialectical. The interanimation, which he proposes, is not a collusion between the discourses, where the one discourse dissolves or wears away into the other. Instead, Ricoeur says that "metaphysics ... seizes the metaphorical process in order to make it work to the benefit of metaphysics" (417:294-295). It is this intersecting that needs to be determined more exactly to clarify the gathering of the truth of the metaphorical reference.

(3) The truth of metaphorical reference.

The section of Study Eight of La métaphore vive dealing with "the intersection of spheres of discourse" (417:295-303) is pivotal for the understanding not only of the referential mode of the metaphor, but also of the interrelationship between biblical discourse and theology which we must consider below.[55] Aided by the research of Jean Ladrière,[56] Ricoeur considers the semantic aim and semantic dynamism of metaphorical discourse in some detail in this section. He shows it to be the condition of the possibility of speculative discourse. But he also shows that this dynamism of the metaphorical expression towards the concept can be examined by speculative thought only with the resources that are proper to

---

54. Art. cit., p.29. Cf. La métaphore vive, (417:293).

55. See below p.251-253.

56. "Discours théologique et symbole", Rev.Sc.relig.49, 1975, p.29.

speculative thought. This transfer of the metaphorical expression into the domain of speculative thought takes place, therefore, at the price of the transmutation of the metaphorical.

Let us examine these positions in greater detail.

(a) From metaphor to concept.

Ricoeur asserts that the condition of the possibility of conceptualization in discourse lies in the semantic dynamism of metaphorical utterance (417:296). In other words, the structure of meaning of the metaphorical utterance itself calls for, or urges, the "passage to the concept" (417:294) of whatever novelty of meaning that has emerged through the clash of semantic impertinence. What the metaphor allows to be seen as..., the dynamism of meaning seeks to grasp, no longer in its similarity, but through the concept. Now, it is Ricoeur's contention that "every gain in meaning is at one and the same time a gain in sense and a gain in reference" (417:297). Ricoeur admits that this contention is a refinement of what we have stated earlier concerning his theory of sense and reference.[57] He says that the dynamism of meaning functions as a criss-crossing of the acts of sense (predication) and of reference.[58] In discourse, the process of meaning follows a course, whose dynamism moves in two intersecting directions. It moves toward concept, but in its very passage towards the concept, it broadens its referential scope.

Ladrière explains the dynamic interplay of sense and reference as follows. He says that in ordinary language, abstract predicates are mastered only by relating them to a specific, concrete object. Since the lexical term represents only a rule for its use in a sentence context, by creating variations in usage towards different referents, one can master the sense of a sentence. In other words, the gain in meaning through the variations of usage is also a gain in sense. Conversely, new referents can be explored by seeking to describe them as accurately as possible. In the process, the referential field is extended by the more and more refined abstract predicates. Thus, predication and reference mutually support and interact upon a process of meaning, either as new predicates in a familiar referential field, or as familiar predicates in a new referential field. The power of signifying lies then in the intersection of two movements. One movement expends its energy by determining the abstract, conceptual traits of reality. The other movement works with these predicates towards making new referents appear. Thus, the power of signifying, by means of the criss-crossing of the predicative and referential acts, is unlimited.

These processes also bring into play an historical dimension. New experiences find their expression by delving into the treasury of

---

57. See above, p.32-34.

58. Ricoeur leans heavily on the study of Jean Ladrière in the statement of his position.

historically established meanings. Because meanings are never firmly established in their use, it is possible for new experiences to find a new outlet by means of accepted meanings. The accepted meanings function then as a guide for new meanings (417:297-298).

If this dual process is valid for ordinary language, in metaphorical discourse, Ricoeur says, this semantic dynamism is carried to an extreme (417:299). Metaphorical utterance operates simultaneously in two referential fields. It links together two levels of meaning: a known field of established meanings and an unexplored field, for which no appropriate predicates exist. For that reason, in order to explore the new field of reference, the semantic aim reverts to the network of familiar predicates and places them in the new field to help explore it. Presupposed in this effort is the existence of the new field of reference and the attraction which its existence exerts upon already established predicates to emigrate to the new field. Earlier, we referred to Ricoeur's position that the metaphor both creates and reveals meaning (417:239,246). Here, he explains that process in which invention and discovery are not opposite. He insists that the energy for the discovery resides in the semantic aim, which is generated by the new field. The new field of reference gives rise to the uprooting and the transferring of current predicates. But, for Ricoeur, this has an interesting repercussion for meaning. Meaning is not a stable staple, but a "dynamic, directional, vectoral" (417:299) form, which links up with the semantic aim of the sentence to forge towards its fulfilment. Hence, there are two energies, two dynamisms, at work. On the one hand, there is the gravitational dynamism of the new field of reference upon meaning. On the other, there is the dynamism of meaning itself as "the inductive principle of sense" (417:299). These two energies are placed in relation to one another by the semantic aim of the metaphorical utterance, so that a semantic potential will insert itself in the movement of the second referential field.

The new meaning, which emerges through the introduction of this semantic potential into the second referential field, is not yet a conceptual meaning. It is not a firmly established meaning, for it can be regained only by reliving the shock of the semantic impertinence. The shock, which makes us see reality as..., seeks to gain, however, the stability of the concept. But it is not as yet a knowledge by means of concepts (417:296). Ricoeur calls the new knowledge a "semantic sketch" (417:299). The metaphorical utterance is sketchy both on the level of sense and on the level of reference.

On the level of sense, the metaphorical utterance can only sketch the new referential field by means of a familiar referential field by reproducing it in the as yet unknown area. On the level of reference, the semantic aim can only provide a sketch insofar as it draws the unknown referential field into the ambit of language through similarity or resemblance.

At the origin of the whole metaphorical process - as well as of ordinary language - Ricoeur posits what he calls "the ontological vehemence of a semantic aim" within an unknown field (417:299). The ontological vehemence is the activator of the field. It kidnaps a meaning from another field, takes its sense-movement, and activates that sense-movement in the new field. Hence, we are presented with a split sense and a split reference. The meaning released in the second field, however, hardly exceeds the figurative. Speculative thought will delve into this figurative sketch to evolve the concept.

(b) Speculative thought and metaphorical discourse.

If the metaphorical process has been shown to be the origin of all semantic fields, how does it relate to speculative discourse? The ontological vehemence of the semantic aim, which generated the metaphorical utterance, also generates the energy, which seeks the concept. But, according to Ricoeur, it is not the metaphorical process that generates the concept. This task is reserved to speculative discourse. Speculative discourse, drawing on its own reserves and resources - driven by the very structure of the mind - explores the space of the metaphor by means of notions and principles, which it derives from itself. For that reason there is no automatic progression from one discourse to another. "One can pass from one discourse to the other only by an époché" (417:300). In this context, speculative discourse will determine the conceptual field by means of its independently established primary notions and principles.

With these resources, speculative thought will tackle the semantic sketch provided by the metaphorical utterance. Speculative thought draws the semantic sketch into the new space of the concept. Speculative discourse is, therefore, the discourse which regulates and systematizes the concept by means of its own primary notions and principles and forms it into a second-order discourse. It grounds the conceptual discourse. The concept is not derived from perception or from images, as in the case of the imagination, but it is supplied by the speculative field or horizon. The speculative is not based on the similar - as the imagination is - but upon an understanding of the same. The speculative seeks from its own angle to ground the similar of metaphorical utterance into the same, knowing that where things are similar there is also identity. Hence, the two levels of discourse, the level of the imagination and the level of the speculative, remain distinct. In fact, it can be said the speculative discourse is the upper limit of metaphorical discourse.

According to Ricoeur, the concept must function in a proper order of discourse if it is to be free of perceptual images.[59] Within the discourse of the speculative logos, the concept can begin to function with the resources provided it by the speculative discourse. In this way, it can

---

59. Ricoeur introduces here Husserl's critique of the image in the conceptual order in order to delineate more clearly the two discourses. Cf. La métaphore vive, (417:302). See also J. Greisch, "Bulletin de philosophie. La tradition herméneutique aujourd'hui: H.G. Gadamer, P. Ricoeur, G. Steiner" in Rev. Sc.ph.th. 61, 1977, p.296.

leave behind the type of schematization, such as double-meaning language and image-work, proper to the imaginative level.

(c) Hermeneutical interpretation: the composite discourse.

The previous discussion ought not to lead to the conclusion that Ricoeur's conceptual order abolishes the metaphorical. His 'inclination', he says, is to posit a constant interanimation and interplay of the order of discourses. The attracting and repelling cannot cease because the one can never dissolve into the other. That which organizes the discourses is 'off-centred' in relation to both of them. This disallows any attempt to establish an absolute knowledge, which would amalgamate the various discourses. It should also be noted that the Kantian concept of the limit, which has governed Ricoeur's philosophy from the beginning,[60] has not been shelved.

The activity and work of the concept is a work of interpretation. By means of the primary notions and principles of the speculative order, the concept interprets the metaphorical sketch. In accordance with the semantic aim of speculative discourse, the concept will elucidate this sketch and seek to arrive at a univocal statement. The suspension and tension will be dissolved, as will the experience of the metaphorical utterance. As such, the concept is a reduction. But, it may be asked, is it not possible to have a non-reductive interpretation beside the reductive one? Ricoeur thinks that this is possible through the discipline of hermeneutics. Hermeneutics, which we shall examine in greater detail in the next chapter, is a type of interpretation which respects both the conceptual aim and the experience seeking to be expressed in the metaphorical aim (417:303).

Interpretation functions at the threshold of two areas: the speculative and the metaphorical. It seeks to respect both the clarity of the concept and the dynamism of the metaphorical meaning. A metaphor "is living by virtue of the fact that it introduces the spark of imagination into a 'thinking more' (Kant) at the conceptual level" (417:303). Interpretation is the 'soul' of this activity.

---

60.   Cf. Don Ihde, op. cit., p.59-80.

CHAPTER FOUR: MEANING AND THE QUEST FOR A HERMENEUTICS.

Bibliography.

139.	"Le sentiment" (1959).
152.	L'homme faillible (1960).
229.	"Existence et herméneutique" (1965).
278.	"New Developments in Phenomenology in France: The Phenomenology of Language" (1967).
286.	"L'art et la systématique freudienne" (1968).
320.	Le conflit des interprétations (1969).
321.	"Philosophie et langage" (1969).
355.	"Langage (Philosophie)" (1971).
374.	"Cours sur l'herméneutique" (1971).
375.	"The Problem of the Will and Philosophical Discourse" (1971).
377.	"Ontologie" (1972).
388.	"The Task of Hermeneutics" (1973).
389.	"The Hermeneutical Function of Distanciation" (1973).
390.	"Ethics and Culture. Habermas and Gadamer in Dialogue" (1973).
398.	"Phénoménologie et herméneutique" (1974).
399.	"Hegel aujourd'hui" (1974).
406.	"Philosophical Hermeneutics and Theological Hermeneutics" (1975).
413.	"Objectivation et aliénation dans l'expérience historique" (1975).
422.	"History and Hermeneutics" (1976).
423.	Interpretation Theory (1976).
433.	"Schleiermacher's Hermeneutics" (1977).
434.	"Expliquer et comprendre" (1977).
438.	"Herméneutique et l'idée de révélation" (1977).

With the ground and the source of meaning no longer immediate and intuitive, but mediated by the language of the poetic text, Ricoeur can return to the perception of Jean Nabert, that reflection is interpretation. But what type of interpretation? If reflection is interpretation, Ricoeur must enter into the hermeneutical debate and forge an alliance between hermeneutics and phenomenology. This develops in two phases.

In the first texts where the need for a hermeneutics arose, namely, La symbolique du mal (153) and De l'interprétation. Essai sur Freud, (227) Ricoeur gave a restricted range to the theory of hermeneutics. His more immediate concern with the symbol as the bond with being led him to insist that the symbol and interpretation were co-extensive. The symbol was perceived as a figure of double-meaning language which required interpretation. The symbol contains a surplus of meaning or, in psychological terms, an overdetermination, which would release itself to understanding only by way of the interpretation of that surplus. That perception of hermeneutics also underlies the articles collected in Le conflit des interprétations, (320) where the surplus of meaning is interpreted as containing conflicting interpretations. However, in the same collection one can notice a new orientation which gains the upperhand in his Cours sur l'herméneutique (374) and in his Interpretation Theory, (423).

In these latter texts, Ricoeur incorporates a discovery about the symbol that his study of linguistics had provided. While his earlier works recognized that symbols were linguistic, Ricoeur had not sought to uncover the semantics of the symbol. Through his introduction into linguistics, he came to see that the symbol, like the metaphor, has a semantic and also a non-semantic moment with the semantic moment as the point of access to the non-semantic moment. With that, the point of gravity of his research became more and more located in the hermeneutics of the language of poetic expressions.

In his quest for a hermeneutics of the language of poetic expressions Ricoeur looks for two dimensions. The hermeneutics is to fulfill the exigency of an ontology and of an epistemology. In other words, the hermeneutics is to assure that the interpretation of the language of poetic texts does not dissolve the bond between language and being, and ultimately the phenomenological concern with the subject. But, at the same time, the ontological thrust may not bypass the epistemological. The understanding and self-understanding through the poetic text may not be isolated from the struggle - so predominant in our culture - between explanation and understanding. The conflict between explanation and understanding was first diagnosed by Kant. His epistemological distinction between explanation and understanding led to the assignment of explanation to the realm of pure reason and understanding to the realm of practical reason. For Ricoeur, a contemporary hermeneutical theory must overcome the dichotomous relationship between understanding and explanation in a dialectical relationship. The hermeneutics of the text must incorporate both a scientific study of the linguistic structures of the text and an existential appropriation of the world of the text (464:xi).

This dual concern aligns Ricoeur's hermeneutics with the mainstream of modern hermeneutics, in which the basic vectors have been the ontological and epistemological axes. To grasp Ricoeur's hermeneutics, one is forced to retrace the outlines of the hermeneutics of the major modern proponents: Fr. Schleiermacher, W. Dilthey, M. Heidegger, and H.G. Gadamer. Only in understanding Ricoeur's reading of that history, can one begin to appreciate his own contribution to the hermeneutical theory and his orientation to the question of meaning and the subject.

A. FRIEDRICH SCHLEIERMACHER.[1]

Fr. Schleiermacher is the father of modern hermeneutics. It is not that there was no hermeneutics prior to him, but Fr. Schleiermacher

---

1. See 374:69-80;433:187-197; and 388:143-144.

gave it its specific modern quality. He achieved this by interlinking two cultural movements of his time: Kantianism and Romanticism.

At the beginning of the 19th century, there was a growing split between the two major regions of interpretation: the exegesis of the Bible and the philology of ancient texts. The thinkers of the Enlightenment had succeeded in creating a wedge between exegesis and dogma by the insertion of philology into the exegetical process. The text of the Bible became a profane text, like any other text. Moreover, philology separated the sense of the text from the truth of the text. Kant, who inverted the relationship between the sign and the thing canonized this situation. He set the priority of the theory of knowledge, the condition of things in the mind, over the theory of being. For a hermeneutical theory this reversal is central. By giving priority to the capacity of knowledge that governs the operation of interpretation, Kant divorced the operation of interpretation from the text itself. Instead of remaining the search for the hidden meaning of the text - since the Middle Ages the task of exegesis - Kant reversed interpretation toward a search for the security of the cognitional operations. Unfortunately, Kant hardly passed beyond the conditions of knowledge of the physical sciences. This will have its effect on subsequent hermeneutical theory, because, in the search for an adequate interpretation, the conditions of theoretical knowledge will govern the operations.

Romanticism, on the other hand, went in search of the conditions of the knowledge of the spirit. In its reaction to rationalism, Romanticism looked not to the conditions of human knowledge, but to the force of the spirit as the source of the creative process. The spirit is the unconscious creator within a human genius (388:144), who is the great creator of human culture. Life, for Romanticism, means to have a living relation to the creative process of the genius. Interpretation in this context loses its epistemological concern and seeks a way to be at one with the creative process. Romanticism has expressed its aim in the hermeneutical slogan: To understand an author as well as and even better than he understood himself (388:144).

Fr. Schleiermacher combined the critical concerns of Kant and the genial concerns of Romanticism. Through them he sought a theory of interpretation that could reconcile the goals of both philology and exegesis. But the resulting Kunstlehre subordinated philology to the problem of understanding. There is a hermeneutics, not because of the diversity or antiquity of the texts, but because there is a misunderstanding. The goal of hermeneutics is to overcome misunderstanding by leading one to the source of the thought that is expressed in language. Schleiermacher's theory of interpretation attempted - without fully succeeding - to show how thought and its linguistic expression were interrelated. Through, on the one hand, a linguistic, grammatical interpretation of the text and, on the other hand, a psychological, technical interpretation of the singularity of another (the genius), he sought to link expression and thought, or Kantianism and Romanticism. When thought and expression have been interlinked, it can be said that one understands the author as well as or better than he or she understands him/herself (374:74).

After a fashion, then, Schleiermacher succeeded in isolating the two major concerns of modern hermeneutics. First, he recognized the need to consolidate the variety of hermeneutical objects into a general hermeneutics governed by understanding. Secondly, he also recognized that the process of understanding involved a divinatory (guessing) aspect and a methodical aspect (grammatical, philological analysis). Both of these gains must not be lost sight of in a current hermeneneutics.

B. WILHELM DILTHEY.

Although Ricoeur mentions that he wishes to remain true to the intention of Schleiermacher's hermeneutics (423:93), the coloration and orientation of his hermeneutics are equally determined by W. Dilthey. Working towards the end of the 19th century, when history had replaced philology as the darling discipline, Dilthey's hermeneutics struggled to discover how one historical individual can understand another. He sought to discover how historical knowledge can exceed intuition and achieve a scientific status. In the understanding of historical reality and of another person, he sought to supply historical knowledge with an equivalent of the experimental sciences' successful theory of explanation. Because of this overriding concern with the scientific status of history, Dilthey's hermeneutics, unfortunately, did not rise beyond the epistemological level.

According to Dilthey - and here he is clearly influenced by Hegel -history is the manifestation or the expression of the movement of the Spirit. It is the deposit of experience, the objectivation of humanity (374:94). The figures of the Spirit, the fundamental expressions of life, form a structured and coherent chain of events (Dilthey's Zusammenhang) that in their objectivation and their coherence are snatched from an irretrievable individuality into the realm of knowledge. It is into this great chain of events that the individual and his works must be inserted in order to gain meaning. Meaning is derived from the Zusammenhang. Through the signs that emanate from the individual, the individual links up with the objective spirit of history. However, while for Hegel the Spirit or mind was not individual, for Dilthey Spirit is first of all individual. From the individual and the works of the individual, Dilthey views the total cultural and historical construct. It is not the objective Spirit but the life-expressions of the individual that constitute the great interlinking of history. And, inversely, because the fundamental expressions of life in history are productions of individuals, one individual has access to the understanding of another (388:147). The great Zusammenhang of history is a form of the individual, and the objectivity of its expression allows us to understand the other. Its manifestation is the objectified product of psychic life.

For Dilthey, hermeneutics is the discipline that delves into the psychic life of another by reproducing the Zusammenhang of the objectified signs of that psychic life. Hermeneutics is a Nachbildung, a recreation of another's life. This hermeneutics can only be undertaken if these manifestations of life assume a durable form. That durable form is writing. Only writing, a text, permits the recreation of another, an entry into the psychic state of another.[2]   Only in the durable form of writing can I recreate the process whereby another has become. The psychic, one might say, becomes fixed.   Hermeneutics becomes the discipline of the understanding of another through the written text of the psychic life of another. For Dilthey hermeneutics is basically a psychology: a science of empathy into the state of another.[3]

But, and here we introduce Dilthey's second concern, the discipline must be clothed with the respectability of objectivity. This, he sought to accomplish by means of the scientific methods of philology. Philology is the science that rules understanding (374:90-91).   Since hermeneutics was to be an interpretation of the written texts of life, philology was the science of the reading of these texts. But this close identification of philology and understanding forced Dilthey to form a theory of understanding that could attain a level of objectivity that approximated that of the physical sciences. Dilthey never ceased searching for ways to increase its objectivity. But he could only do so by making understanding the equivalent of interpretation as a mode of knowing. Understanding then suffers from being approached only epistemologically according to the level of the objectivity that it obtains.

Dilthey's major contribution to hermeneutics consists in his insistence that life can only be grasped in its mediations.   The fleeting moments of history are transcended by the textual expressions of life. Historical understanding does not have to resort to the absolute Spirit of Hegel. Instead it can turn to interpretation. However, Dilthey, according to Ricoeur, destroys what he has gained by determining that understanding does not seek to interpret what the text says but delves behind the text. Hermeneutics seeks to gain an empathetic understanding of the individual behind the text who has expressed him/herself in the text. It is the life of another that is sought. Also Dilthey did not escape the attempt to reduce interpretation to a psychological concern.   Understanding is basically the empathetic reproduction of the structured, living dynamism of another. The fusion of this psychological interest and the scientific intent of the interpretation of the text led to an aporie. What was sought was life and not the meaning of the text of life.   Hermeneutics remained the transference into the psychic life of another. It sought a reality behind or before the text: the illusive psychic reality that, according to Ricoeur, does not communicate itself.

---

2.   After 1900 Dilthey tried to restate this theory in terms of Husserl's theory of intentionality. He saw the psychic as intentional, i.e., as intending a meaning that can be identified again and again. He realized that the psychic itself could not be reached but that one can grasp what the psychic intended. Cf. 499:147.

3.   In his later works Dilthey generalized hermeneutics to coincide with interpretation. The later Dilthey textualized all reality. All reality is a text to be interpreted. Cf. 374:92.

Schleiermacher and Dilthey represent the first phase of modern hermeneutics. They succeeded in bringing hermeneutics under the aegis of understanding as the human sciences' mode of knowing.

This epistemology of the human sciences is sharply contrasted with the explanatory approach that dominates the physical sciences. Accordingly, hermeneutics was accepted as a discipline of interpretation employed in the human sciences, whenever these examine life-expressions in the written form.

With Heidegger and later with Gadamer, a radical re-orientation of hermeneutics takes place. With them hermeneutics moves out of the orbit of the Methodenstreit with its epistemological overtones into the area of a fundamental ontology. Although the historical referent of their philosophy remains the epistemological debacle, hermeneutics does not ask, "How do we know a text or history or another?" but rather, "What is the mode of being of that being who only exists through understanding?" (388:151). Their approach takes one beyond the split of subject and object, that dominates epistemology, to the question of Being. With Heidegger and Gadamer we enter a region prior to epistemology which they have mapped out in an ontology of understanding.

C. MARTIN HEIDEGGER.

Martin Heidegger has been Ricoeur's sparring partner in the development of his hermeneutics more than he appears to be willing to acknowledge. Heidegger appears as the goad of his vision, as his silent interlocutor, in his search for the recovery of the subject. Ricoeur's hermeneutics of the subject is comprehensible only in the light of Heidegger's ontology of understanding.

According to Ricoeur, Heidegger's ontology of understanding undertakes two fundamental shifts in the hermeneutics of Schleiermacher and Dilthey.

1. From epistemology to ontology.

The first shift, to which we alluded above, is the Heideggerean reversal of epistemology and ontology. As Ricoeur says, Heidegger "wanted to retrain our eye and to redirect our gaze" (320(229):10). In Sein und Zeit,[4] he refused to enter into the methodological debate, saying, that prior to any theory of knowledge, prior to the opposition between subject and object, there is a type of inquiry into Being that is more primordial than the epistemological one. For Heidegger Being is Ground. But Being as Ground is not transparent or immediately available. However, Being as Ground does manifest itself. It does so in the being where the question of Being arises.

---

4. Tübingen, Max Niemaeyer Verlag, 1926. See also F. Seeburger, "Ricoeur on Heidegger" in The Iliff Review, 35, 1978, p.49-57.

This being in Being is a being of understanding. This inquirer of Being, for whom Being arises as a question, Heidegger calls Dasein, being-there. Dasein is the subject that is totally open to the question and the manifestation of Being (377:100). Dasein is not only the inquirer of Being, but the very question of Being. Hence, it not only questions Being, but it is also the mode of being guided by the question of Being (320(286):225). In addition, the question of the subject is not primary for Heidegger. The subject must respect the question which it is.

To the extent that I recover myself as the questor of Being, I retrieve, in Heidegger's view, the 'forgotten' center of myself. Hence, by asking about Being, I ask simultaneously about the inquiry which is the mode of Being of the inquirer (320(278):227). Understanding is, therefore, not a mode of knowing, but the mode of being of the being that questions. Or, as Heidegger expresses it, "understanding of Being is itself a definitive characteristic of Dasein's being" (320(278):226).

Implied in this investigation is the priority that Being has over any method of exploration of Being. The neo-Kantian order of method over content is reversed. It is the mode of being that determines the method (374:101-102). For hermeneutics, the consequences are significant. Hermeneutics is the theory that accompanies the process of the unveiling of the Sein of Dasein through all the dissimulations that have led to the forgetfulness of Being. If Being is forgotten, the being in whom Being is understanding must be safeguarded against forgetfulness. For Heidegger, hermeneutics is the guide of the manifestation of being for the being who is the inquirer of Being (388:151).

2. From the understanding of the other to the understanding of the world.

A second reversal of Heidegger's hermeneutics concerns the depsychologization of hermeneutics. Heidegger shifted away from Dilthey's hermeneutics of the understanding of the psyche of another through empathy towards a hermeneutics of the relation of being with the world. According to Heidegger, hermeneutics seeks to understand my position in Being. Consequently, Heidegger's hermeneutics deals with the understanding not of the other but of being-in, more specifically, being-in-the-world. Instead of a concern with the other, Heidegger focusses on the question of the world (388:152).

Heidegger's starting point in Sein und Zeit is the grounding relation of every subject in the being-in-the-world. For Heidegger, a subject must first find him/herself 'there'. One must first feel the world, before one can begin to find one's way. In other words, Heidegger does not start with understanding, but with 'world' and from the 'world' he moves to 'being-in' and to 'being-there'. Heidegger locates understanding in this movement from world to 'being-there'. Heidegger locates understanding within the trilogy of situation (Befindlichkeit), understanding (Verstehen), and interpretation (Auslegung). This trilogy is the existential constitution of 'there' (374:107).

For Heidegger, before ever I come to language, I first find myself in a situation. I feel something, before I face it, before I express myself, before I orient myself. Before I talk, before I move, I am like a plant rooted in a situation. It is feeling that bonds us to a situation. It is feeling that enroots us.

Understanding arises out of this Befindlichkeit. For Heidegger, understanding remains prior to language, prior to the text. For him, understanding is a power of being. Its task is to orient us in a situation. Dasein, for that reason, not only enroots us like a plant in a situation. But like an animal Dasein is also movement. Dasein is a being which orients itself. The task of understanding is to guide this orientation, to sketch projects in which our possibilities, our ownmost possibilities, are projected. Understanding apprehends the possibilities of Being. It reveals the Being-in-the-world, the ontological conditions of our 'being-thrown' by Being itself. In Dasein this is brought to understanding (374:108-109).

For Heidegger, consequent upon understanding is interpretation. Interpretation, however, is not yet an exegetical method, but rather an explicitation (Auslegung), or an unravelling of understanding. The task of interpretation is to bring understanding to itself. In order to develop understanding, however, interpretation does not look to a theory of knowledge, but to something which Heidegger calls Vorhabe, Vorgriff, or Vorsicht. Interpretation, according to Heidegger, works with an anticipatory structure of understanding. In understanding there lies a pre-understanding, a pre-acquisition, a pre-grasping or a pre-vision, of Being-in-the-world. Interpretation explicitates this pre-acquisition of the whole in terms of a particular area under consideration. This is Heidegger's famous hermeneutical circle: in order to explicitate something as being this or that, one must first have an anticipatory understanding of the whole. Interpretation is the explicitation of something as (Heidegger's als) this or that, in relationship to the prior view or pre-understanding (388:153-154).

It is only at this point that Heidegger introduces the question of language in Sein und Zeit (par.33). Language is linked to interpretation at the point, where the als of interpretation passes into articulation or a proposition. Language is, therefore, not principally communication to another, but is disclosure (Aufzeignung). It reveals Being and its link with Dasein. Language is a disclosure of Dasein. A first consequence of this is, that language is not primary but derived. Being is primordial; language is the way we articulate and manifest the understanding of our Being-in-the-world (388:155).

This point is accentuated by Heidegger, when he insists that, what is of importance in the articulation, is not the saying of something, but rather the hearing of something. Because of its relationship to Being-in-the-world, understanding is first of all hearing. Before the word that I speak, there must be the word that I hear. To produce speech, I must first be silent: "Hearing is constitutive of discourse".[5] Before discourse opens to

---

5.   Sein und Zeit, op. cit., p.206.

the world and to the other, it must have its foundation in hearing. In line with this, Heidegger distinguishes between 'saying' (reden) and 'speaking' (sprechen) to designate the difference between the 'letting-say' of hearing (the existential constitution) and the linguistic expression (sprechen) which exteriorizes the Rede. For Heidegger, all linguistics operate on the level of speaking. Linguistics can never attain the level of Rede, nor does it add anything to Rede. He calls linguistics the hypostasized isolation of human speech (374:119).

Ricoeur's critique of Heidegger is radical. If Heidegger proposed to transcend the aporia of an epistemological approach to understanding, he only aggravated it according to Ricoeur. For Ricoeur the aporia is only shifted to the higher plane between an epistemology and ontology. Ricoeur welcomes Heidegger's recovery of the existential and ontological ground of understanding, but he cannot accept Heidegger's refusal to return from this ground to the epistemological question of the status of the human sciences. Heidegger showed that methodological questions, such as those presented by exegesis and historical criticism, are at most derivative questions. But, he refuses to consider these derivative questions. And that failure, according to Ricoeur, is inexcusable today. With the re-establishment of an ontology the epistemological question can no longer be avoided (386:50-51).

D. HANS-GEORG GADAMER.

Ricoeur's summation of the masters of hermeneutical philosophy would be incomplete without H.-G. Gadamer's Wahrheit und Methode.[6] Gadamer undertook to re-open the question of the relationship between ontology and epistemology which Heidegger had largely ignored. That meant re-introducing Dilthey's concern of the epistemological status of the human sciences within the Heideggerean achievement of an ontology of understanding. Gadamer's hermeneutics is founded on the dialectical notions of participation and distanciation. The notion of participation expresses the primordial relationship of things to being. Before things can be opposed to us, they first of all belong - they belong to being. Now in the human sciences this ontological participation, the Zugehörigkeit, is shattered in favour of an objectifying distance. In the distance created between participation and Being the human sciences have established a measure of objectivity. Sciences are founded upon that distanciation. Gadamer elaborates this theme in the three spheres of hermeneutics: aesthetics, history, and language. In each sphere, it is the distanciation that permits a critical judgement to take place. Thus, for instance, in the historical sphere, the distanciation makes possible the consciousness of being carried by a prior tradition. And it is this consciousness, according to Gadamer, that leads to the foundation and differentiation of the historical methodology into the variety of the human and social sciences. But its

---

6. Tübingen, J.C.B. Mohr (Paul Siebeck), 1960. See F. Kirkland, "Gadamer and Ricoeur. The Paradigm of the Text." in Graduate Faculty Philosophy Journal 6, 1977, p.131-144.

consequence is an inevitable impoverishment. The historical experience as a mode of Being, mediated through the method of text-interpretation, is destroyed as a life-experience. For Gadamer, the reality of life and method are irreconcilable: the ideal of method destroys the reality of life (374:97).

Gadamer perceives the objectifying trend of the human sciences as a last-ditch attempt of Enlightenment thinking to retain consciousness as the master and subjectivity as the point of departure. For Gadamer, there is no last refuge for neutral observation. As he says in his Kleine Schriften, "We cannot extricate ourselves from historical becoming, or place ourselves at a distance from it, in order that the past might become an object for us. ... We are always situated in History".[7] Gadamer calls this consciousness of being always inescapably exposed to the effects of history the wirkungsgeschichtliches Bewusstsein.[8] The past does not become available to us as an object of observation. We are never free of the past. We can only become conscious of how it affects us as the past of our experience.

This priority of historical existence over critical reflection will become a dominant problem for Ricoeur and the salient feature of the difference between Ricoeur and Gadamer. For Ricoeur, this is a remnant of the debate between Romanticism and the Enlightenment, in which Gadamer chooses to remain on the side of Romanticism (390:156-157). The interrelationship of participation and distanciation and, subsequently, of understanding and explanation forms the main outline of Ricoeur's hermeneutical philosophy.

E. RICOEUR'S METHODICAL HERMENEUTICS.

The schematic outline of the history of modern hermeneutics touches only the basic vectors which Ricoeur encountered in the development of a modern hermeneutical theory. It is in continuity with this tradition that he wishes to place himself. He considers two lines of that movement to be constitutive of the hermeneutical tradition and indeed of the solution to the problem of the subject in our contemporary culture.

The first movement of the hermeneutical tradition according to Ricoeur is its drive to recall hermeneutics from the number of regions, to which the hermeneutical art applied (exegesis of the Bible, philology, jurisprudence), toward a general hermeneutics. This process was first undertaken by Schleiermacher and then by Dilthey, when they organized the discipline under an epistemology of understanding. The movement was completed by Heidegger and Gadamer, who grounded hermeneutics in an ontology of understanding. Ricoeur's working definition of hermeneutics

---

7.   Tübingen, J.C.B. Mohr, 1967, p.158. Cf. 499:159.

8.   Ricoeur translates wirkungsgeschichtliches Bewusstsein as the consciousness of the history of effects. It is a consciousness of the agency of history.

reflects this orientation. For him hermeneutics is "the theory of the operation of understanding in its relations to the interpretation of texts" (388:141).

The second movement of the current hermeneutical tradition involves the relationship of hermeneutical understanding to the explanatory mode of knowing of the empirical sciences. This issue was raised first by Schleiermacher and Dilthey. Both sought a mode of validation for hermeneutical statements which could compete with the successful methods of the natural sciences. Heidegger and Gadamer shunted aside this objective. But, for Ricoeur, this disjuncture of truth and method can only lead, in the end, to the splendid isolation of the two fundamental areas of contemporary human discourse.[9] The mediation of these two spheres of discourse is the great task of modern philosophy (229:16). Instead of Gadamer's truth and/or method, Ricoeur resolutely opts for truth and method. There can be no understanding without explanation and no explanation without understanding. Instead of the opposition between understanding and explanation, so popular among the neo-Kantians, Ricoeur seeks to expose a complementary and dialectical relationship between truth and method.

In his inimitable fashion Ricoeur manages to interrelate these two movements by retaining both the Heideggerean and the Diltheyan thrust. But he transforms them both in the process. Ricoeur's hermeneutics is a dialectical blend of the ontological and the epistemological. It bridges a new dialogue between hermeneutics and the language of the experimental sciences. Ricoeur hopes, in this manner, to contribute to the stemming of the dispersal of human discourse and to the re-integration of the human and empirical sciences into some kind of unity of speech (229:16). Ricoeur has called the ontology which interrelates with an epistemology an indirect ontology and his hermeneutics a methodical hermeneutics (355:780).

At first glance the hermeneutics of Ricoeur in his linguistic phase seems a radical departure from his earlier, more phenomenological, concerns. But that is only a surface impression. Ricoeur remains faithful to his earlier concern of the 'for me' of the appearances of things. As we shall see, he links the ontological and epistemological thrust with reflective philosophy by means of Gadamer's notion of appropriation. Hermeneutics remains incomplete until it explicitates the subject's desire and effort to be.

---

9. The specific contours of Ricoeur's hermeneutical theory were shaped by two events. First of all, Ricoeur's confrontation with the semiological and semantic analysis of language forced him to a first-ever penetration into explanatory procedures. He recognized the validity and even the necessity of these procedures. But that meant the expansion of the horizon of interpretative methods, and a dramatic re-orientation of hermeneutics. The second event is Ricoeur's still growing awareness of the importance of language in a poetics of the will. Cf. Otto Bollnow, "Paul Ricoeur und die Probleme der Hermeneutik" in Z. philos. Forsch. 30, 1976, p.167-189 and p.389-412.

Hermeneutics mediates the re-appropriation or the recovery of the subject. Only through a hermeneutics of the text is reflection liberated from being abstract. Through hermeneutics reflection becomes concrete reflection.

1. Participation in being.

Ricoeur, we said, abandoned the high road route of Heidegger I which is out of reach of the epistemologists and their concern for validation. His route is much more modest. He denies the possibilitiy of inhabiting the high ground of a direct ontology. For Ricoeur the subject never dwells there. S/he only climbs in its direction, urged on by the very reality that s/he seeks. In place of Heidegger's analytic of Dasein as the mode of being of understanding, Ricoeur opts - as does Merleau-Ponty (321:286) - for an indirect ontology. Instead of taking a primordial ontology of understanding as a point of departure, Ricoeur turned first to the forms of understanding.[10] This is still in harmony with his phenomenological principles. These forms are accordingly derived forms, i.e., derived from the primordial, ontological understanding. It is the task of an indirect ontology to indicate in the forms of understanding the signs of their derivation and to follow up the repercussions for understanding.

What are these forms of understanding? For Ricoeur the most fundamental form is language itself. In that respect he differs rather radically from Heidegger and Gadamer. In the ontologized hermeneutics of Heidegger language was only the interpretative dimension of understanding. In interpretation, understanding comes to language. Language for Heidegger is fundamentally bound to Being before it can be considered as the language of written documents. Language manifests the forgotten Being. Language is the text of existence. Language shows, it lets-be. Heidegger calls this dimension of language sagen (to say). This saying dominates Heidegger's hermeneutics. Its opposite, ordinary and logicized language, he called sprechen (to speak). For Heidegger only sagen unveils Being; sprechen promotes the forgetfulness of Being. In his later works, principally in Unterwegs zur Sprache (1959), the ontology of language was pushed to the forefront even more. Philosophy is said to think in the direction of language and not only in language. Language is not first of all a possession, a tool to be manipulated but a power to say, to let-be (355:779-780). For Heidegger this quality was best expressed and manifested by the poets and the pre-Socratics.

In the footsteps of Heidegger, Gadamer situated language as a region or modality of understanding which comes after history and aesthetics. For Gadamer, language is the universal medium of experiences of meaning. Its principal task is to help overcome the distance, the alienation, and incomprehension that shapes our existence, because of a past

---

10. That is basically the critique of Heidegger and Gadamer by Jürgen Habermas. He also maintains that when understanding becomes a property of being rather than of consciousness, one loses touch with the critical dimension of hermeneutics. See 386:48.

that has objectified itself as a tradition, or document, or aesthetic object. Writing for Gadamer is the major form of alienation or distanciation. The task then of hermeneutics is to overcome - to re-appropriate -what has become alienated in writing. And since both history and aesthetics have become linguistic realities through writing, they must be brought back to discourse (Sprachlichkeit) in order to be understood. But, for Gadamer, this Sprachlichkeit is no more than the letting-say again of our tradition, the overcoming of the gap between the past and the present. In other words, language remains principally within an ontological perspective. From the lofty position of an ontology of language the Methodenstreit is only a game of the uninitiated (355:780).

Ricoeur reverses the downward gaze of Heidegger and Gadamer. With him there is no disdain nor a dazzling circumvention of the epistemological debate. Language not only says out our being, but it equally manifests a structure and a strategy in its very saying. Let us explore this indirect ontology more closely.

To describe the ontological dimension of language, Ricoeur borrows Gadamer's concept of Zugehörigkeit (participation, belonging-to). The notion of participation expresses a primordial relation of things to a source or foundation that is inclusive, encompassing, and global (375:227-228). Participation expresses an ontological pre-eminence which says that a belonging to and a dependence on being is prior to any distinction between subject and object. The concept of participation breaks with any vision of a self-constituting subjectivity. Participation implies, that it is not the subject who is the source of the unity of meaning, but something that precedes the subject. Subjectivity as well as objectivity are, therefore, secondary, derived forms. They are carried by and derived from participation (438:29). Similarly, explanation and understanding in the epistemological sense are derived forms. In the very heart of the epistemological process Ricoeur finds a notion of understanding that points beyond a concern for accuracy and validation to an "apprehension, at a level other than scientific, of a belonging to the whole of what is" (434:165).

Despite the different orientations of ontology and, therefore, of participation, Ricoeur, too, insists that before we speak, before we structure through language, before language is the product of a subjectivity, I am the being through whom existence, Being, comes to language. To say it in Ricoeur's words, "The sense of human experience is made through us but not by us. We do not dominate the meaning, but meaning makes us at the same time that we make it" (399:353, my translation). This condition is an ontological condition. We apperceive it in situations in which I find myself without consciously having chosen them. These are very deep experiences of human finitude (375:228). They are experiences of being affected by things at whose source I do not stand (413:30;386:25).

This notion of participation is borrowed from H.G. Gadamer. But already in L'homme faillible (152) Ricoeur investigated this participation under the notion of feeling.[11]   Feeling, he said there, is a mode of manifesting, not a mode of positing being. It stands in a correlative relationship with knowing.   Feeling and knowing mutually generate each other.   Feeling without knowing can be no more than a word.   Knowing without feeling is no more than sophistry.   Borrowing from Plato, who called the agency of the manifestation of being the thumos, the 'heart'.   Ricoeur holds that feeling (the modern translation of thumos) mediates the participation in being.   In the thumos, the bios, human life-energy, reaches out to consciousness.   In other words already in the early, pre-linguistic phase of his philosophy, Ricoeur had investigated the reaching-out of the bios to logos (152:126).

Basic to feeling for Ricoeur is its bonding power. It mediates between life and thought. It unites the vital, the psychic and the spiritual by relating us to the world in a manner that is much more profound than the relationships established by the cognitive process. The cognitive process by its very nature institutes the split between subject and object (139:263). Feeling unites and bonds us with being by attaching itself to things. It does so, because the intentional correlate of feeling is not an object, but something (the hateful, the lovable, the pleasing) 'meant' or 'felt' on things. Without the things, there would be no feeling. Feeling qualifies reality as desirable, as fearful, as hateful. Because feelings presuppose reality, they do not posit reality. At most, one can say that they manifest reality. They require reality in order to be able to manifest their quality. As 'meant' or 'felt' on things "feeling attests our coaptation, our elective harmonies and disharmonies with realities whose affective image we carry in ourselves in the form of 'good' and 'bad'" (152:133).   In intending reality, feeling expresses my affection. It is an intentional expression of my bond with reality, or of my existence with the outside, through desire and love (152:134).   One may not think of this intentionality solely in subjective terms because feelings are objective, in the sense that through feeling "objects touch me" (152:135), reach out to me and link up with me.

But feeling, while manifesting our participation with beings and with Being, is interrelated with knowing. Our participation in being through feeling is the inverse of objectification. It recognizes, that, before we are fragmented through knowing, before the subject opposes itself to the object in knowledge, there is a primordial belonging to being and the Being. However, human feeling remains indistinct, unconscious, and not human, unless it is informed by the knowing process. And in knowing, what was previously one in a vital affectivity, is split apart. Reason creates the degrees of feeling, and differentiates feeling. Reason becomes the source

---

11.   In the doctoral thesis Mystery and the Unconscious A Study in the Thought of Paul Ricoeur (Metuchen, N.J., the Scarecrow Press and the American Theological Library Association, 1977) Walter Lowe gives a lengthy analysis of genèse réciproque, a term used in L'homme faillible, which, according to Lowe, has a similar weighting as participation. However, Lowe allows that its importance is made more explicit in Ricoeur's later writings. See p.30-82.

of the conflict in life between feeling and reason.

This earlier elaboration of feeling finds its linguistic counterpart in the notion of participation in Ricoeur's later work. The interaction of feeling and knowing in L'homme faillible has its parallel in the process whereby our participation in Being is released from its diffuseness and indeterminateness. In addition, human participation in Being seeks to come to understanding. It can only do so to the extent that the experience of participation is externalized. And this occurs at the moment when we interrupt our participation in order to signify it (398:239).

2. Distanciation.

The externalization of our participation into some form of objectification Ricoeur, again following Gadamer, calls distanciation (434:166). But despite his borrowing of the term distanciation from Gadamer, Ricoeur disagrees with his evaluation of distanciation. For Gadamer, the objectification or distanciation of our participation in Being represent the alienation of our time. For him, this distanciation is our unfortunate exile from the home of being and needs to be overcome. For Ricoeur, our very participation in Being requires distanciation. For him, distanciation is the condition of the possibility for the interpretation of our participation. Zugehörigkeit seeks exteriorization and objectification, "To invoke distanciation as a principle is to attempt to show the very experience of belonging to ... requires something like externalization in order to apprehend, articulate and understand itself" (422:691). It presupposes that the being in which we participate is itself a dynamic principle that seeks not only to exteriorize itself, but also to be understood (386:52-53).

The difference between Gadamer and Ricoeur stand out quite clearly. For Gadamer, distance is to be abolished for the sake of understanding. Ricoeur seeks distanciation to make understanding possible. This distinction becomes even more evident when we take their differing approaches to language into consideration.

Both Heidegger and Gadamer weigh the ontological dimension of language. Language shows or lets-say being. While not denying this ontological dimension, Ricoeur is careful not to distinguish sagen and sprechen so radically. For him, too, language is the basic externalization of being. In language being says itself. In fact, in saying itself in language, being becomes itself (375:237). In the exteriorization of language and or of some other external mark, the experience of being is intensified (422:692). But this exteriorization is, at the same time, a creation of a distance between the speaker and reality. And, since for Ricoeur this distanciation is the transcendental condition of the apprehension of being, he perceives language as the exteriorization not only of our participation, but also of our distanciation. While for Gadamer Sprachlichkeit is itself part of the ontological moment, as the language dimension of all experience (406:15), for Ricoeur, language is at the same time a moment of distanciation. This distanciation through language is constitutive of participation. It is primitive and radical in the full sense of the word (413:34-35). And because the distanciation is itself original, language, and beyond it writing becomes possible and provides us with a medium of understanding.

For Ricoeur, this dimension is strengthened even more. He accepts the position which François Dagognet advanced in Écriture et iconographie,[12] concerning the image and writing. Dagognet holds that an image is not a diminution or a copy of reality, but an intensification of reality. By its ability to concentrate reality and to combine dimensions, exteriorization increases our experience, rather than erodes it. The distanciation by way of language is, therefore, more than a mere distance, for it implies a creation of distance, in order to permit a redescription of reality.

3. The hermeneutics of poetic language.

If Ricoeur follows the indirect ontology of Merleau-Ponty, it must be added that he is much more specific about which expressions or which language can be the bearer of the indirect ontology. Ricoeur's attention is drawn to the creative dimension of language. It is there that he seeks the manifestation of the archê and the telos of being.

Ricoeur, therefore, does not seek the language of being in the language of the physical sciences. In the physical sciences one can forego the emphasis upon the language of participation without creating a crisis. In the physical sciences the insistence upon mathematicizing reality has turned reality into an object vis-à-vis my subjectivity. The primary aim of its language is not to express my participation in being, but my ability to manipulate what the distanciation has enabled me to recognize and articulate. Distanciation is like the fissure across which one can build the bridge of method. But the experience of the physical sciences is not totally devoid of the experience of participation. But, for Ricoeur, it is not the privileged sphere in which our participation in being is manifested. The descriptive language of the physical sciences in its search for exactitude and univocity is less capable of evoking our source or foundation in being.

Now, just as Heidegger proposed that the privileged locus of the manifestation of being must be sought in the pre-Socratic poets, in an ontology prior to metaphysics (377:101), Ricoeur has invested poetics with the charge of relinquishing the secret of our bond. The language of being is, therefore, not just any language. Its logic is the intended ambiguity of poetry. Its form is not merely a word, not merely a sentence, but a poetic text or an oeuvre. In other words we must turn once again to the text, the poetic text, as the manifestor of the ontological ground.

Ricoeur is aware that the approach to being by way of the text appears to break apart the carefully constructed unity of Heidegger's and Gadamer's hermeneutics. Does a text-theory with its multitude of texts not threaten to once again regionalize hermeneutics? Ricoeur's response to the

---

12. See above, p.36.

charge is that the basic issue of hermeneutics remains for him the 'art of understanding', but that he seeks to apply it to the interpretation of texts (406:16). It is not strictly speaking, as he warns us, "A hermeneutics of the text, but a hermeneutics based on the problematics of the text" (406:16). Moreover, as we shall see, Ricoeur's notion of text is not as narrow as it may seem at first. It possesses an universality peculiar to itself since it is not limited only to literary, written texts, but also to any activity that has the qualities of textuality, that is, of inscriptability in signs in the form of a work. Along these lines history can also be considered a text.[13] In fact, 'text' becomes the name for any object of hermeneutical inquiry, even human existence. It circumscribes the hermeneutical field, even though Ricoeur warns that it remains but one point of departure (406:16). In short, one might equate Ricoeur's hermeneutics of the text with his philosophy itself: a hermeneutic phenomenology.[14]

What are the advantages of this point of departure? Mainly two. The first advantage is Ricoeur's brand of ontology. His ontology is indirect and methodical. He refuses the direct ontology of Heidegger, opting instead for the route towards the ontological mapped out by the strategy and the creative leaps of language itself which are inscribed in the text. By opting for this route he circumvents a series of obstacles that confront a direct ontology.

A second advantage, which for Ricoeur is equally important, is epistemological. A hermeneutics based on the problematics of the text allows Ricoeur to rejoin the epistemological concerns of Schleiermacher and Dilthey. Can the interpretation of texts (Dilthey's 'expressions of life fixed in writing') be undertaken with a rigour that brings it beyond guessing or intuition? What is the epistemological status of an interpretation of a text? The theory of the text opens up new possibilities of dissolving the dichotomy between explanation and understanding that neo-Kantianism left as its heritage. Text-theory blends explanation and understanding so inextricably that, according to Ricoeur, there can be no understanding without explanation and no explanation without understanding.

The approach presents Ricoeur, however, with one fundamental problematic. Does the theory of the text allow for making the distanciation occasioned by the text productive? Can the text effect the appropriation, or the re-appropriation, of one's participation in being? Can the objectification of the primordial experience in the text be transcended so that the text is more than an expression of our alienation? It is Ricoeur's

---

13. See, for example, "The Model of the Text: Meaningful Action Considered as a Text" (370:529-562).

14. See David Pellauer, "The Significance of the Text in Paul Ricoeur's Hermeneutical Theory" in Studies in the Philosophy of Paul Ricoeur, edited by Charles E. Reagan, Athens, Ohio University Press, 1979, p.97-114.

gamble that a passage can be found from the texture of the text to the self-understanding of the reader (389:129).[15]

_____

15. In the article "The Hermeneutical Function of Distanciation" (389) Ricoeur proposes the real or imagined antinomy between explanatory procedures and the fundamental reality that we participate in the following way, "Either we have the methodological attitude and lose the ontological density of the reality under study or we have the attitude of truth and must give up the objectivity of the human sciences" (389:129). Ricoeur refuses the antinomy, seeking instead a mediation of explanation and understanding.

CHAPTER FIVE: MEANING AND TIME.

Bibliography.

8.	Karl Jaspers et la philosophie de l'existence (1947).
153.	La symbolique du mal (1960).
156.	"L'antinomie de la réalité humaine et la problème de l'anthropologie philosophique" (1960).
164.	"Le péché originel: étude de signification" (1960).
173.	"Herméneutique des symboles et réflexion philosophique" (1961).
191.	"Herméneutique et réflexion" (1962).
200.	"Symbolique et temporalité" (1963).
227.	De l'interprétation. Essai sur Freud (1965).
229.	"Existence et herméneutique" (1965).
247.	"Le problème du double-sens comme problème herméneutique et comme problème sémantique" (1966).
271.	"Langage religieux. Mythe et symbole" (1967).
294.	"Préface" in R. Bultmann, Jésus. Mythologie et démythologisation (1968).
320.	Le conflit des interprétations (1969).
332.	Les incidences théologiques des recherches actuelles concernant le langage (1969).
337.	"Qu'est-ce un texte? Expliquer et comprendre" (1970).
357.	"Mythe" (1971).
398.	"Phénoménologie et herméneutique" (1974).
399.	"Hegel aujourd'hui" (1974).
404.	"Manifestation et proclamation" (1974).
408.	"Puissance de la parole: science et poésie" (1975).
411.	"Biblical Hermeneutics" (1975).
416.	"Parole et symbole" (1975).
417.	La métaphore vive (1975).
422.	"History and Hermeneutics" (1976).
423.	Interpretation Theory (1976).
453.	"The Narrative Function" (1978).
469.	"Narrative Time" (1979).
474.	"La fonction narrative et l'expérience humaine du temps" (1980).

The marriage of hermeneutics with phenomenology has a number of interesting repercussions. More than any other movement, hermeneutics destroys the idealism of Husserlian phenomenology. But it does not destroy phenomenology itself. In fact, Ricoeur insists that phenomenology and hermeneutics belong together (398:223). Phenomenology remains the foundation of hermeneutics. In Husserl's Logische Untersuchungen, Ricoeur discovers a phenomenology, whose method is described in terms of an Auslegung, an interpretation, an elucidation of significations. And although that does not make Husserl's phenomenology a hermeneutics, it does offer an inroad for the interpenetration of phenomenology and hermeneutics (Cf. 398:242-252). Hermeneutics' searching out for a hermeneutical equivalent in phenomenology, will bear its fruit, when we shall consider how Ricoeur proposes to re-introduce the appropriation of the subject.

For the moment, however, we must consider another aspect of the interpenetration of hermeneutics and phenomenology. Husserl's search for a final foundation of objectivity, according to Ricoeur, encounters its limit in an ontology of understanding. Every effort of justification, that purports to be final, must recognize that it is borne by a relation that precedes it. Every relation of a subject and an object is ultimately grounded in the relation of participation. An ontology of understanding is an ontology of finitude. All understanding is finite understanding. For Ricoeur, that is the very heart of the hermeneutical experience (398:228). To say it in other words, hermeneutical understanding is historical understanding.

At its most universal level, one might say that whenever people communicate with one another in ordinary language, hermeneutics is involved. Ordinary language is by definition ambiguous language, because the words of ordinary language are polysemic and the actual use of these polysemic words does not exhaust the potential meanings of these words. The context of the sentence determines the meaning. This function of the context in selecting the actual meaning is the most extensive application one can give to the notion of interpretation. Aristotle understood hermeneutics along these lines. He called hermeneia the very process of the mediation by way of signs of our relation to things. Language by its nature is hermeneia (337:149). At this level, Ricoeur says, "Interpretation is the process, by which, in the play of question and answer, the interlocutors determine together the contextual values that structure their conversation" (398:229-230).

For Ricoeur, however, this definition of interpretation is too limiting. The model of conversation restricts interpretation to the face-to-face communication. The field of hermeneutics finds its favorite focus not in the short conversational relationship, but in the much broader field of historical intersubjectivity. Hermeneutics seeks out the relationships with our predecessors, our contemporaries, and our successors. That relationship is a relationship of historical transmission or tradition. Hermeneutics brings in the historical connection. It promotes the communication with institutions, social roles, and collectivities (398:230).

This transmission of an historical tradition is mediated by texts, that is, the documents and monuments in which that historical tradition has become fixated. Although these documents and texts have received a certain autonomy, as we saw above, they may not be hypostatized. They remain part of the historical connection. This means that hermeneutics does not place us at the foundation of things, but right in the middle of things: neither at the beginning nor at the end (398:231). Hermeneutics places us in the middle of a conversation which we did not begin, but it helps to orient us in that conversation, so that we can make our contribution, without it being at the same time, the last word. But this is only one dimension of the historical dimension of hermeneutics. For the moment we shall put it aside, in order to return to it in the subsequent chapters. In this chapter we shall examine the more ontological side of the historical dimension.

The interaction between phenomenology and hermeneutics also has ontological repercussions. We saw above that, for Ricoeur, our participation in being is dialectically paired with distanciation. This distanciation, contrary to Gadamer's opinion, is not an alienation to be overcome, but an indispensible condition. Phenomenology confirms that the distanciation is constitutive of participation. It posits that every consciousness of meaning is possible only if there is an époché, a moment of distanciation. As Ricoeur says, "Phenomenology begins when, not content with 'living' - or with 'reliving' - , we interrupt the lived in order to signify it" (398:238). In that exchange between the lived and the signification of the lived, the sign retains its ontological depth as long as it is not forgotten that the époché is only a philosophical gesture. The breach it inaugurates between the sign and the thing is not an absolute or permanent chasm. They remain in dialectical tension with each other (398:238-239).

Now this dialectical tension hermeneutics applies to its region of competence: historical existence. Its lived experience is the historical connection that is mediated by the transmission of the works, documents and institutions of our historical existence. It makes little difference that hermeneutics calls the lived experience, participation, and the époché, distanciation. Corresponding to the consciousness of the meaning in phenomenology, hermeneutics knows of a consciousness of the historical connection. In Gadamer's terms it is a wirkungsgeschichtliches Bewusstsein, a consciousness of the efficacity of history. Hermeneutics owes its existence to the fact that we no longer are satisfied with our participation in existence as historical, but interrupt it to signify it (398:239).

In this Chapter we shall examine how Ricoeur has worked out the temporal and historical dimensions of poetic texts. We shall not turn to specific poetic texts but to genres of texts, going from the most dense to the least dense texts. It is Ricoeur's contention that symbol and myth as well as fiction and history speak to existence as temporal. It should be noted, however, that most of Ricoeur's investigation into symbol and myth antedates his hermeneutical work. For that reason, his insistence on the temporal dimension is not as strongly pronounced in the text of La symbolique du mal (153) and De l'interprétation. Essai sur Freud (227) as it will be in later works. And yet, as we shall see, it is not absent. It is more implicit than explicit. It comes to its full flowering when Ricoeur comes to his analysis of the narrative.

A. THE SYMBOL.

For Ricoeur, the symbol is language at its most intensive level. He began his investigation of the symbol in La symbolique du mal (153) in the context of his philosophy of the will. This philosophy of the will, as he says in Le volontaire et l'involontaire (29:3-34), seeks to clarify the structures and acts of the will according to a threefold game plan. The first work, Le volontaire et l'involontaire (29), examines the eidetic structures of the will, unencumbered by the question of evil and transcendence. The second approach, Finitude et culpabilité (152, 153), removes the époché of evil, while a third work, yet to be written, will re-introduce the sacred. The removal of the époché of evil in L'homme faillible (152) and La symbolique du mal (153) makes Ricoeur look for the locus where the pathétique of evil surfaces in the cultural realm. This locus he takes to be the symbol.[1]

Ricoeur's fascination with the symbol lies in the promise of its linguistic abundance to lead him to the root of language and existence. As he wrote in 1962,

"If we raise the problem of symbol now, at this period of history, we do so in connection with certain traits of our 'modernity' and as a rejoinder to this modernity. ... In the very age in which our language is becoming more precise, more univocal, more technical, better suited to those integral formalizations that are called precisely 'symbolic' logic ... - it is in this age of discourse that we wish to recharge language, start again from the fulness of language (320:288).

The symbol and its interpretation is again the central theme of De l'interprétation (227). In this work Ricoeur looks at the oneiric dimension of the symbol in dream-language through the psychoanalytic theory of Freud. Inasmuch as the psychoanalytic theory of Freud is a cultural theory, Ricoeur is able to discover in symbolics the great cultural struggle between Eros and Thanatos, between the archê and the telos of existence, between freedom and bondage. More and more the symbol becomes for him the rejoinder to our cultural problematic.

The theme is continued in Le conflit des interprétations (320). Here Ricoeur examines in greater detail the difficulties of interpreting the symbol. Because of its intended ambiguity, the symbol can either disclose our bond with being or the sacred or dissimulate or distort it. To clarify this ambiguity, Ricoeur is forced more and more to elaborate the semantic constitution of the ambiguous language. This he does in La métaphore vive (417). La métaphore vive seems from this perspective to be no more than a great effort to bolster his theory of the symbol semantically. But in the semantic analysis of the symbol he suddenly perceived that his definition of the symbol as double-meaning language required a modification. A study of language reveals that symbol is not only language, but a mixed form. The symbol is a mixed form of language and force.

---

1. Cf. A. Cipollone, "Symbol in the Philosophy of Ricoeur" in The New Scholasticism 52, 1978, p.149-167; J. van Bergen, "'Het symbool geeft te denken.' Een studie in Ricoeur" in Tijdschr.Theol. 13, 1973, p.166-188; T. Peters, "The Problem of Symbolic Reference" in The Thomist 44, 1980, p.72-93.

1. The symbol and language.

For Ricoeur, the symbol situates itself at the edge of language. More precisely, the symbol is found at the point where language emerges out of its pre-linguistic ground (416:143). The symbol, then, is already a word. The symbol is already language. But, at the same time, it evokes its pre-linguistic source. Two universes are linked together in the symbol, one of which is linguistic, and the other non-linguistic (416:143). As early as in La symbolique du mal Ricoeur wrote:

> But symbols are already in the element of speech. We have said sufficiently that they rescue feeling and even fear from silence and confusion; in virtue of them, man remains language through and through (153:350).

In "Langage religieux" he writes,

> Symbolism ... places us at the threshold of the word and of silence. That privileged frontier marks perhaps the point of birth of all language, just as it marks the exigency and the operativeness of being. The silence is the ground from which the tenacity of the word loosens itself, in order to break the silence, in order to speak once more, before being silent. It is a plea for the word in the presence of the silence from which the symbol snatches us (271:133, my translation).[2]

Ricoeur is attracted to the symbol, because the symbol is already language, while it sits at the threshold of language. Because of this unique position of the symbol, he calls it the fullness of language (e.g., 227:30). In fact, it is language's first exploration and manifestation of what is not yet language, but which strives toward it. What that language explores is the inexpressible region of what grounds life. The philosopher, seeking entry into that region, may not destroy the delicate balance, the tension, which the symbol maintains between the linguistic and the non-linguistic. Inattention to the delicate relationship could lead to the forgetfulness of being (271:132).

---

2.   "Le symbolisme ... nous place aux confins même de la parole et du silence; cette frontière privilégiée marque peut-être, au même titre que tout à l'heure l'impérativité ou l'opérativité de l'être, le point de naissance de tout langage. Le silence est le fond sur lequel se détache l'opiniâtreté de verbe à convertir l'inexprimable en exprimable, à rompre le silence, à dire encore, avant de se taire. C'est un plaidoyer pour la parole face au silence que le symbole nous arrache."

This warning puts us on guard against a view of the symbol as a free exploration of the pre-linguistic region. Symbolic language is bound language. It is bound in two manners. It is bound to and bound by (416:151-156; 227:31).

First of all, what lies prior to language becomes bound to the language that begins to express it. The language of the symbol is a special type of language. The emergent language is language at its point of birth. The symbol is the moment of the creation of language, the moment when language first captures its own ground. As such, symbol must be defined as a word that effects something in relation to being (271:129).

For Ricoeur, this bond of the non-semantic to language occurs primarily in three fields: psychoanalysis, religion and poetics. In each field the symbolic language is a manner of controlling, regulating, evoking, avoiding, dissimulating, revealing, and participating in its non-semantic dimension.

The clearest example, for Ricoeur, lies in psychoanalysis. For psychoanalysis the dream is the mediator between the conscious and the unconscious. As Freud perceived it, the unconscious is that dimension of our subjectivity that is burgeoning towards language, without it being, as yet, language. It is only latent language (227:453). In the dream-text of the waking hour the unconscious achieves a linguistic dimension. But the high symbolic content of that language shows it to be a language, where desire meets meaning, where drives meet their representations or affective substitutes. The language of the dream-text mixes together desire and language. "The symbol hesitates on the boundary line between bios and logos" (416:153, my translation).[3]

The same bond between the non-semantic and the semantic is present in religious symbolism. In religious symbolism one is confronted with the sacred and the power of the sacred. In their primordial form religious symbols employ the elements of the universe and of vegetation, such as, the heavens, the earth, rocks, water and plants, to figure immensity, power, birth, growth and death. These cosmic symbols are hierophanic. They manifest the sacred. Their power and efficacy, as the phenomenology of religion has indicated, do not necessarily break through in the word. As Ricoeur notes,

> To the transcendent divine there opposes itself a sacred that is near, witnessed in the fertility of the soil, the exuberance of vegetation, the well-being of the herds, the fecundity of the maternal womb. In the sacred universe the living are not dispersed here or there, but there is life as a total and diffuse sacrality which manifests itself in the cosmic rhythms, in the return of vegetation, in the

---

3.   "Le symbole hésite sur la ligne de partage entre bios et logos."

alteration of births and deaths (416:154-155, my translation).[4]

But the rock, the heavens, etc., do not become truly hierophanic, unless the cosmos is imbued with the word. "Only in the universe of discourse do these realities take on the symbolic dimension" (227:14). It is the language that accompanies the cosmic elements that permits the figurative to emerge out of the symbol of Heaven, Earth, Rock and Water (404:62-63).

In other words, these symbols do not come to language except after passing through the elements of the world. "In the sacred universe the capacity to say is based upon the capacity of the cosmos to signify" (416:155, my translation).[5] If a logic exists, it is a logic that finds its roots in the very structure of the universe. By way of the sacred hierophanies of the universe, the sacred reveals itself in the word and the gesture. Religious symbolism brings to language and manifests the power of the sacred more clearly than the oneiric symbols of the recounted dream.

We have already indicated in a previous chapter the bound language of poetic images.[6] The poetic images bind us to being precisely by abolishing and subverting the reference of the describable and manipulable world. The poetic image is a mixture of language and mood, bonding us in feeling to the world of being.

The mixed language of the symbol seems, according to Ricoeur, to principally express something like power, efficacity or force. Symbolic language would then designate the human or being as a power, a force, an efficacity to exist. It does so from below through our dreams as a desire and an effort to be, as a power of drives, and through our poetic images as the power to open up new possible worlds in which we can live, as a power of creative existence. It does so from above in the religious symbols as the power of the sacred to heal and to destroy (416:156). But more about this later.

But, second, once the pre-linguistic is captured by language, it binds that language to itself. The language is <u>bound by</u> the symbolic meaning. The language becomes a weighted language. It bears within it not only its literal meaning, but also simultaneously, in tension with the first

---

4.   "Au divin transcendant s'oppose ainsi un sacré prochain, attesté dans la fertilité du sol, l'exubérance végétale, la prospérité des troupeaux, la fécondité du sein maternel. Dans l'univers sacré il n'y a pas des vivants ici ou là, mais la vie comme sacralité totale et diffuse, qui se laisse voir dans les rythmes cosmiques, dans le retour de la végétation, dans l'alternance des naissances et des morts."

5.   "Dans l'univers sacré la capacité de dire est fondée dans la capacité du cosmos du signifier."

6.   See above p.67-69.

meaning, a second meaning. This meaning is the symbolic, figurative one. The literal meaning is invaded by this second meaning and becomes imbued with the force of the second meaning (320(247):64-65). That is why the first meaning, if taken literally, would be, to use a phrase of Jean Cohen, semantically impertinent. It is filled with another meaning which is not linguistic itself, but which is evoked by the first. In speaking of this force that invades language, Ricoeur points toward an excess, a surplus, an overdetermination, of symbolic language (416:149; 227:496). Its excess or surplus is evocative of what seeks to come to language. That is why a symbol is like a movement. It is not a movement from the literal meaning to the symbolic meaning but it is a transfer from one level to another within and through the literal meaning.

The semantic, therefore, is bound by the non-semantic. A specific language invades the pre-linguistic realm of desire and the sacred. That language not only qualifies and affects desire, force, and the sacred, but is in turn itself qualified. The sacred, desire, and force invade a specific human culture (153:41).

This point is of considerable importance to Ricoeur. The pre-linguistic that comes to language in the symbol is historically, culturally and geographically oriented. For our Western civilization this formulation is Greek and Jewish. In that sense the language limits the symbol. In La symbolique du mal and De l'interprétation Ricoeur recalls that our cultural memory reverts to the symbols and myths that underly our Western consciousness.

> These two cultures, which would contain nothing exceptional for an eye not situated anywhere in particular, constitute the first stratum of our philosophical memory. More precisely, the encounter of the Jewish source with the Greek origin is the fundamental intersection that founds our culture (153:20).

If this appears as something of a scandal in our desire for truth, it remains an unavoidable fact, that an affectively binding perspective of a universal culture is not as yet availale to us (153:24). But the fact does point out the significant factor that in a specific culture desire, force and the sacred manifest themselves in a specific language.[7]

---

7.   Like Philip Wheelwright (The Burning Fountain, op. cit.) Ricoeur recognizes that this contingent linkage of the symbol with language leads to a hierarchy of symbols and furthermore to a gradation of durability and importance (417:352, note 41). On the lowest rung are the images and symbols that predominate in one poem. This is followed by the preferred images and symbols through which a poet expresses him or herself in his/her entire oeuvre. Beyond the single poet we discover a scheme of symbols that may pervade an entire cultural tradition such as the Western civilization. A fourth type of symbol is transcultural, inasmuch as it binds together people

2. The symbol and the metaphor.

The linkage of the symbol with language has a consequence, however, which Ricoeur did not recognize in his earlier works on the symbol. If the symbol is already language, it possesses a form or a structure. However bizarre its predicates may be, symbols operate with ordinary sememes, lexemes and morphemes (320(247):79). In his more recent works Ricoeur has engaged himself, therefore, in a semantic exploration of the figure. And when he does so, he discovers that the semantic structure of the symbol is remarkably similar to that of the metaphor (416:148-151; 421:53-57).

Without repeating what was said above about the metaphor, we may signal here the relationship between the literal and the figurative meaning. The metaphor can help us to focus upon the linguistic affinity of the symbol. The symbol, we have already pointed out, refers to and solicits the non-linguistic by means of language. Its language bears the excess which did not come to language. It is this excess that brings about the tension between the literal meaning and the surplus. It is the tension that brings about the work of interpretation which transforms the semantic impertinence to a pertinence. In other words, semantically the mystery of the symbol is reducible to the functioning of the metaphor.

But to acknowledge that the semantic structure of the symbol repeats that of the metaphor intensifies the significance of the metaphor. The metaphorical utterance of the symbol invests the metaphor with a depth and rootedness which it could not be given in our previous discussion. We are taken beyond the realm of apprehension, because the exploration of the sacred by the symbol assimilates us to that which the symbol refers (423:56; 227:17). This existential quality of the symbol distinguishes it from what appears to be the much freer composition of the metaphor. The metaphor has transgressed into the realm of the logos more fully than the symbol. The symbol is found on the boundary line between the bios and the logos. The symbol binds us to existence. This existential intensity, when it translates itself into a metaphor, permits us to qualify those metaphors as 'root' metaphors (423:64).

The root metaphor like a symbol touches the "durable constellations of life, feeling, and the universe" (423:64). But how can a metaphor remain a living metaphor, that is, how can the metaphor retain the tensile moment, and at the same time attain the durability of the symbol? Ricoeur resolves this dilemna by suggesting that the invasion of

---

of different cultures in certain religious or secular symbols. Finally, there are the archetypes, the great symbols that bind together large segments of humanity. Symbols such as the moon, the shadows, lordship, are common to many cultures and effect humanity's relationship to the depth-structures of life. By the participation of metaphors in that great work of assembling humanity, they attain a durability and tenacity and creativity, that transcends their original instance de discours. Cf. 408:173-174;416:158.

the metaphor by the symbol creates a whole network of metaphors. Thus, for example, the Hebraic tradition calls God King, Father, Husband, Lord, Shepherd, Rock, Fortress, Redeemer. All of these metaphors are gathered into the one metaphor. But also any one of these metaphors suggests the others so that they remain alive by means of their power to signify the other metaphors. The root metaphor is the metaphor that, on the one hand, gathers all the partial metaphors into one, and, on the other hand, allows the scattering into a variety of related fields. This scattering is virtually limitless. This metaphorical scattering is, in fact, the force of the symbolic experience. But to avoid irretrievable scattering, there are root metaphors which organize the particles into a network of intersignifications (423:64). As Ricoeur remarks,

> Everything indicates that symbolic experience calls for a work of meaning from metaphor, a work which it partially provides through its organizational network and its hierarchical levels. Everything indicates that symbol systems constitute a reservoir of meaning whose metaphorical potential is yet to be spoken (423:65).

But the assimilation of things to one another and of ourselves to things which the power of the symbol expresses and effects is not without tension. This is exemplified in the very structure of the metaphor. The tensile structure of the metaphor may itself reflect the tensile structure of reality. The very tensile structure of the metaphor may bring to expression and clarify a dimension of reality which the symbol only confusedly expresses (423:69). We must investigate a little further the tension and profusion of the symbol.

3. The surplus of the symbol.

The _bios_, the energy, force and exigency of life, we have said, reaches the _logos_ in the symbol. But the _logos_ is hardly adequate to encompass the _bios_. There is a surplus of meaning in the _logos_, because it makes available in language form what lies prior to language. For that reason, there exists a relationship of meaning between the meaning of the language of the symbol and the meaning of what lies prior to language. In this relationship between meaning and meaning, the literal meaning of the symbolic word comes to bear some type of analogical relationship to the symbolic meaning.

> In the symbol, I cannot objectify the analogical relation that connects the second meaning with the first. It is by living in the first meaning that I am led by it beyond itself. The symbolic meaning is constituted in and by the literal meaning which effects the analogy in giving the analogue. ... In fact, unlike a comparison that we consider from the outside, the symbol is a movement of the primary meaning which makes us participate in the latent meaning and thus assimilates us to that which is symbolized without our being able to master the

122

similitude intellectually. It is in this sense that the symbol is donative; it is donative because it is a primary intentionality that gives the second meaning analogically (153:15-16).

On the semantic level Ricoeur calls this surplus, or its psychological term overdetermination (320(229):14), polysemy or intended ambiguity.[8] The ambiguity is intended or provoked because the univocal language cannot be adequate to the reality to be brought to language. The language is, therefore, existentially ambiguous.

A first consequence of this ambiguous twisting of language is that symbolic language, like metaphorical language, requires the work of interpretation. In La métaphore vive (416) Ricoeur emphasized the work of interpretation that is required to make an impertinent predication pertinent (416:90-100). For Ricoeur the field of interpretation is co-extensive to the work of unravelling the intentional ambiguity of symbolic language.

Secondly, because of the ambiguity, the symbol is open to more than one interpretation.[9] This quality inheres in the symbol itself. Ambiguity is part of the ontological fibre of the symbol itself. The being that is expressed in the symbol is itself ambiguous. In this context, Ricoeur likes to quote Aristotle's saying that Being is said in many ways (320(247):67). The symbol's ambiguity is expressed in the very tension created by the relationship of meaning to meaning. "It is the raison d'être of symbolism to disclose the multiplicity of meaning out of the ambiguity of being" (320(247):68, my translation).[10] For in analyzing the symbol, one becomes aware that symbols are both regressive and prospective. Thus, for instance, dream symbols take one back to one's infancy. Poetic images, on the other hand, are prospective, inasmuch as they grasp hold of one's personal synthesis or one's future (227:175) in sympathetic imagination (153:9). But this regression to one's archaism in dream symbols and this prospection of oneself in the figures of wholeness are not mutually exclusive. A symbol, as its Greek root says, brings together. By immersing one in one's archaism - which is, in fact, the archaism of humanity

---

8. See above p.63-67.

9. The truth of the intended double meaning language is examined in the semantic study of metaphorical language. While maintaining a bond between metaphorical language and reality, Ricoeur is hardly able to indicate a criteriology of metaphorical truth beyond saying that it is measured by its appropriateness and by the work of resemblance. See above p.83-85; 417:235. It hardly helps in resolving the problem of literary criticism which asks which text is true or which text permits us to glimpse reality in its truthfulness. To my knowledge Ricoeur has not addressed himself to this question.

10. "C'est la raison d'être du symbolisme d'ouvrir la multiplicité du sens sur l'équivocité de l'être."

(153:13) - the symbol explores simultaneously what might be. Hence the symbolism of evil reflects not only the archaism of evil, the beginning of evil, but also the future of evil, that is, its end (227:40). For that reason a symbol has two vectors. It is both a repetition of our childhood and an exploration of our adulthood. The surplus of the symbol manifests itself in this double movement of regression and prospection.

This vision of the surplus of the symbol presupposes that the symbol under consideration be a living symbol. Only a living symbol is prospective and exploratory of my future. The so-called sedimented symbols of our culture have lost that power. Only in the creative moment, in the clash and tension of the poetic production, does the imagination give us a glimpse of wholeness and of the future (227:521ff).[11]

But the surplus of the symbol manifests not only the double movement of regression and prospection but also another movement which intersects with the first. It is the movement of disclosure and disguise. Ricoeur has investigated this movement of revelation and dissembling within the symbol at even greater length than the movement of regression and prospection. Thus, in the three major earlier works dealing with symbolic form and its interpretation Ricoeur investigated the revelatory character of the symbol in La symbolique du mal (153), the dissimulating character of the symbol in De l'interprétation. Essai sur Freud (227), and the tension and conflict of these two interpretations in Le conflit des interprétations (320). He has applied his analysis particularly to the culturally sedimented symbols of the phenomenology of religion and of psychoanalysis.

Thus the symbol investigated by the phenomenology of religion manifests the power of the cosmic symbols to bond one to the sacred. These symbols are fundamentally revelatory. Phenomenology of religion perceives the symbol as a linguistic form expressing and manifesting the sacred. But on the other hand, the dream symbols investigated by psychoanalysis do not fundamentally manifest but disguise and dissimulate. Instead of manifesting our bond with primordial desiring, dream symbols in the narrated form dissimulate. For psychoanalysis the symbol throws us off the track. It hides what it expresses. Within the framework of psychoanalysis, one should not permit the symbol to speak, one should not follow the prospect of the symbol, without first unscrambling the screening process that the dream symbols throw up to block the access to the effort and desire to be. Psychoanalysis perceives its task to be to destroy the disguise of desire in order to permit the symbol to manifest itself.

Here we have two symbolic forms and two differing and opposing interpretations. But the tension that is expressed here between two

---

11. Among the hierarchy of symbols the dream symbol occupies the lowest level, since dream symbols are not creative symbols but take up 'stereotyped and fragmented remains of symbols'. They are "so worn with use that they have nothing but a past" (227:505). Dream symbols are nothing but vestiges, while creative symbols surge with meaning (227:499-500).

distinctive symbolic forms, also exists within the symbol as part of its surplus of meaning. In other words, the conflict and tension is not extraneous to the symbol and present only in its interpretation. The conflict of interpretation manifests an internal struggle within the symbol itself. It is the tension within the symbol itself that gives rise to conflicting interpretations.

The movement of the projection of our possibilities is interlinked with the movement of regression into our archaism. Before the symbols unleash their power to project and guide us into our adulthood, they take us not only through the movement of regression, but also through the painful labour of unscrambling the disguise of our desire. The symbol is, therefore, not only a passive indicator of this tension of regression and exploration, but also an active power in the process of becoming. Symbolic language, to use Austin's expression, is performative language. It effects the bond, the relation which it signifies (271:130-131). Thus,

> culture is nothing else than this epigenesis or onthogenesis of the 'images' of man's becoming adult. The creation of 'works', 'monuments', and cultural 'institutions' is not something projected by a human symbolizing power which is brought to light by regressive analysis. It is the emergence of Bildung... That is how they are paideia, education, eruditio, Bildung. They are open to what they have disclosed (320:118-119).

For Ricoeur, the symbol is precisely the encounter of these two movements (227:494). It mediates the dialectic between regression and projection without which it cannot effect its power. They retain their power as long as the dialectic of regression and projection remain in effect. And the regression is equally a dissimulation:

> But if symbols are fantasies that have been denied and overcome, they are never fantasies that have been abolished. That is why one is never certain that a given symbol of the sacred is not simply a 'return of the repressed'... The two functions of symbol remain inseparable. The symbolic meanings closest to theological and philosophical speculation are always involved with some trace of archaic myth (227:543).

Ultimately, according to Ricoeur, the self depends both on the unconscious, the archê of existence, and the sacred, the telos of existence. The self moves in the tension of the archê and the telos in the process of a summons directed to it to become adult (320(191):333). Symbols point one to one's ground which is at the same time one's end. One can say with Ricoeur that symbols are indeed the prophecy of consciousness (320(191):333). They summon us beyond the present configurations of life in the dynamism of the movement of the symbol (156:120-124).

125

One might even say that, thanks to their overdetermined structure, symbols succeed in inverting the temporal signs of the origin(al) fantasy. The primal father signifies the eschaton, the "God who comes"; generation signifies regeneration; birth analogously stands for rebirth; the childhood - that childhood that is behind me - signifies the other childhood, the 'second naiveté.' The process of becoming conscious is ultimately a process of seeing one's childhood in front of oneself and one's death behind oneself: "before, you were dead..."; "unless you become as little children..." In this interchange of birth and death, the symbolism of the God who comes has taken over and justified the figure of the primal father (227:543).

The symbol in our language makes us touch the relationship of ourselves with beings and ultimately with being. It is a power that is no longer derived from the enslaving curse of our narcissism but a power that calls upon us to be attentive and listen (see 227:551; 8:291).

4. The symbol and interpretation.

For Ricoeur symbol and interpretation are correlative concepts (320(229):13). There can be no symbol without interpretation. In other words, the symbol does not function except when its tension and conflict are interpreted (416:156). Moreover, to indicate that the symbol and interpretation seek each other, Ricoeur holds that the symbol is already interpretation. Here he comes close to the position of Heidegger and his ontology of understanding. Symbols are the language of being and, as such, an interpretation of being. The symbol is a language spoken to us more than a language spoken by us (320(191):319).

In the preceding paragraph we used the word interpretation in the twofold sense that Ricoeur employs that term. Interpretation is both a technique, an application of semiotic and semantic rules of language to the decoding of texts, and an ontological trait of language. For him, interpretation is a dialectic of explanation and understanding. Hence "the sacred of nature shows itself in its being said symbolically. Showing founds saying and in that order" (416:156, my translation). But the saying possesses the structures of language which can be approached through explanatory procedures. Our effort and desire to be - existence, Being, the sacred, or whatever name one seeks to give to this reality - is itself imbued with a drive toward meaning and language.[12] It finds its first articulation in the ambiguous language of the symbol. Despite its ambiguity, it is already an expression, and in a derived sense, an interpretation of fundamental reality. But the very enigma of the symbolic expression provokes our understanding.

---

12. Ricoeur understands this drive toward meaning and language as a drive towards self-understanding. It is the drive by which meaning makes us while we make it. For Ricoeur, as for Hegel, the progress of meaning is the progress of the subject (See 399:353). This will be taken up again below in Chapter Seven.

It seeks to be unfolded (227:18). It is through interpretation that the symbol's power enters into the wider framework of language.

This unfolding takes two directions. One direction is the symbolic proliferation, about which more will be said below. The symbol expresses its exuberance in an ever expanding wealth of metaphorical expressions. The other direction is toward ever more elaborate forms of interpretation. This movement of interpretation takes us first to the myth and from there to more discursive forms of reasoning up to the density of the concept (320(164):269-286). Once the pre-linguistic plenitude enters into language and the framework of interpretation, the process of interpretation is unending.

5. The symbol and totality.

Symbols in their exuberance do not stand alone. One symbol calls forth another in an unending process of interpretation and re-interpretation. Thus symbols link together and gather existence in its symbolic affluence. Now Ricoeur maintains, that only within a total economy of gathering the symbolic values into unity can the individual symbols be recognized and differentiated. Hence, the symbol becomes tied to an 'economy' or order of symbols (320(200):58).[13]

The delimitation of symbols comes forth only in their being brought together into an economy of symbols where their interrelationships and differential functions manifest themselves. Only an economy can attract, sift out, purify, and coordinate the ebulience of the symbolic forms. In this economy there stands revealed an intentionality towards a totality of meaning or toward a total meaning of the universe. For the signifying power of the symbol is virtually limitless. In its search, totality is, however, only aimed at. It is never completed. The symbol conjures up the wholeness of existence without giving us the totality as a perception or as a knowledge (153:170-171). It is only this economy that can orient us in our aim toward this totality.

If the originary unity out of which the symbol comes forth and to which the symbol returns us is shattered in the variety of symbols, it is even further disjointed by the limitation that language and its operations place upon it. With language and its interpretation the symbol enters into the historicity of language. Through interpretation the symbol is sedimented. It begins to install a tradition and a history of the transmission of the tradition (320(200):55). The interpretative process of the symbol is, therefore, also a historical and cultural process. This tradition will be kept alive only by the constant renewal of the interpretative process of a community of interpretation, who will safeguard the tradition and retain the exuberance of the symbol within its economy. Without this process the symbol can easily "solidify into an idolatry" (320(173):293).

---

13. See D. Rasmussen, Mythic-Symbolic Language and Philosophical Anthropology, op. cit., p.113-128.

6. The symbol and the myth.

Since the symbol is already a type of interpretation, the very surplus of meaning of the symbolic form has become a dynamism of meaning that searches out further possibilities of expression. In line with that development myths are "symbols developed in the form of narrative and articulated in a time and space that cannot be coordinated with the time and space of history and geography according to the critical method" (153:18). Certain dimensions of the symbol are accentuated in the myth such as its temporality and narrativity. In other words, what breaks forth in the myth as "what is beyond known and tangible reality" (320(294):391) breaks forth in the linguistic form of a narration (153:166). Although unique to the myth, its temporality and narrativity can also be attributed to the symbol because of its link with the myth (320(200):28). Also the symbol has a temporal and narrative dimension that the symbol by itself does not display. This linkage of the symbol with narrativity will assume greater import as Ricoeur's philosophy unfolds.

In order to locate the myth in the thinking of Paul Ricoeur, we must think of it as one step further removed from "the indivisible plenitude, in which the supernatural, the natural, and the psychological are not yet torn apart" (153:167). Myth like the symbol, but at one pace removed from the symbol, seeks to express the reality that lies prior to language in the broken language of narration. As a development of the symbol the myth is equally a reduction of the symbol. It is an unravelling of the symbol and a reduction of the tension of the symbol. For the myth to retain its power to reveal it must not lose its relation to the symbolic field. Without the link with its ground a myth will quickly evolve into a fable or a gnosis (320(164):272; (173):304).

B. THE MYTH.

1. The myth and language.

Etymologically a Greek word, myth brings with it a specific Greek philosophical problematic. In Greece the word myth (muthos) emerges in direct opposition to logos. In contrast to the pre-Socratic myths of Homer and Hesiod, there developed in Greece the word of the philosopher. Western consciousness has inherited this opposition of muthos and logos. The approach to the myth in the West has been either a denial of the truth value of the myth or some type of acceptance of the myth. As a result of this fundamentally Greek approach, Western thinking has tended to approach the other mythic strains from Babylon and contemporary civilizations in a similar manner. This approach is fundamentally epistemological. Because of its opposition to the logos, the muthos was considered the approximate equivalent of folklore, fables and legends (332:28-29). This dominant current of philosophical thought must not be allowed to overshadow another tradition which links the myth with the creative and productive imagination. The Kantian schematism and productive imagination produced the pattern for the understanding of the myth in Romanticism and Jungian psychology. This strain of thought was much more appreciative of the power of the myth. According to this tradition, myth is not opposed to the logos. It expresses the power of the imagination to explore the realms inaccessible directly to speculative thought (332:30-31).

Ricoeur's approach to the myth attaches itself to the latter tradition. According to this understanding of the myth, the myth comes to philosophy, first of all, as an issue of meaning (357:530). Language is the medium whereby the fullness of experience, the invisible and unsaid, receives its tangible form (153:169). For the myth is also a form of discourse. This discourse is the analogue, the contingent form, of what the myth signifies.[14] The myth intends to say something about the reality in which we live. It commits a subject to its vision (357:532). It is this referential thrust of the myth that interests us here.

For Ricoeur this referential function of the myth is founded upon its metaphorical surplus of expression. The narrative interpretation of the symbol, which we said is the myth, assumes the form of metaphorical language. It is active, inasmuch as it brings about a transfer of meaning. Its process is foundational in establishing new semantic fields. Its reference is a metaphorical reference and hence an inverse reference. What does it say? To what reality does it bond us?

2. Ontological dimension of myth.

Ricoeur's definition of the myth follows that of Mircea Eliade.[15] According to Mircea Eliade, a myth is a story of origins. Its primary

---

14. The structural analysis of myth such as undertaken by Cl. Lévi-Strauss in La pensée sauvage indicates a logical coherence in the myth of kinship which is similar to the linguistic relationships of differences and oppositions in langue. However, Ricoeur warns against over-generalizing the method of Lévi-Strauss. He points to the exclusive use by Lévi-Strauss of totemic thought in which the arrangements of thought predominate over content of thought. The Semetic, Hellenic and Indo-European traditions show a preference of content over structure. Totemic thought is much more conducive to a structuralist analysis than the Semetic and Hellenic strains. Nevertheless, he acknowledges that a structural approach to the latter tradition is both welcome and necessary. Cf. 368:533; 320(200):40-49. Ricoeur suggests that the mythic tradition upon which our civilization is founded functions and reacts to the future out of the excess of meaning discovered in the mythic and symbolic substratum. Here there is a minimum of structuration and a maximum of meaning. Cf. also P. Riggio, "Paul Ricoeur et l'herméneutique des mythes" in Dialogue 35, 1967, p.73-89; Boyd Sinyard, "Myth and Reflection: Some Comments on Ricoeur's Phenomenological Analysis" in Can. Journ. Theol. 16, 1970, p.33-40.

15. Le myth de l'éternel retour, Paris, 1943; Traité d'histoire des religions, Paris, 1949; Aspects du mythe, Paris, 1963; La nostalgie des origines. Méthodologie et histoire des religions, Paris, 1971.

function is the establishment and institution of the main traits of human existence. A myth tells how things began. It does not tell it in terms of historical times but in terms of primordial time: in illo tempore. The myth relates how the institutions, ethical rules, and reality in whole or in part has its ground, its root, in the time of the myth. This relationship of historical time to the mythical, primordial time is essential to the myth (357:533). In fact, historical time is grounded in a mythical time. As such the ontological dimension of the myth is laid bare in this relationship of human existence to a depth structure of time. Existence is defined in this relationship of our historical time with our essential being (153:163).

Three corollaries follow from this first aspect.

1. What is invariable in the myth is its function of establishing things. Who does the establishing and what is established varies. It is secondary to the myth whether these figures are gods or heroes or a first ancestor. It is a misrepresentation of the myth, therefore, to make the figures of the myth autonomous. The myths are not the story of the gods but the stories of the origin of things. It is this quality that distinguishes the story form of the myth from other story forms (357:533-534).

2. A myth has a practical function. Anthropology has pointed out the link between a myth and a rite. In other words, the myth cannot be understood outside of its linkage with a ritual action. The myth is the founding act of ritual. In the sense that a myth is the story of origins, it is linked with a paradigmatic action that links the story of origin with the existence and praxis of the present. The rite stands as a model for the myth and activates it in the present. The implication of the praxis is most clearly present in the Babylonian celebration of the New Year. The celebration is essentially a ritual of the enthronement of the king, in which the great story of creation is told. The enthronement of the king and through him the establishment of the order, justice, and harmony of his realm is the ritual re-enactment of the story in which the original order and harmony was established (332:33). Here the myth assumes the function of a guardian of existence (332:33). But what was said in the first corollary also applies here. It is possible to expand the representations of the myth into an autonomous story of the gods and the great heros. In the same way it is also possible to separate the ritual from its roots and give it an autonomous existence in which the myth is perceived as subservient to the rite. For Ricoeur the relationship of primordial time to historical time must be retained as central (332:45).

3. The third corollary concerns the psychological implications of the myth. The linkage of historical time with primordial time also has an affective, emotional character. Ricoeur, following Rudolf Otto, calls the affective character of the myth, the sacred.[16] The myth brings us into touch with the ambivalent feeling of fear and attraction, which Otto said

---

16. Das Heilige; über das Irrationale in der Idee des Göttlichen und sein Verhältnis zum Rationalen, München, C.H. Beck, 1917.

constitutes the realm of the sacred. In the myth the historical person is linked with the primordial times through the ritual action. Ricoeur calls it an 'emotional reactivation' of the primordial times. "To live according to a myth is to cease existing only in daily life; the narration and the rite trigger a sort of emotional interiorization which generates what one might call the mytho-poetic core of human existence" (357:534, my translation).[17] The linguistic character of this affective link with the sacred through the myth should not be overlooked. Here again, the affective moment should not be considered autonomous from its mythical narrative. The core is mediated only in and through the mythic recitation. Its recitation together with its ritual component instructs our affectivity in relationship to the sacred (332:46).

3. Myth and time.

Myth reveals not only the narrative dimension of the symbol, but also the temporality of the symbol. The temporal charge of existence that is present in the symbol is manifested more clearly in the mythical strain. In its relating of historical time to a primordial time, the myth suggests that the wealth of the symbolic content is imbued with temporality.[18] The temporality appears then as a result of the symbolic affluence. In "Structure et herméneutique" Ricoeur has called this temporality of the symbol and myth 'historicity' (320(200):58).[19] Because of its historicity the symbol and the myth reach out to understanding first of all by being sedimented or institutionalized in a tradition and secondly by entering into a history of interpretation.

Ricoeur maintains that because of the relationship of the myth to the symbol, the time of the myth is already a time that has lost some of the symbol's fullness of time. He calls it a time on its way to exhaustion (320(200):33).

But the myth explicitates another dimension of time which is only implicit in the symbol. The narrative form of expression of the myth

---

17. "Vivre selon un mythe, c'est cesser d'exister seulement dans la vie quotidienne; le récitatif et le rite amorcent la sorte d'interiorisation émotionelle qui engendre ce qu'on peut appeller le noyau mytho-poétique de l'existence humaine."

18. In the structuralist approach to the myth by Lévi-Strauss, the diachronicity of the myth has been replaced by the synchronicity or the a-chronicity of the deep structure. While recognizing the validity of such an approach, Ricoeur will not follow Lévi-Strauss in his a-chronical reading. Like Greimas, he retains a diachronic 'residue' which seeks an interpretation toward the time dimension of the myth (411:57).

19. At the time of writing "Structure et herméneutique" (1963) Ricoeur had not yet undertaken the study of Heidegger's three levels of time. For a discussion of these three levels of time see below p.138-146.

signifies that the reality aimed at by the symbol and the myth is itself a thing "woven of happenings and personages" (153:169).

The narrativity and temporality of the myth make Ricoeur describe the original reality that reaches language in the myth as dramatic (153:169). The myth cannot encompass that original fullness and dramatic content - the <u>fantastique transcendentale</u> as he also calls it (357:531) - except in the form of a narration of the beginning of an experience and of its end in a primordial time. By its very expression of reality in a tension of time: of historical time and primordial time, of the present historical existence with what might be, the narrative aims at existence as dramatic. Existence is an intention and an effort that is never fulfilled (320(173):293).

4. The economy of myths.

As with symbols, the surplus of the myths comes to expression in the great variety of myths that we find within cultures. This multiplicity of myths can be tamed only when these myths are placed within, what Ricoeur calls a typology (320(173):293). Like the symbols, the myths can be understood in an order or an economy of myths. Thus, a myth does not stand alone. It communicates with other myths in a climate of struggle and affinity. The myths too aim at a totality of meaning by the very rich diet that they place before us. In the myths of evil, for example, this wealth is ordered in a typology and dynamics of myths which, according to Ricoeur permit us to situate myths on a scale in which myths run the gamut from those in which evil is seen as purely external to the human individual to those in which evil becomes almost exclusively anthropological (153:232-278). Thus, for instance, because the anthropological Adamic myth is more phenomenological than the other near-Eastern and Greek myths, it is the key to the understanding both of the dialectic of exteriority of evil and interiority of evil, and of the dynamic of an interpretative process among the myths. In Ricoeur's analysis of the symbolism of evil the Adamic myth becomes the key to open the maze of mythic exploration. The Adamic myth helps to decipher and uncover the latent dimensions of the other myths.

This breakdown of the totality of reality into the maze of myths should not make us lose sight of the totality that these myths aim at. In Ricoeur's perspective, the myth, both in its internal plenitude and in the plenitude of its proliferation, signifies the totality out of which the myth has come forth. Myths signify and aim at that totality. But it becomes available only in its broken form. they are no longer the full experience of what they express. Their great variety fragments the reality out of which the myths come forth. That reality is now glimpsed only through the broken fragments:

Because it is aimed at only symbolically, it requires special signs and a discourse on the signs; their heterogeneity bears witness to the significant whole by its contingent outcroppings. Hence, the myth has the function of guarding the finite contours of the signs which, in their turn, refer to the plenitude that man aims at rather than experiences (153:169).

5. Myth and interpretation.

If for Ricoeur myth continues the interpretative process that comes to language first in the symbol, the process of interpretation does not stop with the myth. Although at this point we cannot go into a full examination of the notion of interpretation, one aspect of that interpretative process of the myth needs mentioning. And that is the notion of demythologization.

The interpretation of myth has been influenced in our century by the work of demythologization of the New Testament by Rudolf Bultmann.[20] For Ricoeur the process of interpretation of the myth, leading to a phenomenological reflection upon the myths, is fundamentally a process of demythologization (320(173):300). The myth's power to reveal is uncovered in the same process whereby its non-essential qualities are eliminated. If myth is already an interpretation, the dynamism of meaning which is found in its linguistic expression searches out and seeks to bring to understanding the true tension of the myth. Hence, the demythologizing process of interpretation will eliminate from the myth all attempts to conceive it as an explanation of reality. It will also refuse to accept all attempts to objectify the features of the myth. In hermeneutical reflection "to demythologize is to interpret myth, that is, to relate the objective representations of the myth to the self-understanding which is both shown and concealed in it" (320(294):391).

Myth is the bringing to language in narrative form of our bond with being. To the extend that this is released for us in terms of self-understanding the true function of the myth is safeguarded. To demythologize is to interpret so that the powers of the myth be set free for our own self-understanding.

---

20. Bultmann's intention to remove the mythological representations of the universe from the New Testament, in other words, to demythologize the New Testament, in order to let the true 'Scandal of the cross' be revealed, need not be rehearsed here. For Ricoeur there is a twofold approach to the interpretation of myths. First of all,there is the work of demythologization which is the work of interpretation inherent in the myth, i.e., to think the myth. But beside a demythologization there is also the work of demystification. Demystification approaches the text not with a sense of belief and openness but with suspicion. The text also dissembles. The relationship of demythologization and demystification will be taken up again below. Cf. "Préface à Bultmann" in Le conflit des interprétations (320:373-392).

C. THE NARRATIVE: FICTION AND HISTORY.

On the surface the distance between myth and story appears vast. The story is an even freer composition, i.e., less bound to reality, than the myth. The openness to an ontological depth is even less evident. However, the distance between the myth and the story is not a chasm. The narrative story also shapes us in our existence prior to our intentional consciousness. If, as we saw above, existence is dramatic, it is the story above all that brings its drama to language.

Our analysis of Ricoeur on this point must remain tentative since he is at the time of writing still elaborating the narrative and its temporal dimension. However, the articles "The Narrative Function" (453) and "La fonction narrative et l'expérience humaine du temps" (474) and an unpublished lecture "Narrative Time" (469) give sufficient indication of the direction of Ricoeur's theory of the story.

The story is a broad category. Ricoeur includes in this not only the enormous variety of fictional narratives but also historical narrative. It is his thesis - derived from W.D. Gallie[21] - that history too must be gathered under the genus of story. Both the historical narrative and the fictional narrative in all their variety articulate our insertion in the temporal dimension of life. This approach implies the need to break down the positivistic approach to history of Carl Gustav Hempel.[22] For Hempel the narrative dimension of history is diverted into an epistemological debate concerning explanatory laws of history. On the one hand, Ricoeur will seek to establish that a synchronic or a-chronic analysis of the story such as that undertaken by the Structuralists, could be rescued from a-chronicity by the linkage of the story with history. On the other hand, he will strive to link the narrativity of fiction with a theory of history, rescuing it from the anti-narrative efforts of the positivists. By recharging history with its narrative thrust, Ricoeur hopes to retrieve a temporal dimension in history that links it closely with the fictional story (453:179).

1. The story and the structuralist code.

The major hurdle to Ricoeur's approach to the story as a narrative comes from the school of French Structuralism. We have seen that this School shows a great interest in the narrative tradition.[23] The structuralists concentrate their efforts in analysing a code or structure underlying the narrative. They recognize a relationship between this code

---

21. Philosophy and Historical Understanding, New York, Schocken, 1964.

22. "The Function of General Laws in History" in Aspects of Scientific Explanation and Other Essays in the Philosophy of Science, New York, Free Press, 1965 (1942), p.231-243.

23. See above p.44-46.

and the narrative structure of the story. However, in their search for a depth-structure of the narrative, they look behind the narrative features of the story. The meaning of the story lies not in the narrative dimension, which they call its surface feature, but in the underlying code. The code is the real meaning of the story. The surface features are only the dressing, the envelope, for the underlying structure. The reference of the story, to use another terminology, is the logical sequence or the binary logic of the actants.

In his critique of structuralism Ricoeur warns against a structuralist ideology, which he calls the 'for-the-sake-of-the-code-fallacy' (411:69). Ricoeur denies validity to a structuralist approach to the text that takes us from the surface structures to the depth-structures of the narrative, but refuses to undertake the journey back to the surface. He judges this type of structuralism to be fixated upon the dead-end of the code that has broken its link with the story as discourse. Thus, for example, V. Propp maintains that the depth-structure of the Russian folktale consists of the closed system of a limited number (31) of functions.[24] All folktales bear the same structural invariant built upon an unchangeable sequence. For Greimas the depth-structure is provided, not by the functions in their sequential order, but by the actantial model, governed by R. Jakobson's binary opposition. According to him an actantial logic rules the story.

But if the return to the story as told, read, or heard is blocked, it leads to a suffocation of language in its capacity to communicate. Ricoeur refuses to acknowledge a narcissistic language that has broken its contact with language as discourse. Only to the extent that a semiotic analysis aids in the understanding of the story as told, read, or heard, i.e., in making the story more 'followable', does the story warrant such a thorough analysis of linguistic procedures (411:67). In other words, Ricoeur remains convinced that "the surface-structure of the 'plot' is not an epiphenomenon, but the message itself" (411:71).

Positively, however, he recognizes the structural analysis as an indispensible tool within the household of hermeneutical procedures. The breach between a semiotic analysis and an existential understanding is bridgeable. In fact, without the mediation of a structural analysis a proper reading of a text may well be impaired. The possibility of such an analysis lies, first of all, in the distanciation, created by the inscription of discourse, and, secondly, in the fact that all discourse is produced discourse. Discourse is inscribed in a certain code, a certain literary genre. These codes generate the epic, the poem or essay. These generative codes reveal the text to be a work. The text is encoded. It is the unique product of an individual, who produced this text as a poem or an essay. A structuralist analysis is possible and even necessary to unravel the discourse or even the text as a production. Since the production is inscribed in the very text, a text can and must be decoded in order to be understood. To understand a text one must be able "to identify the individual discourse (the 'message')

---

24.   See above p.46-47.

through the modes of discourse (the 'codes') which generate it as a work of discourse" (411:70).

But beyond his concern for the validity and even the necessity of structuralism, Ricoeur has tested the ability of structuralism to leave space for the temporality of the story. A structuralist approach defines itself by the achronicity or more properly the synchronicity of the system.[25] The diachronical elements are systematically excluded. This achronicity also extends itself to the structural analysis of the narrative. Thereby it deprives the narrative of its most constitutive characteristic. However, the factual structural analysis of the narrative of both V. Propp and A. Greimas failed in its attempt to remain achronical. V. Propp, for instance, retains a diachronical level by his insistence upon a sequential order for the thirty-one functions. And although Greimas discards the sequential structure for his actantial model, he is left with a measure of chronicity which he calls a 'diachronic residue' (411:49).

In line with what we have already said about the purpose of the structuralist analysis in its relation to the existential dimension of the text, Ricoeur maintains that it is the function of structural analysis to highlight this diachronic residue. The diachronic residue, in fact, would constitute the depth-semantics of the text (411:50). It is to this emphasis of Ricoeur upon the time dimension of the narrative text that we must now turn our attention. What does the story say about our fundamental existence?

2. Narrativity and emplotment.

The dimension of time which in a structuralist analysis of the story is merely a residue becomes a central theme in Ricoeur's analysis of the narrative. He introduces the temporality of the narrative by way of the plot. He refuses, therefore, to bury the narrativity and the temporality of a story under the weight of the system or the deep structure (411:65). Fundamentally it is in the plot that temporality achieves its narrative form.

What is the plot? In the paper "Narrative Time"[26] Ricoeur defines the plot as "the intelligible whole that governs a succession of events in any story" (469:4). The plot is a device connecting events into a specific succession to form a whole called a story. The plot "makes events into a story" (469:4). The emphasis here is on the poietic character of the plot. The plot is not an accidental structure of a story but it is a deliberate structuring. Rather than speaking of plot we might speak of emplotment. It is a poiesis, a craftsmanship, by which events and a succession of events are crafted into a pattern to form a whole (453:191-195).

A number of points need to be accentuated here.

---

25. See above p.45-50.

26. Art. cit.

1. Basic to a story is both that it be told and that it be heard or read. Not only must the plot be crafted by the story-teller but on the part of the listener or reader the story must be followed and followable. The story must possess 'followability'.[27] This followability is the correlate of the development of the story. To follow a story one must understand the sequence of actions or experiences of a number of characters who find themselves in a number of situations, who react to these situations, and who in the ensuing crisis bring the story to its conclusion. The following of the story consists in being taken along by the sequence of actions, in being challenged by its options, and in grasping proleptically the possible conclusions. The attraction of the story lies obviously in its conclusion. But the conclusion must be reached by passing throught the entire story. Only then is it an acceptable conclusion. One must pass through the story, one must follow the story to its conclusion, for it to be effective and understood (469:10).

2. In a narrative a distinction clearly exists between the episodes or events and the configuration of events (469:16).[28] A story is created out of events, perceivable as units. To make these events intelligible they need to be taken out of their individuality and placed in an encompassing configuration. The act of the plot is to elicit such a schema. Ricoeur calls this act a reflective judgment, because emplotment is a reflection upon events within the context of a configuration (469:17). The act of the plot, in crafting the configuration, leads to, what may be called with Aristotle, the 'theme' or 'thought' (dianoia of the muthos), or the 'point' of the story (469:19). The configuration, envisaged by Ricoeur, is not the same as the achronical depth-structure of the structuralists. The configuration does not suppress the episodes but heightens them by means of the narrative sequence and pattern. Hence, the point of a story or the theme is not to be torn from the narrative context nor from the temporal aspect of the story. The thought of the story is itself both narrative and temporal.

3. Finally, a narrative also touches on the need for totality. The mere crafting of a configuration upon the sequence of events forges a specific closure upon the myriad possibilities of the sequence of events and upon the open-endedness of the episodes. Episodes can gather to themselves a variety of perspectives that are virtually limitless. But the configuration, by patterning the sequence, brings the open-endedness to a conclusion. It ends the open sequence. And in ending the open sequence, one might say that the ending rules the story. By imposing a certain resolution on the crisis of the story, it gives intelligibility to the specific pattern of the sequence of events. Retrospectively the resolution of the story colours the pattern of events that led up to it. A story seeks to be complete and it is the resolution, the ending, that allows it to be complete.

---

27. The source here is W.B. Gallie, op. cit.

28. Ricoeur borrows here from Louis O. Mink, "Interpretation and Narrative Understanding" in The Journal of Philosophy, 69, 1972, p.735-737.

3. Emplotment and temporality.

The interrelationship of temporality and the plot is no mere accident. It is Ricoeur's thesis that narrativity and temporality are reciprocally related. It means, that for Ricoeur narrativity is that form of language whose ultimate referent is temporality. But, conversely, it also means that temporality is a structure of existence that receives its linguistic expression in narrativity (469:2). The ontological dimension of narrativity surfaces here. Narrativity expresses, to use Wittgenstein's term, a 'form of life'. The human experience of time is, therefore, inextricably, but mostly unconsciously, bound up with narrativity.

In order to manifest this temporality of narrativity, Ricoeur maintains that temporality and narrativity intersect in the plot (469:4). It is at the level of the emplotment of the narrative that the temporality of the narrative is, therefore, to be made conscious.

Borrowing Heidegger's analysis of time in Sein und Zeit,[29] Ricoeur retains a threefold level of time, each corresponding to a level of narrativity.

a. Narrativity and within-time-ness.

Correlative to the development of the narrative and, therefore, of the followability of the story, there is a time dimension which Heidegger has called 'within-time-ness'. This level of time is closest to what is ordinarily known as linear time. Within-time-ness is often reduced to linear time, because it is so easily linked with the observable. It is time that is datable; it is public and measurable (469:3). But in a significant manner it also goes beyond linear time.

'Within-time-ness' is primarily an existential determination of time. It reflects our thrownness among the objects of our care. The objects of our care are the things that are available to and manipulable by us. We are thrown among these objects and they are the source of our pre-occupation and circumspection. This existential dimension of our pre-occupation with these seemingly external objects has also a temporal dimension. It is not a linear time such as we find in a sequence of events, but a being in time. Our being in time makes us reckon with and, therefore, measure time. But time receives its meaning not from the objects but from our pre-occupation. But since our pre-occupation is with objects, it is datable and measureable time. However, the 'now' of time is not the measured second of the clock, but the time to do something as an expression of our thrownness in existence (469:6-10; 422:369-371).

It is Ricoeur's thesis that the Heideggerean 'within-time-ness' is best brought to light in the narrative. We have pointed out above the importance that Ricoeur attaches to the diachronicity of the narrative. He

---

29. Op. cit.

thinks Structuralism's attempt to dechronologize the narrative is due to its inability to perceive narrative time as more than linear, chronological time. Ricoeur hypothesizes that there are as many as three levels of time - Heidegger's three levels - in the narrative (422:348). Limiting ourselves for the moment to the first level of time, 'within-time-ness', we wish to indicate how Ricoeur develops this notion by attaching it to the development of the plot.

Now within the development of the plot there is a certain temporal directedness. We mentioned that the attraction of the story lies in its conclusion, which, although not predictable, intrigues us with its varying possibilities. The interaction of the conclusion of the story upon the development of the plot is such that a dimension of time emerges which is hardly linear. The narrative structure confirms the 'within-time-ness' as Heidegger proposes it, but in a significant point also amends it (422:350).

The confirmation of 'within-time-ness' in the narrative is apparent in the surface text of the story. Story-telling and following a story throw us in time. By the use of such words as 'then, now, next, after, while,' the story places us in time. The hero or heroine is presented with all the characteristics of 'within-time-ness'. There is a pre-occupation with things. There is time for ... and a lack of time for... Although measureable in terms of days and hours, the emphasis is upon the pre-occupation with things, with care, and not upon the abstract, objectifiable time of the clock that can date the pre-occupation. The time of the story is 'now'. It escapes ordinary time in two ways. It is first of all a 'now' that is shared each in their own way by the characters of the story in the telling of the story. But, secondly, it is as well a 'now' that clings to the hearer and reader of the story. The story's saying of 'now' is, to use Heidegger's term, a way of 'making present' that is more than the 'now' of ordinary time.

For Ricoeur the narrative category of the epic,[30] as expressed in the genre of the story of the quest,[31] is the 'privileged discursive expression' of this dimension of time (469:14). Ricoeur here amends Heidegger by insisting that an analysis of the quest in the narrative is better able to account for the 'making present' of time. The 'saying now' of the narrative, more so than Heidegger's 'reading of the hour', shows the 'now' to be a time of intervention, a time in which a character actively tests his or her existence. The 'now' is a moment of actively wrestling an orientation from life, a time in which the possible becomes actual (422:352). This time-dimension is most clearly enshrined in the quest narrative. It manifests most clearly how the 'now' is a 'making present', an interpretation of our care. Ricoeur calls the quest 'the narrative par excellence of preoccupation' (422:352).

---

30. Ricoeur here refers to the work of Robert E. Scholes and Robert Kellogg, The Nature of Narrative, New York, Oxford University Press, 1966.

31. Both V. Propp and A. Greimas use the story of the quest as the paradigm of the narrative.

But there is another contribution that the narrative of the quest makes to bring forward the 'making present' of time. This contribution will bring us to the threshold of a deeper dimension of time which Heidegger calls historicality.

This contribution to our understanding of time devolves from the relationship we have described above between the episodic aspect and the configuration activity of the story. This interrelationship of the episodes and the configuration of the episodes pulls the story out of the chronological succession of events into a unified whole, where the conclusion rules the plot. Upon the completion of the reading or hearing of the story we in fact reread the succession of events and the transformation of the characters in the light of the ending. That is why the point of the story or its theme remains bound not only to the narrative but also to the time of the narrative. The episodes are retaken in the conclusion and through the conclusion they become locked into a certain sequence and receive a specific meaning. The ending repeats the episodes and takes them out of their contingency. We are enabled to read time backwards from the end to the beginning. This type of configurational activity is a type of recollection or repetition. But this activity is brought to language more expressly in what Heidegger has called historicality (422:355).

b. Narrativity and historicality.

In his analysis of time in Sein und Zeit, Heidegger developed the theme of time starting from time at its most authentic and unified level, which he called temporality, to time at the point of its scattering in 'within-time-ness'.[32] Historicality, according to Heidegger, is the intermediate level of time. It manifests itself on three levels (469:21).

(1) Time as 'extension' between birth and death.

Historicality, where it most closely approximates 'within-time-ness', is first of all the 'extension' of time between birth and death. If temporality is time in its deepest unity, historicality distends or extends that unity of time. It is in its extension that the time of historicality can become time as care, as time for ... and time to ... of 'within-time-ness'. Historicality is the stretching of time between past, present and future or, in existential terms, between 'having-been', 'making present', and 'coming-forth'. Historicality represents, therefore, the cohesion, the Zusammenhang, of life as stretched between life and death. Heidegger's word for this extention of time is Geschehen. By means of this word Heidegger attaches to the notion of extension the aspect of mobility, of movement, of extending. Geschehen in Ricoeur's translation is to 'make

---

32. In line with his general approach of Heidegger's ontology, Ricoeur reverses Heidegger's ordering of time. He begins with 'within-time-ness' and works toward temporality. Heidegger begins with the deep unity of time and works toward the dispersal of time in 'within-time-ness'.

history'.[33]   Its close association in German with Geschichte links the extension of time with history.   Geschehen constitutes the grounding of historiography.

But this grounding of historiography upon Geschehen is impossible according to Ricoeur. It reveals a basic deficiency in Heidegger's concept of history. Heidegger was faced with the task of incorporating historiography into his scheme of time which has started with the densest ontological time of temporality and worked towards a time that is closest to measurable time: within-time-ness. Heidegger tried to resolve the dilemma by grafting historiography directly upon an ontology of Geschehen. According to Ricoeur, Heidegger fails because such a direct ontology cannot provide a foundation for an epistemology of historiography (422:357). Ricoeur proposes to correct this deficiency by once again taking an indirect route. Once again narrativity is the intermediary to deepen an aspect of time.

What Heidegger overlooked is that fundamentally history is a species - as Gallie has maintained in his Philosophy and Historical Understanding - of the genus story (453:182).[34] If the thesis of Gallie is correct, it means, according to Ricoeur, that the epistemology of historiography, that is, the character of historical explanation, must resemble the traits that are attached to the intelligible emplotment of a story or to the followability of the story. Historical explanations are given us only in a narrative dress or, to use Ricoeur's statement, "an epistemology of historical knowledge (is) grounded on a phenomenology of following a story" (453:183). History, then, employs the same type of explanation as the story. It is an 'explanation by emplotment' (453:189). The thesis, that history is a species of the genus story is borne out by the application to the realm of history of all the traits attached to the story, such as, emplotment, the configuration applied to the events and to the sequence of events, and the sense of an ending. On a structural level there is a homology. The only distinction that one might draw is on the basis of their

---

33.   Ricoeur finds the translation of Geschehen with historial (H. Corbin) to reflect insufficiently the verb character of Heidegger's Geschehen. See 420:357.

34.   Op. cit. The refusal to acknowledge this narrativity in history is derived from Carl Hempel's "The Function of General Laws in History", art. cit. Hempel tried to draw an analogy between the scientific laws and the historical laws. The statement of the law in the determination of an historical event constituted for Hempel an explanation of an event. Both Heidegger and Ricoeur consider the attempt to be a failure, but for different reasons. Heidegger attempts to reroute the epistemology away from the explanatory mode by way of a direct ontology. Ricoeur refuses, on the other hand, to bypass the epistemological stance but grounds it instead in a theory of narrativity. Heidegger overlooked the narrative of history and for that reason failed to find the link between the levels of time and the variety of narrative levels.

referential quality. History claims to represent actual occurences, while the fictional story deals with possible events (453:178).[35] Historicality, therefore, finds its outward expression in two narrative modes, the fictional and the historical. The historical brings historicality to expression indirectly through documents, memoirs, letters and other traces. The fictional narrative brings possible reality to expression by means of the split reference. As Ricoeur notes, historicality appears to require narrativity and narrativity appears to require "the intersecting interplay of two narrative modes. Historicity is <u>said</u> to the extent that we <u>tell</u> both stories and histories" (453:195). Both stories and histories belong to the <u>Wirkungsgeschichte</u> - Gadamer's term for the history of the efficiency - of historicality.[36]

On the basis of this thesis Ricoeur maintains that both the fictional story and history refer to <u>Geschehen</u>, to 'making history'. Both do so by way of narrativity. In other words, what expresses itself in the form of the fiction and history as narrative is existence and time as historicality.

(2) The backward orientation of time.

Historicality, as the extension of time, is further characterized by the weight that it places upon the past. Within the schema of Heidegger, who proceeds from temporality to 'within-time-ness', this orientation of our care to the past is enigmatic. The orientation of care in temporality according to Heidegger is toward the future. This hardly explains why historicality which flows from temporality reverses this orientation from the future to the past (469:22-23). But when placed in a narrative context, the backward orientation of historicality is less enigmatic.

(3) The illimitation of the extension of time.

A third trait of historicality is its illimitation. The extension of time both backward and forward knows no limit. The history of nature and humanity stretch in both directions indefinitely. Again we meet a paradox.

---

35. The ability to attach explanatory procedures to history is not thereby denied. Hayden White indicates that a variety of levels of conceptualization can be added to the "explanation by emplotment". Among others he mentions the explanation by formal argument, the explanation by means of the form of its discursive argument, (e.g., formacist, organicist, mechanistic or contextualist), and the explanation by ideological implication, (e.g., anarchism, conservatism, radicalism, or liberalism). Cf. 453:189-190.

36. Accordingly, Ricoeur recharges history with the power of the imagination. History is a type of story that probes the region of the possible. In history the imagination is made productive on the basis of the analogy of the intersubjective recognition of the other in history as another I. See the informative article of M. Gerhart, "Imagination and History in Ricoeur's Interpretative Theory" in Phil. Today 23, 1979, p.51-58.

While historicality extends indefinitely, temporality out of which historicality flows places a limit upon the experience of time. Temporality, Heidegger argues, is limited, first of all, to the time experience of the individual and, secondly, to the time extension of the individual between birth and death. Temporality is structured by its 'being-toward-death'. Ricoeur will try to correct this too subjectivist and monadic trait of temporality of Sein und Zeit by once again linking these temporal dimensions with a theory of narrativity (469:23-24).

The linkage of the notion of historicality with narrativity is effected by Ricoeur by means of Heidegger's understanding of repetition. For Heidegger, repetition is the fundamental experience whereby historicality as extension, as retrospection, and as limitless is grounded in temporality. For Ricoeur this notion of repetition will help to highlight a dimension of narrativity which might have been overlooked otherwise. On the other hand narrativity can help correct a deficiency in Heidegger's understanding of historicality.

Briefly, the notion of repetition according to Heidegger can best be approached through the notion of heritage. Something is transmitted from the past from which one can draw. This resource is drawn on by going back into the past, by repeating the past, drawing on one's existential possibilities that lie expressed in the past. Heidegger, however, perceives this repetition very individualistically. Rooted in the 'being-toward-death' of temporality, repetition individualistically identifies the source of the heritage to be the self: each one draws from him- or herself the resources of the past and transmits them. In the same vein the past and its repetition approach us as a fate (Schicksal): each one receives him- or herself as fate. This linkage between the repetition and fate is the heart of his historicality.[37]

Despite this limiting character of Heidegger's historicality, which Ricoeur will attempt to heal, the notion of repetition reaffirms the primacy given to the past by history. The retrospection towards the past as fate cannot, however, be divorced from the transmission of that fate as a project. What we receive as heritage is our possibility of Dasein, that is, our project as a movement towards the future. Our future, our project, is what Heidegger calls an 'Ent-wurf', a thrownness. The future is bounded by retrospection, that is, "a re-taking in the manner of being affected by that which we can be" (422:358, my translation).[38] Here again, according to Ricoeur, the limitation of Heidegger's approach is its individualism. It is only after Heidegger has delved into historicality on the level of the monadic individual that he extends fate to a communal destiny (Geschick). But the priority remains with individual fate (Schicksal) over destiny.

---

37. This analysis of Heidegger bears a close resemblance to the relationship that Freud established between the movement of regression and the movement of projection.

38. "Reprise sur le mode de l'être-affecté de ce que nous pouvons être."

Now, by linking historicality with narrativity, these narrowing dimensions can be eliminated. Ricoeur seeks to do so, first of all, by indicating a certain genre of narrative where this is most apparent. He excludes the genre of the quest narrative as the paradigm. He does so, despite the fact that the narrative of the quest brings us to the threshold of historicality. He recognizes that several quest narratives include a measure of repetition. But the success at dechronologizing these stories by the structuralists ought to be a warning against extending the story of the quest as the paradigm of the narrative. Instead, Ricoeur opts for the genre initiated by Augustine in his Confessions (422:362-363).

What form does repetition take in Augustine's account of why he became a christian? Unlike stories of a quest where the repetition tends to be a preparatory phase of the story, in the genre of Augustine's Confessions the temporal form itself is one of repetition. It tells how someone "becomes who he was" (422:363). The movement of time can hardly be confused with ordinary time. It is a "spiral movement which, by way of anecdotes and episodes, brings one back to the almost motionless constellation of the potentialities that the story repeats. The end of the history makes the present the equivalent of the past, the effective the equivalent of the potential" (422:363, my translation).[39] Or as Ricoeur says elsewhere, "The hero is who he was" (469:31). What is repeated in this genre is no more than what I can be. I can be what I have been. Repetition applies equally to historical accounts. They too express how the project of our communal possibilities has reached us (422:363).

But the perspective that this genre of narrative brings to historicality can also add a decisive corrective to a number of Heidegger's themes relating to historicality. These must be examined because they reflect some basic themes of Ricoeur.

First, Ricoeur insists on the priority of the communal destiny over the individual fate. Both Ricoeur and Heidegger agree that repetition is presented to us in the narrative form. However, Ricoeur maintains that the chronicle as an articulation of the destiny of a people is not derived from the private form of fate. Repetition is first of all a repetition of communal destiny. For Ricoeur narrative time is right from the start public time or time with and for others. Narrative time is not monadic and individual time.

Second, this correction, in turn, affects the much more decisive theme that characterizes temporality, namely, communication. If historicality is from the start a being-with-others can temporality remain within the limit of 'being-toward-death'? Does narrativity not also question this private experience which is the foundation of the deep understanding of

---

39. "Le mouvement en spirale qui, à travers anecdotes et épisodes, reconduit vers la constellation presque immobile des potentialités que le récit répète. La fin de l'histoire est ce qui égale le présent au passé, l'effectif au potentiel."

time for Heidegger? Ricoeur hardly takes it beyond this question when he asks rhetorically,

> Does not narrativity, by breaking away from the obsession of a struggle in the face of death, open the meditation on time to a radically different horizon than that of death, namely, to the issue of <u>communication</u>, not only between the living, but also between contemporaries, predecessors and successors...? (422:365, my translation).[40]

Ricoeur insists that by the very fact that the narrative time takes us beyond the death of the antagonists, it also takes us beyond the individual fate and introduces us to public time (422:365). Ricoeur seeks, therefore, to bring temporality beyond the framework of death and struggle and into the realm of communication. In his article "The Narrative Function" (453) Ricoeur provides another suggestion that may help overcome this monadic pre-occupation with death. He introduces the notion of <u>interest</u>. The notion of interest, borrowed from J. Habermas, is the power that underlies and rules the variety of human cognitive undertakings. Applied to the area of historical inquiry, the underlying interest is the interest in communication. History's ultimate interest is perceived as the enlarging of our sphere of communication. According to Ricoeur, the historian does so in two ways. He gleans from the past what needs to be remembered, i.e., the values that rule actions, the life of institutions and the social struggles. And the historian also enlarges communication by creating a distance between one's desires, and, by extension, one's pre-occupation, in order to perceive what is different. In these two ways the pre-occupation with one's own death is engulfed by an interest that supercedes it.

Third, priority must be given not to the self but to the other. The repetition of the heritage is not from self to self, but from the <u>other</u> to the <u>self</u>. It is this that Gadamer has elaborated under the notion of tradition, as the transmission of the heritage from one generation to the next. For Ricoeur this approach of Gadamer has a better chance of building a bridge between the ontology of historicality and the epistemology of historiography. It is the community who ultimately determines and takes up its tradition. This act of the community is a repetition of its origin but at the same time a new beginning. In that sense it is a <u>Geschehen</u>, a making-history. The writing of history, historiography, is the outflow of this historicality.[41] Historiography is founded, then, on repetition which, as

---

40. "En l'affranchissant de l'obsession du combat face à la mort, la narrativité n'ouvre-t-elle pas la méditation sur le temps sur un tout autre horizon que celui de la mort, sur la problématique de la communication, non seulement entre vivants, mais aussi entre contemporains, prédecesseurs et successeurs...?"

41. As Ricoeur says in "Narrative Time", "Historiography, in this sense, is nothing more than the passage into writing, then to critical rewriting, of this primordial constituting of tradition" p.35.

Ricoeur insists, always has a narrative form. But the repetition is of the founding acts of the community that need to be communicated in order to insert me into its otherness. Historiography turns this narrative repetition into a critical inquiry (422:366).

c. Narrativity and temporality.

In the three articles upon which we have based the previous analysis of the ontological dimension of the story, little was said concerning temporality itself. Temporality is the deep unity of time of past, present, and future, or in existential terms, a 'coming-forth', a 'having-been', and a 'making present' before its extension and repetition of historicality and its dispersal of 'within-time-ness'. Its emphasis, as we have remarked above, is future rather than past. Its future is marked by the limit imposed by 'being-toward-death'. As we have seen, Ricoeur transforms this into the giftedness of the other in the interest of communication. At issue for Ricoeur is whether temporality can also be linked to a theory of narrativity. Can narrativity lead us to the depth dimension of time? Ricoeur suggests that this possibility may not be excluded especially since the concept of tradition, death, and repetition may well lead us to a point that breaches the boundaries of extension to its genesis (422:367).[42]

Symbol, myth and narrative have uniquely interlaced meaning and time. To use the terminology of Aristotle's Poetics,[43] these genres are a mimesis of human action. They shape, embellish, and express what is of deepest significance for human existence. To the extent that this mimesis is an active redescription of human existence, they achieve the discovery of our self and of the human community as historical and temporal. A phenomenology that does not shy away from a hermeneutics and an ontology has the added advantage of incorporating the temporal dimension into the process of meaning.

---

42. We need to emphasize once again, that with the linking of temporality and narrativity we find ourselves with the most recent texts of Paul Ricoeur. The work is by no means complete. It is somewhat surprizing, for instance, that despite his hermeneutics of the biblical text he has made no attempt to link the third layer of time, temporality, with the apocalyptic and eschatological genres of the Old and New Testament. The fulfilled time of the stories and proclamatory statements of the Kingdom of God in the New Testament is the time of the giftedness of God's rule of justice and mercy entering into the 'now' of our time by way of the narrative proclamation. The proclamation of the future of God has all the characteristics of what Heidegger called temporality. However, the most recent publications of Ricoeur indicate that his meditation on temporality and narrativity has not ended.

43. See above p.81-82.

CHAPTER SIX: MEANING AND PRAXIS.

Bibliography.

6.   "Le chrétien et la civilisation occidentale" (1946).
8.   Karl Jaspers et la philosophie de l'existence (1947).
12.   Gabriel Marcel et Karl Jaspers. Philosophie du mystère et philosophie du paradoxe (1948).
15.   "Dimensions d'une recherche commune" (1948).
19.   "L'expérience psychologique de la liberté" (1948).
24.   "Le yogi, le commissaire, le prolétaire et le prophète" (1949).
29.   Philosophie de la volonté. I. Le volontaire et l'involontaire (1950).
33.   "Une philosophie personaliste" (1950).
51.   "Note sur l'existence et la foi chrétienne" (1951).
62.   "Vraie et fausse angoisse" (1953).
75.   "Sympathie et respect. Phénoménologie et éthique de la seconde personne" (1954).
79.   "Philosophie de la personne. I. L'existence d'autrui" (1954).
83.   Histoire et vérité (1955).
93.   "Négativité et affirmation originaire" (1955).
95.   "Que signifie 'humanisme'?" (1955).
105. "État et violence" (1957).
108. "Phénoménologie existentielle" (1957).
112. "Le paradoxe politique" (1957).
114. "La philosophie politique d'Eric Weil" (1957).
140. "Introduction" in M. Weber, Éthique et politique (1959).
152. L'homme faillible (1960).
157. "L'antinomie de la réalité humaine et le problème de l'anthropologie philosophique" (1960).
183. "Nature et liberté" (1962).
184. "Affirmation, différence et médiation" (1962).
185. "L'acte et le signe selon Jean Nabert" (1962).
186. "L'humanité de l'homme" (1962).
190. "Préface" in J. Nabert, Éléments pour une éthique (1962).
191. "Herméneutique et réflexion" (1962).
197. "Morale de classe - morale universelle" (1963).
212. Histoire et vérité (2nd ed) (1964).
222. "Prospective du monde et perspective chrétienne" (1964).
227. De l'interprétation. Essai sur Freud (1965).
229. "Existence et herméneutique" (1965).
232. "Demythiser l'accusation" (1965).
234. "Tâches de l'éducateur politique" (1965).
235. "Sciences humaines et conditionnements de la foi" (1965).
236. "De la nation à l'humanité: tâche des chrétiens" (1965).
238. "Prospective économique et prospective éthique" (1965).
246. "Une interprétation philosophique de Freud" (1966).
264. "Philosophy of Will and Action" (1967).
270. "Postscript" in J. Paupert, Taizé et l'église de demain (1967).
284. "Liberté: responsabilité et décision" (1968).

290.	"Aliénation" (1968).
297.	"Approche philosophique du concept de liberté religieuse" (1969).
309.	"La paternité: du fantasme au symbole" (1969).
320.	Le conflit des interprétations (1969).
322.	"La philosophie et la politique devant la question de la liberté" (1969).
324.	"Croyance" (1969).
325.	"Religion, Atheism and Faith" (1969).
355.	"Langage (Philosophie)" (1971).
356.	"Liberté" (1971).
363.	"Le conflit: signe de contradiction ou d'unité" (1971).
367.	"La foi soupçonnée" (1971).
370.	"The Model of the Text: Meaningful Action Considered as a Text" (1971).
373.	"Sémantique de l'action" (1971).
374.	"Cours sur l'herméneutique" (1971).
375.	"The Problem of the Will and Philosophical Discourse" (1971).
376.	"Discours et communication" (1971).
380.	"L'herméneutique de témoignage" (1972).
385.	"Volonté" (1972).
386.	"Herméneutique et critique des idéologies" (1973).
390.	"Ethics and Culture. Habermas and Gadamer in Dialogue" (1973).
391.	"A Critique of B.F. Skinner's Beyond Freedom and Dignity" (1973).
395.	"Le 'lieu' de la dialectique" (1973).
396.	"Science et idéologie" (1974).
399.	"Hegel aujourd'hui" (1974).
405.	"Le problème du fondement de la morale" (1975).
409.	"Phenomenology of Freedom" (1975).
414.	Political and Social Essays (1975).
423.	Interpretation Theory (1976).
422.	"History and Hermeneutics" (1976).
424.	"L'imagination dans le discours et dans l'action" (1976).
430.	"L'herméneutique de la sécularisation: Foi, idéologie, utopie" (1976).
434.	"Expliquer et comprendre" (1977).
440.	"Préface" in R. Celis, L'oeuvre et l'imaginaire (1977).
444.	"The Question of Proof in Freud's Psychoanalytic Writings" (1977).
446.	"Toward a Theory of Narrative Discourse" (1977).
451.	"My Relation to the History of Philosophy" (1978).
452.	The Philosophy of Paul Ricoeur (1978).
464.	"La raison pratique" (1979).
472.	The French Historiographical Tradition (1980).

Ricoeur's original project to construct a philosophy of the will ought to be a warning not to exhaust his work within the representational framework of the previous chapters. Priority in his philosophy must be granted not to theoretical reason but to practical reason. Beside a recovery of the subject on the level of seeing, there is a prior recovery of the self on the level of doing. The home of meaning is not dwelt in and explored only by perception. It is a home not merely to be contemplated or viewed. The home of meaning gathers us even more in action, in a doing, that is properly human. If in perception we encounter a subject who constitutes meaning, after first being constituted by meaning, in the world of praxis we are presented with a subject of praxis which is both source and not source of itself. It is this praxis and the subject of this praxis which we will explore in this chapter.

The realm of praxis, however, is not to be divorced from the realm of theory.[1] Before we delve into practical reason we do well to indicate their points of convergence. In several ways there is a parallel between the creativity of the imaginative variations of the poetic and the realm of possibilities (Heidegger's "my ownmost possibilities") that human action effects and creates. Both my speech and my action are grounded in something anterior to speaking and doing.[2] Both my speech and my action bespeak a freedom and bondage. If poetic speech is bound by what it says, my action too does not shape reality arbitrarily. It too as freedom is bound.

The human speaking and doing, human theoria and praxis, express a human existence that is ambivalently both a nature and an act. Both theory and praxis enroot us in our original world according to which we are not only a subject of perception but also a responsible subject (452(264):61). But in their relationship to one another we must give anteriority to praxis over theory. Ricoeur provides as the reason for this anteriority the new-found precedence in the notion of being of act over nature, essence, or form. The real meaning of being, as Aristotle had already perceived, is being as act. Being is primordially the act of existence. Human freedom finds its source, therefore, not in some type of "essential being, the already completed being, the dead being" (414(183):32), but in a primordial dynamism, in being as act. This chapter will probe this act of being in order to appropriate this primordial dynamism not theoretically but practically. A theoretical appropriation at this level can only be secondary to the practical appropriation. Theory only expresses and orders the emergence of our primordial existence. Praxis is the true realm of the emergence of freedom or of the subject as free and responsible.

---

1.   In "Le "lieu" de la dialectique" (395:95) Ricoeur defines praxis as "la sphère entière de la réalité humaine, considérée sous l'angle de ses prédicats historiques." The insistance upon the historical dimension colours the treatment of praxis throughout.

2.   The questions which Ricoeur asks in his article, "Explanation and Understanding" (434:158) express well the tenour of his concern with praxis, "How can a project change the world? What must be, on the one hand, the nature of the world in order that man can introduce changes? What must be, on the other hand, the nature of action that it can be seen in terms of changes in the world?"

Ricoeur has expressed the priority of the practical over the theoretical in other ways as well. In fact, initially his philosophical project as set forth in the introduction to his doctoral dissertation was toward a practical philosophy.[3] His philosophy of the will which still stamps his philosophical career most decisively remained dominant until his practical philosophy encountered the problem of the symbol and, through the symbol, the problem of language.[4] His linguistic studies diverted his practical project towards the realm of the theoretical. But his proposed "Poetics of the Will" with which his concerns have constantly been baited remains the original horizon of his philosophical oeuvre. In this context, his linguistic studies appear as a great detour to a poetics of the will.

Because of this original horizon, the later writings of Paul Ricoeur have begun to show the inroads of these linguistic studies into the practical realm. Thus, for instance, in the article, "The Problem of the Will and Philosophical Discourse" he voices a dissatisfaction with his analysis of the will in his doctoral dissertation (375:273) by recognizing that an application of a theory of discourse and of the text can be fruitful in the analysis of practical reason.[5]

This search is not yet complete. It is possible, however, to show the principal areas of the incursion of language studies into Ricoeur's philosophy of the will. In his latest writings Ricoeur acknowledges three levels of discourse of the will. The first discourse is the phenomenological discourse of his earlier writings which has now listened to and passed through the findings of the linguistic analysis of the Anglo-Saxon School of Ordinary Language.[6] The first discourse is a discourse on human action. It

---

3.   Le volontaire et l'involontaire, op. cit., p.4-34. In his doctoral dissertation Ricoeur transformed Husserl's phenomenology of perception into a vehicle for an eidetic of the will, i.e., of the affective and volitional aspects of the world, the other, and the body.

4.   The impasse that his phenomenology encountered in his study of symbol and myth in La symbolique du mal makes Ricoeur wonder at the end of the work, "How shall we continue?" (p.347).

5.   Cf. "Explanation and Understanding" (434) and "The Model of a Text: Meaningful Action Considered as a Text" (370). These attempts are still too lapidary and tentative to give a firm foundation to such an attempt. The present chapter will attempt to study this area of practical reason in Ricoeur's latest writings. We have to base our work on a number of articles and the stencilled version of a course, taught at the University of Louvain in 1970-1971 entitled, "La sémantique de l'action" (373). See D. Pellauer, "The Significance of the Text in Paul Ricoeur's Hermeneutical Theory" in Studies in the Philosophy of Paul Ricoeur, op. cit., p.108-114.

6.   "I would say that today the future of this first type of discourse lies in an interpretation of phenomenological description and the conceptual analysis of ordinary language" (375:276).

is an analysis of the variety of ways in which we say our doing. Its discourse is pre-ethical. It examines the various ways in which human beings use language to express actions which have the human 'I' as subject.[7] The second discourse is an ethico-political discourse. This is the discourse of human meaningful action in which we act out our existence and transform existence into concrete freedom. Ricoeur qualifies this discourse as in essence dialectical. The third type of discourse is the ontological discourse on freedom. Here again as on the perceptual level Ricoeur's ontology of freedom is indirect. It is a discourse in the form of an interpretation. Once again, the ontology is fundamentally a hermeneutical discourse (cf. 375:273;396:352).

Before proposing Ricoeur's three levels of discourse of human freedom, I want to indicate where Ricoeur, as an historian of philosophy, situates the problematic of the will and of freedom. Ricoeur finds five major signposts in the history of philosophy that isolate the major thread of this philosophy. They are Aristotle, Augustine, Descartes, Kant and Hegel.

1. Aristotle: the ethico-political context.

Influenced by the tragic poets and orators, Artistotle was the first to force a reflection on human action. He concluded from the deliberations of the courts and of political assemblies that there is a distinction between actions done 'willingly' and actions done 'unwillingly'. Two types of actions are distinguished: on the one hand, actions that depend on me, or done knowingly, and, on the other hand, actions done under duress or constraint or through ignorance of the circumstances. An action willingly undertaken is an action whose roots lie in me and whose circumstances are known to me. Among these actions Aristotle distinguished between those actions which are simply wished, i.e., actions not depending on me, and actions which are preferred, i.e., actions depending on me. Preferred actions are deliberated actions. Voluntary actions are predeliberated. But this deliberation can only be about the means towards an end. The end is proposed by the wish, but it does not depend on me.

Ricoeur signals three contributions that Aristotle brought to a philosophy of the will.

1. Aristotle enrooted the will both in human vitality or desire and in rationality. It is this vitality that feeds our motivation. But it speaks at the same time to our reason. The notion of preference speaks to both dimensions. This joining of desire and reason can be called practical reason. It reveals, however, the double temptation of voluntarism and intellectualism that will plague the subsequent philosophy of the will. The voluntary is a 'deliberated desire' for Aristotle.

---

7. The course, "La sémantique de l'action" examines this discourse at length. Because our concern is merely to indicate the inroads that linguistic theories have made into a phenomenological analysis, the remarks below can provide only the sketchiest of presentations. The real recovery of the subject takes place not in this discourse but in the discourse of freedom.

2. Aristotle placed this discussion of deliberated desire in an ethical and political context. Deliberated desire is involved in the debate of the 'good life'. As deliberated, it seeks a mean between excess and deficiency in actions. This life according to the mean, this life of practical wisdom, leads to a life of excellence[8] and happiness. This ethico-political context was largely overlooked in history, until it was taken up again by Hegel.

3. Aristotle's approach opens the discussion of the will both to a linkage with linguistic analysis and to an ontology. The linkage with linguistic analysis is provided by Aristotle's point of departure: the poets and orators and their discourse on human action. On the level of a psychology of the will there is is a specific language which expresses that psychology, making it accessible to a linguistic analysis. But human decision is also rooted in an ontology because for Aristotle, decision as a human work or task, is an outpouring of the energeia of being itself. Being as power and act is revealed in the will's activity (385:943-944;356:981-982;409:174-175;375:274-277;373:109-112).

2. Augustine: the theological context.

The second decisive moment in the philosophy of the will occurred in the theological reflection of Augustine. Augustine introduced an infinite dimension into the power of the will. In contrast, Aristotle's philosophy of the will, concentrating as it does upon the means rather than the end, stands out as a metaphysics of finite action. Augustine enriched Aristotle's metaphysics by his metaphysics of the desire of God and by his meditation on evil. As Ricoeur says, "Here, voluntas is revealed in its terrible splendour in the experience of evil and sin; the will has the power to deny being, to say 'no', to 'turn away from' God and to 'turn towards' his creatures" (409:176). This posse peccare introduces the notion of freedom into Western consciousness which had been lacking in Aristotle. The will is the power to deny what is true and good. S/he can choose the true and good because s/he can deny this. But as his meditation on the origin of sin and evil revealed, this freedom to act is limited by an impotence in the very nature of man. Freedom is bound freedom.

Medieval theological speculation, according to Ricoeur, aggravated the problem of the will by introducing a parallel divine 'psychology' of God's knowledge, will and power. The absolute knowledge and power of God became the dialectical opposite and source of the finitude of human knowledge, will and power. Consequently, the will was perceived both as the infinite power to say 'no' and the finite power to say 'yes'. The will is finite because of the poverty of the illumination of the will by the intellect and the resisting obedience of the body. This philosophy of the will's finitude was heightened by the speculation concerning the relationship of this all-powerful creative, divine will and the creaturely dependent

---

8. The 'life of excellence' is Ricoeur's translation of Aristotle's areté (virtue).

human will. Is it still possible, it was asked, to speak of a human act-center in the face of this divine will or must one speak of a predetermination or predestination? The paradox which emerges for the Christian West is a human freedom that is bound by something over which we have no control. Freedom is then perceived as a gift, not as the source of itself (Cf. 409:176-177;264:10; 356:984;385:994-945).

3. Descartes: the epistemological context.

Descartes placed the philosophy of the will in the context of the first truth of his philosophy: Cogito, ergo sum. In his search for an indubitable truth to give foundation to knowledge, Descartes subordinated the will to this search. The basic question governing the Cartesian enterprise is "Why is there not only truth?" In seeking the cause of error, Descartes was the first to investigate a psychology of assent. Freedom is the power to be mistaken and the power to give assent to what we truly know. That places the weight of truth as well as of error on the will. The power of knowledge is innocent. When I do not keep my will within the limits of my intellect, it is the source of error.

This represents a dramatic shift in the philosophy of the will. Descartes drew away from the ethical and political realm and limited the perspective of the will to that of judgment, choice and consent, i.e., to a psychological dimension. In the process he isolated the will from the intellect and introduced the problematic of a faculty psychology. But although Descartes transformed Augustine's problem of sin and evil into the problem of error, Descartes and Augustine remain linked in that the will remains for both the power of alternating between yes and no. Thereby Descartes retained the tension between an infinite and finite pole of the will (Cf.264:63;284:156;322:42;385:945).

4. Kant: the critical context.

Kant is the fourth signpost in Ricoeur's philosophy on the will. While for Descartes there is still an experience of the will, Kant removes the will and freedom from the realm of knowledge and experience (373:142-148). Pure reason is operative in the knowledge of the natural sciences. With their natural causality, with regular successions without an absolute beginning, the natural sciences are antinomical to the will and its free causality. This means that for Kant a cosmological point of departure for the free will is excluded. But that also means that pure or theoretical reason can gain no access to the will and to freedom. Moreover, there is no longer a knowledge that would encompass both natural causality and free causality (264(270):63). Natural causality and free causality are antinomical.

But if excluded from theoretical reason, the will is open to practical reason. It is possible to determine the practical conditions of a good will (385:945). For Kant the will can never become a knowledge. It must forever remain practical. But his practical philosophy remains a philosophy. And for Kant philosophy is fundamentally a theory of law.

Hence, at the theoretical level he posits a law of thought founded on the law of nature. On the practical level, there is not a natural law, but something similar: the moral law. Freedom cannot exist -cannot be thought - outside of this law. The moral law is to freedom what the natural law is to nature. As a critique, practical reason's task is to define the necessary conditions of moral judgments.

Because of this constellation the correlate of Kant's will is not, as in Descartes and Augustine the power of contraries,[9] but duty. Because duty is non-empirical, the will is known only as determined by law. The free will and the moral law are inseparable: the free will is the basis of moral law and the moral law is the presupposition of our knowledge of the free will (409:180). Freedom is, therefore, like a third term that is the ground of the will, but which can only be known by way of the law.

But because Kant saw the will as a type of reason, his practical reason banished desire as pathological. The careful corelation of desire and rationality by Aristotle is broken. This exile of desire forces Kant, however, to situate it elsewhere. He does so by instituting a distinction in the will between moral law and desire. Ricoeur suggests, that thereby Kant's critique comes very close to opposing the practical will to the idea of an arbitrary will (Willkur) that is not determined by reason at all. Thus the practical will, governed by law is an objective will, while the arbitrary will is a subjective will. Ricoeur severely critiques this bonding of will and law precisely because Kant's position ultimately leads to arbitrariness: in order to introduce radical evil, Kant had to rely on the arbitrary will, because to the good will of practical reason the 'bad will' can only be a scandal (see 385:945-946;356:982;409:179-180;375:277-279;373:IX.1-14;232(239):   336-341; 29:130-134;373:128-148).

5. Hegel: the dialectical context.

The deep divisions that Kant instituted between nature and freedom, between rationality and desire, between duty and desire, between the objective will and the subjective will, led Hegel to seek to transcend these antinomies. Hegel's dialectical concept of the will healed the divisions by preserving them in a higher unity.

In the abstract terms of the Philosophy of Right the dialectics of the will supposes three moments: a moment of indetermination to an empty

---

9.   Ricoeur sees the will as the power of alternatives also returning in Kant's philosophy but in a manner different from Augustine and Descartes. The alternatives are provided by creating a division in the will itself between Wille, the will determined by duty and law, and Willkur, the subjective will which is the power to obey or not. For Kant this awesome power is purely subjective (289:157). For Kant philosophy is fundamentally a theory of the law. Hence, he posits a law of thought and a law of nature. So there is also a law for freedom. Freedom cannot exist and cannot be known outside of the law. The moral law is to freedom what the natural law is to nature.

universality, a moment of determination by a limited project, and a moment of bringing together the indetermination and the determination into a singular activity. The human will is the encounter of a moment of universality and a moment of particularity. In the words of Ricoeur, "In the concept of singularity the opposition of the universal and the particular is the source of the concrete power of determining oneself" (385:946). For Hegel the will became thinkable again by way of dialectics. Thus Hegel approached the antinomy of rationality and desire by accepting Aristotle's view of will as deliberated desire. For Hegel the will is desire that is overcome by a reasonable project. And, in the antinomy of the subjective and objective will, Hegel proposed that the subjective will must pass through the objective will in order to become itself.

The concrete form of a proper discourse of freedom is examined by Hegel in his Phänomenologie des Geistes. He recognized that the discourse of freedom must pass beyond the Cartesian psychology of faculties or the Kantian concept of duty and law. A concrete dialectics insists that the will in order to become itself must first confront another will and other wills in the form of institutions. There is no free will, until it has been touched by the will of another (Hegel's abstract right or contract). In the passage towards the objective mind, the will internalizes the institutional contract. And, in the passage, the objective mind becomes subjective. But, at the same time, arbitrary freedom becomes concrete freedom or reasonable will. According to Hegel the institutional forms through which the subjective mind must pass are successively the family, the economic collectivity and the political institutions. Only in this successive dialectical process is freedom realized. The highest form of freedom is realized in the State.

Hegel's dialectics will allow the elements Kant separated to be thought together. Thereby, he also returned freedom to thought. For Hegel the will has its own discourse - a dialectical discourse - which philosophy can analyse to obtain its underlying logic. This logic is the logic of being. Hegel discovered a discourse in which nature and freedom can once more be thought together. The other of freedom is internalized. Substance becomes subject. This concrete freedom by way of the institutions is Hegel's greatest contribution to a philosophy of the will. It is practical reason, par excellence (see 385:946;409:181-182;464:235-241;297:413-414;375:286-287).

A. THE LINGUISTIC-PHENOMENOLOGICAL DISCOURSE OF HUMAN ACTION.

Prior to any discourse on meaningful action or on freedom Ricoeur insists that there be an underlying discourse that articulates the conditions of the possibility of that discourse on freedom. He had elaborated such a philosophy in his Le volontaire et l'involontaire (29). But Le volontaire et l'involontaire is strictly a phenomenological discourse, applying to the will Husserl's phenomenology of perception. It was written prior to the development of Ordinary Language Philosophy (Linguistic Analysis) and its theory of action in English speaking countries. The first

155

phase of that development occurred between 1955-60 (434:155f). In his writings on the will after 1960, Ricoeur began to incorporate the analysis of this action theory into his philosophy of the will, bringing about a considerable change in texture.

But, in accordance with a trademark of Ricoeur's philosophy, the introduction of linguistic analysis did not lead to the supplantation of phenomenology. It led instead to the recognition of a number of levels on which the will might be brought to discourse. For him the first level became a discourse of human action. It comprises an interanimated discourse of linguistic analysis and phenomenology. Although linguistic analysis and phenomenology find themselves on different strategic levels, their interanimation can cure their mutual short-comings (373:122).

It is impossible to repeat here Ricoeur's extensive analysis of the phenomenology of the will as he worked it out mainly in his Le volontaire et l'involontaire and of linguistic analysis which he developed most extensively in his La sémantique de l'action (373). We must be content with a few basic points that have bearing on our concerns. The first paragraph briefly outlines Ricoeur's phenomenology of the will. The second paragraph will touch on some aspects of a linguistic analysis of the will.

1. Phenomenology and the philosophy of the will.

The contribution of Husserl's phenomenology of perception to a philosophy of the will concentrates on three dimensions.

1. Ricoeur has shown that one can apply Husserl's justly famous époché to the will. As an abstraction, the époché reduces the naturalistic world of things, facts, and laws first of all to a world of meaning (385:946). In other words, phenomenology is basically an analysis of significations and not of immediate experiences. In order to understand the meaning of willing, phenomenology seeks the 'essences of the lived' or the structures of the experience of willing. Phenomenology seeks to uncover, therefore, the meaning of the lived. It operates out of the awareness that the lived, as constitutive of reality, is pre-predicative (385:947). It is not yet language and at the same time it is on the way to language. For Husserl, these essences are the a priori structures of lived experience. The lived is not bottled up within an individual as incommunicable according to Husserl but it emerges in understanding and even more so in language (373:114). Thus the will also manifests itself in phenomena that exteriorize its life and that possess a specific logic (264:14-16).

Ricoeur's phenomenology of the will is patterned upon this intentionality analysis of Husserl's phenomenology of perception. This means that willing - its acts, its aims and its intentions - becomes available for analysis in its objects. In phenomenology the 'objects' of the will are identified as the world, my body, and others (264:16).

2. What does such an intentionality analysis of the will manifest? The intentional act of the will, the 'vécu de volonté', shows itself

primarily in an act-done-by-me or, more strictly, an act-to-be-done-by-me. It points to a project or pragma to be undertaken by me. The act of decision implies a world that is as yet a possibility and that can be filled with my action. The project of my decision is a project that lies within my power and is attainable in the world. The project says as much about the world as it says about the I by whom the project is undertaken. In the words of Ricoeur,

> The project is inserted into a future of the world, which world includes voids, the indeterminate, the non-resolved; this possible is projected upon the course of events, some of which do not depend upon me and others of which do, to speak as the Stoics... The world is such that a responsible agent bears the weight of a certain number of events which happen because of him; the world is such that it can be the object of provision and of projects (264:17-18).

On the poetic side, the pragma or project is a commitment of the 'I'. The pragma or project brings to language a dimension of self-imputation. In decision the pragma reveals a binding of the 'I'. The pragma is a to-be-done-by-me. I determine a world and in turn am determined. The action can be ascribed to me. "In making up my mind, I impute to myself the action, that is, I place it in a relation to myself such that, from then on, this action represents me in the world" (264:19). I decide but in the very act of deciding - to use a French idiom - Je me décide: I decide myself (29:58-62). This is not a speculative or perceptive act but a practical act. In deciding, I reveal myself to myself as a being of action, as a being of possibility, "It means that what I shall be is not already given but depends on what I shall do. My possible being depends on my possible doing" (29:64). Hence, not only my world is shown to be a world of possibility, but also I stand revealed as a possibility: the possibility of acting (264:19).

3. A third dimension of a phenomenology of the will that we must point out briefly in the light of the above history of the philosophy of the will is the problem of motivation. Phenomenology points out that motivation is another link between the project and the 'I'. It shows this bond with the project to be not a causal link, based on a natural necessity, but a reasoned link. I decide because... The link is called motive.[10] A motive is not ascertainable outside of the decision that reveals it. The meaning of a motive is "tied in a basic way to the action of the self on the self which is decision" (29:67). By the very act by which I project myself into the world as practical being, I also invoke a reason: I do this in the light of...

A motive is not a cause because unlike a cause a motive is inseparable from what is done. A cause, on the other hand, can be known

---

10. On a number of occasions Ricoeur has gone to considerable lengths to differentiate between motive and cause. Cf. 29:66-72;29:347-353;373:II-18 - II-54.

without knowledge of the effect. Motives are, therefore, not pure rationalizations or intellectual arguments but they are supports to willing.[11] At the upper level of motivation we may find rational justifications to give support to willing. But at the lower extremity there lie the needs and drives that almost void the will as a power of projection and make the will appear as a determined movement. For Ricoeur what becomes central to the problem of motivation is that motives make a specific subjective reference appear. The motive, as reason for action, reveals the body as a partial source and an ultimate referent of the will (373:124). But the body that emerges out of this reflection is not the body as object, as separable from my action and, therefore, knowable by itself as a cause, but the body as subjective or as a personal or I-body.[12]

Aristotle had already recognized this dimension when he said that the will is moved by desire. The body is a type of involuntary that is not fully pliable and at our disposition, but which, nonetheless moves us not as foreign to our willing but as the human dimension of our willing (290:81-82). As a consequence the body as 'corps propre' becomes the organ of the act of the will (29:212). In the words of Ricoeur, "This means that the will actually decides about itself only when it changes its body and through it the world. Inasmuch as I have done nothing, I have not fully willed" (29:202). The body is brought to language when the 'I will' becomes expressed as the 'I can' (385:947). For Ricoeur the personal body that emerges out of the analysis is on the level of the vécu - the lived experience. It pertains to the ontological structure of being-in-the-world. It expresses the human manner of being-in. Once again, the phenomenological operates on the level of the meaning of the lived as manifested in the exteriorizations. It is through these that we can read the original constitution of the self (374:126).

2. Linguistic analysis and phenomenology.

According to Ricoeur, linguistic analysis does not add greatly to the analysis of phenomenology. In order to escape the finely honed, artificial language of the sciences, Ordinary Language Philosophy turned to the expressions found in ordinary usage. In the area of human action this means that Ordinary Language Philosophy turns to the language with which people articulate their action. Like the phenomenology of willing, the discourse of action, as analysed by linguistic analysis, is pre-ethical. It is thought - more implicitly than explicitly, because Ordinary Language Philosophy is in principle incapable of reflecting its own presuppositions - that ordinary language is the depository of the human experience of action. It refuses to start with an intuition of human action, but concentrates on the concepts and propositions which language displays to say our doing. The contribution of linguistic analysis to the philosophy of the will consists

11. Ricoeur refuses to see motives only as a type of Kantian practical reason. Cf.373:123.

12. "I-body" is D. Ihde's translation of corps propre. Op. cit., p.28, footnote 2.

primarily in concretizing the analysis of phenomenology, safeguarding it from intuitionism, or more precisely, providing another procedure to reach the same end (373:105-106).

The strategy of Ordinary Language Philosophy presents itself at three levels.

Ricoeur places the conceptual analysis of the expressions used when speaking of human action on the first level of discourse. The concepts that ordinary language uses are intention, aim, reason for doing, motive, desire, preference, choice, etc. The originator of this codification of our language's capacity to say our doing is L. Wittgenstein in his Philosophical Investigations (par. 611, 660). In his recognition of the organization of language in language games, he realized that the language of action is distinct from the language in which we describe movement. Thus, for instance, we speak of an action in the following proposition, "I raise my arm to indicate that I am going to turn left". Movement, on the other hand, is expressed in a proposition such as the following, "The arm is raised". It is, therefore, in a specific language space with interlinking concepts that the question of human action and motivation is expressed. Through this conceptual analysis of action, one learns that the language game of action is entered by a carefully selected series of questions and answers (What are you doing?, Why?, How?) and that this questioning and responding itself takes place in the even larger language game of interaction (373:3-6,21-35;II-1 - II-54).

The second level of discourse of action stems again from Wittgenstein. The second discourse is not a conceptual analysis but a logical analysis of the propositions of action. It is related to the propositional logic of Frege and connected to the work of Austin (How To Do Things With Words), Strawson (Individuals, e.a.), and Searle (Speech-Acts. An essay in the Philosophy of Language). It is termed the theory of speech-acts. Instead of examining the concepts used in our discourse of action, the theory of speech-acts examines the logic of the propositions that articulate action. As we saw above,[13] the theory of speech-acts uncovered the force of language in Austin's distinctions of the locutionary, the illocutionary and the perlocutionary dimension of a proposition. Along these lines the category of promise and intention best express what is known as willing: one promises or intends something to be done into a type of void, which can or cannot be filled. But the theory of speech-acts zeroes in only on the declaration of that intention or promise. The theory of speech-acts submits all the ways in which propositions express the act of willing to an exhaustive examination (373:6-9,36-90;385:947).

There is also, however, a third level of the discourse of action which moves beyond the conceptual analysis and propositional logic. For Ricoeur that level is a type of discursive discourse, a syntax of action. In this discursive discourse one discovers the line of argumentation that a

---

13. p.27-34.

complete discourse of action utilizes. An intention is never a simple act that can be expressed in one proposition. Generally it finds itself expressed in a chain of propositions. It expresses itself in a syntactical form such as "to do p in order that q", i.e., beyond a semantic, propositional "to do p" to a syntactical interlinking with another action, "in order to do q". The discourse of action displays a certain strategy, a sighting of an end through the arrangement of means. This discursive discourse is worked out by C. Perelman's theory or argumentation[14] and in what has become known as the decision-theory and the game-theory (373:9,91-104;385:947). In his conference "La raison pratique" (469:228-229) Ricoeur calls this syntax of action practical reasoning (raisonnement pratique).

3. Critique of the theory of action.

Ricoeur's evaluation of the discourse of action of linguistic analysis is rather harsh. He allows that as an analysis of the concepts, of the logic, and of the argumentation of action, linguistic analysis can throw light on the lived experience of the phenomenology of willing to the extent that that lived experience is an expressed experience. But strategically phenomenology and linguistic analysis operate on different levels. The former operates on the level of the lived, because it seeks to reach the level of the Lebenswelt. The latter operates only on the level of the articulation of discourse without reflecting on its presuppositions and its carrying ground. There is a level, therefore, on which phenomenology and linguistic analysis are contiguous, but the interanimation of both is minimal. Linguistic analysis cannot think its own presuppositions. It is too bound to a positivistic logic to recognize the need to enter into the pre-predicative source of willing. Ricoeur says that the description and analysis of the will of linguistic analysis is unproblematical. It fails to understand that the problem is not the analysis of the concepts, the propositions, and the argumentations of the discourse of action, but the realization of our freedom (385:947). Only when a will is confronted with other wills, with historical norms and with institutions, does the problem of the will surface not as psychological but as philosophical (373:105-127).

B. THE DISCOURSE OF MEANINGFUL ACTION.

1. From solipsism to meaningful action.

The discourse of action of phenomenology and linguistic analysis is not yet an ethical discourse. The phenomenology of decision, motivation, and self-imputation provides the conditions of ethical discourse, but it does not enter the real arena of ethics or of meaningful action. Ricoeur calls the phenomenological moment the "solipsist moment of freedom" (322:42). The phenomenology of the voluntary and the involuntary hardly leaves the circle of my decision, my motivation, my action, my limitation imposed by my

---

14. See C. Perelman and L. Olbrechts - Tyteca, Traité de l'argumentation, Paris, 1958, 2 vol.

character, my birth, and my unconscious. While it reflects my action and my power, it remains abstract and arbitrary. The phenomenological reduction to help open up the lived experience neutralizes another dimension of action which is called meaningful action (373:130-132;322:42-47).

If in his earlier philosophy Ricoeur was not so aware of this negative dimension of the phenomenological époché, in his later philosophy he frequently expresses the limitation of a phenomenological approach to the will as it is based on a phenomenology of perception. He realizes that every phenomenology in the final analysis remains bound to a phenomenology of perception, even his own Le volontaire et l'involontaire. It cannot loosen itself from the subjective view of decision, suggesting that freedom is ultimately a subjective self-determination. As such it explores only one dimension: the Kantian Willkur which, as we saw above, must be distinguished from an objective Wille (284:161-163). This philosophy of the will has its roots in Stoic philosophy, according to Ricoeur. Stoicism was not able to place choice and preference in a political context, as Aristotle had done, but located them instead in a psychological and moral context, based on the power to give or refuse assent. Strengthened by Descartes and Kant, this philosophy of interiority came to exist alongside a political philosophy that concerned itself almost exclusively with power and sovereignty (Machiavelli, Hobbes), but which lost all reference to the life of excellence and the rule of prudence as Aristotle had first perceived it (322:45).

If the ethical moment is not found in a phenomenological or analytic framework, the discourse on meaningful action will, of necessity, take on a fundamentally different mode of discourse. It must transcend the phenomenological solipsism and confront human reality from the perspective of what it is not but might become. Such an approach is dialectical, because what is not yet opposes itself to the what is in such a manner that the former can be productively appropriated by an individual in his process of becoming (see 395:92). This dialectical discourse of ethics is thoroughly historical. It falls, therefore, under the regime not of action but of praxis, that is, the regime of human reality precisely as historical (395:95).[15]

Despite this Hegelian note in the discourse of meaningful action, Ricoeur maintains that Kant still determines the discussion today beyond Hegel. The criticist approach of Kant, in spite of its limitations, released the problematic of freedom in the clearest terms. The Kantian antinomies of nature and freedom, of duty and freedom, of subjective and objective will, of desire and practical reason, will for that reason return in Ricoeur as the touchstone of an authentic analysis (264:20-21). Once again, a philosophy of the will is to be achieved for Ricoeur only within a history of philosophy (451:54).

---

15. For Ricoeur the core dialectical reality is the human reality. Hegel had refused to give priority to any of the three dialectical realities of logic, nature, and human reality. Ricoeur is less cautious. Without falling into the trap of an Hegelian type of absolute knowledge, Ricoeur points to human praxis as the privileged area of dialectics (395:94).

2. Ricoeur's reflective context.

Kant's moral philosophy, weighted as it is by the problematic of theoretical reason, constituted the notion of duty and law as the non-theoretical pole of freedom. In opposition to this antinomy, which has set the tone for the contemporary discussion of morality, Ricoeur indicates a point of departure for ethics that precedes a moral philosophy. He grounds ethics in a movement anterior to duty and law. For Ricoeur the Kantian a priori structure of duty and law is only a derived structure. Ethics is not first of all obedience to a law but an affirmation of life and existence. Before we enter into the objective moment of ethics, where Ricoeur will introduce the notion of law, we must attempt to construct the conceptual network that might indicate the proper moment for such a discussion of law.

a. The ethical point of departure: the human desire and effort to be.

Ricoeur's ethical quest begins with an affirmation or a belief (cf.324:171-176). It is affirmed against all the philosophers of negation since Hegel that the first human reality is not a denial or void or nothingness but being and existence (212(93):305). Ricoeur calls it the primary affirmation. He has borrowed the notion of this primary or originary affirmation from J. Nabert, a philosopher who has had a pervasive influence upon Ricoeur's thought, even in his latest writings (see 405:178).[16]

The originary affirmation is not an a priori. For both Nabert and Ricoeur it is diffusely present in our experience through feeling (152:209). Its diffuseness in our feeling does not permit us to grasp this originary affirmation immediately or directly. As Ricoeur shows at length in L'homme faillible (151) and elsewhere, such a belief or affirmation is only recovered in experiences of negation and lack, e.g., K. Jasper's limit-situations. It is the experience of anguish, of death, of fault, failure, and solitude, that calls for an exercise of reflection that seeks to reconcile or, at least, to confront within ourselves a seemingly contradictory feeling. On the one hand, the experience of fault, failure and death appear to confirm a relationship within ourselves to non-being, to negation. On the other hand the experience of the threat to our existence underscores an "intense passion for existence" (83(62):288). The anguish of death, the non-necessity of my being there, the experience of my finitude, the experience of my

---

16. The major works of Nabert that have stimulated Ricoeur's reflective philosophy are L'expérience intérieure de la liberté, Paris, P.U.F., 1924; Éléments pour une Éthique, Paris, P.U.F., 1943, for whose second edition (Paris, Aubier, Éditions Montaigne, 1962). Ricoeur wrote the preface (p.xvii - xxviii); Essai sur le mal, Paris, P.U.F. (Collection Épiméthée), 1955, of which Ricoeur wrote a review ("'L'essai sur le Mal' de Jean Nabert" in Esprit 25, 1957, p.124-135). After Nabert's untimely death Ricoeur helped to edit his unfinished manuscripts in a volume entitled, Le désir de Dieu. For other articles in which the influence of Nabert is evident cf. 83(62),83(93),184,185,190,380.

violence, cannot hide that at the core of my existence there is also another dimension: my passion to exist. This passion to exist is more original than the dread and anguish of existence. For Ricoeur this passion to exist is the root of all acts (83(62):301). It is the root of the regulative idea that being is primordially good and that evil is not co-original with ourselves. Accordingly, the human being is a power of affirmation, a "Joy of Yes in the sadness of the finite" (152:215; see 212(93):305). But the human attests to this passion only in negation.

For Ricoeur this negation is not founded on the Hegelian limitation and denial of the absolute in its exteriorization, but in the operation of distinguishing. The language of negation is the language of otherness. For instance, in perception the act of signifying means to make distinctions, e.g. between form and substance or between substance and qualities. On the level of existence too there is the otherness of distinction. We differ from ourselves, i.e., we are not ourselves. Spinoza called this otherness the "sadness" (212(93):318). This "sadness" affects the very passion for existence. For Ricoeur, this contingency, this lack of existence in the very desire for existence, is the constitutive dimension of my existence as finitude. The human being is a being that needs to be. Freedom manifests this nothingness at the very heart of existence (414(183):32). It apperceives itself as being without that which necessitates it, as being without a cause, and yet as an exigency to be itself a source. It is this affirmation of being that grounds human existence, but only in the experience of a difference, of failing to live up to itself. Human existence is an act, therefore, whose meaning is not immediately available, but which must constantly be recovered in its negations (186:322). This act of existence always remains a task of understanding, without ever achieving itself (380:59). Or as Ricoeur says it cryptically, "I am not what I am" (212(93):311).

Ricoeur articulates this foundation of the "I am", "the being in question in man's being" (152:210), particularly subsequent to his analysis of Freud, as the desire and effort to be. Human existence, he says, is both an effort and a desire. It is an effort - Spinoza's conatus - because existence must be posited only out of itself (320(246):170). Effort is the positive act whereby we constitute or posit our existence and being. This affirmation of our existence seeks nothing other than the duration of existence. We are this constituting affirmation. However, in a variety of ways, this affirmation is threatened. Human existence consists in the constant effort to appropriate and the reappropriate this original affirmation, even though it is in fact inalienable, since it is our being itself. It is the energy of human existence (320(232):342). But in the light of the presence of non-being in our very being, the effort (conatus) of existence, in its alienation from itself, is at the same time a desire (320(325):462). Desire here has the meaning of Plato' and Freud's eros, i.e., a lack or need. It is the non-being, the negation of being, in the very heart of existence that makes the self-constituting effort simultaneously a desire to be in the face of the manifold alienations of life (320(325):452). Human existence is the effort and the desire to be (320(229):21).

But having established this primary affirmation, we have not yet attained the ethical dimension. For Ricoeur two further dimensions need to be added. First, as the effort and desire to be stretch into human duration it is forced to speak and manifest itself in human works (444:185;320(229):20-21). Energy and desire attain meaning through their transformation into the words and works of human action and ultimately into the production of human culture.[17] For Ricoeur this externalization and objectification is essential. There is no direct intuition of our existence, no immediate grasping of our existence, except through its coming to be in the language and the works of our effort and desire to be. Secondly, it is this appropriation in words and works of the effort and desire to be that Ricoeur, following Nabert and Spinoza, calls ethics. In ethics we encounter the attempt to recover our existence as desire and effort by means of the signs (significations) of existence. Across the lack of identity, the alienation, the negation of being, ethics seeks to appropriate and re-appropriate our existence. Ethics leads, therefore, from alienation to freedom (227:45), from slavery to beatitude (320(232):340). That is why in these writings Ricoeur identifies ethics with philosophy, i.e., with the "exemplary history of the desire to be" (320(185):219;227:45;326(191):329).

This ethical philosophy bears the stamp of reflective philosophy. It sets itself as task to take hold of existence, of the "I am" of the effort and desire to be, by way of the signs by which it manifests itself (190:xviii). Because we do not possess ourselves immediately in one total act of existence, we have to take the long and arduous route of the "I am" in which the "I" has objectified itself. The "I" must lose itself in order to regain itself (320(191):327). The reflective task to gain oneself through the detour of the interpretation of the signs and works in our history is essentially the ethical task (190:xxi).[18] The ethical task is the becoming of what one is, (186:322), the "education of desire" (320(309):474).

b. The condition of meaningful action.

The project of the recovery of the self through the pathway of an appropriation of that which we lost, or of that from which we have become separated through our history, our guilt, or our forgetfulness, is also a pathway to the realization of our freedom. Freedom is the second notion at the source of ethics.

Kant made us aware that freedom is beyond the realm of knowledge and pure reason. It does not add anything to our knowledge. Freedom is practical without ever being able to supply a proof of itself.

---

17. Here again we encounter the enigmatic relationship between bios and logos. Again Ricoeur turns to the language of Nabert to discover its language.

18. According to Ricoeur, Kant created an illusory ethics by dumping desire from his moral philosophy in favour of reason. It is the major drawback to Kant's moral project:320(232):336.

Freedom must, therefore, be constituted in the works of freedom (375:281-282). But before I can undertake the positing of my freedom, I must believe that I am free, "I can only begin from the belief that "I can," and that I am what I can do, that I can do what I am" (405:176). The unfolding of our effort and desire in action is a task of this freedom and this belief. Freedom is a power to be that shows itself in a doing and not in a knowing. Freedom is a doing that is not in possession of itself except by means of the long duration (405:177) and through what the doing establishes in the world (264:19).

The belief of freedom is that it can contest the "real" (212(93):322). Therefore, that from which freedom wrests itself cannot be such that it is immutable. Reality must be such that freedom is possible. It cannot be an immovable nature, but it must be a dunamis, a potency, a lack in the wealth of existence. Freedom implies a void that the project of my decision can fill. Freedom is therefore, a conquest of our humanity over a nature which is antinomical to it without being an irreconcilable opposite. That is why the will, according to Ricoeur, is the terre natale of dialectics (395:98). What Kant had so diligently dichotomized, a philosophy of freedom must relate dialectically (373:ix -13). The dialectic of nature and freedom makes nature both the "other" of freedom and the mediator of freedom (see 414(183):24).

This dimension of freedom becomes even more paradoxical when we consider that not only is freedom a conquest of nature, but also that freedom must first assume nature before it can realize itself as freedom. Freedom must become like a second nature. Freedom is its own task to realize itself. This too is the ethical project. In the words of Ricoeur,

> I will call ethics therefore this movement (parcours) of actualization, this odyssey of freedom across the world of works, this proof-testing of the being-able-to-do-something (pouvoir-faire) in effective actions which bear witness to it. Ethics is this movement between naked and blind belief in a primordial "I can", and the real history where I attest to this "I can" (405:177).

Freedom does not exist, therefore, outside of its objectification in works. Freedom that does not take on the form of a habit, that does not solidify itself in works and institutions, that does not first lose itself, remains an arbitrary freedom. Only at the conclusion does freedom become my own and ethics the flowering of my nature (414(183):37;414(95):75-76).

c. The imagination as the power of the possible.

If freedom is the irruption of the possible into our world, the power of that projection lies in the imagination. It is in the imagination that the movement of our effort and desire to be takes form. We noted above that for Ricoeur, following Kant, the imagination is the power of opening up meaning, the mediator between the bios and the logos, the

creative intrusion into the realm that lies prior to our language.[19]   As
Ricoeur says in "Hegel aujourd'hui", "The project of being free of man is less
dependent on knowledge than on the imagination" (399:353).

Without repeating what we developed earlier concerning the
linkage between imagination and semantic innovation, it is obvious that the
imagination, as the mediary function, extends beyond the theoretical
dimension into the practical.   The semantic innovation, operative in the
metaphor and by extention in fiction, implies a redescription of reality not
solely in the area of perception but also in the realm of human action.

For Ricoeur the images, the possibles, of imagination are first of
all linguistic realities.   The emergence of the new in the imagination is a
linguistic phenomenon.   The new is apperceived in the semantic clash upon
the ruins of the first reference.   It is, therefore, the power of the metaphor
and of fiction to bring about a redescription, a remaking, of reality, opening
up the realm of my ownmost possibilities.   Now some fictions possess the
power to remake human action.   This power lies first of all not in the
structure of the story but in the narrative act.   In the telling of the story,
we activate not only the force of language, its illocutionary power, but also
the power of the imagination.   The referent of the story is the human
action, even though, in the case of already existent narratives, it repeats for
the reader/listener what has been redescribed already (424:216-217).

Ricoeur extends this power of the imagination to the realm of
action by relating the imagination to the project and the pragma, to the
motivation, and to our being-able-to-do-something.   Phenomenologically I do
not appropriate these powers except by the long route of the
exteriorizations of this power.   These exteriorizations are the imaginative
variations of the "I can".   Hence, as Ricoeur says, one may discern "in the
freedom of the imagination, that which might be the imagination of
freedom" (424:218).

But, with what we have said thus far about the imagination, we
have gone only part of the way.   We must pass beyond the imagination
perceived on the level of the individual and attempt to immerse the
imagination in the social realm as well.   After all, it is not in my solipsism
that freedom realizes itself, but in myself as social being.   In a philosophy
such as Ricoeur's, where understanding is equated with self-understanding,
the movement from the subject to the other and from the other to
institutions and collectivities is weighted by a number of problems.   The
state and the other can be approached only from the perspective of a theory
of intersubjectivity.   In this Ricoeur remains faithful to Husserl as the latter
developed this concept of intersubjectivity in his Fifth Cartesian Mediation.

This theory of intersubjectivity requires some attention because
it has become central to a number of theses in Ricoeur's work.   The passage
from the individual subject to the other and the collectivity cannot be

---

19.   See above p.75-79.

brought about by some means of argumentation or by an empiricism. For Ricoeur, the movement toward the other and others is first of all an historical movement.

Historical experience involves a number of temporal fields (472:10-11). These fields, whether perceived at the individual level as a type of "histoire événementielle", or as the history of "slow rhythms" with its "long time-span", or as the history of what has become known as the "geographical time", are related to one another. As Husserl remarked, these temporal fields can be paired. In the pairing of one temporary field with another, the subject apprehends the subject of another temporal field as having the same capacity to say "I" as I have. This coupling of temporal fields relates me therefore not only to my contemporaries but also, as Alfred Schutz saw, to my predecessors and to my successors (422:686-689).

The transcendental principle that governs this historical chain is the principle of analogy.[20] It proposes that temporal fields are not unlike mine, or that "others, all these others, before, with, and after me, are egos as I am an ego; that is, they, like me, can ascribe their experience to themselves" (422:688). It is the imagination that plays a constitutive role here. Just as in the theory of metaphor the imagination is the operative power in forging new meaning, so in the practical sphere it is the power of forging intersubjectivity through an analogical apperception. The imagination must keep alive intersubjectivity on the basis of the analogy of the ego, preserving it from sliding into reified relations or into causal explanations.

But what is the form and the role that the other, the institution and the state play in the realization of my freedom? How does our social imagination operate to forge my ownmost possibilities?

3. The building-blocks of an ethical theory.

a. The ethical point of departure: the other.

For Ricoeur the ethical moment of freedom must move us beyond the subjective description and analysis into the realm of what he has called "the ethic of the second person" (75:380, cf. also 79:289-297). What was presented in the previous praragraph was solely the ethical principle. The ethical content has not been injected yet (405:178).

How does the other, the second person or my alter ego - introduce the ethical moment? The other encounters me not as an object that I can make my own (108:211-212). I cannot see the other (75:381). That is why Descartes failed to recover the other after his doubting

---

20. Gadamer's wirkungsgeschichtliches Bewusstsein, says Ricoeur, is equally subject to this principle. It helps to apprehend why we can have an historical experience and why we can continue to be affected by the effects of history. Cf. 424:221.

experiment. I can only apperceive the other (75:381;440:11). The other encounters me as an other "I". The other is other and yet similar. The other is linked to me, yet is not "I". Kant identified this link (Husserl's term was Paarung) as respect. Ricoeur borrows this notion of Kant (152:105-121). For Kant the other is an event of practical reason. The other is given to my attention as a duty to recognize him or her as other and yet equal. The other is a call to recognition, "The other is a center of obligation for me, and the obligation is an abstract abridgement of possible behaviour toward another" (76:388, my translation).[21] Ricoeur terms this respect person. In other words, he does not develop respect in the direction of law and obligation.[22]

This meeting of another as person is fundamentally a self-limitation. It calls upon me to recognize him or her. Ricoeur accordingly calls the person a project (152:107), an "is-to-be" (152:110), which his or her presence asks me to accomplish. A person can never be a means, only an end. "I ought to treat myself and others as an end" (157:399). This is the task that Kant called humanity: to let the other and myself be as my ultimate project (75:389). In letting you, the other, be, I let your freedom be. Fundamentally, this is an auto-limitation. In letting your freedom be, I will to limit the extent of my own desires. I will to respond to the other as person, as task to establish his or her freedom.

For Ricoeur, ethical existence begins where I curb my desires in the recognition of the other.

Ethical freedom is not a claim which proceeds from me and is opposed to any control, it is, rather, a demand which is addressed to me and which proceeds from the other: allow me to exist in front of you, as your equal! (391:174)

I recognize the right of the other to exist and thereby oblige myself to exist according to that right.

---

21. "Autrui est un centre d'obligation pour moi, et l'obligation est un abrégé abstrait de comportements possibles à l'égard d'autrui."

22. Ricoeur borrows the notion of respect from Kant and places it in the context of person. Kant himself, however, had developed respect in the context of law. Cf. Adri Geerts, "Het fundament van de ethiek en de opbouw van de ethische intentie volgens Paul Ricoeur," in Tijdschrift voor filosofie, 40, 1978, p.270-305, esp. p.282. See also Stephen Skousgaard, Language and the Existence of Freedom. A Study in Paul Ricoeur's Philosophy of Will. Washington, D.C., University Press of America, 1979. This work presents a chronological analysis of Ricoeur's Philosophy of the Will up to La symbolique du mal. The author passes too quickly, however, to the kerygmatic perspective of freedom, bypassing Ricoeur's notion of concrete freedom.

The curb that I place upon myself by letting your freedom become my task must take into account that this self-limitation takes place in the context of conflict. Negation also mediates here. Within the ethical context it is not sufficient to focus on the inadequacy of ourselves to become. This lack of selfhood is only one aspect. To it must be added that the realization of my freedom through your freedom has taken place, as Hegel realized so clearly, in the struggle and conflict of the other to be recognized. Therefore, the dialectic of freedom and conflict has a very specific history: the history of the struggle for freedom in the face of oppression (405:179). Freedom emerges in history as a demand for emancipation from oppression and for mutual recognition (75:394-396).

It might be important to note that Ricoeur thinks that the word has a powerful influence upon the history of our freedom. Ricoeur believes that our will and our quest for freedom can be fundamentally touched by the word. As a "positive, vital reality", the word is bound to the very core of my existence.

> Word has the power to change our understanding of ourselves. This power does not originally take the form of an imperative. Before addressing itself to the will as an order that must be obeyed, word addresses itself to what I have called our existence as effort and desire (320(325):454).

The power of the word and its relation to existence will be taken up more extensively in the final chapter.

b. The duplication of wills.

With the recognition of the freedom of another we have not yet reached the full dimension of ethics, only its point of departure. Ricoeur's second step in the direction of ethics is to begin to introduce the objective will beyond the subjective will and intersubjectivity. To realize itself, freedom must insert a dimension of nature in its bosom. Thus, for instance, the confronting of two wills over a piece of property can lead to a common will whereby the one commits him/herself to the other. That situation we may call a duplication of wills or a contract (356:980-981). In a contract a will agrees to bind itself before another will in a type of mutual recognition. That mediation by another will in a contract makes me become objective - a nature - before myself.

This second step shows us a freedom that moves away from abstraction and wild freedom to a freedom that realizes itself in action. It is a freedom that does something. It is a freedom that assumes the form of a work. It relinquishes its indetermination - its desire to be everything - and chooses to become something. It is a choice to accept one's existence as finite

Hence concrete freedom is a freedom which assumes the law of work which is the law of the finite courageously and joyously; to give form and, in giving form, to take form, that is freedom (322:52).

For Ricoeur finitude is an achievement, not a destiny, "Man is man when he knows that he is only man" (414(95):86).

This process whereby the universal, unrestrained will limits itself through work to become a singular will Ricoeur describes by means of Hegel's Philosophy of Right. For Hegel the will is fundamentally dialectic. Freedom comes into existence through assuming what negates it. According to Hegel that is what Kant had failed to recognize (464:236). Kant left behind the irreconcilable antinomies of freedom and nature. Hegel brought together in a dialectic on the one hand the "I" that refuses any content in order to remain free (wild freedom), and on the other, a finite existence. By dialectically relating the two dimensions Hegel brought freedom into the concrete realm of human work, of institutions, and of the state (322:52-53).

In his more recent works Ricoeur has turned to Max Weber's notions of social action and social relations to articulate the inclusion of the other in the work of freedom (396;464:230). For Weber social action is an action that is meaningful to an individual because it takes the other into consideration. This social action must, however, have a certain stability and predictability. This stability is provided by what Weber calls social relation. A social relation is "a course of action in which each individual not only takes into account the reaction of another, but motivates his action by the symbols and values which no longer express only the private characters of desirability made public but specifically public rules" (464:230, my translation).[23]

But with these public symbols and values we have arrived at the third building-block of ethics: the institutions.

c. Freedom in an institutional framework.

The third step in ethics is probably the most difficult step. At a time when freedom demands to be set free from the oppression of institutions (464:238), it seems reactionary to maintain that institutions are the royal road to freedom (322:62). Ricoeur makes this third step by articulating freedom as a duplication of wills and as a work through Hegel's concept of right. Right he defines as "that region of human action in which work is presented as institution" (322:53, my translation).[24] For Hegel the

---

23. "Un cours d'action dans lequel chaque individu non seulement tient compte de la réaction d'autrui, mais motive son action par des symboles et des valeurs qui n'expriment plus seulement des caractères de désirabilité privés rendus publics mais des règles elles-mêmes publiques."

24. "Cette région de l'action humaine où l'oeuvre se présente comme institution."

system of right is the realm of realized freedom. For him right is the concept that links both institutions and freedom. Through the concept of right it becomes possible to have a philosophy of freedom that is at the same time a philosophy of the institution and a philosophy of the institution that remains a philosophy of freedom (322:54). According to this view an institution is defined as "the whole of the rules relative to the acts of social life that allows the freedom of each to be realized without harming the freedom of others" (322:53, my translation).[25] Hence the institution is an organ of freedom that is acknowledged by others, guaranteed by laws and protected by public order (322:54).

The institutions of our culture are to be perceived first of all as the concrete realizations of freedom. They are the "being-there" of freedom. Before being sources of conflict (363:189-204), institutions guarantee the flowering of freedom. Hence the familial, juridical, economic, policitical and cultural institutions are fragmentations - liberties - of freedom en route to realizing itself. In the complex task of thinking together freedom and institutions, freedom and the state, Ricoeur seeks the highest realization of freedom - as did Hegel - in the ever expanding and encompassing institutional structures of the family, the economy and finally the state. Hegel's Sittlichkeit, his ethics in the institutional framework, achieves its apex in the political institution because the political realm is the highest realization of the co-ordination of the individual good and the good of the community. It is the task of a political ethics to incorporate the decision-making process and the force to enact the decisions at the level of the community (234:144;114:412-429; cf. also 112:721-745).

Ricoeur, however, refuses to go the full way with Hegel. Hegel absolutized the modern liberal state as the highest realization of the objective spirit. In doing so, he hypostatized the spirit totally out of reach of the subjective spirit. The state as hypostatized becomes an absolute reality, beyond the reach of individuals, closed to intersubjectivity, and subject to the supreme temptation of totalitarianism. To counteract the divinization of the state, Ricoeur suggests that only the principle of intersubjectivity, as developed above, can safeguard the undue reification of the institutions (464:238-240).[26]

---

25. "Un ensemble de règles relatives aux actes de la vie sociale permettant à la liberté de chacun de se réaliser sans nuire à celle des autres."

26. In this linking of ethics and politics Ricoeur follows Aristotle. Yet, he will at a further level, which we must examine in the final chapter, inject an evangelical ethic into this political context. Many of Ricoeur's articles that have a bearing on his political and social views have been collected in Political and Social Essays, collected and edited by David Steward and Joseph Bien, Athens, Ohio, Ohio University Press, 1974, 293p. In these essays one notes the influence of the personalist views of E. Mounier (Cf. also "Emmanuel Mounier: une philosophie personnaliste" (83(33):135-163) and the movement of Christianisme social. See also Politiek en Geloof. Essays van Paul Ricoeur, translated with an introduction of A. Peperzak, Utrecht, Ambo, 1968, 199 p.

Ricoeur's development of the institutionalization of our freedom is quite similar to Max Weber's notion of the social relation, that is, action structured according to certain rules. Action within an institutional framework is action set within a system of conventions. Actions are not private or purely individual, but assume a meaning within the social code in which they take place. Clifford Geetz speaks of symbolic mediation in this context (464:230). As cultural entities, the social code of conventions proposes what is to be done. They are the media through which humans act and interact socially through which they interpret one another's activity. The institutions insert themselves in my realization of freedom as agencies that I have not created and which may not even coincide with my desires, but which are inscribed in norms and values that say to me what I ought to do.27

Accordingly, if free action is action governed by rules which I have not set, we must examine the relationship of the subjective will and the objective will at the institutional level. Ricoeur undertakes this through the examination of value (see 234:145-148;390;405:182-184).

It is in his analysis of value that Riceour confronts head-on the concrete human dimension of freedom. It is the anomaly of value that it realizes my freedom, although value is not the creation of my freedom. For Ricoeur this is the central antinomy of moral philosophy (390:153). Values seem so much the work of freedom, the work of creative spontaneity. Yet, there is an objective dimension to values that makes them appear as a vis-à-vis of my freedom: as duty and obligation. For values are not made by me; they are discovered by me. Even those who appear to be the creators of value in our history, admit that they are not the inventors but the discoverers of value. To live in accordance with values becomes thereby

_____

27. It is important to note that the ethico-political discourse is not necessarily an univocal discourse. On a number of occasions, Ricoeur introduces into this discourse the distinction of Max Weber between an ethics of conviction (Gesinnungsethik) and an ethics of responsibility (Verantwortungsethik) or the ethics of power. The two levels of ethics are indispensible to the well-being of the human community. The ethics of conviction is borne by the communities such as societies and the churches. They seek what is humanly desirable, the moral epitome. In "Tâches de l'éducateur politique" (cf.234:78-93), Ricoeur points to the Sermon on the Mount as the highest realization of such an ethics of conviction. But an ethics of conviction can degenerate into fanatical moralism or clericalism, when it demands sole right in the realisation of freedom. And ethics of conviction must learn to live and interact with an ethics of responsibility and power. This is the ethics of the use of power, or regulated violence and calculated guilt. This ethics of power must respect the ethics of conviction and not identify with it, lest it fall into Realpolitik or a type of Machiavellianism. Cf. for example, 105(83):234-246;140:225-230;235:141; 236;238;270:251;222:141-142;367:74; 405:192;428:64. Ricoeur wrote an introduction to the French translation of Weber's Politik als Beruf (Cf. "Éthique et politique" in Esprit 27, 1959, p.225-230).

more an obedience than a creative spontaneity to situations. But must we leave value as an antinomy between obedience and creative spontaneity? Is there a way of mediating between the vision of value as uncreated essences in the heavens and value as completely originating in the will? Throughout his work Ricoeur has struggled with this antinomy. In his writings contemporaneous with Le volontaire et l'involontaire (29)[28] he frequently raises the issue, but as A. Geerts notes, Ricoeur became more and more pessimistic about being able to determine values more objectively.[29] In the more recent article, "Ethics and Culture. Habermas and Gadamer in Dialogue,"[30] he moves toward another solution. He transposes the antinomy from the axiological level, where the dilemma appears to be unsolvable, to the philosophy of culture, where a parallel antinomy exists. He ventures that a discussion of the antinomy in cultural philosophy between traditions and reason can throw light on the antinomy of values. The discussions in its modern dress is between Hans Georg Gadamer[31] and Jürgen Habermas.[32]

The transposition to cultural philosophy reveals one new dimension. Values are historical. Culture like value is a human work. But, like value, culture approaches us not as an ever original creation but as a heritage, that is transmitted to us in the form of a tradition. Culture is a transmitted heritage that comes to us with a certain force that is experienced as binding. A cultural tradition is, therefore, the authority of the past upon the present. It is in this capacity that tradition comes in conflict with enlightened reason. Tradition is perceived as the violence against reason. In historical terms this conflict is translated into the debate between the Enlightenment (Aufklärung) and Romanticism. The Enlightenment, best articulated in Kant's sapere aude, was a protest against

---

28. "Le chrétien et la civilisation occidentale" (6); M. Dufrenne and Paul Ricoeur, Karl Jaspers et la philosophie de l'existence (8); Gabriel Marcel et Karl Jaspers. Philosophie du mystère et philosophie du paradoxe (12); "Dimensions d'une recherche commune" (15); "L'expérience psychologique de la liberté" (19); "Le Yogie, le Commissaire, le Prolétaire et le Prophète" (24); "Note sur l'existentialisme et la foi chrétienne" (51).

29. Art. cit., p.290.

30. 390:153-165.

31. Wahrheit und Methode, op. cit. and particularly, "Rhetorik, Hermeneutik und Ideologiekritik. Metakritische Erörterungen zu 'Wahrheit und Methode'", in Hermeneutik und Ideologiekritik, Frankfurt a.M., Suhrkamp Verlag (Theorie-Diskussion), 1971, p.57-82.

32. See esp. his Erkenntnis und Interesse, Frankfurt a.M., Suhrkamp Verlag, 1968; "Erkenntnis und Interesse" in Technik und Wissenschaft als Ideologie, Frankfurt a.M. Suhrkamp Verlag, 1969, p.146-167; and "Zu Gadamers 'Wahrheit und Methode'" in Hermeneutik und Ideologiekritik, op. cit. p.45-56; and "Der Universalitätsanspruch der Hermeneutik", idem, p.120-159.

the power of traditions and a call to a revamping of existence along the patterns set by reason. The subsequent Romantic movement was a protest against the destructive powers of reason and an impassioned retrieval of prejudice, authority and tradition. If the position sketched here appears solidly antithetical, Ricoeur will argue that the split is not as radical as it may have appeared in the terms of the nineteenth century.

In the debate between Gadamer and Habermas this antinomy becomes the antinomy of a hermeneutics of tradition, schooled by Heidegger, and a critique of ideologies from its nesting-place in the Frankfurt School. The former views tradition as an authentic dimension of historical consciousness. The latter views tradition as the source of distortion and alienation. The focus of the debate is the historical origin of values. For Gadamer tradition is a dimension of our human historicity and it is grounded in the experience of participation. He argues that in the hermeneutics of tradition there is brought to expression our original belonging to things and to being. Thus historical experience is the consciousness of being carried by traditions. Gadamer points to the distanciation that the modern sciences have interjected between ourselves and our participation in being as the modern tragedy. In terms of tradition one ought to recognize, therefore, that we can never extricate ourselves from history and its effects. There is no a-historical situating of ourselves in a space and time where we might be an uninvolved spectator or an absolute origin. All we can do is to become conscious that we are inserted in historical becoming (390:156-157;386:33).

Habermas' position is that such a captivation by prejudice, authority, and tradition is a distortion of our freedom. He allows that to permit oneself to be assumed by the hermeneutics of prejudice, authority, and tradition is to forget that hermeneutics itself is governed by an interest. In fact, all knowledge production is ruled by an interest. Thus instrumental activity is ruled by a cognitive interest. The sphere of the historico-hermeneutical sciences is ruled by the interest of communication. The sphere of the critical social sciences is ruled by the interest in emancipation. It is the thesis of Habermas that the sphere of instrumental activity, the realm of the modern sciences and technology, has gained such an ascendency today that it has invaded the properly human realm of the historico-hermeneutical sciences and is distorting communication. For Habermas the scientific and technological venture has become ideological in the Marxian sense of the word. As a consequence the tradition of the historico-hermeneutical sciences is not a bearer of the value of freedom, but it distorts the communication of freedom.

Habermas assigns the task of unblocking the distorted communication to the critical social sciences. These critical social sciences are guided by their interest in emancipation. The interest in emancipation, according to Habermas, is not derived from the past tradition. For him it is a regulative idea. It is an anticipation of a future in which the violence, presently hiding the real interests from our consciousness through a censored communication, is unmasked. The process of emancipation as a demand for an unconstrained and unlimited communication is guided, therefore, by the anticipation of freedom. "The critical thinker does not speak as the poet does of "the dialogue which we are," but of the idea of communication which we are not, but which we ought to be" (390:159). For Habermas value comes not from the recovery of past traditions but from the future, from the regulative idea of a communication without limit and constraint.

The obvious antinomy of Gadamer and Habermas' view calls for a dialectic approach. Against Gadamer, Ricoeur suggests that there is a need to interject a critical agency in his hermeneutics of reminiscence. Ricoeur has provided such an agency by indicating that the distanciation from our participation that takes place in the historico-hermeneutical sciences is not a harmful alienation but an indispensible and productive distanciation. By placing a positive face on distanciation, one provides the necessary opening for a critique and hence a critical recuperation of past traditions. On the side of Habermas, Ricoeur urges that the critique of ideology requires a more sympathetic reabsorption of the past traditions. The past, he says, is more than a distortion of communication. He rejects, therefore, the idea that only the critical social sciences are the praxis and knowledge that bring about emancipation. He insists that the interest of emancipation must be linked with the historico-hermeneutical sciences. Habermas' position is based on the mistaken assumption that the historico-hermeneutical sciences operate only on the level of understanding, and not on the level of explanation, while the emancipatory praxis demands that it operate both on the level of understanding and explanation. As we have seen, for Ricoeur the historico-hermeneutical sciences are interpretation-sciences, operative within a dialectic of understanding and explanation. But even more pertinent to our problematic is the fact that the misunderstanding that hermeneutics seeks to clear up is not far removed from the ideology that the critique of ideology seeks to unmask. Both hermeneutics and the critique of ideology recognize that there is no absolute zero point from which we can survey our bond with history and from which we can start anew. Both a critique of ideology and the elucidation of our pre-understanding are consciously inserted in our historical becoming. Hence both seek to emancipate by enhancing the competence of our communication. For Ricoeur this competence can be strengthened only by a recouping of our cultural memory. If our heritage contained no reference to an unconstrained communication, our emancipatory interest could itself become an illusory dream.

On the level of the appropriation of value this type of interpenetration of a hermeneutics and the critique of ideology would mean that one would insert a critical moment in the very process of appropriating a value. It would assert a value as historical, i.e., found within the very historical process of realizing our freedom. Our world is already qualified as ethical (320(325):453-454). And yet the discovery of a value requires not an unequivocal surrender to it, but a critical re-appropriation. Only a value that has been tested for its illusory and distortive aspects and content is worthy of human appropriation. Only a value, in other words, that has been 'transvaluated" by the interest in emancipation is truly a human value. The ethical life today demands that we move beyond an unmediated ethics into a life process that constantly seeks to achieve its freedom throught the re-appropriation of our past heritages.[33]

The solution to the antinomy of values is fundamentally a practical solution (390:164-165). Let us take the example of justice. In Ricoeur's view justice is "the institutional instrument by means of which several freedoms may co-exist" (405:182). Justice says that I want you to be free. But that means that justice is not a theoretical construct or some type of ethical essence but a "schema of actions to be done to make institutionally possible the community and communication of freedom" (405:182). Justice as a value says that your freedom should be as my freedom should be. That is the supreme ethical situation. But that recognition lies within an institutional and social order. Consequently,

> the concept of value is a mixed concept which assures the compromise between the desire for freedom of individual consciousnesses and the situations which are already qualified as ethical situations. Furthermore, this is the thrust of an action that intends to produce a new institution, but to do so beginning from an already sedimented institutionalized state of affairs. Every value is situated in an order already "stamped" as ethical. In this sense, every value is a compromise among an exigence, a recognition, and a situation (405:183).

To maintain that value is historical is to raise the question of the truth of a value. Can we commit ourselves to an historical value? Is all value not ideological? That is the question that we must now raise.

d. Ideology and utopia.

With the notion of value, historically and institutionally motivated, we touch on an issue that becomes prominent in the later writings of Ricoeur, namely, ideology. The preceding analysis has indicated one level of the discussion. Before we leave this section we must take up the matter of ideology in the broader context of Ricoeur's theory of praxis and of the realization of human freedom. We have left the ethical thrust in the political realm. We cannot leave this political realm without taking cognizance of the mode in which political society receives its social motivation and self-image and promotes itself. Since Ricoeur wishes at all costs to avoid the tyranny of an absolute knowledge, it should not surprise us that even at the level of praxis there is not an absolute appropriation of the self. All understanding is fundamentally historical understanding. All

---

33. The question of evil and the original breach in human willing between desire and the humanly preferable will be dealt with below. For Ricoeur the fault that creates a chasm in human existence (the human as 'intended for good' but 'inclined to evil') is best read through the religious affirmation of the believer in the confession of evil.

understanding is of the long duration. It must be retaken in an endless process of losing oneself in order to gain oneself. A discussion about ideology and utopia can articulate that desire and effort on the cultural and social level.

For Ricoeur, ideology and its correlative concept utopia are the ultimate proof that human action is mediated, structured and integrated by symbolic systems. It is that dimension of the debate that attracts our analysis. Ideology is first of all an epistemological and political concept. We introduce it and utopia here to accentuate three points. First of all we must bring the integration into culture by means of a symbolic mediation into focus. Secondly, this symbolic mediation and integration is to be related to power. And thirdly, the whole area of human praxis must be correlated with ideology in the sense that all understanding is properly speaking historical understanding.[34]

(1) Ideology and social integration.

By introducing values into a social, institutional and cultural context, Ricoeur has no difficulty in linking values with norms, imperatives and laws. Value which promotes the praxis of your freedom, my freedom and our freedom does not always coincide with my desire. Consequently, value appears as the preferable over the desirable. Then value approaches my desire as a force and is expressed in negative terms as a prohibition: Thou shalt not... Because of this tension between desire and preference, I experience value as a norm. This does not mean that the value is negated. It means very succinctly that I will to be one will in the face of desires in order to protect value from subjective arbitrariness. Through the mediation of norms I change from an arbitrary will to a rational will (405:184-185).

The imperative attaches to this norm the element of command: "Do this!" (405:185). At this level values are objectified into a system and a hierarchy of values and appear as the other of my freedom. In the imperative I lose the consciousness of being author of my freedom. I relate to value in a relationship of command and obedience (405:186-187).

Law, according to Ricoeur, inserts itself into the ethical process only at this juncture. Law is the "terminal moment of a constitution of meaning" (405:187). Law adds to value, norm and imperative the demand for universality. By law we manifest that our human actions cannot be so far removed from our natural environment that we cannot place our praxis and rationalization in the neighbourhood of the rationality we seek in nature (405:187). The test of universality lies in the ability to make a value generally applicable according to the Kantian criterion, "Would I want everyone else to do the same?" (405:187). But the law of nature is only an

---

34. The discussion of ideology and utopia enters Ricoeur's work following the intense debate in the latter part of the 60's and the early 70's on social and university reforms. It is the version popularized by the neo-Marxist Frankfurt School that Ricoeur here interjects into his hermeneutics.

analogon; human law can never take on the solidity that Kant found reflected in the order of nature. By placing law at the conclusion of the odyssey of freedom, Ricoeur has inverted Kantianism. Law is not the first realm but the terminal moment. For Ricoeur the Kantian law is too formal; it is only a didactic criterion. Between freedom and the law Ricoeur felt it necessary to interpose the concrete odyssey to the other, the institution and the state.

One can also express the process from norm to law in sociological terms. There meaningful action can be expressed in the Weberian terms of social action, i.e., the orientation of action to the other, and of social relation, i.e., the motivation of that orientation to the other by means of public symbols and values. Public meaningful action is action governed by a public code that specifies the cultural structure in which my individual action must take place. Hence every culture possesses a system of interacting symbols that regulate and govern the actions of individuals in an institutional framework. Because these systems of interacting symbols resemble a code, they possess what Ricoeur calls a "readability-character", i.e., they can be committed to writing so that in an analogous fashion the texture of action also resembles a text (464:231;370:529-562).

It is at this level of the codification of a political society that the notion of ideology enters. Ideology is bound to the need that every social group has to form an image of itself so as to settle its identity or in order to present itself to itself. This image mediates the relationship of the group to its being. Lévi-Strauss stresses that this symbolism is not an effect of society but that society is an effect of this symbolism (424:223). This self-image is grounded in the founding event that brought this historical community into being. The primary task of ideology is therefore to ground an historical community in its founding act as a type of perpetuation of its dynamism. It is by constantly returning to its origins in a creative re-actualization that a community stabilizes or, one might say, domesticates, itself. Ideology mobilizes an historical community by means of the representations of its own identity (396:331-332;464:230).

Beyond this primordial role of social integration, Ricoeur points to four other traits of ideology. 1. The dynamism of ideology is derived from its role as social motivator. It is a force driven by the desire to show that this historical community has a right to exist. Its project is to keep the community alive in the light of its foundation. 2. It retains this motivating force by simplifying and schematizing the human totality into a recognizable, ritualized, stereotyped prism. Ideology is the kingdom of 'isms':socialism, liberalism, capitalism... The ideology is the view of the whole through a specific prism. Epistemologically ideology is at the level of opinions. 3. The interpretative code of an ideology is not a deliberate creation but much more something "in which men live and think" (396:333). It is operative behind our backs so that fundamentally it is not critical. In fact, it is socially efficacious because it operates unconsciously. 4. This third trait explains why ideologies are by nature difficult to budge. Social groups tend to be orthodox and intolerant of dissenters. The social self-image is deeply ingrained and socially desirable. But this hardening of the social reality can also become a stumbling block in the realization of freedom.

(2) Ideology as legitimation.

There is, however, a second concept of ideology. Beyond being a symbolic mediation of social integration, ideology is also an instrument legitimizing a given system of authority. What ideology does best is to interpret and justify the human relationship to authority and power. Max Weber again provides the analysis. All authority, he says, needs to legitimate itself. Every phenomenon of domination brings together, on the one hand, the claim to legitimacy and, on the other, the belief in that legitimacy by the individuals subject to that authority. The relationship between the claim and the belief is dissymetrical in the sense that the claim to legitimacy surpasses the belief in the legitimacy. It is this surplus - Ricoeur calls it the "plus-value de créance" (430:54, note 11) - that the ideology needs to legitimate. But his legitimation is never apparent or transparent because the phenomenon of authority operates of necessity with an opacity (396:336). In fact, ideology legitimates and therefore motivates best when it is not perceived as a legitimation.

(3) Ideology and illusion.

The above concept of ideology is untainted by the pejorative connotation that ideology has received from Marxist philosophy and in the critique of ideology of the Frankfurt School. The Marxist concept of ideology adds to the preceding concepts the notion of distortion and the reversal of the real into an illusion.[35] For Marx there is a reversal of the real because a certain social production reverses the real. For Marx, as it was for Feuerbach before him, this reversal of the real takes place in religion. Religion is ideological because it reverses the heavens and the earth. Religion makes us walk on our heads. Real life is replaced by these reversed religious images, so that the religious ideology represents life. Marx, therefore, sought to reverse the reversal.

For Ricoeur's Marx' concept of ideology is valid only if one is not forced to look for a reality that is not ideological. The reversal of the reversal is possible only if the distortion of ideology is exposed. Marx' emphasis is best supported when we see it founded on the need of every social group to be integrated by a symbolic mediation. In addition Marx' recognition that the legitimation of authority which is ideology's principal area of activity is tied to specific social classes and the struggle between classes is valuable only in the context of the task of ideology to provide that legitimation of authority. For Ricoeur ideology is indispensible to social

---

35. Ricoeur insists that Marx' concept of ideology as reversal and distortion gains its validity only on the basis of the two previous concepts of ideology. The very efficacity of ideology in establishing and maintaining social links is the foundation of the dissimulation of ideology. Cf. 424:223-224.

existence. Social existence is founded upon a symbolic constitution and requires an interpretation of itself in and through the images and representations of its social links (396:336-338).

(4) Utopia.

This function of ideology as integration, legitimation, and distortion, is confirmed when ideology is placed in conjunction with utopia. Following the lead of K. Mannheim's Ideologie und Utopie, Ricoeur maintains that the polarity between ideology and utopia is primarily a dialectic relationship.[36] Three concepts of utopia dialectically correspond to the three concepts of ideology.

1. The constituent function of utopia is not to integrate and ground the social relations in the founding act, but to disrupt the order mediated by ideology by means of a project of an order that differs from the ruling order. Utopia is the literary genre that translates the project to a new social order into a type of discourse. Although principally a written literary genre, as first created by Thomas More's Utopia (1516), it is not essential that it be written (430:57). In contrast to ideology, Utopia has a high profile. It does not hide itself as ideology does. Utopia, as described by Thomas More, is the "no-where" (u-topia), where a different social order is established. It is a project of the imagination that creates a new space and time from which one looks at existence as it is ruled by the dominant symbolism and injects into that dominant reality the vision of new possibilities. By rethinking in radical fashion the family, sexuality, government, religion, etc., it contests that which is. Utopia's function of social subversion is exactly counter to ideology's function of social integration (424:225).

2. Utopia's relationship to the legitimation of authority is equally subversive. The literary products that have come from the utopic imagination indicate that the principal area of concern of the utopic genre is power. Utopia, by projecting another society, shows the fragility of the ideology that seeks to bind together the claim of legitimacy and the belief in that legitimacy. By its imagination of another society, utopia exposes the obfuscating game ideology plays to bolster its credibility. Here again, the need of legitimation is kept in check by the projection of another mode of social relation (430:58). The legitimation as well as the power it serves is never absolute.

3. But there is also a pathology of utopia, similar to the pathology of ideology. Utopia can degenerate into the mad dream that seeks to submit reality to itself. Utopia can become fixated into

---

36. The dialectics of ideology and utopia repeats in many ways the dialectics of archaeology and the teleology of the subject which we have developed above. The dialectics of ideology and utopia isolate the historical dimension more clearly than the dialectics of the archaeology and teleology of the subject, however.

perfectionistic schemes and uncompromising refusals to undertake the concrete means to realize the aim of the utopia. Utopic imagination can lead to unrequited nostalgia.

For Ricoeur utopia cannot function outside of an ideological context. Mannheim had indicated that the possibility of thinking together ideology and utopia is based on the concept of non-congruence. Together ideology and utopia refer to the dissonance and incongruity of social and historical reality (424:222). Left without the complementarity of the other, ideology or utopia would hide this fundamental position of historical reality from view. Both point to that essential dimension, ideology despite its attempt to repeat and stabilize, and utopia despite its excentricity, its being "no-where" (424:227). For Ricoeur the tension of ideology and utopia must remain, "The dialectic of ideology and of utopia is open and without end" (430:60, my translation).[37]

e. A non-ideological discourse?

The ultimate question to be asked, therefore, is whether there is a non-ideological approach to reality and to social relations? Could science be such a non-ideological approach? It has often been suggested that it can fulfill that role. But if science assumes such a position, it would remove ideology from its mediating role and ideology would become the mystification of a false consciousness (396:339). For Habermas the sciences that fulfil this non-ideological role are the critical social sciences. Ricoeur rejects the claim that the critical social sciences defuse the system of ideology, because they cannot fulfil the requirements of scientific explanation and verification. Also science as critical science has not shown the capacity to rise above the ideological debate. If, as Ricoeur says, the social link is itself symbolic, it is vain to look for something that might be anterior to images. There is not something like the real, or real activity, or real life, to be found prior to images, if the images are that whereby the social link is constituted. In the final analysis an absolutely radical critique of ideology is impossible because there is no non-ideological place from which such a critique can be initiated.

That brings us to the point that needs to be made about the whole realm of the realization of freedom. There is no possibility of a reflection or a knowledge that is total (464:239). Every reflection implies a point of view, an historical stance. Every social stance is an ideological stance. And that creates an agonizing situation. How does one avoid becoming a cynic or a sceptic, incapable of concretizing one's freedom because every thing is relative? If a total synthesis or a total point of view is not possible, if every view is a point of view, must we renounce all claim to truth and any claim to a critique of ideology? Ricoeur does not think so. There is a middle road, he suggests, between absolute knowledge and absolute relativism. It belongs to the hermeneutical discourse on the

---

37. "La dialectique de l'idéologie et de l'utopie est ouverte et sans fin."

conditions of historical understanding (396:352). For Ricoeur, as we shall see, our naiveté has been savagely jolted out of its complacency. Only a knowledge that has passed through the critique of knowledge and through the explanatory procedures of our time can safeguard us from sterility. Only a second naiveté, chastened by the modern suspicion, is yet open to us (464:241).

But the discussion of this hermeneutical discourse links the ethical discourse to the discourse of perception. For Ricoeur the symbolic text -understood in its broadest sense - is the indispensable detour, whereby the self recovers the conditions of its own installation. If story and history insert us in historical time (355:536), and if ethics too is the realization of our freedom in history, the hermeneutics of perception and action find themselves on a common ground. Both seek to discover the conditions of historical understanding. Because Ricoeur sees this as bound up with the most fundamental problematic of our time: the relationship of explanation and understanding, we must take up this issue at greater length in the next chapter.

C. THE DISCOURSE OF FREEDOM.

Even with the development of a discourse of human action and decision, and the discourse of meaningful action, the discourse of freedom has not yet been plumbed completely. Ricoeur points to a third level of discourse that more strictly examines the enrootment of freedom in being and the various modes in which this enrootment has been expressed in our history. Ricoeur points to three phases of the philosophy of the will in history to indicate three basic modalities of the will. Today we find ourselves in the crisis of the third phase. This discourse on freedom provides a prime example again of how the history of philosophy is itself a mode of doing philosophy and why philosophy for Ricoeur is fundamentally interpretation.

The third discourse of the will is an ontological discourse, i.e., it is a discourse underlying the two previous modes of discourse. Human action, as Aristotle reminds us, speaks to us of a mode of being. Being, he remarked, is an act, an _energeia_, that is manifested in the human _erga_ (works). Being itself is activity. The human 'being' or _energeia_ is manifested in the life lived according to excellence, the life of virtue. In other words, the ethical quest itself refers back to being as act and the ontology of potentiality (Metaphysics, Book 9; 414(183):32-33).[38] This third discourse of an ontology of freedom does not know a smooth transition from

---

38. Ricoeur suggests that the reason why Aristotle lacked a notion of freedom was his inability to co-ordinate being as act with his ethics. In the final analysis Aristotle predicates being as act not of human individuals but of the divine being. As a consequence the ontological and the ethical discourse remain distinct. For the same reasons it can be said that Aristotle lacked the concept of subject and subjectivity. Cf. 356:983-984.

the first and second discourse of the will. It is not a phenomenological nor a dialectical discourse, but an ontological discourse. But as we have pointed out a number of times, Ricoeur insists that today's ontological discourse can only be a broken, indirect discourse. Ontological discourse is fundamentally hermeneutical, passing through the historical signs and traces in search of its roots and its aims.

This hermeneutical ontology of freedom possesses the curious dimension of historicizing the ontology of freedom. The hermeneutics of freedom passes through the history of its modes of being. There it reveals a number of phases which we can identify as cultural phases of freedom's mode of being. As Ricoeur notes, "The history is, in a certain way, the history itself of the modes of being, the history of the manifestation of being" (375:284). This is the deep history of the will that has found a number of ways of surfacing in our history. Ricoeur points to three thresholds that the deep history has crossed. The crossings of these thresholds were axial cultural moments in our history. As we shall see, the terminal point of the historical journey of the will is the will as subjectivity. For Ricoeur subjectivity is the pre-dominant mode of being (375:285).

The first threshold in the perception and functioningof the will occurred when the Greek culture was transformed into Christian culture. It was at this crucial point that the Aristotelian psychology of the will as the choice of means towards an end was confronted by Augustine's view of the will as infinite. Augustine saw the power of the will in the experience of evil and sin. In the possibility of sin the will shows itself to be a power to deny being. The power of the will is an infinite power (375:285;356:984).

The second threshold emerged at the crucial moment of the beginning of modern consciousness. It was articulated in the Cartesian cogito. Here the subject appears as the one before whom the world is a spectacle. The world is the representation before the subject in search of certainty. The ego is the first truth. It is the power to say "yes" and "no". Freedom becomes part of the ego cogito. The "I will" pertains to the "I can". The experiment of doubting is an experience of my freedom. To will and to be free are inextricably related. By snatching us from doubt, the cogito is a profession of freedom: the freedom of thought (356:984).

The third threshold was the achievement of Kant and Hegel. Freedom as subjectivity emerged through the recognition of the antinomy of freedom and nature. Kant's Critique of Pure Reason which presented a nature entirely subject to laws that brooked no exception forced the secession of freedom from the realm of nature. Freedom and nature fall under different regimes. Freedom lies beyond a cosmological framework. Kant therefore placed freedom in the realm of action of an ethical subject. This antinomy of freedom and nature is unresolvable on the speculative level. Speculative reason cannot unify the twofold causalities. It can only know them antinomically. Freedom presents itself as a power that is not cosmological but that can be an originator of phenomena. For Kant freedom is the transcendental condition of ethics and moral reflection (284:163).

But Kant only obtained this transcendental condition at the expense of a ruined cosmology. By distinguishing, Kant separated and left us a split world. Hegel attempted to heal that split. As we know Hegel's philosophy attempted to articulate this in a dialectics. For him the dialectics of the objective and subjective Geist articulates the process whereby substance (nature) becomes subject. If Geist is dialectic, then freedom too is dialectic.

According to Ricoeur, this achievement of Hegel is the completion neither of the philosophy of the will nor of the ontology of freedom. Hegel's Geist remains but one moment in the emergence of subjectivity. It is not the absolute moment: substance has not yet become subject (356:984). Hegel's difficulty lies in his relating of the will and truth. Hegel's truth, we saw, lies not in the present moment but in the succeeding moment, where the present contradictions are reconciled. The final moment has the distinction then of being the decisive moment. It becomes the moment of truth: the final reconciliation. The philosopher who penetrates the succeeding moment more deeply than any other is, therefore, in a position of advantage in the progression of truth (375:287). But history did not prove the truth of Hegel. History subsequent to Hegel - Ricoeur's deep history -reveals the weakness of Hegel's truth. It is labelled Idealism.

With Kierkegaard, Marx, and Nietzsche a new mode of being came to history. In one way, they bring this historical manifestation of freedom full circle. Nietzsche, in particular, shows the ground of being again as an act and power and not primarily as form or essence. But this rediscovery of being as act and power has brought the philosophy of subjectivity to a head, according to Heidegger, and opened up another mode of being. Nietzsche injected into history the will to power as a mode of being. However, the symbols by which Nietzsche brought this will to power to language are not the symbols of subjectivity but cosmic symbols: the Eternal Return of the Same, Zarathustra, Übermensch, Dionysus. The new mode of being was not yet in his grasp - he only announced it. Nietzsche saw subjectivity destroying itself in nihilism (375:288).

But Nietzsche also accomplished something else. This is at the level of philosophical discourse. The problem that Hegel deposited with us was the relationship of will and truth. If for Hegel the truth of freedom is always in the succeeding movement, for Nietzsche that relationship is inverted. He states that truth itself or the search for truth manifests a quality of the will: the will to truth. If truth lies in the will, where do we search for the manifestation of truth and of freedom? Here Nietzsche pointed to the philosophy of interpretation. Hegel's philosophy had attempted to stand at the apex of history, or perhaps more accurately, in the next phase of history from which he could glance back at the present. Nietzsche's philosophy seeks to stand in the midst of an ambiguous history. As we have seen Ricoeur is more sympathetic to this stance. With Nietzsche he can turn only to all the signs that attest to the power of being. And these are found in the play of every-day existence, in its display of intentionalities and in its quest for meaningful action in the ethical and political sphere. Although Ricoeur has not worked out this sympathetic

184

reading of Nietzsche in any great detail, he too seeks only a discourse in the form of interpretation. Only the interpretative discourse can discern the depth-history of human freedom. Only interpretative discourse will avoid the temptation to be more than an historical understanding and to resort to totalitarian violence (375:288-289;356:984-985).

CHAPTER SEVEN: <u>THE APPROPRIATION OF THE SUBJECT.</u>

Bibliography.

83.	<u>Histoire et vérité</u> (1955).
93.	"Négativité et affirmation originaire" (1956).
95.	"Que signifie 'humanisme'?" (1956).
139.	"Le sentiment" (1959).
155.	"L'homme et son mystère" (1960).
186.	"L'humanité de l'homme" (1962).
214.	"Technique et nontechnique dans l'interprétation" (1964).
220.	"Le langage de la foi" (1964).
227.	<u>De l'interprétation. Essai sur Freud</u> (1965).
232.	"Démythiser l'accusation" (1965).
246.	"Une interprétation philosophique de Freud" (1966).
247.	"Le problème du double-sens comme problème herméneutique et comme problème sémantique" (1966).
248.	"Le poétique" (1966).
319.	"Interrogation philosophique et engagement" (1968).
320.	<u>Le conflit des interprétations</u> (1969).
325.	"Religion, Atheism and Faith" (1969).
337.	"Qu'est-ce qu'un texte? Expliquer et comprendre" (1970).
355.	"Langage (Philosophie)" (1971).
356.	"Liberté" (1971).
357.	"Mythe" (1971).
358.	"Du conflit à la convergence des méthodes en exégèse biblique" (1971).
360.	"Esquisse de conclusion" (1971).
362.	"Événement et sens dans le discours" (1971).
370.	"The Model of the Text: Meaningful Action Considered as a Text" (1971).
371.	"From Existentialism to the Philosophy of Language" (1971).
373.	"Sémantique de l'action" (1971).
375.	"The Problem of the Will and Philosophical Discourse" (1971).
381.	"La métaphore et le problème central de l'herméneutique" (1972).
386.	"Herméneutique et critique des idéologies" (1973).
388.	"The task of Hermeneutics" (1973).
389.	"The Hermeneutical Function of Distanciation" (1973).
390.	"Ethics and Culture. Habermas and Gadamer in Dialogue" (1973).
396.	"Science et idéologie" (1974).
397.	"Philosophy and Religious Language" (1974).
399.	"Hegel aujourd'hui" (1974).
406.	"Philosophical Hermeneutics and Theological Hermeneutics" (1975).
408.	"Puissance de la parole: science et poésie" (1975).
411.	"Biblical Hermeneutics" (1975).
413.	"Objectivation et aliénation dans l'expérience historique" (1975).
414.	<u>Political and Social Essays</u> (1975).

417.   La métaphore vive (1975).
420.   "Gabriel Marcel et la phénoménologie" (1975).
422.   "History and Hermeneutics" (1976).
423.   Interpretation Theory (1976).
424.   "L'imagination dans le discours et dans l'action" (1976).
434.   "Expliquer et comprendre" (1977).
438.   "Herméneutique et l'idée de révélation" (1977).
440.   "Préface" in R. Celis, L'oeuvre et l'imaginaire (1977).
444.   "The Question of Proof in Freud's Psychoanalytical Writings" (1977).
453.   "The Narrative Function" (1978).
463.   "Preface: Response to My Friends and Critics" (1979).
472.   The French Historiographical Tradition (1980).
475.   "Herméneutique et sémiotique" (1980).

What has emerged out of Ricoeur's theory of discourse and the text is a dislocated and despoliated subject, who is no longer either the Cartesian self-constituting subject or the Kantian transcendental principle. The subject does not know him or herself. The subject does not know the I that accompanies all representations. Self-consciousness is false: I am not who I am. I am in fact disbonded from my self to which I constantly seek to be rejoined. But the meditation on Ricoeur's indirect ontology warns us that this is not the total story. This dethronement of the subject as the master of consciousness is only the negation through which must come a rediscovery of the subject beyond the Cartesian Cogito. Now while the contours of the world in which the subject dwells have been sketched, it remains to highlight the process whereby this world shapes a new I. The word 'new' is used advisedly. The demise of the Cartesian subject is a cultural event of high significance, because it marks at the same time the advent of a new cultural I.

According to Ricoeur, the process of the recovery of the subject consists of three moments which are dialectically related. The grounding moment consists of participation which is dialectically related to the moment of distanciation. Both moments are taken up into the moment of appropriation. This chapter will examine these three moments and the process that links them. The first section will examine the correlative pair of participation and distanciation. It will focus specifically upon the historicity of human existence. The second section will consider the textual dimension of the distanciation. The third section inaugurates the movement in which the interpretion of the world of the text reveals a subjective dimension of that world. The process whereby this 'for me' of the text forges a new self is called appropriation.[1] The appropriated self is a self mediated by the reading of the text.

---

1.   In the language of Jean Nabert's reflective philosophy, the appropriation is called concrete reflection. Gadamer calls it application.

A. THE HUMAN MODE OF PARTICIPATION.

For Ricoeur, hermeneutics in the broadest sense means the making of the human mode of existence my own. We have insisted in the previous chapters, that the human mode of existence has an ontological ground which is our true being but with which we do not coincide. We are not who we think we are or who we might be. In the previous chapter we have described this enrootment of ourselves and our non-coincidence with our ontological ground with Nabert's concept of originary affirmation and with the hermeneutical concept of participation. As a consequence, all human activity, all human knowing, all human experience, all objectivity and subjectivity, are taken up in this all-encompassing relation of participation (398:227).[2] In other words, the belonging of ourselves to being and to beings - Heidegger's Being-in-the-world - is the primordial hermeneutical experience.

However, the experience is not intuited. It is not grasped in all its immediacy. Participation is human only to the extent that this primordial participation is intercepted and exteriorized, so that it becomes accessible to understanding. In Ricoeur's view, for participation to be human it must be correlated with distanciation (398:228). Distanciation is, therefore, equally constitutive of human existence (413:34). What for Gadamer is the "scandal of modern consciousness" (390:156), is in fact the transcendental condition of every human science, and for Ricoeur the challenge of the contemporary human mode of being. By disrupting the primordial core of participation, distanciation establishes us as historical beings. In other words, the correlative concepts of participation and distanciation are the foundation of historical understanding and historical existence (412:29-30). What does Ricoeur mean by historical existence and historical experience?

Above it was noted, how, for Ricoeur, the historicity of human existence is brought to language in narrativity.[3] In narratives, whether fictional or historical our historical existence and experience is found exteriorized (453:195). What we wish to examine here, however, is the epistemological status of our historical experience. This must be undertaken to set the stage for a proper understanding of the appropriation of ourselves as historical beings.

The principal difficulty of historical experience is that it does not lend itself to conceptualization. Its externalization in narratives is but

---

2. See above p.106-109. That condition of participation is valid for the natural sciences as well. The object of the natural sciences can be apprehended in a primordial sense, because I am first of all among things that I did not make (422:686). It is the ideology in the pejorative sense of the natural sciences that they can be forgetful of their historical constitution.

3. See above p.138-146.

one indication of this. Terms such as objectivity and even experience do not apply with equal rigour to historicity as they do to the objects of the physical sciences. Ricoeur shows this by his exposition of the conditions of historical experience. He does this by means of a critique of Kant's analogies of experience in his Critique of Pure Reason.

In his analogies of experience, Kant concerned himself with the ordering of time. He instituted there the distinction between an objective succession of time in the object and a subjective succession in the representations of the object. In other words, he recognized two successions, one that is ordered and one that is not ordered. Accordingly, there are two temporalities. For Kant, objectivity consisted in the capacity to keep distinct these different successions and temporalities in every experience (413:28). Now, for these successions and temporalities to be an experience, they have to possess two further qualities. For Kant, these temporalities and successions must first of all be ordered, i.e., interlinked into an order; and secondly, be unified in such a way that I can attribute them to me. An experience is ordered and one. An ordered experience is an experience that can be imputed to one consciousness (413:28). Only then can one call an experience one's own.

In this context, is it possible to speak of an historical experience? For historicity to be an experience Kant demanded that the order of the experience be subordinate to the unity of the experience, and, we might say, the unity of the experience subordinated to the ability to ascribe the experience to myself. Ricoeur disputes this. The final condition of experience, he maintains, is not the ability to ascribe something to myself. This self-ascription of any experience must be preceded by the ontological dimension of participation. The self-ascription, Ricoeur says, is not a first, sovereign, constitutive act of experience. The experience is constituted by participation (413:29). With that we are back on familiar ground. In fact, as we have seen, this participation is constitutive not only of historical experience but also of the physical sciences. The initial situation of both is receptivity rather than the imperious constituting by a subject. But how then does the experience of participation in the object of the physical sciences differ from the participation in the object of historical experience?

In the physical sciences, the object can be set over and against me for analysis despite the participation. In historical experience, however, the object is a temporality that I cannot oppose to myself. For it is a temporality like my own. The historical object is not an over and against but a paired (Husserl) object. The other temporality is a subject-temporality, not an object-temporality. The other is subject like me. That means that my temporality is accompanied by other temporalities, all of them analogous to my own. For Ricoeur, therefore, following Husserl, historical experience is first of all an intersubjective experience. This intersubjective experience extends not only to my contemporaries but to my predecessors as well and even to my successors. The contemporary intersubjective experience is, in other words, caught up and encompassed in a larger temporality that relates my history to the temporality of those who preceded me and those who will succeed me. In the language of participation, my temporality belongs to this great temporality. This encompassing temporality is history (422:686-687; 413:29-31).

This encompassing temporality escapes the rule of objectivity proposed by Kant. The historical field escapes the ordered and unordered succession because it is constituted by the immense number of temporal fields which can be placed into the threefold relationships of contemporaneity, precedence and descendence. But, if it escapes objectivity, historical experience does not thereby become irrational. All that it means is that history is not nature, and that history has its own rationality (413:31). It is not the rationality of the ordered sequence. Its rationality is the rationality of human praxis, which, as we said above, is based on the principle of analogy. For Ricoeur analogy is the transcendental principle that can provide intelligibility for the relationship of different temporal fluxes. The analogy does not establish the relationship of our contemporaries, predecessors and successors. It is only a transcendental principle signifying that all others, whether they are contemporaneous, or whether they came before me or will come after me, can, like me, say 'I' and ascribe experience to themselves (413:31-32; 422:687-689).

However, this primordial constitution of my historical experience in participation achieves, as in all cases of human participation, a measure of exteriority. The distanciation of historical experience is most apparent in our relations with our predecessors. Our relations with our predecessors are accessible to us in the archives, documents, letters and monuments that are the external mark of their presence. These present the "facts" of history, never to be reified, but always kept alive in the dialectic of participation and distanciation. It is through these externalizations that our participation with our ancestors becomes understandable. It is also the condition of the possibility of historiography (472).

But our historicity pervades all human existence. Human existence is fundamentally intersubjective. The recuperation of ourselves as historical is a recuperation that keeps alive the intersubjective bond of communication attaching us to our contemporaries but also to our predecessors and to our successors. A hermeneutics of the subject will guard against any reification of this intersubjective rapport, as well as the reduction of the narrative of that rapport to a physical object.

B. THE OBJECTIVATION OF OUR PARTICIPATION: THE TEXT.

For Ricoeur, the act of distanciation from our primordial participation pertains to the necessary condition of the appropriation of ourselves. Appropriation is not a simple, intuitive procedure. There is no appropriation that reintroduces the subject prematurely, before it has been tested in the fire of the various modes of analysis and of the critique of the representations in which our participation manifests itself. In other words, our participation requires a mode of self-communication. Without this self-communication, an appropriation of ourselves is impossible (420:73).

For Ricoeur, the most constitutive mode of this self-communication of participation is the text. For him, the text is "the paradigm of the distanciation of all communication" (389:130). The text is the narrows through which the water of human existence must pass. This philosophical hypothesis is the biggest gamble of Ricoeur's hermeneutical theory. He has to prove that "the entirety of human existence is a text to be read" (220:223). At issue, therefore, is not only that our participation in being exteriorizes itself, but that the texture of that exteriorization resembles that of a text. It presupposes that fundamentally human existence has a languagistic character (320(246):68; 398:237), that this dicibilité can be written or inscribed (413:34), and that the discourse of existence can be fixated in a text. Accordingly, the text is the point of access to our self-understanding (389:141). Existence is understood or appropriated, not in the immediacy of the lived experience, but as said or inscribed in a text (396:354). Without this intermediation of the text, self-understanding is effectively blocked.

Ricoeur's text-theory, as we have seen, extends itself not only to the realm of perception but also to the realm of human action. In the latter sphere, however, the hold of the text is more tenuous. In the one article in which Ricoeur has dealt explicitly with the textuality of human action "The Model of the Text: Meaningful Action Considered as a Text" (370:529-562), he maintains that, both on the level of the object and of the methodology, human action displays similarities to the textuality of the world of human perception. In referring to Max Weber's definition of the object of the human sciences as sinnhaft orientiertes Verhalten (meaningfully oriented behaviour), he suggests that the "meaningfully oriented" ought to be translated into "readability characters" in order to emphasize the possibility of engraving meaningful action into a text that can be read (370:537). Also, in his more recent writings on fiction and history, he emphasizes the capacity of the fictional and historical text to redescribe human reality and human action. Since the theory of speech-acts has indicated that doing can be inscribed in language as the force of language (illocutionary act), it has opened up the further possibility of perceiving the other characteristics of textual writing in action. According to Ricoeur, these characteristics include 1. the autonomy of action vis-à-vis the author,[4] 2. the autonomy of the action vis-à-vis the initial situation in which it took place,[5] and 3. the autonomy of the action vis-à-vis its original addressee.[6]

---

4.   One might call it the social dimension of action. In the words of Ricoeur, "Our deeds escape us and have effects we did not intend" and they enter into social actions that leave an imprint in history (370:541).

5.   An action can become a paradigm and as such extend to a transhistorical relevance: the world of meaningful action.

6.   On the level of praxis this autonomy becomes evident when we realize that human action is not evaluated by its initial setting, but that its meaning is open to anyone who can re-enact it in a new praxis.

At first sight, this linkage of hermeneutics with the text theory could easily be interpreted as a limitation of the broad perspective that Heidegger and Gadamer brought to hermeneutics. Gadamer's hermeneutical key of history and the historicity of human existence is narrowed to that of the text. Ricoeur recognizes this. But he counters this charge by pointing out that the return to the text is also a return to the hermeneutical concerns of Schleiermacher and Dilthey. Dilthey in particular concentrated on the text as the "expression of life fixed by writing" (406:16). Moreover, Ricoeur has not abandoned Gadamer's concern for historicity. However, he emphasizes that the text is not just a medium through which our historicity is alienated but a productive medium for the historicity of human existence. Yet, Ricoeur also admits, that the point of entry provided by the text is narrow. Hermeneutics and interpretation do not take in the total field of interpretation that comes into play in the question and answer dialectic of human existence. Hermeneutics is not the interpretative exercise called for in every human communication. For Ricoeur, it is the interpretation of written discourse: written discourse in the form of a text (388:142-143).

If at first sight Ricoeur's hermeneutics appears limiting, his linkage of the text with self-understanding and human existence brings him back into the fold of a general hermeneutics (220:223). The catch word of this modern hermeneutics has been understanding in search of a victory over misunderstanding. By defining hermeneutics as "an inquiry about the act of understanding involved in the interpretation of texts" (406:16), Ricoeur has attempted to link up with this general hermeneutics from the perspective of the text. In his own inimitable way he has linked the hermeneutics of Schleiermacher and Dilthey and their concern with texts with the ontology of understanding of Heidegger and Gadamer.

The productive distanciation of our participation brings into play the full theory of the text within hermeneutics. The immediacy of the experience of participation is interrupted in favour of the mediation of the text and its threefold autonomy. As we saw above,[7] the fixation of discourse in the text liberates the text from the original psycho-social condition of its production, from the dialogal context of its original situation (depsychologization of the text), and finally, from its original addressee (desociologization of the text). What the text confronts us with is not what lies before the text, or what surrounds the text, but the text itself and its production of reality (397:80). The object of the text is precisely the world of the text, where a new dwelling place of the self emerges. The reference of the text is not the tangible world but a possible world, a new way or orienting ourselves in existence (355:780; 381:107; 337:148; 389:140). The text hermeneutics of Ricoeur is, therefore, not merely "a hermeneutics of the text but a hermeneutics based on the problematics of the text" (406:16).

---

7.   p.35-41.

C. APPROPRIATION.

If distanciation is the objectification of participation, appropriation is the subjectification of participation. Appropriation is the Zueignung, the making-one's-own, of the ground of one's existence, the home of the subject. Appropriation is the becoming of the self. Since the appropriation is by way of the text and in no sense a direct, unmediated work, the task of appropriation pertains to the hermeneutical exercise or the work of interpretation. There is no appropriation without interpretation. In fact, appropriation is interpretation (337:145).

1. All understanding is self-understanding.

Ricoeur's indebtedness to Husserl's phenomenology crops up repeatedy in his hermeneutical theory. With Husserl, Ricoeur maintains that all understanding is self-understanding, i.e., the comprehension of the condition of the appearance of things is related to the structure of human subjectivity (186:317). For Ricoeur, this subjectivity is not the correlate of an objectivity, that is, a subjectivity that constitutes an objectivity, as Husserl had perceived it, but a subjectivity grounded in participation (398:227). All objectivity and constituting subjectivity is founded on the ontological participation of Being-in-the-world.[8] The subject can provide an epistemological justification and operate methodologically, only because it is grounded primordially in participation. All understanding flows out of this ontological constitution where the finite self dwells in Sorge and Dasein (398:228).

To say, therefore, that all understanding is self-understanding is not to return to a self-constituting subject. In fact, a wedge exists between the self of self-understanding and the ego of self-consciousness (423:94-95). Consciousness has its meaning, not from the ego, but from something outside itself (398:235). Understanding at this primordial level is not epistemological, nor methodical but ontological, i.e., it attests to the fact that we belong to being. It is not the Diltheyan epistemological understanding of the Geisteswissenschaften but the Heideggerean Verstehen (434:165).

2. All understanding is interpretation.

This becoming of the subject in understanding is not, however, immediately obvious. Here again Ricoeur follows vintage Heidegger. He assigns the same breadth to the notion in interpretation as to understanding. Heidegger perceived Auslegung (interpretation) as the development of understanding according to the structure of "als" (as). In other words,

---

8. Ricoeur prefers Gadamer's term, Zugehörigkeit (participation), over Heidegger's Being-in-the-world, because it expresses more directly the conflict of the relation of subject to object. It also makes the dialectical concept of distanciation, without which participation cannot be, more visible (389:228).

interpretation adds nothing to understanding except that it allows it to become itself. Interpretation is not a translation into another language but the bringing to itself of understanding (398:229). Interpretation is, therefore, like a second step in the process of the being-there of Being. Consequently, interpretation depends totally upon understanding, because both come forth out of our participation in Being (434:165). Interpretation is not, first of all, a method of the Geisteswissenschaften, but a moment of the ontological constitution of human existence. Interpretation is as universal as the projection of meaning.

Since interpretation flows from understanding, what Heidegger calls Vorhabe is operative in interpretation. One has a prior grasp or view of the object, not as a sovereign subject, but through an anticipation of the object. It is this that allows the interpretation to have the structure of "als". The 'as' of interpretation corresponds to the anticipatory grasp, the prepossession of the object in participation. The 'as' of interpretation only explicitates this pre-understanding (398:229;232-233). We understand ourselves by beginning with these anticipations, this pre-understanding (355:779).

Where does interpretation manifest itself? Its favourite field of operation is that of intersubjectivity (440:11) or communication (398:232). In intersubjectivity one understands when one shares in the same meaning. This occurs in a conversation, when the dialogal and dialectical process of question and answer unfolds the field according to which the conversation is structured. Interpretation, accordingly, is the process through which this mutual understanding proceeds (398:230) and the original ambiguity is overcome. What needs to be stressed again is that it is not the subject who is in control of meanings; s/he is not the origin of the intersubjective meaning, but meaning comes to be in him or her.

However, the model of conversation is not paradigmatic of interpretation. Conversation is too limited an intersubjective relation. It is bound by two interlocutors sharing a situation in the here and now. The dialogal intersubjective relation is only a 'short' relation. For Ricoeur to introduce the notion of interpretation, this relation must move out of its situation of immediacy and enter into the realm of the 'long' relation that encounters us in social, cultural, political and religious institutions. These long relations are basically historical relations. It is, therefore, at the intersubjective level with our contemporaries, our predecessors, and our successors that interpretation, properly speaking, manifests itself.

3. Interpretation and the text.

The third moment of the unfolding of Being for Heidegger is language. Here again Ricoeur follows Heidegger. As we saw in the previous paragraph, Ricoeur concentrates his efforts concerning the language dimension of interpretation, not upon the 'short' inter-subjective relation, but upon the 'long' relation. That long relation finds its point of identity in the text. What the text adds to the dialogal relationship is precisely the inscription of the discourse. Inscription fixates a discourse and produces for us an autonomy of a text, not only vis-à-vis its author/speaker, but also vis-à-vis its immediate ostensive context and its addressee. This unmoored text, floating through history toward whomever can read, is for Ricoeur the cardinal depository of meaning.

The text is, therefore, the outlet of understanding in interpretation. It must not be divorced from the process of understanding and interpretation, because it is not unmoored from participation. But in the text we do have the surfacing of participation in distanciation. As such the text is also the dialectical opposite of participation. But that does not permit us to forget that whatever objectivity the text can muster, its objectivity is grounded in the being of the text and ultimately in the dicibilité of life itself (475:II).

But, as inscribed discourse, the text has durability. The text displays a structure of meaning. For Ricoeur, this is a central moment of hermeneutics. It is central because it is the moment in which two types of hermeneutical practices meet. It is the moment that Dilthey split into explanation and understanding, and which Heidegger and Gadamer were not able to bring together again in their attempt to renew hermeneutics. For Ricoeur, the text is, therefore, both an outflow of understanding and interpretation in the Heideggerean sense, and a structure of meaning that is open to analysis and to explanatory procedures. This means that, for Ricoeur, interpretation implies a dialectic of understanding and explanation (423:92). Understanding becomes enriched in that it assumes, beyond the moment of the apprehension of our participation, a moment in the process of the science of interpretation. In that context, understanding is the non-methodical pole, the dialectic opposite of explanation (434:165). As to interpretation, it becomes the process that moves between the pre-understanding and the exegesis of the text, between understanding and explanation (475: IV-VII). The dialectic of understanding and explanation is grounded in the dialectic of participation and distanciation. It states that the self of self-understanding is effected not by sharpening my subjective capacities intuitively or without mediation, but by recourse to a more objective discourse that we believe to be the objectification of our Being-in-the-world or of our 'forms of life'. The text as a form of life permits an approach that has two poles.

The first pole is that of understanding. Contrary to all attempts to devise a method for understanding, Ricoeur maintains that understanding is non-methodical. Non-methodical understanding takes the form of a guess (423:75). We first guess the meaning of the text, because at first the text does not speak: it is mute (423:75). Since we seek to understand our 'forms of life', a hermeneutics of understanding refuses the challenge of Romantic hermeneutics which sought to restore the relationship between the author and the reader to a dialogue situation, to a genial communication. For Ricoeur, the text itself as a form of life must be brought to understanding. The text as a form of life must be moored, not to its original author or his or her Sitz im Leben, but to the life of the reader. Understanding is the first step of bringing back to life a particular text. Consequently, understanding takes place in the semantic space of the text (423:76). Understanding as guessing concerns this semantic space of the text. And as Ricoeur remarks, "There are no rules for making good guesses" (423:76), just as we must say of the empirical sciences that there are no rules for making good hypotheses.

The second pole is that of explanation.[9] The guesses of understanding regarding the relationship of parts of the text to the whole, of the determination of the individuality of the text and of the possible actualizations of the text need to be validated. This is the task of explanation, but always as the dialectical counterpart of understanding. "Understanding precedes, accompanies, closes and thus envelops explanation" (434:165). The one cannot be thought without the other because "explanation develops understanding analytically" (434:165). Together they constitute the hermeneutical circle: one explains what one understands, and one understands what is explained (390:163). What breaks apart here is the Diltheyan epistemological dichotomy. Explanation is not the hegemony of the physical sciences. Structural analysis has clearly demonstrated that explanation pertains also to the realm of language (337:139).

Of the two poles, only explanation is truly methodic. And although the validation of the guesses can hardly exceed, as E.D. Hirsch remarked, beyond probability (423:78) - Ricoeur calls it a method of 'converging indices' (423:79) - the method of explanation is nonetheless methodical. For Ricoeur, this methodic pole is the necessary intermediation between pre-understanding and self-understanding. Together they form the hermeneutical arc (423:87;505:IV). Its most frequently mentioned form is that of structural analysis, provided by the semiotics of the Structuralist Schools.[10] Structural analysis seeks to guard against a superficial, naive reading of a text. Its explanatory procedures can help uncover the depth-semantics of the text and, therefore, a more critical reading of the text (423:87). By remaining within the oppositions and differences of the lexical entities of the text, structural analysis can help to determine whether one reading is more adequate than another. The explanatory procedures may not validate absolutely, but they validate nonetheless (337:146-148).

Moreover, the interpretation of the text must refuse to hypostatize the text. Interpretation is not interpretation of the text, i.e., an application of a series of explanatory procedures. Rather, it is an interpretation based on the text (406:16). By this Ricoeur wants to warn the interpreter not to fall into the trap of remaining within the strictures of the code. It is not the code but the message that one is after. The

---

9.   See above p.109-112. For an evaluation of Ricoeur's use of explanatory procedures - in Le volontaire et l'involontaire Ricoeur calls them diagnostics - see Mary Gerhart, "Paul Ricoeur's Notion of 'Diagnostics': Its Function in Literary Interpretation" in Journal of Religion 56, 1976, p. 137-156.

10.   Ricoeur does not intend to point exclusively to semiotics. Any approach that uses explanatory procedures can provide the methodic pole.

interpretation of the text presupposes that every text has a reference. Interpretation is in pursuit of the reference of the text, i.e., the world of the text. Ricoeur focuses on the "open state of the universe of signs" (320(247):65), their ability to say something about something, while recognizing at the same time that the reference is mediated by the sense (406:29).

Here, too, the control of the conscious subject is limited. The subject's task is to permit him/herself to be guided by the movement of the text toward its reference. The subject must seek to dislodge him/herself before the text. Explanation does not mean control.

4. Interpretation and the world of the text.

We saw that interpretation is a process in pursuit of the reference of the text. But Ricoeur's pursuit is limited to the reference of poetic texts (357:533). The reference of these texts is properly described as a double reference or split reference. By abolishing reference at its ordinary level in descriptive or didactic texts, poetic texts forge a reference in the logical absurdity of a first level reading. In the clash of the semantic fields one catches sight of the world of the poetic text. The referential visée of the poetic text provides a glimpse of an ontological sphere. It is from this sphere that a return to the subject can be made.

By breaking with the surface of reality, poetic language show us a deeper mode of belonging to reality. In a paradoxical manner poetic language links us with that foundational reality through the very discourse that it creates.[11] By its capacity to create mood it reveals new ways of being in the world. These new ways of dwelling in it have not originated with a subject, but are first of all outpourings of the very reality that poetic texts express.[12] It is poetry that makes that reality appear for the first time (248:113). It evokes 'the mythico-poetic ground of man' (408:174), which ordinary language tends to dissimulate. By tearing a fissure in language, it forces a new world into view. It is the poet's task to let that reality speak to us. Outside of the poetic creation it is not perceivable. It alone breaks open a world as a possible way of seeing and doing things. Into

---

11. Ricoeur likes to quote the phrase of Bachelard in his La poétique de l'espace according to which the poetic image "Becomes a new being in our language; it expresses us by making us what it expresses." see 227:15-16;155:121; 417:214-215.

12. See the text of "Le poétique" (278): "Elle est l'expressivité du monde; et parce que l'expressivité va des choses vers nous, et non l'inverse, on peut parler d'une signification de la poésie, dans une acception du mot signification qui, pour n'être pas logique, n'est pas pour autant 'subjective': la signification, c'est la venue à la parole de l'expressivité même du monde. C'est de cette manière anti-subjectiviste qu'il faut entendre le primat de l'expression sur la signification en poésie: loin d'éliminer la signification il lui donne une assise." (248:109)

this world we can project new possibilities of becoming a self, or becoming "what one was" (422:363).

The name attached to this world of the text varies immensely. Ricoeur borrows very freely from the words that have covered this reality for the major philosophers. Without clear preference we discover Husserl's Lebenswelt alongside Heidegger's Being-in-the-world (e.g. 397:79) and 'my ownmost possibilities' (e.g. 436:495), Nabert's 'originary affirmation' (93:101-124), Spinoza's 'conatus' (320(232):336), Freud and Plato's 'eros' (320(232):336), Levinas' 'infini' (373:101), Aristotle's 'Being' (356:983), Dufrenne's 'Nature' or 'God' (248:111-112), Schelling's 'Grund' (248:112) and Plato's 'idea of the good' (373:95).

But no matter what name we give to the realm out of which the poetic arises - the names of the previous paragraph are by no means the only ones - the poetic extends that source to us. It fuses a bond between us and the source. It touches us not by its description or didactic power but by the mood that the poem has shaped by its language. The mood affectively binds us to that world (423:60). It is a feeling that the world of the poetic text is not totally alien; in fact, that its 'space' and its 'time' is our originary space and time, thanks to which we can continue to exist (139:269;450:176). But it is only the poetic that extends that source to us. By following the movement of the poetic text, a fusion of our space and time with the originary space and time takes place. Gadamer calls this phenomenon Horizontverschmeltzung - a wiping away of horizons. In this fusion of horizons I am enabled to transgress my previous boundaries and limits towards a world of my ownmost possibilities as it is projected in the poetic text (362:23).

It is evident that for Ricoeur the reference of the poetic texts bonds us to a world in which the split between subject and object has not yet occurred. Its reference towards a world of the text is not to a world of essences, but to a world in which I can dwell. The reference of the poetic text is, therefore, also auto-referential, without becoming subjective in a transcendental sense (381:100). The world which the text opens and discovers projects an increase of my possibilities of existing.

The realm of the world of the text pertains to the power of the imagination. The imagining power enables or mediates the opposition between the world of ordinary discourse and the world of poetic discourse (463). It is the imagination that enters into the world of ordinary discourse and disrupts its tranquility, its self-assuredness, its logic, and seeks to reshape it in accordance with the images and signs that pertain to what is possible. More positively, the imagination is the dynamism of the ground as it surges into our language and into the concreteness of our human existence. It grants us a new reference after the breakdown of the first and thus opens the primordial reality for us. It is this capacity of saying that redescribes our reality (424:215).

Hence, the poetic finds its source not in the subject but in this ground. This ground manifests itself in the poetic.[13] The ground itself is, therefore, perceived to be incapable of remaining unmanifested. The ground seeks to reveal itself, to let itself appear (248:116). With Hegel, Ricoeur says, "Art is that which makes matter sing" (399:345). Consequently, the ground which the poetic brings to expression, cannot be a passive essence, to be contemplated, but it must be, as Aristotle perceived already, an act. Being or the ground is dynamic. This means, moreover, that the emergence of the ground cannot remain solely at the level of perception but must find its expression in human action. The analysis of the symbolic language has hinted at this on several occasions. Poetic language is mimetic language. It not only redescribes reality but it is also an enhancement of human action. The emergence of this ground in poetic language lets the ground of the subject be seen as well.

The reference of the text probes the Being-in-the-world, the realm of my ownmost possiblilities. It is this that attracts the interpretative quest (358:53). Interpretation presupposes that reality is possibility, that our world and ourselves are not ready-made. It presupposes that reality can be redescribed, that mimesis means not an Eternal Return, an amor fati, but an exploration of the essentially real. The interpretation of the world of the text is therefore an aggression against the so-called real and a subversion of the established order (475:VIII).

It is before this world of the text that the subject must make its appeal. It is in this world of refashioned visions and redescribed actions that the subject is beckoned to dwell and to become. To understand oneself before the text is to perceive the text as opening up the world of my possibilities. Interpretation is not an empathetic or congenial understanding of the psychic life of an author, but allowing oneself to be overtaken by the posibilities of the text.[14] To appropriate the meaning of the text by making one's own the signs sedimented in the written texts of our culture is, therefore, a becoming of the subject. Text-interpretation is not just a process of the subject and, therefore, arbitrary, because the subject does not control the world of possibilities. These are offered to me as the gift of the text. Instead of a projection of my subjectivity into the text, the subject receives a new possibility of knowing him/herself from the text. The self is not the foundation nor the condition of interpretation but its endpoint (406:30). "If the reference of the text is the project of a world, then, it is not the reader who primarily projects himself. The reader rather

---

13. In "Religion, Atheism and Faith" he expresses this as follows, "In terms of its total extension and radical comprehension, poetry is what locates the act of dwelling between heaven and earth, under the sky, but on the earth, within the domain of the word" (320(325):467).

14. In his "Cours sur l'herméneutique," Ricoeur writes, "L'interprétation consiste à produire le mode d'être qui donne à ce monde possible la dimension de ma propre existence. La capacité du texte d'ouvrir un nouveau monde, c'est-à-dire d'ajouter à mon existence de nouvelles possibilitiés, voilà sa référence." (374:30)

is enlarged in his capacity of self-projection by receiving a new mode of being from the text itself" (423:94).

Here too a hermeneutical circle is operative. The understanding of the world, projected by the text, is correlative to the understanding of oneself before the projected world (381:100:375:122-123). The Sache of the text must become the self: "Thus I exchange the "I", master of itself, for the self, disciple of the text" (398:236, my translation).[15] For Ricoeur, it is the final defeat of the constitutive subject (438:30;358:53;381:108-109). Human unity lies, therefore, not within the subject but without. It is purely intentional. As projected in the world of the text, that which brings together the object and the self, i.e., the self of oneself, can be presented only in the form of imaginative variations. The imagination as productive is the tenuous reach towards the unity that we are not yet except in the imagination. Our Self is the "art hidden in the depths of the human soul". The text as the inscription of this productive imagination thus becomes the source of self-understanding.

5. The act of appropriation: reading.

The act of appropriation which is the completion of interpretation passes far beyond a mere linguistic analysis of a text. For Ricoeur appropriation is an act whereby one is playfully seduced into letting go of the ego-subject, the narcissistic and imperialistic subject. It is accomplished through the act of reading. Interpretation is complete, when the objectivity and the autonomy of the text is transformed once again into an event of discourse for a reader. The accomplishment of reading is its power to transform the otherness of the text into an event of discourse for me (362:22;411:67;423:92). The event of discourse of the reader is a new event; that is, not a repetition of the original event, but a creation produced at the behest of the text.

The unmooring of the text from its original situation also allowed the text to drift away from its original addressees. Gadamer proposes, therefore, that the text is addressed to anyone who can read. A text loses its restriction; it is basically open (337:144). The text of the Letter to the Romans is mine to read just as at one time it was the Romans! The letter assumes a new time dimension. Paul's original writing takes on a universal dimension, always ready to take on new readers and to actualize its reference in new situations.

This actualization of the textual discourse in reading bears a number of interesting characteristics.

1. The possibility of reading lies in the text itself. The text is open to a new discourse and to a new actualization of its referent. It is not the subject projecting him/herself into the text or reading him/herself into

---

15. "Alors j'échange le moi, maître de lui-même, contre le soi, disciple du texte."

the text. The reader is shaped by the act of the text (406:29). The invitation and the dynamic come from the text and not from the subject (337:144-145). As Ricoeur remarks, reading as an interpretative activity is "a work of the text before being a work of the reader" (360:293). Or more strongly, "Interpretation is a prolongation of the work of the text on itself. It is a re-saying, the reactivation of the work of saying" (360:293). It is not the subject who activates the meaning of the text; it is an act of the text itself (337:148). Ricoeur's analysis has consistently called for this approach to the text. The act of the text is, in fact, the movement of sense to reference in the text. In accordance with its semiotic structure, the text calls for a "reader of codes", i.e., a reader awakened by the codification of the text, by the grammaticality of the text, and by the narrativity of the text (475:IX). The reader must have a competence that resembles that of the author in order to be taken by the dynamism of the sense of the text to its reference. But again these demands devolve from the dynamics of the text and not from the reader (371:93).

2. Reading, as a re-enactment of the text as a discourse, links together two discourses: the text as discourse, and reading as a new discourse. Ricoeur borrows Gadamer's term, the fusion of horizons to describe the broadening of the understanding of the subject by his or her being taken up into the world of the text (371:93). In reading I am being taken where I was not before. I take up a new dwelling in the world of the text. Both my situation and the mute text are transgressed and interlinked.

3. The third characteristic of reading attaches itself to the very activity of reading. Reading is a form of playing. When we read, the imaginative variations of the text have a way of capturing the reader in much the same way as the activity of a game engrosses the player. Even though we can be transformed by the play activity or, in the case of reading by the 'thing' of the text, we are not conscious of the transforming process until, in a reflective moment, we return to it. To read is to be taken up into the metamorphosis of reality (Gadamer's Verwandlung). In a playful fashion, the ego is transported by the metamorphosis of reality toward a deeper self (406:31). Hence the metamorphosis of reality by means of fiction is, at the same time, a metamorphosis of the reading subject. There is no esthetic judgment that accompanies the reader when s/he is absorbed by the to-and-fro of a narrative. The reader is not the conscious subject; s/he is as much "being read" as being a reader (375:218).

This ludic dimension of reading corresponds to the ludic dimension of reality brought about by the split reference of literary and poetic texts. The play of literary texts is a heuristic fiction. In its playfulness and seeming arbitrariness, it opens up a realm of meaning as a playspace for anyone who trusts enough to enter it. In the play within the space of the meaning of its imaginative variations, the really real displaces not only the ordinary real but also the ordinary conscious self (375:218). "The reader is this fictive I, created by the poem and a participant in the poetic universe" (375:222, my translation).[16]

---

16. "Le lecteur est ce moi fictive, créé par le poème et participant à l'universe poétique."

6. The critique of the illusions of the subject.

If, as Ricoeur says, the world of the text metamorphizes the subject, the world of the text is also the source of the critique of the subject. The world of the text, as the heuristic fiction of the real and as the exploration of the truth in the very metamorphosis of the reader, also exposes the illusions of the subject. It is in reflection that these illusions are brought to consciousness. For Ricoeur, this despoliation of the subject of its illusions is today's great cultural task. Freud has made us realize that the critique of the subject is an arduous work - a Durcharbeiten - because it entails the overcoming of the narcissistic ego. The resistance to be conquered is the defence that the subject has mustered to ward off reality (Cf.320(214):180).

The introduction of this subjective critique is decisive for Ricoeur. It fulfills two functions. First of all, it presages a radical modern shift of emphasis. It veers the attention away from the object - the world - which Descartes and Kant had placed under the radical question and directs it instead to the subject. What was so clear and unquestionable, the last stance of certainty for Descartes in a world distanciated from myself by the doubt, the subject, becomes now the question. Who is the subject? That is today's core question. Secondly, the critique focusses on the world and reality as an answer to the quest for the subject. But, as Aristotle reminds us, Being is said in many ways. What reality says and calls me to is ambiguous. In interpretation that ambiguity breaks into our world of consciousness. And the ambiguity becomes the conflict of interpretation. Reality itself is thoroughly symbolic, i.e., impervious to an absolutist or unique approach. Reality will not let go and unlock its ambiguity, Ricoeur admits, by a merely passive attentiveness to the world of the text. Ricoeur's introduction of a critique within interpretation is accompanied by the metaphor of conflict (Cf. Le conflit des interprétations). Understanding and self-understanding is to be won by wading right into the midst of the battle for understanding that is waged all around us. No one has the supreme vantage point for the conflict, because it is not a battle for points but the struggle for an authentic existence.

Ricoeur's earlier hermeneutical work made frequent references to the critique of the subject that was imparted as a cultural heritage by the three masters of suspicion: Marx, Nietzsche, and Freud.[17] Although Ricoeur has written about Freud, he has hardly elaborated the content of the critique of Nietzsche and Marx. Freud became paradigmatic for the dispossession of the constituting subject. I introduced this critique in Chapter One to orient our interpretative work of Ricoeur. Basically Ricoeur has retained this vision (see 444). However, his writings since 1973 gather this critique of the subject under the heading of the critique of ideology (398:233). While still referring to the masters of suspicion, the critique of ideology places its focus, according to Ricoeur, upon the

---

17. See De l'interprétation. Essai sur Freud and Le conflit des interprétations.

historicity of human existence and of the human subject. The critique of ideology incorporates the critique of the subject more adequately within Ricoeur's most fundamental concern, namely, human existence as existence within a limit. For Ricoeur, human existence, human truth, human self-consciousness, human power, human freedom is only human (414(95):86). Human existence is bound to time. It is always somewhere in the flow of the past, present, and future of time. It is without an absolute for its point of departure and for its future. Finitude is the measure of our existence (362:26).

The critique of ideology is derived from a different cultural tradition than the hermeneutical rememoration of tradition. From Ricoeur's own perspective, it qualifies as a counterposition. The critique of ideology has its cultural roots in the Enlightenment, while the recovery of the self in prejudice, authority and tradition looks to Romanticism. As we saw above, Ricoeur recovers the contemporary clash of these two great cultural movements in the work of H.G. Gadamer and J. Habermas (390:155).

We have already briefly presented the critical theory of ideology of J. Habermas. Our focus here will be the critique of the subject of the critical theory. Because Habermas' position runs counter to Ricoeur's own hermeneutical stance, Ricoeur has some difficulty in introducing the critical theory within a hermeneutical consciousness.[18] But again Ricoeur feels impelled to listen to an antithetical tradition, and seeks to be healed by it.

The point of intersection, where the critique of ideology questions a hermeneutics of reminiscence, is at the level of communication. Within a hermeneutics of finitude, the constitution of historical experience, according to Ricoeur, is intersubjectivity. I am consciously inserted into the historical becoming within a process of communication with my contemporaries, predecessors, and successors. The critique of ideology seeks to bring to consciousness the distortions that affect this communication. If the hermeneutical tradition is characterized by its attentiveness to the communication, the critique of ideology judges the present state of communication negatively as a disrupted and blocked communication that must be destroyed.

What, according to the critical theory, is the source of the blockage and distortion? Habermas recognizes a dimension of human knowledge that the hermeneutical theory has often overlooked; namely, that

---

18. Habermas does not dissociate himself from hermeneutics altogether. He is wary of a hermeneutics that recuperates past tradition. He operates with a meta-hermeneutics, derived from Freud's meta-psychology. He perceives this meta-hermeneutics to be a critical science whose aim is to set free the distorted and violence-ridden communication. He thinks that Freud's meta-psychology is less dependent on the sedimentations of tradition and more upon a regulative idea of a communication without distortion. His meta-hermeneutics is a projective, rather than a recuperative hermeneutics. (See 386:59)

all knowledge is ruled by interests. According to Habermas, there are three governing interests: the technical, instrumental interest that governs the knowledge production of the physical sciences, the communicative interest of the historico-hermeneutical sciences, and the emancipative interest of the critical social science. Prior to any submission to authority, the historico-hermeneutical sciences must recognize that they are governed by a practical interest in communication.

It is, however, to the third body of science, the critical social sciences, that Habermas extends the most dramatic task. It is their task to unmask the forms of the relations of dependence that have distorted communication. It is the task of the critical social sciences to unblock relations of dependence that have become "ideologically frozen" or reified (386:44). According to Habermas, these relations can be transformed only critically, i.e., not hermeneutically. And this critical work is guided by the interest in emancipation or by what Habermas calls "self-reflection". The critical social sciences seek to set the subjct free from dependence upon all hypostacized powers - also from the ontology of Heidegger. For Habermas this critique is more primordial than the hermeneutical consciousness. Its task is to unmask the interests at work in the spheres of knowledge particularly since it will show that the theoretical subject is subject to institutional constraints which will distort his/her communicative competence (386:45).

In Habermas' view the notion of ideology enters at this point. Ideology functions in the philosophy of Habermas in a fashion similar to the notion of misunderstanding in Gadamer's hermeneutics. In hermeneutics, understanding must overcome misunderstanding. In Habermas' philosophy, it is the ideological, i.e., the reified relations, that must be overcome and set free. For Habermas, ideology is connected with blocked or distorted communication. The distortion is not an epistemological misunderstanding but a political action of repression by an authority. In other words, distortion is the result of violence. This ideology and its violence particularly affects the area of work, power and language. Ideology enforces a type of domination in the realm of communicative action, where, because of the inverted relationships between work and power, the conditions of the use and the competence of communication are distorted (386:46). The lack of recognition of this changed relationship between work, power and language creates the ideological condition according to which the subject lives under an illusion, projects a false transcendence, and rationalizes this new arrangement of work, power and language. Accordingly, the communication of the subject is systematically distorted (386:46).

In order to set the subject free from his or her ideological illusion, Habermas refuses to take the route of a hermeneutics of understanding. Instead he chooses the critical social sciences. The paradigmatic science that can break the hold that ideology has on the subject is psychoanalysis. But since psychoanalysis also remains in the sphere of understanding, a type of hermeneutics cannot be avoided. Habermas calls it a Tiefenhermeneutik, a depth-hermeneutics. But this

205

depth-hermeneutics of desymbolization and resymbolization can only achieve the goal of healing the self-consciousness of the patient by explanatory procedures. The competence of the critical sciences to overcome the communicative distortions by explanatory procedures becomes understandable in the light of the failure of ontological hermeneutics. For Habermas, ontological hermeneutics, based on the experience of participation, too easily overlooks that communication with that experience is blocked by ideology. One can hardly turn to the texts that inscribe our understanding if these same texts do no more than exteriorize our distorted communication.

Habermas seeks, therefore, not a hermeneutics of traditions but a regulative idea. That regulative idea does not come from a past heritage, but is a projected idea. The regulative idea is not behind us, but is projected ahead of us. the regulative idea operates as an interest in communication. It seeks a communication without bounds and constraints. This regulative idea of unlimited and unconstrained communication is more what ought to be than what is. As such, it appears as the diametric opposite of the more ontologically oriented hermeneutics (386:48-49).

Ricoeur acknowledges the distance between Habermas and himself, but at the same time he discovers points of interpenetration. He mentions four. 1. Hermeneutics does not exclude a critical moment within the process of understanding. That is precisely Ricoeur's critique of Gadamer's inadequate dialectics of participation and distanciation. 2. Because of his notion of distanciation, the explanatory procedures are not foreign but indispensable to understanding. 3. The world of the text is not solely a recuperation of the past but is, at the same time, a projection of my possibilities. Central to Ricoeur's hermeneutics is his theory of the productive imagination. 4. And finally, the subjectivity of hermeneutics is released by the world of the text as an "imaginative variation of the ego.". The emancipative interest lies, therefore, within the confines of a hermeneutical theory (386:56). A critique of ideology as a type of meta-hermeneutics, however, can safeguard the hermeneutics of traditions from a premature appropriation.

However, for Ricoeur, the point of closest convergence between a hermeneutics and a critique of ideology lies in the concept of prejudice and ideology (386:57). Both concepts pertain, according to Ricoeur, to a hermeneutics of finitude. Both express that there is no escape from the historical conditions of understanding. Even the critique of ideology which seeks to operate from a principle prior to hermeneutics, namely, the interest of knowledge, is not immune from the insurmountable character of ideology (398:232).[19] Habermas' theory of ideology addresses itself to the contemporary ideology, which he says is the dominating and intrusive

---

19. Ricoeur maintains that the interest cannot be derived from an empirical description, but must have its origin in a philosophical anthropology. Otherwise what determines that there are three interests and not one? (See 386:57)

position of science and technology (389:59). However, to state that the sphere of instrumental action has ceased to be a subsystem but has instead begun to dominate the sphere of human communication, is to admit at the same time that the critique of ideology is situated somewhere and views its task from a specific perspective (396:354). Both hermeneutics and the critique of ideology themselves remain no more than an ideology (386:61). The quest for liberation is, therefore, not from some lofty, supra-historical position, but for emancipation that, according to Ricoeur, on the one hand listens to the Greek and Judeo-Christian story of freedom and liberation, and on the other projects a less distorted communication with contemporaries, predecessors and successors into the future (412:37). The interest in communication is fundamentally a practical interest.[20] In Chomsky's terms it is a competence for communication. Its charge is, not to reduce the immense numbers of temporal relationships into some type of reified form, but to keep open the communication which is history. As a competence, it is allowing ourselves to be affected by the effects of history, to remain open to intersubjectivity, and to the analogy of the ego (413:37-38).

Accordingly, both in hermeneutics and in the critique of ideology, the subject begins somewhere. S/he has no absolute beginning, is never identical with her/himself, and will never complete the project (396:354). The subject is always inserted somewhere in the process of historical becoming (398:233). That is the finitude, proper to human existence and to human belonging (398:228). The possibility of a fusion of horizons toward an expansion of our self-understanding can never be so extensive that an absolute knowledge emerges. Ricoeur rejects Pannenberg's Universalgeschichte for the same reason (362:30).[21] A universal horizon within which the events of history become understandable is not available. All that is available, according to Ricoeur, is the process of fusing the horizon of the text and the horizon of our experience. This process is one that must be undertaken again and again in a never ending search for our subjectivity. Our finitude does not allow us to go beyond this hermeneutical condition (362:31). To refuse our historicity is to seek to be totalitarian and ultimately to enforce the totalization by means of violence (83:10, 165-166).

---

20. In other words, Ricoeur does not accept that this interest in communication must be placed outside of the historico-hermeneutical sciences. Because the historico-hermeneutical sciences can incorporate a critical and explanatory dimension, there is no need to sediment the emancipatory interest in the critical social sciences. For Ricoeur the interest in emancipation is principally a practical interest.

21. See Pannenberg's "Hermeneutik und Universalgeschichte" in Grundfragen Systematischer Theologie, Göttingen, Vandenhoeck and Ruprecht, 1967, p. 91-122. It is Pannenberg's thesis that only in a Universalgeschichte, i.e., in a horizon of all the events of history, that historical understanding becomes meaningful.

CHAPTER EIGHT: THE HERMENEUTICS OF HOPE.

Bibliography.

20.   "Le renouvellement de la philosophie chrétienne par les philosophies de l'existence" (1948).
44.   "Vérité et mensonge" (1951).
79.   "Philosophies de la personne. I. L'existence d'autrui" (1954).
87.   "Aux frontières de la philosophie. II. Philosophie et prophetisme" (1955).
101.   "Karl Jaspers" (1957).
109.   "Philosophie et religion chez Karl Jaspers" (1957).
153.   La symbolique du mal (1960).
164.   "Le péché originel: étude de signification" (1960).
173.   "Herméneutique des symboles et réflexion philosophique" (1961).
186.   "L'humanité de l'homme" (1962).
191.   "Herméneutique et réflexion" (1962).
198.   "Préface" in B. Rioux, L'être et la vérité chez Heidegger et Saint Thomas d'Aquin (1963).
200.   "Symbolique et temporalité" (1963).
203.   "Philosopher après Kierkegaard" (1963).
216.   "Le symbolisme et l'explication structurale" (1964).
220.   "Le langage de la foi" (1964).
227.   De l'interprétation. Essai sur Freud (1965).
228.   "La psychanalyse et le mouvement de la culture contemporaine" (1965).
232.   "Demythiser l'accusation" (1965).
233.   "Discussione" (1965).
235.   "Sciences humaines et conditionnements de la foi" (19650.
236.   "De la nation à l'humanité" (1965).
251.   "La parole, instauratrice de liberté" (1961).
256.   "L'athéisme de la psychanalyse freudienne" (1966).
267.   "Ebeling" (1967).
270.   "Postscript" in J.M. Paupert, Taizé et l'église de demain (1967).
273.   "Interprétation du mythe de la peine" (1967).
291.   "Tâches de la communauté ecclésiale dans le monde moderne" (1968).
294.   "Préface" in R. Bultmann, Jésus (1968).
297.   "Approche philosophique de concept de liberté religieuse" (1968).
299.   "Contribution d'une réflexion sur le langage à une théologie de la parole" (1968).
309.   "La paternité: du fantasme au symbole" (1968).
320.   Le conflit des interprétations (1969).
324.   "Croyance" (1969).
325.   "Religion, athéisme, foi" (1969).
332.   Les incidences théologiques de recherches actuelles concernant le langage (1969).
338.   "Hope and Structure of Philosophical Systems" (1970).
357.   "Mythe 3. L'interprétation philosophique" (1971).

358. "Du conflit à la convergence des méthodes en exégèse biblique" (1971).
360. "Esquisse de conclusion" (1971).
362. "Événement et sens" (1971).
365. "Préface" in O. Reboul, Kant et le problème du mal (1971).
367. "La foi soupçonnée" (1971).
375. "The Problem of the Will and Philosophical Discourse" (1971).
396. "Science et idéologie" (1974).
397. "Philosophy and Religious Language" (1974).
400. "Stellung und Funktion der Metapher in der biblischer Sprache" (1974).
404. "Manifestation et proclamation" (1974).
406. "Philosophical Hermeneutics and Theological Hermeneutics" (1974).
410. "Listening to the Parables of Jesus" (1975).
411. "Biblical Hermeneutics" (1975).
417. La métaphore vive (1975).
423. Interpretation Theory (1976).
426. "Entre Gabriel Marcel et Jean Wahl" (1976).
427. "Le "Royaume" dans la parabole de Jésus" (1976).
430. "L'herméneutique de la sécularisation: Foi, idéologie, utopie" (1976).
434. "Expliquer et comprendre" (1977).
436. "Nommer Dieu" (1977).
438. "Herméneutique et l'idée de révélation" (1977).
448. "Response to Karl Rahner's Lecture: On the Incomprehensibility of God" (1978).
452. The Philosophy of Paul Ricoeur (1978).
470. "The Logic of Jesus: the Logic of God" (1980).
476. "A Response" (1980).

According to Ricoeur, the route of the despoliation of the Cartesian and modern subject has not yet run the full course of the destruction of the imperial subject. To complete Ricoeur's route one has to include the world of the poetics of the will: the world of transcendence. The world of transcendence is the ultimate world, the ultimate home of meaning. This chapter proposes to explore this world of transcendence in Ricoeur's writings. The task is delicate because Ricoeur himself has not provided a coordinated analysis. We are still in the prolegoumena of his poetics of the will, although something of its vista has been opened up. It is this vista and its corresponding self-understanding, despite the obvious limitations imposed by its incompleteness, that will round off our study of Ricoeur's textual world and the subject in that world.[1]

---

1.   For an analysis of Ricoeur's earlier reflections on religion and salvation from a philosophical perspective see D. Vansina, "Het heil in de filosofie van Paul Ricoeur" in Bijdragen 27, 1966, p.484-510.

How does one gain entry into this world? If we are permitted to apply here what we have stated above, namely, that we do not forge our entry in any sphere from point zero, we must look for a starting point right in the midst of things. All understanding - also religious understanding - is historical understanding. One is inserted somewhere in the process of historical becoming. As Ricoeur remarks in La symbolique du mal, "The beginning is not what one finds first; the point of departure must be reached, it must be won... The first task is not to begin but from the midst of speech, to remember; to remember with a view of beginning" (153:348-349).

That "midst of speech" in the realm of transcendence is for Ricoeur our Western, Judeo-Christian and Greek tradition. I believe, that one might say that it is Ricoeur's own adherence to that tradition. He makes no apologies for that. His own participation in this tradition receives no grounding justification other than the Anselmian credo ut intelligam. He is a believer, a Christian believer, who proposes to think his faith (320(294):389-390). But he proposes to think his faith not as a theologian, but as a philosopher. As he says in "Guilt, Ethics and Religion",

> By sympathy and through imagination, the philosopher adopts the motivation and intention of the confessing consciousness; he does not "feel" but "experiences" in a neutral manner, in the manner of "as if," that which has been lived in the confessing consciousness. (320(326):426)

This position requires a further explanation.[2]

Ricoeur's hermeneutical phenomenology proposes to take the historicity of human existence seriously. As we saw, that implies that every position is ideological - including Ricoeur's own hermeneutics. It is inserted somewhere, and the philosopher does not stand outside the process of historical becoming. Without his or her commitment and belief, no philosophy is possible. It is only from this somewhere - this second naiveté - that the question of truth can be raised again. An absolute position, from whose lofty perspective history can be perceived to unfold according to some deterministic plan, is only destructive of existence. Throughout his philosophical career, Ricoeur has remained faithful to the combination of

---

2.   See also, H. Wells, "Theology and Christian Philosophy: Their Relation in the Thought of Paul Ricoeur," in Studies in Religion/Sciences Religieuses, 5, 1976, p.45-62. See also the citation of E. Schillebeeckx on the occasion of the conferral of an honorary Doctoral Degree in Theology by the University of Nijmegen in 1968, "Le philosophe Paul Ricoeur, docteur en théologie" in Christianisme Social 76, 1968, p.639-645, and R. Bergeron, op. cit., p.118-159; H.J. Heering, "Paul Ricoeur als Godsdienstwijsgeer" in Nederl. Theol.Tijdschr. 25, 1971; M. Gerhart, "Paul Ricoeur's Hermeneutical Theory as Resource for Theological Reflection" in The

histoire and vérité.[3] That is also why the book of collected articles, Histoire et vérité (83) contains a number of articles that could only come from a deep awareness of and a personal commitment to the Christian faith. In checking the complete bibliography of Ricoeur one notes at least one hundred titles, averting to one or another dimension of Judeo-Christianity.

Here is what Ricoeur himself says about this situation,

The task of the philosopher appears to me...to be distinguished from that of the theologian, in the following manner: biblical theology has the function of developing the kerygma according to its own conceptual system; it has the duty of criticising preaching, both by confronting it with its origin and by reorganizing it in a meaningful framework, in a discourse of its own kind, corresponding to the internal coherence of the kerygma itself. The philosopher, even the Christian one, has a distinct task; I am not inclined to say that he brackets what he has heard and what he believes, for how could he philosophize in such a state of abstraction with respect to what is essential? But neither am I of the opinion that he should subordinate his philosophy to theology, in an ancillary relation. Between abstention and capitulation, there is the autonomous way which I have located under the heading "the philosophical approach" (320(297):403).

The issue is obviously of concern to Ricoeur. Time and again he returns to the issue to assure his readers that he has not departed from the philosophical fold.[4] He justified his listening to the texts of faith by insisting that Christian faith has sedimented itself in the religious texts of our culture as our heritage. And his encounter with them "gives rise to thought" (153:347). It is his wager, in other words, that in listening to the Christian and Jewish texts he can come, as he says, to "a better

<hr>

Thomist 39, 1975, p.496-527; A. Dumas "Savoir objectif, croyance projective, foi interpellée" in Sens et existence; en hommage à Paul Ricoeur, G. Madison (ed), Paris, Seuil, 1975, p.160-169; P. Gisel, "Paul Ricoeur" in Études théologiques et religieuses 49, 1974, p.31-50; H.J. Dijkman, "De wijsgerige en wetenschappelijke mogelijkheidsvoorwaarden voor een verantwoord theologisch taalgebruik in het denken van Paul Ricoeur", in Vox Theol. 42, 1972, p.40-53.

3.   Thus, for example, his stance with regard to the symbols and myths of evil is determined by his own Judeo-Christian reading of history. He admits that he believed in order to understand, "I entered that circle as soon as I admitted that I read the ensemble of the myths from a certain point of view, that the mythical space was for me an oriented space, and that my perspective angle was the pre-eminence of the Jewish confession of sins, its symbolism, and its mythology" (153:354).

4.   Cf. 79:292;153:353;203:307-308;227:29;270:247, e.a.

understanding of man and of the bond between the being of man and the being of all beings" (153:355). This "giving rise to thought" is for Ricoeur first of all a philosophical endeavour.

But one cannot avoid wondering from time to time whether Ricoeur has not in fact passed beyond the boundaries of philosophy and entered into the world of theology. In explaining his philosophical approach, Ricoeur states his task to be an attempt, as a philosopher, to stay close to the kerygma and theology. He listens as an autonomous thinker: "If there is only one _logos_, the logos of Christ requires of me as a philosopher nothing else than a more complete and more perfect activation of reason; not more than reason; but the _whole_ reason" (320(297):403). In listening to the kerygma of faith, Ricoeur seeks to take reason to its limit, by pressing it to think in accord with language in its greatest wealth and intensity.

The first approximation of this thinking in accordance with the kerygmatic text is provided for Ricoeur by Kant's philosophical discourse of religion "within the limits of reason alone". It was Kant who first thought religion from the perspective of hope. For Ricoeur this approach of religion in terms of hope and promise in history coincides with a number of recent attempts to elaborate a philosophy and theology of hope. In this context he affirms his indebtedness to Jürgen Moltmann's Theologie der Höffnung which permitted him to articulate the eschatological dimension of the kerygma in terms of hope.[5] Ricoeur is indebted to Karl Barth even more so than to Moltmann. Despite his early distaste for K. Barth, Ricoeur has been profoundly influenced by the verticalism and transcendentalism of Barth's theology.[6] He has not written any articles about K. Barth, but Barth is to him the theological giant of the 20th century who most clearly understood the avenues open to faith after the ravages of the radical critique of 19th century Liberalism. But, as we shall see, Ricoeur cannot accept Barth's extreme diastasis. He applies here what he recognized as the deficiency of Heidegger's lofty ontology: its lack of mediation. In the realm of faith which can never be the work of language, Ricoeur is more aware than K. Barth ever was of the intermediation and power of language. The

---

5. München, Chr. Kaiser Verlag, 1965. See also Ricoeur "Le Dieu crucifié de Jürgen Moltmann" in Les quatres fleuves. Cahiers de recherches et de réflections religieuses (Le Christ, visage de Dieu) 4, 1975, p.109-114.

6. According to E. King (Interpretation of Pastoral Experience. A Study in Hermeneutical Theory and Practice, (unpublished dissertation defended at the University of Notre Dame, November 1980), Notre Dame, Department of Theology, 1980) Ricoeur posits a Barthian-type foundational faith-expression upon which all further expressions depend. Ricoeur, however, cannot go all the way with Barth. He refuses to recognize a free zone, where interpretation and critique cannot intervene. Cf. 411:109. On the other hand, he recognizes a similarity in aim in the Krisis-theology of Karl Barth. Barth's great contribution to this century was his effort to break the pretense of humanity to be its own foundation (cf. 233:390 and 320(232):344).

message of hope is not located in a zone free from the turmoil of human language. But it must remain a language of hope, i.e., a language that comes as a gift over which the subject has no control. Accordingly, Ricoeur asks how the transcendent enters into our human realm as hope and how philosophy can think religion (faith) as hope.[7]

A. RELIGION WITHIN THE LIMITS OF REASON ALONE.

The first aspect that needs to be clarified is to specify the type of discourse proper to religion. Since Ricoeur proposes to think religion in the light of the hope of the kerygma, while at the same time professing that this thought is an autonomous thought, he needs a philosophy that sets free the categories of hope and promise. The kerygma seeks to be thought, not along lines of a recuperation of past meaning or of a return of the same, but along the lines of "what never was before" (Is 41:23). For Ricoeur, the kerygma deposits in our midst novelty and innovation of meaning (320(297):411). Is it possible to link this innovation of meaning of the kerygma with the autonomous thought of reason? If it were impossible, Ricoeur says, then hope would be a

flash without a sequel; there would be no eschatology, no doctrine of last things, if the novelty of the new were not made explicit by an indefinite repetition of signs, were not verified in the 'seriousness' of an interpretation which incessantly separates hope from utopia (320(297):411).

By bringing it to thought, Ricoeur hopes to manifest what constitutes religious discourse and to avail himself of a critique of religious discourse.

His thinking on hope is characterized by Ricoeur as a post-Hegelian Kantianism (320(297):412;411:138-139). His post-Hegelian Kantianism is basically a rethinking of the philosophical system of both Kant and Hegel in the light of hope. This thinking in the light of hope suggest a reading of Kant and Hegel that inverts their chronological order whereby the intelligibility of hope is more starkly exposed.[8] In this reading of Kant

---

7. Ricoeur does not turn directly to the language of theology to manifest the power of the sacred. He writes, "What is more, it is an old conviction of mine that the philosopher's opposite in this type of debate is not the theologian, but the believer who is informed by the exegete; I mean, the believer who seeks to understand himself through a better understanding of the texts of his faith" (438:2).

8. Ricoeur borrowed this idea from Eric Weil. He insists, however, that the reasons for the inversion are not only theological but also philosophical. But the philosophical reason is not very cogent. Merely because we are post-Kantian and post-Hegelian can, of course, allow us to

after Hegel Ricoeur discovers an approach to hope that does not give content to hope but that gives us insight into the limits of reason or into the closing of the discourse of reason. According to Ricoeur, a post-Hegelian reading of Kant can give the contours of the farthest reach of philosophical discourse. Through the inverted reading, Ricoeur will take both Kant and Hegel a step beyond themselves. The inverted reading will allow him to interject his theory of the power of poetic or metaphorical language. The poetic approach not only confirms the limits of language proposed particularly by Kant, but it also affirms beyond Hegel's representation of religion, a power of representation by way of poetic language that is not absolute in Hegel's sense. The more poetic approach will not only confirm the limits of language as proposed by Hegel and Kant, but also reveal a power of language unknown to Kant and Hegel.

Ricoeur begins with Hegel's horizon of philosophical discourse. For Hegel, the farthest reach of philosophy is absolute knowledge. Despite Hegel's openness to the future by means of the successive mediations, the mediations themselves are ultimately ruled by a closure. He proposes a final reconciliation of all oppositions. In the final analysis, it is Spirit that determines all the previous mediations. Hegel's universe is a closed universe. Within such a system hope is short-circuited by its entrapment within a totalizing Spirit. In the absolute knowledge of Spirit, Hegel's truth comes to itself. Truth is the final adequation that rules the system from beginning to end: "The Hegelian system is a system written from the end towards the beginning, from the standpoint of totality, towards the partial achievements of the system" (338:60). Consequently, for Hegel, the discourse of philosophy and religion are identical because there can be only one discourse of the absolute Spirit and in both discourses one reflects the ultimate return of the Spirit to itself as self-consciousness.

Ricoeur seeks to salvage one unique contribution from this closed universe of Hegel. Hegel was the first to undertake to write the history of the stages of the representation of the absolute. He perceived a world of 'representations' that possessed a certain autonomy and a proper dialectic which, in his view, led to a speculative conceptualization. Hence, the world of religion also presents a certain 'representation': a process of forms and their negations, leading toward a concept. Like all representations the religious representations are recognizable as forms that must first be overcome in order that they may become a concept. What Hegel proposes, in other words, is a speculative content to religion whose moment of truth lies in the final mediation of absolute knowledge (411:140-141). The religious realm is not totally cut off from the speculative.

Ricoeur's critique of Hegel focusses on Hegel's linkage of the process of religious representation with absolute knowledge. The philosophers of suspicion have seriously jeopardized such a linkage. Thus, while he accepts Hegel's analysis of religious representation, he asks

---

read the one through the other, but that does not indicate that we ought to read the one in the light of the other.

whether one cannot posit a religious representation that refuses the claim of an absolute totalization of reality by knowledge, and nevertheless retain a level of knowledge or conceptualization. To give hope an outlet, Ricoeur must break through the absoluteness of the process of Hegel and re-establish the dynamism of reality, that is, reality as possibility, without, at that same time, abolishing everything of Hegel's speculative dimension. If he were not to succeed, Ricoeur thinks that he would have to identify religion with the absolute point of convergence of the movement of history. If unsuccessful, a religion of hope would have to be banished as illusory.

It is to Kant's philosophy of limit that Ricoeur constantly turns, whenever he legitimates his aversion to totalizing systems. But it is a post-Hegelian Kant. Moreover, Ricoeur is drawn to Kant because he defined religion by the question, What may I hope?

But we cannot understand the Kantian philosophy of religion, unless we first comprehend the two questions that precede the religious quest. Prior to the question of hope lies the question of pure reason, What can I know?, and the question of practical reason, What must I do? And underlying these questions is Kant's revolutionary distinction between Verstand (understanding) and Vernunft (reason), between Erkennen (to know) and Denken (to think).

Kant's Vernunft is a function of the unconditioned, while Verstand remains a function of conditioned knowledge. When Kant speaks of the limits of knowledge, according to Ricoeur, he implies "not only...that our knowledge is limited, has boundaries, but that the quest for the unconditioned puts limits on the claim of objective knowledge to become absolute" (411:142). Vernunft functions as a limit and not as an absolute in the area both of knowledge and of action. In the realm both of pure reason and of practical reason, reason seeks to be total, but simultaneously recognizes the impossibility, even the prohibition, of this totality. In pure reason, the object - das Ding-an-sich - is sought but is unattainable, except as the conditioned of the unconditioned. In practical reason, God, immortality, and freedom is sought but they too are not practically attainable. Theoretically and practically, according to Kant, humanity is limited. And yet, despite the limitation, humanity is also the exigency of totality. It is out of this tension that religion emerges as a hope for completion and fulfillment.

On the level of knowledge, pure reason exposes a transcendental illusion. The self, freedom and God are not absolute objects. In fact, knowledge destroys the absolute object. Religion, therefore, stands under the critique of the transcendental illusion. The nouminal order is closed off to pure reason. For Kant this order is not an order of knowledge, since sensibility does not reach into the noumenal. The realm of hope is closed off to knowledge, and, for that reason, what I hope I must first despair of reaching and grasping through knowledge, in order that a true hope may emerge. What I hope is not subject to the conditions of space and time. Speculative reason cannot achieve the thought of the unconditioned.

For Ricoeur, this critique of absolute knowledge through the theory of the transcendental illusion is central to his perception of a thinking in the light of hope. The limit of knowledge operates as a closure on a number of attempts to organize a metaphysics or an onto-theology (365:XIV). At the other extreme, even atheism's attempt to set up the human individual as an absolute is subject to the same critique. For Ricoeur, a rational and speculative theology - onto-theology - cannot maintain itself against the critique of the transcendental illusion (338:65; 320(297):415; 320(325):445). Hence the God, who is supreme being, ultimate intelligibility, the watchmaker, the first mover, falls before the onslaught of the critique of the transcendental illusion (373:96; 436:496; 186:51; 367:68). The God of metaphysics is dead, so is the God as moral legislator, and the God whose existence must be justified in the face of evil (320(325):448 438:19; 436:495-497). For Ricoeur, in this context, the usurping of God by Being is a dangerous but subtle seduction (436:496).

In addition, on the level of practical reason, our reason is confronted with an illusion similar in nature to the illusion of pure reason. While pure reason seeks totalization on the level of knowledge, practical reason seeks to be completed on the level of practical moral living. Its goal for the will is the supreme good. The will asks that it be completed in happiness, but happiness must coincide with the achievement of the duty and law of the moral life. But the desire for totalization, i.e., for the complete nexus of happiness and morality, is frustrated by the critique of the transcendental illusion. Totalization is not granted here either. And for Kant there is the added problem that if happiness is to coincide with morality, morality is no longer free of desire. Because the goal of the will is happiness, morality itself is invaded with an interest, which Kant's objective morality had excluded in principle (320(297):416-17).[9]

However, the coincidence of morality and happiness is not attainable under the conditions of practical reason. While the expectation for a nexus is there, happiness and morality can only meet in a term that is transcendent and heterogeneous and which lies at the horizon of rationality (338:66; 324:175). It is, as Ricoeur remarks, "necessary yet not given, but simply demanded, expected" (320(297):417). For Kant, happiness is not our achievement. It is a gift. Hence, here too the totalization, as an actualization of my freedom, is not available to my power. Here Kant differs radically from Hegel, who saw the actualization of our freedom realizable in the ideal State.

On this point Ricoeur agrees with Kant. While acknowledging Hegel's successful mediations in history, and the measure of freedom which has emerged out of the negations, he says "Are they not rather sorts of islands of rationality, surrounded by irrationality? Is not the Hegelian philosophy of action a kind of extrapolation based on the limited experience of the fulfilled achievements of mankind?" (338:63). Hegel's claim of totalization, of fulfilled achievement, must not be allowed to overshadow

---

9. See above, p.154.

the sea of unfulfilled claims. Hegel's failure to convince makes Ricoeur return to Kant.

Kant's awareness of the gap between the exigency of totalization and its lack of fulfillment is much more respectful of reality. But the antinomy of practical reason can also make us recognize the illusions of the will. For Ricoeur, this illusion of the will of an actualized happiness can form the basis for a further critique of religion. On the practical level, this critique confronts the instinctual aspects that attach themselves to religion, such as security, protection, consolation, fear of punishment, and accusation.[10] For practical reason, the nexus between morality and happiness is a transcendent synthesis that excludes all premature and violent syntheses on the part of institutions either of Church or of State.

While both the realm of pure reason and the realm of practical reason operate out of an exigency of hope in so far as they demand a reconciliation of a desire and its achievement, it is particularly religion that, for Kant, is governed by hope. Religion is the area of the question, What may I hope? Ricoeur approaches Kant's question. What may I hope for? from two angles: from the angle of Kant's postulates of practical reason, and from the angle of radical evil.

The Kantian postulates of practical reason are beliefs, theoretical in character, but dependent upon practical reason. In fact, they flow directly from practical reason. What our theoretical reason and practical reason seek by way of totalization demands a transcendent realm to which we know we belong and which installs the totality that we seek. But the transcendent realm is a postulate, not an object. That it be an object has been excluded by theoretical reason. There is no new access to a rational theology. For Kant there are three postulates: freedom, immortality, and God.

The freedom postulated here is the freedom of a being who effectively can realize the willed good. It is freedom objectively capable of actualizing itself. Freedom is postulated as a real causality. As Ricoeur says, "But that our capacity be equal to our will, that we exist according to this supreme vow, that is what can only be postulated" (320(297):419). Immortality as a postulate only confirms the concreteness of the postulate of freedom. Immortality is a condition for the possibility of the actualization of freedom. It specifies that our postulated freedom can only be real, if there is temporality, if there is continued existence. Like freedom, this need to persist in existence is not ours to give. It can, however, find us. That is the hope that religion holds out to us like a philosophical equivalent of the hope of the resurrection (320(297):420). Equally the postulate of God attaches itself to the postulate of immortality and freedom as the power to effect what is not in our power to realize, namely, immortality and freedom. As Ricoeur says, God is "a concept for

_____

10. For a brief reflection on the work of demystification, see below p.245-246.

the origin of a synthesis which is not in our power" (320(297):421). In God the highest good of a realized freedom is postulated. But the postulate must remain a postulate, that is, it must remain an exigency of our will in its search for the fulfillment of the highest good. In this search Ricoeur recognizes in Kant a fellow Christian, who postulates philosophically the practical possibility of the highest good. This hope is articulated out of the analysis of the practical and theoretical reason, which indicates that the hope of religion lies beyond the dimension of knowledge and praxis.

But the question, What may I hope? of religion must also confront itself with the question of evil. Kant opens his Religion Within the Limits of Reason Alone with the problem of evil, because it is the greatest threat to the realization of freedom. Our freedom is only a powerless freedom. In the words of Ricoeur,

> Evil makes of freedom an impossible possibility. In spite of the fact that evil proceeds from our freedom, it is no longer within our power to change the maxims of our actions, we cannot change the nature of our freedom. Here we reach the bottom of the abyss. As Karl Jaspers has noticed, Kant carries to termination his philosophy of the limits; not only our knowledge but our power has limits (338:68).

Where we think we have power in our freedom, we encounter the powerlessness of the power of freedom. This is the crisis of practical reason, because real freedom is available only as hope. Freedom in its true nature manifests itself only when it has passed through the powerlessness both of theoretical reason and of practical reason. The negation manifests, that the thwarted totalization of our knowledge and of our power can be overcome by a transformation of the will that is neither ethical nor political. For that reason, radical evil, according to Kant, appears not as a transgression of a law - what we might have expected from an ethics of duty - but as a work of totalization (320(232):345). In other words, evil in its true visage appears with religion in the tension between the desire for totality and its illusion, in the perversion of premature syntheses both of knowledge and of power. For that reason, a totalizing system of knowledge is a seductive temptation to be resisted at all costs. Also the institutions of recapitulation and totalization, the state and the Church, must be safeguarded from the radical evil of totalitarianism (320(297):423).

Kant has provided Ricoeur with the lower boundary beyond which a religious discourse can take place. By way of his critique of hope, the delimitation of that discourse by theoretical and practical reason provided a good critical instrument in determining the perimeters of an authentic religious discourse.

A good example of such a critique of religious language is found in Ricoeur's analysis of the concept of Original Sin (320(164):269-286). For Ricoeur, the concept of Original Sin is the farthest probing of thought of Israel's confession of sin. But to the extent that Original Sin is presented as a concept, as theoretical knowledge, to explain our human condition, or to explain the origin of evil, it looses its power to reveal and it becomes a gnosis - an illusory knowing in the realm of the transcendent. Similarly, a totally practical, ethical approach to Original Sin is invalidated by Kant's critique. Kant's critique breaks with a purely ethical vision of the world, since it readmits a moment in evil that is not reducible to the ethical. Kant linked this moment with the serpent in the Adamic myth. Evil is something which is begun by freedom and is, simultaneously, the 'always already there' for freedom. Evil has always already been chosen by freedom. For Kant, evil takes us beyond the ethical into the realm of the failure of our power to be free, where hope brings us to the expectation of a regeneration (320(173):306-309). It is in this new realm "where everything can begin again...where freedom discovers itself as something to be delivered - in brief...where it can hope to be delivered" (320(326):434-436).

B. THE LANGUAGE OF THE SACRED.

Kant's postulates of God and the problem of radical evil do not yet constitute religion. Kant himself realized as much, when he indicated that real religion is born with, what he called, representation. The total object of the will, the good principle, sought by practical reason finds expression in religion in an 'archetype', i.e., a representation of the totally good. For Kant this archetypal representation must be a man according to the heart of God, the Christ.

At this level Ricoeur's entry into the realm of the transcendent turns away from Kant and returns to Hegel. Kant still belongs to the metaphysical age. While Ricoeur is appreciative of the close approximation of Kant's analysis of religion to the kerygma of hope, Kant's religious representation allows no room for any epistemic content outside of the practical or ethical. While not wishing to fall back to Hegel's absolute knowledge, Ricoeur seeks to find a mediation between knowledge and thought. Must the thought of the unconditioned remain empty, or, may we seek at least a partial entry into the realm of the transcendent? As has become evident from the analysis of poetic and symbolic language, Ricoeur does not leave the space between knowledge and thought completely empty. He postulates that the space is invaded not by a direct discourse but by an indirect discourse. It is the discourse of the sacred in the form of the symbol, the myth, and the biblical forms of discourse. As we saw above, Ricoeur infused this indirect discourse with the ontology that originated with Heidegger. However, he inverted Heidegger, principally to underline that we are not dealing here with some type of objective language, but with a figurative, metaphorical language. It is first of all this language that can reach out to hope. Before we can examine what sort of self emerges from the realm of hope, we must examine the language of hope (cf. 417:142-143).[11]

---

11. Ricoeur's ontology of hope is inspired by the work of Gabriel Marcel, who gave Ricoeur his first hunger for a return to the ontological (426:68; cf. also 373:101).

1. Hope and language.

a. Beyond ontology?

After the Kantian delimitation of religion beyond knowledge and morality, the question must be raised whether, in fact, Ricoeur can retain the ontology that ruled his hermeneutics of perception and action at the level of religion?[12] Can an indirect ontology, patterned upon Heidegger in reverse, be an adequate approximation of the realm of hope? Is religion also an outflow of Being? May we equate Being with God? To avoid falling into the pitfall of an onto-theology must we not seek this God beyond Being? In the conclusion of this article, "Ontologie" (cf. 373:100-101), Ricoeur refers to the contemporary philosophers, such as Merleau-Ponty and Heidegger, who, after having re-introduced the ontological discourse begin, in their final positions, to break down what they themselves built up. Being, or that which lies beyond being, is for Merleau-Ponty that "to which no name can be given" (373:101). Heidegger, too, seeks to break with his earlier position by no longer referring to the 'da' of Dasein which humans are, but to an exigency of Being with no direct reference to the Being that we are. In this context, Ricoeur refers to Heidegger's return to the pre-Socratics and their pre-metaphysical ontology and to the strange act of Heidegger's Zur Seinsfrage of crossing out the word Being (373:101).[13] Ricoeur asks with Jean Wahl: "What is the meaning of this crossed-out Sein? Either no name fits being, or else being is only a name. And both views are tenable" (373:101). Is the 'beyond' Levinas' infini, which the latter opposes to the totalizing word Being?, or, is it Derrida's Difference?

From what we have seen of Ricoeur's philosophy, he hardly can take that step. For how can he identify the 'beyond' without at the same time abandoning the indirect approach to which he had committed himself? And yet, on the other hand, the position of a 'beyond' being seems to follow logically from Ricoeur's acceptance of Kant's critiques and of the category of hope. But Ricoeur does not let being off the hook that easily. In the same article, "Ontologie", he makes a remark that more than any other expresses Ricoeur's own position: "And must we say one thing? In the same

---

12. For this and a further reflection on the contribution that Ricoeur makes to the issue of the philosophical underpinning of evil and salvation see Chr. Depoortere, "Mal et liberation. Une étude de l'oeuvre de Paul Ricoeur" in Studia Moralia 14, 1976, p.337-385.

13. In the preface which Ricoeur wrote for B. Rioux' L'être et la vérité chez Heidegger et St. Thomas d'Aquin, (Montréal, Paris, Presses de l'Université de Montréal. Presses universitaires de France, 1963) he acknowledges that Heidegger is not a theologian but a radical thinker in the face of all theology and perhaps even of philosophy. But Heidegger, for all that, does not know how to pass from being to God. Ricoeur, while unable to surpass Heidegger, seeks another route to being, without letting go of the decisive contribution that Heidegger made toward a theology of revelation (198:111).

way as we spoke in the beginning with regard to Platonic Ideas of a polytheism of being, so one could conceivably speak of the post-ontological polytheism" (373:101). For Ricoeur, we must assume that being still encompasses the realm of the transcendent, that God and being are not outside each other (cf. 87:1938). That if being is polytheistic, or, in Aristotle's words, Being is said of many things, it is not necessary to assume an univocal concept of being. We have insisted above,[14] that Ricoeur rejects such an univocal concept of being, that in fact, there are multiple discourses of being. As a consequence of this multiplicity he is forced to examine at length whether the discourses of being are not so disparate that all communication between them is to be excluded. As an avenue to a solution he insists that an interpenetration of discourse occurs, but that the principle, guiding such an interanimation, is lacking. Even the famous analogia entis does not serve as a true bonding power that keeps the discourse of being from scattering irretrievably (cf. 227:22).

If, for Ricoeur, God is not beyond being, it must be admitted, however, that God strains the concept of being almost to the breaking point. And yet, when he admits with J. McQuarrie that there is more meaning in the word God than in the word being, he does not wish to move the word God into an incomprehensibility that blocks all reference to him (299:348). Without an analogia entis to regulate and properly control the discourse about God, Ricoeur hypothesizes that we must search in language and in the semantic aim of language for the key to the proper discourse of hope.[15]

In other words, as he has done all along, Ricoeur backs away from the lofty heights of a direct ontology and speculation and proposes the long route of an indirect ontology. He seeks to penetrate the realm of religion with the power of language. Here too, discourse is "like an army fighting on a moving battlefront: fighting to conquer the not yet expressed on behalf of the expressed" (448:127).

b. Hope and event.

Before we can explore the power of creative language in the realm of religion, we must overcome a hurdle presented by a prominent trend in theology. In their theology Pannenberg, Metz, and Moltmann assume the precedence of event - the historical event - over the word. They concentrate on the events of history, namely, the Exodus event and the Resurrection event as moments par excellence of the revelation of God. For them, history is the basic source of meaning. God is first of all event and manifests himself in the events of history (320(294):394). He is not primordially a word and, therefore, it is not the word that is first in meaning, but the event. The historical event in which God reveals himself is a historical fact before it is a word or a proclamation. What comes first is

---

14. See p.85-87.

15. Cf. A. Cipollone, "Religious Language and Ricoeur's Theory of Metaphor" in Phil. Today 21, 1977, p. 458-467.

an otherness that has the nature of an event. And in order to keep the event of history from being drawn too quickly into an existential application, these theologians insist, moreover, that the event of history must first be placed into a larger historical framework. The event is said to obtain its meaning by way of its nexus with other events or with their consequences. An example of such a nexus is Jürgen Moltmann's linkage of the death of Jesus with the solidarity with the oppressed of history (362:28).

A second dimension of the revealing event, according to these theologians, is the eschatological character of the event. The temporality of the Exodus event and of the event of the Death and Resurrection of Jesus is not encompassed by the past of the event but it is determined by its openness toward the future. Even as having taken place, the event is not exhausted but remains an event of hope as the future of the fulfillment of the promise. Thus, Moltmann, for instance, speaks of the future of the resurrection of Jesus (cf. 362:32). As future, it determines that the possibilities that propose themselves to me are not dependent upon my decision and power. For him, that is the Christian Kairos, the favorable time, in which a new epoch of being can emerge (362:34). Where hope is accomplished or is regrounded, it is done through an event in history, where the hope and the promise took place.

What Ricoeur retains of the reading of these theologians is the event-character of Christianity. That which manifests itself in our history, they maintain, is God as event, or, more strongly, what is manifested is history in God. In Ricoeur's view this confirms the modern acceptance of being as act (417:276). It corresponds to his own discovery of an active notion of being. It predisposes him favourably to their point of departure (362:25).

But Ricoeur departs from Pannenberg, Metz and Moltmann in their assessment of the meaning of the event. They insist that the meaning follows from the historical nexus of events and lies in the historical consequences of the event. Ricoeur's proposal is more tangible. The meaning of the event lies in the conjoining of these events with language. In other words, he proposes that the dialectic of event and meaning in the theory of discourse also apply to the revealing event of history (375:31). The event is a crystallization of meaning (251:504). The event passes into the meaning; it becomes inscribed in the meaning, and, thereby, escapes the illusiveness and evanescence of the event. The event is captured in significations and preserved. Through the interpretation of the discourse, one can re-activate the deposit into a new event of meaning. But without its sedimentation in meaning, and, beyond oral discourse, in a written text, no retaking of the event is possible.

What we gain from this analysis is that the realm of hope, for Ricoeur, is first of all founded upon and grounded in a dynamism, an event. But, secondly, this event is mediated by the word. In fact, language must be said to be co-original with event, although language draws its power from the event (362:25). And, thirdly, the word must take on the tension of the event toward the future of the promise.

223

c. Hope and language.

The word that flows from the event of God, as co-original with the event, is first of all the word (parole) that says God (271:132). Before God enters into human language, it is presupposed that there is a languagistic dimension or a dicibilité of reality.[16] Here too the influence of Heidegger continues to be felt (267:36-38). The language of the texts of religion - the texts of the Scriptures -are an inscription, an exteriorization, of the reality prior to the external word. If the Bible is called the word of God, the fixation of this text bespeaks a word prior to the text. In line with Christian tradition and under the more immediate influence of G. Ebeling, Ricoeur calls it the Word of God or God as word (251:499).[17]

What is meant by Word of God or God as word? Following Ebeling, Ricoeur makes a number of precisions.

1. The Lutheran tradition of sola fide, according to Ebeling, allows nothing to intervene between the original event and the present event in which the original event is interpreted. The interpretation of the word is an event that is homogeneous with the first event. Ebeling, as a church historian, perceives the history of the Church as a history of the continuous exegesis and actualization of the original event. The Church is the history of interpretation, a history of the reactivation of the original event (267:42-43).

2. Ebeling understands this word itself to be dynamic. He calls it a Wortgeschehen, not in the sense of an instantaneous event, but as a process, an unfolding, a development, a maturing.[18] It is a word that matures in time. To the extent that the word has become text, this unfolding in time is the event in which what has become text becomes word once again. The text must continuously open up to a new proclamation. The

---

16. In his "Préface à Bultmann" he says of this approach, "There is no shorter path for joining a neutral existential anthropology, according to philosophy, with the existential decision before God, according to the Bible. But there is the long path of the question of being and of the belonging of saying to being" (320(294):400).

17. In his presentation Ricoeur attempts to bridge the Reformed and Catholic categories. The Reformed position, in wishing to escape the more realistically oriented ontology of Catholicism, centered its vision on a theology of the word. Ricoeur's position shows that although the orientations differ, the respective positions can be correlated with one another in a Heideggerean style of ontology that safeguards both an ontology and the power of the word. It is significant, however, that Ricoeur distanciates himself from a theology of the word that attempts to be too directly linked to an existential decision (cf. 267:48).

18. Ricoeur translates the German Wortgeschehen with the French échéance.

word exists only in this movement - this Geschehen (267:43-44: 332:5).

3. The word is, therefore, not an object either in this world or in another world but a movement, a becoming. It is a word that says nothing about our world as it is. It does not describe; it is not didactic. It does not give a cosmology, nor a physics, a biology, a psychology, or a politics. It is a word that is completely given over to the event of God: God as word or the word of God. An onto-theology cannot find a point of access here (267:44). And yet, the word of God is not to be situated in a world beyond, having a separate existence, attainable only by a sacred knowledge.

4. For Ebeling, there is only one point of access and that is the general hermeneutic of the word. The word of God is of God, that is, it is not my word. But it must become my word, incorporating human language, to be word of God (332:16). Therefore, it requires no supra-human method to approach it. It is structured as human language is structured: it does not escape the dialectic of sense and reference. Moreover, the word is not for the sake of itself. Through the word we are deposited in something beyond language (267:45). The word is for the sake of that to which it refers. That is its power. It effects an encounter with that reality by making it word-present. But it obeys the 'laws' of language and the process of a general hermeneutics such as we have worked out above (cf. 299:334).

5. A fifth and final point brings us to the heart of the issue. To speak of the word of God, in accordance with this line of reflection, is far removed from an objectified or even subjectified word of God. The word is not a person. The word of God for Ebeling is a fulfilled word:

> a word which creates communication, which creates existence, which creates lucidity. We might say that we are before a word of God to the extent that we are before a word that instigates a self-understanding and an understanding of another, that generates a history, and, consequently, is alive, efficacious, because it is a word that generates man (267:47).

It is an active, dynamic word that addresses itself to humanity, as to the source of its existence (251:506). It touches us at the core of our very desire and effort to be (320(232):336). A word of God is a word that fully gives birth to humanity. It is a word that is an effective communication. Hence, a full word: our language at the point of its full potential. God's word is not opposed to the human word. It is the accomplishment of this word. For Ebeling, the moment in history, where this human word was God's word, occurred in Christ and occurs again and again in the Christian kerygma (299:333; 267:48). Here the word becomes flesh. A true word is spoken. The word of God or God as word means, therefore, that God is the source from whom or from which a Wortgeschehen is possible.

For Ricoeur, the movement, the event of hope as not our creation is a movement that is thoroughly immersed in the movement and the power of language itself. It is not originally our word. It is a word that is addressed to us and interpellates us. Over it I have no power (251:499). But it is captured by us in another word that seeks to re-activate the power of the original event, and as such is homogeneous with the event. It is the original word that finds us and reactivates us at our act-centre by granting us a new understanding and a new self-understanding and thus changing us (251:506). It is this word that accompanies our existence and draws us to that which is essential in us (220:224). The word that speaks or says us is also in the deepest sense the power that gathers us. But this word that gathers us, that speaks us before we speak it, must pass through the word that we speak, in order that the power of the word to bond us with being and with our hope may be experienced (299:346). For that is Ricoeur's presupposition: the experience of hope is experienced in language, a language that has a cognitive, practical, and emotional dimension (436:490). The mediation of the human spoken or written word to the gathering word must be examined in greater detail, for it is this human word in its fulness that captures and preserves for us the hope that is addressed to us.

d. Hope as Kerygma.

The event of hope does not have its origin in us, but by the language that accompanies it, it is addressed to us, to our very source or ground. Taking Heidegger as the closest philosophical approximation of the process of the word, Ricoeur says that the language of being is not what is first said by us but primordially constitutes us. It touches our knowing, our willing, our action, and our existence at the point where we become (232:75). Our first relation to that language is, therefore, not one of speech but of listening. Since all control over this word is denied us, the attitude before this word can only be that of a common and communal listening and hearing (251:499). That is the reason why for Ricoeur the problematic of faith finds its home in a poetics of the will, in the word addressed to me that touches the radical origin of existence. Ricoeur calls this word a word of sollicitation (227:525).

Hope comes to us, therefore, as a kerygma, as a 'good news'. It enters our sphere as a proclamation that seeks our listening obedience. It is in the silent space of our attentiveness, where a listening and hearing can take place, that we are formed and shaped by what comes to us 'of God' (332:15). The Kerygma is the God-event that in our language and time has become sedimented in the proclamation and the history of the proclamation of the ecclesial community (291:249). The proclamation does not devolve from our experience. It is like "an eruption of something from the other side, from the totally other into our culture" (220:210).[19] And yet this

---

19. Here the Barthian side of Ricoeur shows itself. But one cannot extend the parallel too far. Ricoeur's theory of discourse intervenes too decisively to retain the diastasis between God and the human being of Barth in the same measure.

kerygma and proclamation is also a cultural fact. For Ricoeur, it is very concretely the Christian kerygma. Hence, the language of hope is the language of Christian proclamation. The primary activity of hope for Ricoeur is preaching (20:52; 109:640; 44:177; 396(236):15). By means of preaching, the kerygma of hope enters into the concrete history of human existence, right into the midst of the 'forgetfulness of being'. By means of preaching, the word that gathers and constitutes us establishes the historical community of the word. In the deepest sense, preaching is the activation of the event that constitutes us in the fullest measure in an historical and ecclesial context. In the language of preaching what is 'of God', the Wholly Other, becomes discernible and immanent in our language and structures. But since hope cannot enter our history and language in a directly discernible fashion, because its meaning is necessarily hidden, the texture of that language needs further examination.

e. Hope and history.

Riceour perceives an inalienable relationship between faith and religion. He is attracted by the suggestiveness of Bonhöffer's religionless Christianity, because of the latter's insistence upon the centrality of faith and hope,[20] but he refuses to subscribe to a notion of faith that has no point of exteriorization (320(228):185). Ricoeur's reservation about Bonhöffer is similar to his difficulties with the viewpoint of Barth and Bultmann. For Bultmann, for instance, the objectivation of faith is, of necessity, a reification. His demythologization process brings him to a non-mythical core of faith which, he said, was God as act, the word of God, the call of summons of the word of God, the future of God, or justification by faith. Since this core is an existential and personal summons that is not mythological, this core is pure faith which is meaningful only in the context of the surrender of the will. For Ricoeur, there is no such free zone of faith. Also faith enters human language and human history (320(294):394-396). Faith enroots itself in religion (291:246). Religion is the historical and cultural expression of faith, or, as Ricoeur says aptly, the disposable believable (291:246). Religion is faith's historical dimension, dialectically related to it. Thus there is a discourse of faith due to a distanciation from the participation in the act of God. Faith enters the polyvalent realm of human discourse, where the interanimation and the delimitation of the variety of human discourses take place (396:338).

But religion must always be overcome by faith (324(331):441). A critique of religion is indispensable, because in its historical articulation religion is endangered by the seduction of mystification and illusion (452(220):213-218). Faith can never be fully made into an object, because the transcendent, as hope, cannot be encompassed by its historical dimension (216:96; 235:143). This surplus of the meaning of faith over its historical forms manifests itself whenever the critique destroys one

---

20. The influence of K. Jaspers is also evident here. Religious faith for Jaspers is a betrayal of the world. Only transcendence respects the world. Cf. 109:620-621, and 101:377ff.

historical form only to have faith resurface in another form (235:143). Here, too, the content regulates the language and the form, and not vice versa (320(200):48). In the Judeo-Christian tradition the tension of the 'now' of religion and the 'not yet' of faith and hope is expressed by the insertion of the 'Last Day.' Thoroughly eschatological it is, christianity's faith is a hope that proclaims a yes to history as the primary focus of the manifestation of hope, but, at the same time, a no to any attempt to equate the moment of history with totality. Accordingly, the "Church is the place where religion endlessly dies, where this death is lived as an auto-suppression" (235:142). And yet this community is itself a religious form where this tension of faith and religion is lived where "the death of religion is lived as a religious form" (235:142-143). Hence, for Ricoeur, faith is the source of the constant uprooting of religion by means of eschatology (430:68). The eschatological, as the invasion in our history of the beyond history, demolishes the structures and language that might otherwise become totalitarian or gnostic (357:535). Religion is ever under the critique of premature totalization (20:59). Religion must be constantly safeguarded from the transformation of faith into a relic.[21] A relic makes of religion an object that can be manipulated. Religion as relic deprives religion of its power to evoke the possible. For Ricoeur, the same movement that condemns any attempt to objectify religion into a stable configuration as irreligion also forces the religious discourse to stretch human discourse to its limit (227:530).

In the realm of religion language remains the focal battle-ground, where religious hope calls humanity forth to open up new life, to perceive a new time, a new creation, a new existence. Theology's first task, according to Ricoeur, is that the language of the proclamation be kept as a proclamation, so that it does not deteriorate into an accusation or into an undue search for security and consolation (cf. 291:250-251).

The paradox of Christianity for Ricoeur is its confession that its hope and the language that expresses that hope are linked to contingent events of history: the Exodus, the life, death, and resurrection of Jesus, the Christ (436:490). The uniqueness and the contingency of these events does not run counter to what we might call the universal unveiling of being.

---

21.   In a text of De l'interprétation, Ricoeur expresses this at some length, "Thus there is a never-ending task of distinguishing between the faith of religion -faith in the Wholly Other which draws near - belief in the religious object, which becomes another object of our culture and thus a part of our own sphere.   The sacred, as signifying separation or otherness, is the area of this combat.   The sacred can be the sign of that which does not belong to us, the sign of the Wholly Other; it can also be a sphere of separate objects within our human world of culture and alongside the sphere of the profane.   The sacred can be the meaningful bearer of what we described as the structure of horizon peculiar to the Wholly Other which draws near, or it can be the idolatrous reality to which we assign a separate place in our culture, thus giving rise to religious alienation.   The ambiguity is inevitable: for if the Wholly Other draws near, it does so in the signs of the sacred; but symbols soon turn into idols" (227:531).

Though our reason may find this impossible to prove and though it may appear to contradict our experience, Christianity confesses nonetheless that the hope is carried by the fragility of events, the ambiguity of language, the tenuousness of the lives of people. The power of these contingent events and words is not easily fathomed. But what seems impossible to prove in the court of knowledge, the power of its expression manifests a wealth of meaning that has the capacity to reshape reality. These central moments of faith and hope assure a force that appears inexhaustible. These events have the gathering force of symbols that permit a rereading of existence and of our communal history (see 220:210). In that sense, even events in history can have the force of the 'Last Day'.

2. Biblical hermeneutics.

With the prohibition of an onto-theology and a metaphysics of the sacred, Ricoeur peceives only one avenue to be open to a philosophical approximation of the realm of hope. And that is the hermeneutical one. The realm of hope comes to language in our discourse. The gospel itself has become a text (320(294):387). It offers itself to our discernment as any discourse. Our hope, then, becomes an interpreted hope. The rest of this chapter proposes to examine this hermeneutics of the sacred in the texts of the Judeo-Christian tradition. It is in these texts that Ricoeur proposes to discover the mediation of our attachment to the God of hope.

Ricoeur's exegesis of hope is applied to the constitutive texts of the Judeo-Christian tradition: the Bible. He refuses to start with theological propositions such as a number of Anglo-Saxon theologians have done. He believes that before one can undertake to analyse theological propositions, one must first examine the more originary expressions of these theological propositions. Theological propositions are second-order language in relation to the first-order language of the biblical text. Ricoeur believes that in the hermeneutical quest of the biblical texts one can arrive at the "most originary expression of a community of faith" (397:73).

But how does this biblical hermeneutics differ from a philosophical hermeneutics? On a formal level, biblical hermeneutics appears as only a particular case of a general hermeneutics. At the formal level there is no talk of a subordination of one hermeneutics to another. Biblical hermeneutics is subject to the same procedures as a general hermeneutics. For that reason, philosophical hermeneutics is not an ancilla, the handmaid, to a biblical hermeneutics. But because of the uniqueness of the world of the biblical text, since it seeks to express the unnameable, Ricoeur calls biblical hermeneutics the limit of all hermeneutics, the non-hermeneutical origin of all hermeneutics (397:84). As such, biblical hermeneutics is unique. It has a point, where it gathers all its texts. It has one reference that it forges that can never be complete. The reference is a name that is given as not given, a name that is refused as a name (320(309):485-486).[22] It is the power of the hope that issues from this name

---

22. Ricoeur accepts the statement of G. Ebeling concerning the Bible as the word of God, "It is only in listening to this book to the very

that creates the space of a biblical hermeneutics. In line with this, biblical hermeneutics borrows the hermeneutics, based on the problematics of the text, from philosophical hermeneutics. But, because of the unique referent, Ricoeur perceives theological hermeneutics to be more encompassing than philosophical hermeneutics, transforming it according to its own exigency 9406:17).

a. From oral proclamation to the Scriptures.

The Judeo-Christian proclamation, which we have described above as a Word-event, has, however, not only found its way to language but also to writing. As inscribed in language, the discourse of hope becomes subject to the structures and procedures of all language (360:285-288; 358:36-46). In being transformed into a written text, the discourse of hope accrues the same characteristics as any written text.[23] It is significant, however, that from the beginning the Christian proclamation has had a strict relationship with the Writings. The Christian proclamation is fundamentally a hermeneutic. Thus, it is, in the first instance, a hermeneutics of the law and the prophets of Israel's covenant. Also the proclamation of Jesus as the Christ by the first community is a hermeneutics of the figures of the written Hebraic and Hellenic cultures. What is novel in Jesus is made available to a community through an interpretation and an exegesis of what had already become sedimented in a written culture. Furthermore, the proclamation as interpretation became a new written text - the New Testament - at a certain stage of its development (406:19-20).

A number of points ought to be made regarding the Bible as written text.

(1) The distanciation, made by writing, permits the insertion of all the explanatory procedures that we have examined earlier. The interpretation of the proclamation must be mediated by its code and the theory of language (406:20).

---

end, as one book among many, that we can encounter it as the Word of God" (397:82).

23. Ricoeur's text-theory cuts a swath through the exegetical practices of today. Because of the decontextualization of the text from the author, the original situation, and the original addressees, he relativizes the historico-critical method. Instead, he accepts structural exegesis, but only to the extent that it help us read the narrative structure better. With regard to the historico-critical method, he recognizes its irreplaceable value because by retaining an historical accent, the method remains a formidable protest against the Hegelian totalization of history in the absolute spirit (see 358:36). See also the introductory article of L. Dornisch, "Symbolic Systems and the Interpretation of Scripture: an Introduction to the Work of Paul Ricoeur" in Semeia 4, 1975; L.S. Mudge, "Paul Ricoeur on Biblical Interpretation" in Biblical Research, 24-25; 1979-1980, p.38-69.

(2) The interpretation which these writings give of the Word-event is not univocal. The variety of writings open up a multiform interpretation of the event of Jesus Christ. The Christian New Testament provides as many interpretations as there are distinct documents (406:20).

(3) Ricoeur accepts a closure upon the writings of the Bible. The closure made by the ecclesial community is proposed by Ricoeur as the horizon of the proclamation. The Church imposed the closure when it closed the canon of the scriptures. All other testimonies and writings are of lesser stature and are not perceived as primary sources of preaching (406:20).

(4) The interpretative chain does not end, however, with the closure of the scriptures. The interpretation becomes tradition and forms the history of the Church, which is best described as the insertion of the proclamation in time. It is as this power of the word in history that the original word-event reaches our time (406:20;403:57;320(200):47).

(5) This power of a text to infuse and orient a living tradition does not create a closed universe. On the one hand, Ricoeur refuses to hypostatize the text. It is not the text as text that is its force, but the power of the text to say out a world. The reference is the issue, not the literary hypostasis. On the other hand, the gathering power of the text brings the text into contact and communication with other texts. Ricoeur calls this the play of intertextuality. By this he means that every text inserts itself somewhere in historical becoming. Every text relates to other texts that precede it, accompany it, and succeed it. A text is part of a communicative chain (436:491-492). Hence, no text is absolute, because no text is solely for the sake of its sense, but every text exists for its reference that breaks this self-enclosedness.

b. The configuration of biblical discourse.

(1) The work of discourse of the Bible.

In Ricoeur's view the interlinking of the realm of hope with language, and, through the Bible, with texts, brings about a very specific bonding of the confession of faith with the variety of literary configurations that are found in the text of the Bible. The biblical text presents the reader with all the complexities of composition, literary genres, and style.[24] As produced texts, as a work on language, they present us with a number of styles and genres.

For Ricoeur, the number of forms or genres of texts found in the Bible are not accidental. They are determined by and issue forth from what is the issue of the text. Here too Ricoeur perceives a certain closure. He would like to view the closing of the Canon of the Bible as a "fundamental structural act" which delimits the space and the variety of the forms of discourse and their possible interplay (397:760). The number of forms of

---

24. See above, p.41-44.

discourse are factually limited to the forms found in the complete text of the Bible.[25] The total configuration of the text of the Bible forms the space of the full interpretation. However, Ricoeur is careful not to absolutize this closure of the canon. As he says,

> But perhaps this hypothesis is unverifiable and confers on the closing of the canon a sort of necessity which would not be appropriate to what should perhaps remain a historical accident of the text (397:78).

Two further presuppositions needs to be mentioned.

First, Ricoeur proposes that certain forms of discourse are more suited than others to express certain modalities of the confession of faith. Again with caution he states,

> Perhaps an exhaustive inquiry, if one were possible, would disclose that together all these forms of discourse constitute a circular system and that the theological content of each of them receives its signification from the total constellation of the forms of discourse. Religious language would then appear as a polyphonic language sustained by the circularity of forms (406:24).

Second, certain forms of discourse form binary pairs and require one another to complement the reference of their texts. Ricoeur makes specific reference along these lines to the complementarity of the narrative and prophetic genres of the Old Testament (406:22-23).

The total rationale of these characteristics cannot be given until one has considered the reference of these texts. As we saw above, for Ricoeur, it is the backward influence of the power of the Name that determines the forms and the interplay of forms (438:26). But the forms of discourse themselves are traditional, recognizable forms. Thus we discover narratives, parables, proverbs, gospels, letters, hymns, etc. All these forms, however, are infected with the power that they seek to say out. In what follows we shall state briefly which forms Ricoeur has found in these texts and how they interrelate.

---

25. Ricoeur's indebtedness to Von Rad's Theologie des Alten Testaments (München, Chr. Kaiser Verlag, 1960, 2 vol.) is apparent in all his references to the Old Testament. It is Von Rad who introduces Ricoeur to the close link between the literary genre and theological content (406:23;358:43;332:59-760;20(200):45; 222:93). The centering of Von Rad's Old Testament theology on the narrative mode of Dt. 26 has become a central perspective for Ricoeur's own approach to the narrativity of the Old Testament.

(2) The literary genres of the Bible.

Ricoeur's enumeration of the biblical genres is not intended to be exhaustive. His concern is rather to establish the principle that the religious experience which these texts articulate has a specific form and that this form is counterbalanced by other forms. These other forms are either their dialectical counterparts or their extensions, communicating with that form by disrupting or delimiting it. Whether there are more literary forms than the ones he has examined is not discussed. The closure of the literary forms of the biblical text may be more extensive than these which Ricoeur has analysed.

The biblical polyphony to which Ricoeur has listened includes the symbolic and mythical discourse,[26] narration, prophecy, legislation, proverbs, prayers, hymns, liturgical formulas, and sapiential writings of the Old Testament. In the New Testament his attention has been mainly focussed on the parables, proverbs and Kingdom sayings of the Synoptic Gospels (see 400, 406, 410, 411, 427, 436, 438, 470, 476). In their own way each of these forms are confessions of faith or name God in an originary way, but they do not carry equal weight. The literary form that organizes this polyphony of point and counterpoint into a fragile analogical unity is the narrative genre. For Ricoeur the starting point of his entry into the naming power of both testaments is the narrative, upon which he believes the testaments are built (332:59-60).

(a) Narrative discourse.

Von Rad's theology of traditions based on the Hebrew credal story of Deuteronomy 26:5b-10b serves to lead Ricoeur to the insight of the centrality of the narrative. The traditions of the Old Testament, Von Rad believes, are founded on a few key transcendent events, such as, the call of Abraham, the Exodus, the anointing of David. These stories name the reality of God through the historical drama as a God covenanted with a people and their ancestors. God is the great Actor of the call and of the deliverance of a community of people. He is a God who both established and rooted the community and protected it in the moments of danger. God is named in and through the very narration of the great events that grounded the community (436:496). This also applies to the New Testament. The gospels and the Acts of the Apostles are stories of the same nature. The stories of the resurrection, for instance, name God in the story of the raising of Jesus from the dead. This narrative is the story of the establishment and the grounding of a community. For Ricoeur, the narrative mode of naming God confirms the position outlined above of the event-character of God. The narrative is first of all a narrative of the

---

26. The symbolic and mythical discourse of the Old Testament was examined in La symbolique du mal, Le conflit des interprétations, and Les incidences théologiques des recherches actuelles concernant le langage (332).

event. It points beyond its language to history (438:6).[27] In their transcendence, these events have become the gathering points of a new history.

In the story's telling is effected not only the founding of the community, but also the active insertion of the hearers into the movement and time of the story. As the story expresses the originary participation of what it names, my belonging to the community of the story is redescribed by the very reading of the story in the community (438:154; 411:73). Here the narration becomes a confession of faith in God as the great Actant - to use Greimas' phrase. The theology that such a forms allows can only be a theology that is respectful of the narrative structure. Ricoeur calls it a theology in the form of a <u>Heilsgeschichte</u> (397:77; cf. also 87:1928-1930). The name of God is linked with the structure of an historical drama. A theology that seeks to bypass the historical drama, in order to arrive at a generalized concept of God, can only do so at its own peril.

The power of the faith of God as event in Israel's history was so incisive that it drew to itself the mythological strain borrowed from Babylon and in the process transformed it. In itself, this is not surprising, for, according to Ricoeur, the function of the myth is to install historical time (357:536). Ricoeur accepts, therefore, the thesis of Von Rad that the history of God's deeds incorporated the Babylonian creation myths and, by inserting them in Isreal's history, allowed them to become events of salvation (332:65;357:534). Hence, the narrative even touches and remakes cosmology (358:43-46). But the narrative does not totally overcome the cosmological and the mythical. Mythic time returns in the feast and in civic life, in the celebration of the Pasch and of the Sabbath, where it is placed in constant tension with the narrative (332:89). On the other hand the re-introduction of the myth, as well as our recognition that the events recounted are not necessarily chronologically as they took place, shows the temporality of these events to lie at a level deeper than mere linearity (332:81).

(b) Prophetic discourse.[28]

The God of narrative discourse threatens, however, to become immanent to history. The God, who establishes a people by instituting them in freedom, could easily be absorbed into the past of a people as a memory. The confession of this God is bound to the structure of the story. A God of memory dissipates the tension of hope. As Ricoeur says, "The God of the exodus must become the God of the exile if he is to remain the God of the

---

27. To date Ricoeur has not explicitly linked the structure of the narrativity of the bible to a specific temporality. The eschatological dimension of the biblical narrative is mentioned but hardly exploited.

28. Von Rad has also been instrumental here particularly in Volume II of his <u>Theologie des Alten Testaments.</u>, <u>op. cit.</u>, entitled, <u>Die Theologie der prophetischen Überlieferungen.</u>

future and not merely the God of memory" (406:24). He perceives among the forms of discourse one that radically disrupts the story of God as the Actant of history. It is the prophetic oracle with its resounding 'no' to an excessively narrow identification of Yahweh with Israel's story. The prophetic oracle re-infuses the tension into Israel's existence. The prophetic oracle dislocates the time of Israel's story and places it under the threat of death and extinction as a people (397:77-78;153:50-99;357:534-535). In the midst of Israel's story with God, the prophets hurl the Day of Yahweh, the judgement and the wrath of God. The prophet's time is not a time of events, but the time of discourse. In their discourse, they propose another time. But in order to propose a time of Yahweh other than the historical one, the prophets presuppose the God of history. The prophet cannot speak as he does, unless the historical time had already been established (332:89). In his words these times collide: the time of the imminent threat and the memory of the founding events. Time and history become both a time to relive and a threatened time.

There is, however, another distinctive trait of prophetic discourse. The narration speaks of God in the third person. The prophetic discourse has God speak as the I behind the prophet's voice. The prophet does not speak; he speaks in Yahweh's name. The prophet knows himself as called and sent. Behind his voice is the voice of God. As Ricoeur remarks, "God is named in a double first person, and as the word of another in my word" (436:498, my translation).[29] The danger of misunderstanding the prophetic oracle, when dissociated from the narrative, is great. The naming of God can be lost in the search for a God behind the voice and in search of a plan for history that such a voice proclaims. Prophecy's insertion of the Last Day into the process of history can become a divinatory instrument, a manipulative word, that claims to know the path of history, if one does not remember that prophecy's task is to prevent the relationship of Yahweh to history from becoming thingified or petrified (4378:3-4). Only by keeping this tension alive can the dimension of a new time emerge. Prophetic time becomes eschatological time. The time, beyond the threat that destroys this time, is the time of the 'perhaps' of God, the 'not-yet' of the Day of Yahweh, which is also a day of deliverance and promise for his elect (332:82;153:68-70). Drawing on Israel's events with God, the prophets call for a new exodus, for a return to Israel's days in the desert, etc. The prophetic oracle, therefore, both destructures the narrative, and, in recalling the narrative theme, trans-structures it in a new time as an immeasurable promise. In Ricoeur's words,

> The action of the prophecy on the story is its complete metaphorisation of the events themselves since they do not saturate them with accomplishment; that is why, moreover, every occupation of the Promised Land is ultimately eschatological (332:83).

---

29. "Dieu est nommé en double première personne, comme parole d'un autre dans ma parole."

In fact, for Ricoeur, the prophetic dimension attached to the narrative and, through the narrative, to the mythical, metaphorizes the whole tradition into a story of the promise. The end becomes the focal point. The story becomes eschatologized. It is prophetic. The historical events become events from the perspective of the God who comes (332:83,86). Beyond the dislocation of the events through the prophetic oracle, therefore, there is a relocation through the eschatological infusion.

(c) Prescriptive discourse.

A third type of discourse which attaches itself to the two previous is the prescriptive discourse of the Torah. Ricoeur designates it as the practical, ethical discourse of revelation (438:8). In this discourse, God is named as the giver or author of the law. And to the extent that it is addressed to me, Ricoeur says, I perceive myself as designated by God in the second person: You shall...(436:499). On the practical level the prescriptive discourse places my existence and my life in a new type of relationship with God: a relationship of dependence. But what sort of dependence? Is it to be understood along the line of Kant's imperative or as heteronomy, or as divine law?

Ricoeur makes a lengthy meditation of the Torah and its history in La symbolique du mal.[30] There he qualifies the heteronomy of the Torah by linking it with the other forms of discourse. The Torah does not stand on its own. It is the instruction of Yahweh in the perspective of the story of Israel's liberation and the prophetic menace (153:119). The instruction is thoroughly historical: it is intended to be the ethics of a liberated people. The negative connotation of heteronomy is dispersed by the covenantal context of Isreal's dependence upon Yahweh. Life in the convenant is Israel's promise; its breakdown is Israel's menace. Moreover, the link of the Torah with Moses - it is the law of Moses - retains for the Torah its narrative basis in Israel's founding events. The giving of the Torah takes place in the Exodus event from Egypt. The narrative and prophetic discourse interfere, therefore, with too narrow an interpretation of the divine imperative according to a prescriptive discourse. In Ricoeur's words,

If we may still apply the idea of God's design for humans to it, it is no longer in the sense of a plan that we could read in past or future events, nor is it in terms of an immutable codification of every communal or individual practice. Rather, it is the sense of a requirement for perfection that summons the will and makes a claim upon it (438:10-11).

Accordingly, because this discourse also speaks out the name of God, but as the holy one, the prescriptions of the Torah have become both innumerable commandments that fracture that holiness in human living and

---

30. Op. cit., p.118-150.

the supreme commandment of love: "Be perfect as your heavenly Farther is perfect." (Mt 5:48) The new law or covenant is built upon the old according to an ethics of prophecy: "I shall give you a new heart and place a new spirit within you, taking from your bodies your stony hearts and giving you natural hearts" (Ez 36:26).

(d) Wisdom discourse.

Wisdom discourse adds a universal dimension to those already mentioned. The wisdom discourse addresses itself to the sense and nonsense of human existence in general. It is not specifically Jewish, as Ricoeur notes; it overflows the framework of the covenant, because it touches a core of human living that no one people can capture completely. Wisdom views the great variety of human situations in which humanity is touched in its misery and greatness. It is the struggle of humanity to keep alive the hope that in the sea of the meaninglessness of life's tensions, suffering and death, meaning dominates. According to wisdom, humans are faced with life's incomprehensibility; wisdom shifts that incomprehensibility towards God. Wisdom discourse names God as the silent and absent one, especially in the dichotomy experienced between justice and happiness in human suffering (438:11-12;436:499-500).

The suffering of human existence can stand as paradigm of the accomplishment of wisdom. Suffering lies not in the realm of ethos - especially when it is unjust. Rather it links the ethical order with the order of things: the ethos with the cosmos. The whole of the book of Job and especially its conclusion, orients the reader to seek for a horizon of meaning, where suffering actively assumed ties together the cosmos with human action. It does not prescribe what Job must do, but how he must endure. Nor does the response of God provide him with a vision of a justice or an order of the world, where suffering can be understood or justified. This wisdom asks Job to repent even his questioning. For this wisdom, existence makes sense and for Job to dare to question it is an offense. The book of Job places existence within a context of meaning that human intelligence and language cannot fathom.

How does this discourse interanimate with the previously mentioned narrative, prophetic and prescriptive discourses? Ricoeur's key notion is the incomprehensibility of God. When wisdom tries to fathom an impenetrable world of suffering, it refuses to see a clearly visible plan or design of God in human affairs. If there is a design - and here it rejoins the narrative, but as a broken narrative - it is a secret design of God. It is the wisdom of God - a wisdom that the book of Proverbs personifies in a feminine figure who is with God as the accompaniment of creation. Wisdom is similar to prophecy, according to Ricoeur, because the sage like the prophet speaks as an inspired human of the way of things with God. Prophecy and wisdom have a further parallel in the eschatological breakthrough of language. The prophet often speaks of the Day of Yahweh in apocalyptic terms. In the later stages, e.g. the book of Daniel, and much of the writings of the intertestamentary period, wisdom too speaks of a Day of Yahweh, when the apokalupsis, the revelation, of the design of God will take place (438:13).

(e) Hymnic discourse.

The psalms and hymns of praise, supplication and thanksgiving, are the final form or genre of the Old Testament which Ricoeur examines. The hymnic discourse affects the other discourses, inasmuch as here God is addressed in the second person. Humans are a You before God. It is as a You that they respond. Narration in the context of hymnic discourse is transformed into an invocation. The Exodus story and the creation are celebrated in such a manner, for instance, in the ritual celebration of the Pasch. And without the supplication of the psalms, the suffering of the just person would be left in mute imcomprehensibility. Through the invocation, the mute world of affairs is pierced by the cry of the sufferer addressed to a transcendent and incomprehensible You (438:14-15).

How do these hymns name God? Ricoeur warns against a false hypostatizing of the hymn. He urges that we must look for a way of naming God that takes place in accordance with feelings:

> The sentiments expressed here are formed by and conform to their object. Thanksgiving, supplication, and celebration are all engendered by what these movements of the heart allow to exist and, in that manner, to become manifest... The word forms our feeling in the process of expressing it. And revelation is this very formation of our feelings that transcend their everyday, ordinary modalities (438:15).

(f) Parabolic discourse.

Nowhere has Ricoeur shown more clearly the quality of language used in religious discourse than in his analysis of the Hebrew maschal (parable) in the text of the New Testament gospels. If in the text of the Old Testament he discovered, through Von Rad, a number of forms of discourse and their interpretation, it is in studying the genre of parable that Ricoeur clarifies the texture of religious discourse.[31]

Ricoeur defines the parabolic discourse according to three traits: (1) it has a narrative form; (2) it makes use of the metaphorical process; and (3) its religious quality is governed by a qualifier. On the level of the genre a parable is a form of discourse, which applies a metaphorical process to a narrative form. But this linguistic genre requires a specific qualifier in order to bring it to the limit of the possibilities of language and thus make it a religious discourse. This qualifier, according to Ricoeur, is not provided

---

31. Cf. J.D. Crossan, "Paradox gives Rise to Metaphor: Paul Ricoeur's Hermeneutics and the Parables of Jesus" in Biblical Research 24-25, 1979-1980, p.20-37; J. Alexandre, "Notes sur l'esprit des paraboles en réponse à P. Ricoeur" in Études théologiques et religieuses 51, 1976, p. 367-372.

by the parable itself, except in conjunction with two other modes of discourse of the New Testament that attempt to bring the Kingdom of God to language: the proclamatory statements and the proverbial statements. This third trait of the parable: the ultimate referent of the parable, will be examined below. I will concentrate here on the literary genre of the parable, because, according to Ricoeur, it can serve as a model of a form that mediates the Christian existence (411:30).

Since both the narrative form and the metaphorical process, as Ricoeur perceives them, have been worked out extensively, we only need to elaborate how the parable is a conjunction of these two forms.[32]

1. Parables are, first of all, stories with a surface meaning that is obvious. They are stories about ordinary people, doing ordinary things: selling and buying, fishing, loosing and finding, sowing... They are narratives of normalcy (452(410):239). This narrative structure of normalcy, however, is invaded by the metaphorical process, that is, a transfer of meaning is forced upon the text by means of a semantic clash that bids the narrative of apparent normalcy to deliver another, non-literal, figurative meaning. It is Ricoeur's thesis - following the parable research of J.D. Crossan,[33] N. Perrin,[34] A. Wilder,[35] and W. Beardsley,[36] that parables are fictional compositions with a unique metaphorical tension that appear to retain their semantic tension longer than regular metaphors. The power of the parabolic genre is that, by means of the tension in the fiction, it gives a glimpse of another reality which is not accessible to us, except in the release of that reality by way of the imagination in the moment of the semantic tension. But what constitutes the abnormalcy, the shock, in the parabolic narrative that unleashes another world into our existence?

2. The shock is provided by the invasion of another world into the narrative structure. But where does this other world display itself? In his answer, Ricoeur diverges somewhat from Crossan, who immediately passes to the reference. For Ricoeur, there must be traces of metaphoricity within the very structure and the process of the story text itself. However, he is aware that these traces of a symbolic reference of the narrative text-structure are not so convincing that they impose themselves upon us.

---

32. See above p.134-137, and 57-69.

33. In Parables, New York, Harper and Row, 1973.

34. "The Parables of Jesus as Parables, as Metaphors, and as Aesthetic Objects: A Review Article", in The Journal of Religion 47, 1967, p.340-347.

35. The Language of the Gospel, New York, Harper and Row, 1964.

36. Literary Criticism of the New Testament, Philadelphia, Fortress Press, 1097, p.30-41, and "Uses of the Proverbs in the Synoptic Gospel" in Interpretation 24, 1970, p.61-76.

Ricoeur calls the inner clues implicit and elusive. Nevertheless, he remains faithful to the principle of the dialectic between sense and reference. In addition to looking for traces of the metaphoricity in the text, he will also look for clues that lie outside the parabolic text in the larger text in which the parables are found. He calls these contextual clues (411:97).

The inner clues of metaphoricity must be provided by the narrative plot (434:501). For Ricoeur, the plot is not an epiphenomenon of the code, as we saw, but it is the very temporal structure of the narrative. We must search for the metaphoricity in the action of the narrative - what happens in the story.[37] A plot's center is the crisis and its denouement; there existence is said to be found or lost. In other words, Ricoeur suggests that within the closure of the narrative form, i.e., in the setting, crisis, denouement, there is a dimension that breaks open the closure toward a metaphorical reference (434:152;436:501). That dimension he calls the extravagance of the parable. Every parable has a critical, surprising moment either tragic or comic that is unexpected: the mustard plant in which birds nest, a Samaritan who is 'good'...the abandonment of 99 sheep in the desert for the one lost sheep, this moment of excess, of extravagence, introduces the extraordinary into the story of the ordinary and creates the metaphoric tension and surplus (427:17). This tension transforms the closedness of the narrative structure into a figurative referent (411:99).

But according to Ricoeur this inner clue would hardly be recognizable without a number of contextual clues. Of these he gives four.

a. The narrative impertinence is heightened first of all by the whole corpus of the parables which are introduced in the gospel text by an enigmatic word concerning the teaching in parables ("To others outside it is all presented in parables, so that they will look intently and not see, listen carefully and not understand, lest perhaps they repent and be forgiven." (Mk. 4:12) and with the injunction, "let those who have ears hear". Ricoeur proposes that parables make sense only in the whole network of intersignification produced by the whole corpus of parables. The closure of the corpus of the parables by the early ecclesial community provides a network of clashing significations among the parables. The network forces a metaphorical interpretation.

b. In addition to the parabolic discourse the sayings attributed to Jesus also include the eschatological sayings and the proverbial sayings. According to N. Perrin, all of them have a common horizon, provided by the symbol Kingdom of God. For Ricoeur, this means that the parabolic discourse communicates with and can be translated into the eschatalogical Kingdom sayings or the proverbs. Once again, this intensification of the parable strengthens its metaphoricity at the expense of the narrative closure (411:102,109-114;404:67-69). The proclamatory, or Kingdom,

---

37. The parables are not stories about persons, such as, the father, the judge, the mother, the woman, the sower, but about the action of the story. The Kingdom is like a father, who...

statements, for instance, assume a very pronounced temporal tension. Thus, Mark's saying, "The time is fulfilled, and the kingdom of God is at hand; repent and believe the Gospel" (1:15), is said in the apocalyptic genre which presumes a certain temporal order. If taken into a literal temporal schema, the statement breaks apart at a chronological level. Here a new time invades the present time and shatters it: the fullness of time is now. By their interaction with the parables the proclamatory statements infect the extravagance of the parables with a singular type of intensification. The same can be said about the proverbs. The proverbial wisdom sayings of the New Testament offer a similar type of intensification. While wisdom sayings generally seek to create a continuous human project of existence, the New Testament proverbs seek to shatter any such attempt. This is done by making use of paradox ("The last shall be first, and the first shall be last" (Mk. 20:16) or of hyperbole ("whoever loses his life will preserve it" (Lk (17:33). Through the interanimation with the other sayings of Jesus, the proverbial sayings offer their intensification of life to the understanding of the parables.

c. A further extension of the intersignification is given by situating the parabolic discourse within the text of the 'deeds' of Jesus. These texts of the deeds of Jesus speak not only of Jesus "going around doing good" but also of Jesus' extraordinary deeds: the miracle stories. These, too, introduce a rupture of extravagance into ordinary life. The deeds manifest the possibility of the impossible. The intersignification inserts a similar structure of expectation into the sayings of the parables (411:102-103).

d. The insertion of the parables within the gospel as a narrative also sets a context for the intersignification. The gospel provides the total framework and sets the limit of interpretation. The parable is a metaphorical narrative within a metaphorical narrative. Ricoeur calls the parables quotations within a text (411:104), that is, they are parables of Jesus. This factor creates a unique intersignification of the parables with the text of the words and deeds of Jesus, including the narrative of the passion. This intersignification is mutually reinforcing: the metaphoricity of the parabolic narrative is intensified by the larger context, but the subsequent metaphoricity of the parable intensifies the metaphoricity of the Gospel narrative, particularly of the passion. The parables are the parables of the crucified one. For Ricoeur, a new space of intersignification is thereby opened which allows one to perceive the parables not only of Jesus but also of God. They are proclamations of Jesus about God (411:105). But at this point we have introduced the point of highest tension, to which we must return.

3. Following this line of thinking, it is not surprising that as the metaphor is the paradigm of poetic discourse, the parable becomes the paradigm of religious discourse for Ricoeur. Ricoeur compares the parable to the function of the scientific model as perceived by Mary Hesse.[38] The

---

38. See above, p.79-83.

parable explores the reality beyond language as a model explores an uncharted scientific realm. It is a heuristic fiction, redescribing the field of human experience, where the originary reality is brought within the momentary glimpse of the imagination (410:95). As a redescription of human experience, the parable might be only one form of discourse among others, were it not for its aggragation of the supreme referent. Because of the intrusion of the religious realm beyond language, it redescribes human language, experience, and existence at its deepest level (404:66-70).

But as an existential model, its exploration of the realm called the Kingdom of God can be said to operate on a threefold level. The story in orienting our existence by the very normalcy of what it proposes in its images, disorients us in the crisis and in the impertinence of the semantic clash. But in the very tension of the orientation and the disorientation, the imagination reorients our existence in line with the experienced tension. It is through this strategy of discourse that our imagination is directed toward new possibilities according to Ricoeur. The parables exemplify the fact that religious language is "a word addressed first to our imagination rather than our will" (410:245).

C. THE BIBLICAL WORLD OF THE TEXT.

After the examination of the biblical forms of discourse and their interanimation, we must examine what, in Ricoeur's view, gathers these texts into this specific polyphony. How can we qualify the language that says out its source, and what is its logical or epistemic status?

1. The language of revelation.

For Ricoeur, the variety of forms of biblical discourse function as a type of generative poetics of the name of God. God is the ultimate referent of the totality of the discourses: their naming of God is homogeneous to a specific genre and, at the same time, challenged and negated by another genre. According to Ricoeur, it is this notion of a generative poetics in the interplay of genres that governs the idea of revelation (406:26-27). What is revealed is what is displayed before the text. Revelation is not what lies behind the text along the lines of a source of inspiration, but what lies before the text, as opened by the text, or, as a letting-be of that which the text displays. As we have seen, what the text displays is a world proposal, a realm of my own-most possibilities (436:495). Hence, the forms of discourse which we have examined are not forms where truth is verified in some type of process of adequation, but forms where one manifests what lies prior to language (438:20). Revelation, accordingly, is a "feature of the biblical world proposed by the text" (438:26). It is the force of the text that makes it epiphanous.

We have noted above, that, for Ricoeur, the various forms of biblical discourse are related analogically. That means that no form is absolute and that the idea of revelation cannot be elevated to the level of knowledge. It remains in the tension of the forms. Revelation also remains its negation, in the sense, that, like the burning bush, the God who reveals himself in it is a hidden God. In the revelation of the name of God in Ex 3:14-15, the God who reveals his name, and the God whose name signifies the act of deliverance is simulaneously the God who refuses to give his name (436:501). Ricoeur calls this a flight to the infinite of the God-reference of the text. But, because these texts do signify something, it can be said that revelation takes place "between the secret and the revealed" (438:18). Accordingly, in a parabolic fashion, God is 'like'...that is, he 'is' and he 'is not.' God, as referent of all these texts, is the religious name that gathers all these texts and coordinates them. He is, at the same time, the reality that is never totally captured by them. That is why Ricoeur can say that if "God is the religious name of being, still the word 'God' says more... To understand the word 'God' is to follow the 'direction of meaning' of the word" (406:25). The name God is the opening up of an horizon that discourse tends to close.

When Ricoeur qualifies this revelatory language, he calls it a variety of poetic language. Revelatory language is poetic in the sense that it brings to speech the fictions of the imagination, whereby reality is redescribed. But not all poetic language is revelatory in the religious sense. Not all poetic language lays open the New Being (Tillich). Religious language is a peculiar intensification of poetic language. In other words, it is not because it is metaphorical or poetic that it is religious, but because of the intensification (411:108). In the parables, for example it is because the parabolic discourse is contextualized by the ultimate referent of the Kingdom of God and the eschatological dimension of the Kingdom sayings and the paradox and hyperbole of the proverbial discourse that it becomes religious language. The intentional aim of religious discourse appears to take language itself to its limits of expressabiliy. Within the normalcy of life, it inserts the extraordinary, the paradoxical, the disruptive. As a first approximation of religious language, Ricoeur characterizes it as a limit expression (411:108).

How does such a limit expression function? Ian Ramsey describes the process through his theory of models and qualifiers.[39] According to Ramsey, there is a mode of intervening in the use of language which qualifies the language. In biblical New Testament language it might be said, that the paradoxical, the hyperbolic, the extravagant, and the eschatological are qualifiers of traditional wisdom, the apocalyptism, and the discourse of ordinary living of the Hebrew maschal. The qualifier forces, what Ricoeur calls, a logical scandal upon the text. Thus, for example, the proverbs of Jesus, in their destructuring of our life project, leave us with the enigma of how to create a wholeness of life beyond the disorientation. The New Testament qualifier is logically scandalous. If God is the ultimate qualifier of all these texts, i.e., their ultimate referent, it is

---

39. See Religious Language, New York, MacMillan, 1957, p.105-122. Ramsey applied the process of qualifiers only to theological language. Ricoeur, however, transfers the process to biblical language, because it is more primordial than theological language.

suggested that his reality is logically scandalous (411:120-121). Limit expressions are expressions that by means of the logical abuse shatter the normalcy of discourse and reorient language to a hyperlogical dimension. For Ricoeur, the functioning of the New Testament religious language is determined by what it tries to bring to language, namely the Kingdom of God. The Kingdom of God becomes the limit referent of all these limit expressions (411:122). The Kingdom-of-God symbol is the primordial qualifier of the religious language of the New Testament. The naming of God, through this qualifier, gathers the variety of the sayings of the New Testament (436:505).

It is at this level that the uniqueness of biblical hermeneutics becomes most evident. We noted above that, for Ricoeur, biblical hermeneutics is one hermeneutic among others. Yet, it is also a unique hermeneutics. It is unique, because the bible is not only one of the great poems of existence, but also "because all its partial forms of discourse are referred to that Name which is the point of intersection and the vanishing point of all our discourse about God, the name of the unnameable" (438:26).

The centrality of Jesus in the New Testament does not in any way remove the God-reference of the biblical texts (397:83;406:28). The poem of Christ is as much as any a poem of God (436:503). But the poem of Jesus acts as a qualifier of the poem of God. Jesus himself is a parable of God. He is the extravagance that shocks the traditional understanding of God as all-powerful, as immutable and impassible. The cross of Jesus is a shock of a God abandoning the just man, a God of weakness and kenosis. The God, who raised Jesus, is the power of God revealed in the powerlessness of the cross, or the power of powerlessness, also referred to in other God-references.

2. Symbolic language.

As a unique poetic and symbolic language, religious language also functions to create resemblance. In bonding us with the sacred, it also brings the sacred near by the creation of a fruitful tension between the archaism of our existence and the projection of our possibilities. Without repeating what has been said above about the symbol, I wish to touch on two of Ricoeur's points.

a. The sacred and human existence.

The parable, we said, presupposed the normalcy of life or the myth of human existence. The same must be said of the proclamatory and proverbial statements. They touch the ordinary understanding of human existence. The work of resemblance toward the imaginative variations in the realm of religion does not lead to supernaturalism. But the poetics of New Being aims to be a harbinger of true human existence within an ordinary, profane self-understanding. The analogates are derived from ways of inhabiting space and time and from human activity (423:62-63;406:26-27). But in their weighing of this existence, no specific world is privileged: the religious text speaks of a cosmic creation, of a people, of a history and culture, and of individual joys and hopes and trials. But at the same time the religious text draws these experiences to the moments of their greatest intensity. In other words, the world that these texts project is not the world of ordinary experience, even though it uses ordinary experience to express it. In his La symbolique du mal, Ricoeur proposes three symbolic realms, the cosmic, the oneiric and the poetic.[40] Humans, he maintains, express their existential dimension by expressing their world. They project their ownmost possibilities in the cosmic dimensions of the sky, earth, water, vegetation, or stones and in fragments of their own past. By drawing humans to their origin, they become at the same time prophets of consciousness (320(191):332-33;271:133). For Ricoeur, a correlation or a correspondence exists between the structure of the sacred universe and the logic of meaning. It is the sacred time and space of the cosmos, manifested in the human psyche that enables us to explore both our origin and our limits through symbolic language (423:61;404:58-63).

For Ricoeur, this forces upon us a discussion of the role of the sacred in our time which is so characterized by desacralization. Moderns no longer relate to the cosmos, and the sacred manifests itself nowhere in consciousness except in substitutes. Ricoeur suggests that the relationship of the sacred and the power of the word must be correlated. But it is not sufficient to relegate the sacred solely to the kerygma, as Bonhöffer has done. Ricoeur insists on a sacral residue elsewhere, but he insists at the same time, that it be placed in relation to the kerygmatic word that is addressed to us. For him, the word is the sacred power par excellence. The word of the Bible will assume the cosmic symbolism - our originary orientation - but it informs and transforms it by the word (404:75). Thus Ricoeur will point to the language of the synoptic parable, proverb, or proclamatory saying as rooted in a sacred symbolism of the Kingdom of God, and of God as shepherd, father, and king, but this sacred symbolism receives its religious intensity in Christianity by its being taken up into the cycle of words that derive from the death and resurrection, new birth, new creation, the coming of new being and of a new world, that the proclamation says out (404:76). The proclamation retakes the cosmic images and transforms them into a proclamation.

b. The critique of religious symbolism.

The cosmic and the oneiric aspect of the symbol thus become subject to the power of the poetic word. The poetic imagination expressed in the symbol transforms the symbol from being solely a manifestation of the sacred - a reverting to the psychic archaic or to the cosmic - to a power of the future and an exploration of the possible. The stress is constantly placed upon the poetic power of the imagination over the cosmic and the oneiric. In line with J. Moltmann's differentiation between Greek religion as a religion of manifestation or epiphany and Hebrew religion as a religion of hope and a word of promise, Ricoeur seeks the power of the religious symbol in the projective power of the poetic to put us in touch with human wholeness.

---

40. Op. cit., p.10-14.

The power of the religious word is at the same time a critique or a cleansing of the cosmic and the oneiric. Ricoeur has provided an extensive coverage of a number of archaisms which stand under the critique of the kerygmatic word. The grounding of the religious in the cosmic, psychic, and poetic has, therefore, its counterpart in a number of prohibitions that the kerygma places upon a cosmic, purely ethical, archaic, infantile, or neurotic expression of religion. Thus, for example, in the name of a kerygma of hope, he distinguishes the religion of proclamation from a religion in which too great an emphasis is placed upon the cosmic manifestation of the sacred (see 404). Similarly, to liberate religious discourse from the archaic, infantile, regressive and neurotic, Ricoeur has examined guilt (256,326), fear (320(232):347-353), consolation (256;227:550), punishment (273;232;325), the father as phantasm (325,309,227:549). In all these instances, it may be said, "An idol must die so that the symbol of being may begin to speak" (320(325):409).

Ricoeur believes that the religious philosopher and theologian is forced to undertake this labour, because Marx, Nietzsche, Freud, and other philosophers of suspicion show convincingly that religion as discourse can be illusory discourse (367:64-65). In listening to them, Ricoeur detected a conflict in the interpretation of the same phenomenon. It is a conflict not only from without brought on by unbelievers and atheists, but, he insists, also from within by the Christian's own self-understanding. As he says of Freud, "He has already reinforced the belief of unbelievers; he has scarcely begun to purify the faith of believers (256:36). In the article, "L'herméneutique de la sécularisation. Foi, Idéologie, Utopie" 9430), he affirms that the need for a critique of religion becomes inevitable when religion begins to be described, as it is done today, in the alternative terms of either ideology or utopia. However, Ricoeur reminds us that the critique of religion that has come forth from this tradition is overshadowed by the more original critique that the Wholly Other places upon our religion when it enters our sphere and grasps hold of us (227:530).

The question that needs to be asked in this context of a conflict about the interpretation of the world of religion is whether one can transcend the alternatives. Ricoeur believes this to be possible, because for him the critique of religion and the complementary functions of ideology and utopia are themselves founded upon the much more constitutive reality of faith itself. Religion may be called ideological and utopic, and, in some ways, rightly so, because, for example, it gives identity to faith. But religion needs to be constantly infused with the eschatological dimension of faith, in order to prevent it from distorting and reifying hope. Here too the eschaton breaks into human language and structures and makes it the 'odd' language and structures of the Kingdom to come. Accordingly Ricoeur remarks, faith enroots in the manner of religion and unroots in the manner of an eschatology (430:68).

CHAPTER NINE: THE WITNESS OF HOPE.

Bibliography.

24.	"Le yogi, le commissaire, le prolétaire et le prophète" (1949).
25.	"Le christianisme et le sens de l'histoire. Progrès, ambiguité, espérance" (1951).
75.	"Sympathie et respect" (1954).
78.	"Kant et Husserl" (1954).
80.	"Morale sans péché ou péché sans morale?" (1954).
83.	Histoire et vérité (1954).
115.	"Faith and Culture" (1957).
124.	"Les aventures de l'état et la tâche des chrétiens" (1958).
152.	L'homme faillible (1960).
153.	La symbolique du mal (1960).
164.	"Le péché originel: étude de signification" (1960).
186.	"L'humanité de l'homme" (1962).
191.	"Herméneutique et réflexion" (1962).
202.	"Kierkegaard et le mal" (1963).
214.	"Technique et nontechnique dans l'interprétation" (9164).
220.	"Le langage de la foi" (1964).
227.	De l'interprétation. Essai sur Freud. (1965).
232.	"Demythiser l'accusation" (1965).
234.	"Tâches de l'éducateur politique" (1965).
235.	"Sciences humaines et conditionnements de la foi" (1965).
245.	"Préface" in J. Nabert, Le désir de Dieu (1966).
251.	"La parole instauratrice de liberté" (1967).
270.	"Postscript" in J.M. Paupert, Taizé et l'église de demain (1967).
271.	"Langage religieux. Mythe et symbole" (1967).
273.	"Interprétation du mythe de la peine" (1967).
291.	"Tâches de la communauté ecclésiale dans le monde moderne" (1968).
294.	"Préface" in R. Bultmann, Jésus (1968).
320.	Le conflit des interprétations (1969).
325.	"Religion, athéisme, foi" (1969).
326.	"Culpabilité, éthique et religion" (1969).
338.	"Hope and Structure of Philosophical systems" (1970).
360.	"Esquisse de conclusion" (1971).
362.	"Événement et sens" (1971).
367.	"La foi soupçonnée" (1971).
380.	"L'herméneutique de témoignage" (1972).
397.	"Philosophy and Religious Language" (1973).
404.	"Manifestation et proclamation" (1974).
405.	"Le problème du fondement de la morale" (1975).
406.	"Philosophical Hermeneutics and Theological Hermeneutics" (1975).
407.	"The Metaphorical process" (1975).
411.	"Biblical Hermeneutics" (1975).
435.	"Préface" in J. Dunphy, Paul Tillich et le symbole religieux (1977).

436.   "Nommer Dieu" (1977).
438.   "Herméneutique et l'idée de révélation" (1977).
470.   "The Logic of Jesus: the Logic of God" (1980).
476.   "A Response" (1980).

While we discovered the qualities of the world of the religious text in the previous chapter, we will now attempt to expose the characteristics of the appropriation of that world in the view of Paul Ricoeur. The limit-expressions, by which that world is brought near, call for an existence in the light of hope. The appropriation of the religious text in a self-understanding of faith and hope will consider four aspects of Ricoeur's text-theory in the realm of hope. 1. Religious existence as a limit-experience; 2. speculative religious self-understanding; 3. practical or ethical recovery of self in religious discourse; 4. the subject as gift. We hope to show that the I that emerges out of the politics of hope is an I that is not just and free by its own power, but is an I that is justified and set free. It is an I who becomes in hope despite contingency and despite an immersion in the human history of sin. In short, we seek to grasp what Ricoeur means by understanding ourselves before the religious text.

A. EXISTENCE AS A LIMIT-EXPERIENCE.

Correlative to the limit-expressions which we encounter in religious language, Ricoeur posits what he calls limit-experiences at the level of existence. Limit-experiences are the existential response of the individual to the singular intensification of language that strains to capture the infinite. The language of hope does not leave existence untouched. We might call it, with Ricoeur, a performative language. Confronted in the text with the absolute and infinite, human experience undergoes an intensification, comparable to the intensification of religious language. The limit-expressions unleash a limit-experience. The ultimate referent of religious language of the New Testament, the Kingdom of God, not only affects human language, straining it to its limits, but also works upon our human experience (271:130-131).

Borrowing the language of Ian Ramsey,[1] Ricoeur holds that this intensification of religious language brings about an 'odd discernment' experience. It is an 'odd discernment' experience, because its effect is the bonding of the individual with the referent of the religious text, i.e., with God, in a manner that is beyond language. Its power can find its human outlet only in a total commitment. The commitment is total not only in its assumption of the whole of existence but also in the perception that it is universally valid (411:124). The religious limit-experience is both a total involvement of the individual and a universal meaning.

---

1.   Op. cit. See 411:124.

248

For Ricoeur, these limit-experiences remain within the ambit of language. The experience occurs in the power of the word to say out the Kingdom of God. It remains, therefore, within the power of the symbol to effect and to coordinate the relationship with God (271:131). The intensifying qualifier of religious language brings about in the heart of ordinary experience a disorientation of that ordinary experience, releasing it toward a new referent. In the disruptive overturning of ordinary experiences by means of the word, a new way of being is disclosed. But, just as the referent is metaphorically indicated in the limit-expression of religious language, so also the new way of being of the limit-experience is shown metaphorically. It is not mapped out; it is not described, but is rendered open to the imagination.

The disruption or the dislocation of ordinary experience by the limit-expressions of religious language accomplishes two aims. First of all, it intercepts the normal attempt of human existence to create a whole out of life. The human project to tell a continuous story of its own existence is interrupted by the extravagance of religious language. The limit-experience, for that reason, is not an extension of normal experience, but a questioning of such an experience. It brings an element of discontinuity into the human project. The limit-experience extends toward us a wholly new life-project. That is why, secondly, limit-expressions bring about a new orientation of existence right in and through the breach in our normal experience. This re-orientation, touching the 'heart of our heart' (152:160), is called conversion (251:506).[2] This conversion, or re-orientation through disorientation, can only be a total commitment. In L'homme faillible, Ricoeur describes this feeling of the infinite as joy, happiness, and the 'vehemence of the Yes' before existence.[3]

This re-orientation affects every experience and project. It touches the speculative, as well as the practical, ethical and political. No human project is left undisturbed by this paradox (436:508). But, at the same time, no human project can lay claim to encompassing or satisfying the power of the symbol of the Kingdom of God. It is a realm of the impossible demand, calling forth the limit of human existence. No program, no praxis, can exhaust it, because religious language redirects every program and experience (411:125-127, cf. also 220:221). The human experience that is intercepted is intercepted with all the broadness of the world of the religious text. If the biblical text projects a world that is cosmic, ethical, political, as well as individual and personal, the reorientation of experience by that text will have the same amplitude. The religious touches all. It calls for total commitment (cf. 152:209).

---

2. In the article, "La Parole, instauratrice de liberté" Ricoeur gives a psychological description of conversion in the following terms, "Une nouvelle 'articulation significative' de notre manière de nous comprendre dans le sentiment de notre situation" (251:506).

3. See 152:120-161, and 207-224.

What seeks to come to existence, therefore, is the new being of the text. The new being is a matter of 'ultimate concern' (Tillich), because the new being of the text is, according to Ricoeur, the completion of my desire and effort to be. The new being invades my life through the text as the foundation of my life (406:31-32). This means, however, that the ultimate referent of the text of the Bible is not God or the Kingdom of God, but a dimension of human reality. In the reading of the biblical text the God-reference of the text ultimately signifies human experience (411:128). And since it touches the 'heart of the heart' of human existence, the text signifies our human wholeness (360:72).

This human wholeness is also called faith. For Ricoeur, faith is linked to the self-understanding that emerges out of the text. As Ricoeur says, "Faith is the attitude of one who accepts being interpreted at the same time that he interprets the world of the text" (397:84). Faith is the existence modelled on the re-orientation of the text. Faith is the existence of the larger, more complete self, opened up and founded on the text. Faith is the reality of the possible self (397:82; 220:224). Faith is 'ultimate concern', the 'feeling of absolute dependence (397:84; see also 435:12), the mytho-poetic core of existence (408:174).

This faith is beyond the power of conscious subjectivity. For Ricoeur, this revelation of the possible in the text of the Scriptures delivers the severest critique of self-constituting subjectivity. God cannot become an object of my subjectivity, or, obversely, I an object to God's subjectivity, (438:30). Where the power to manifest the realm of the possible touches the human individual is not there where the subject is in control. Where one is grasped by the poetic, religious word, is in the imagination. The imagination is the power of the possible. As Ricoeur says, "Imagination is the dimension of subjectivity which corresponds to the text as a poem" (406:33). The imagination is the place where the figurative power of the word captures the realm of hope and existence (367:72). The power of the imagination is precisely the power to bring near the inexpressible (271:134).

For Ricoeur, then, a deep link exists between faith and the imagination as the power of the possible. Faith, too, is not an instrumental power, but an openness to listen and to be transformed by the New Being that is announced to us by the word, in whose power we exist (367:72). Faith, imagination, the word: three aspects which are inseparable for Ricoeur. Instead of being master, the human individual is borne and created by a generative word which 'says' me rather than is controlled by (220:224). The foundation of the I is to be discovered more by silence, therefore, than by speech, since by the imagination we are placed at the boundary-line of silence and the word (271:133). It is poetic language that breaks into that realm of silence and becomes the word for our listening.[4] Here is language at its most non-violent level. I do not dispose of it; it has me at its

---

4.   See also L. Dornisch, "Symbolic Systems and the Interpretation of Scripture: An Introduction to the Work of Paul Ricoeur," in Semeia, 13, 1975, p.3-4.

disposition. It invites me to listen, to hear. It opens up an experience of reality as a gift. In a deep sense, it reveals (438:25). Revelation is the gift of the text. It is not a knowledge, nor a praxis; perhaps, it can best be expressed in such terms as imagination, feeling and mood (406:32; 436:495).[5] As a consequence, faith becomes a mode of dwelling according to that gift. Or, as Ricoeur puts it, faith is "the experience of being created by the word" (367:72). Elsewhere, Ricoeur calls this existence a 'love of creation' (320(325):467). It is the gift that searches in me by means of my imagination for the self that is most open to dwell in this world according to my ownmost possibilities.

B. CONCEPTUAL RECOVERY OF THE SELF OF FAITH.

If the explorative power of existence lies mainly in the imagination and not in knowledge or praxis, is there any space left for a speculative recuperation of the self of faith? This is a highly sensitive problematic for theology, the scientia fidei. Ricoeur discusses this issue of the relationship of faith and knowledge along lines similar to the discussion of the relationship of the truth of the imagination and speculative knowledge.[6] We said above, that, for Ricoeur, the work of the imagination and the dynamism underlying it seeks not only to express itself on the level of the glimpse provided by the semantic clash, but also seeks to be explored by speculation and theoretical conceptualization. What the imagination constructs as similar, speculation wishes to gather in the sameness of the concept. Ricoeur suggests that there is a type of interanimation between these two discourses of the imagination and of speculation, whereby, what the imagination has brought within our reach, the speculative power seeks to gather into the concept. That same dynamic is a work in the religious realm. What our imagination explores and brings near in the religious text, speculation seeks to bring to knowledge. In Chapter Three we indicated, that, for Ricoeur, there is an intermediary discourse between imagination and speculation, namely the hermeneutical discourse.

A number of points might be recalled here:

1. Any speculative knowledge of the self as gift remains a second-order discourse. It reflects the work of interpretation that shaped it. It only seeks to transfer to another order of discourse what primordially belonged to the work of the imagination. As Ricoeur proposes with regard to the 'concept' of Original Sin, what we might ultimately arrive at is most adequately called a rational symbol.[7] It should not be permitted to become

---

5. Ricoeur calls this feeling or mood the philosophical approximation of revelation. See 436:495.

6. See above, p.85-93.

7. See his "Le 'péché originel' étude de signification" in Le conflit des interprétations, op. cit., p. 265-282.

hypostatized into something objective, cut off from the process that gave shape to it. In other words, the attempts at conceptuality and speculation must not be divorced from their original enrootment in the symbolic order of which they are no more than a speculative interpretation (320(164):282).

2. In line with Ricoeur's post-Hegelian Kantianism one should shun any attempt at the great symbiosis of religion and philosophy. Hegel's absolute knowledge has crumbled under the onslaught of the philosophers of suspicion. Hegel's system will remain, however, the constant seduction that must ever be resisted. The work of the concept can only be a work of interpretation. The move toward knowledge by way of indirect discourse which seeks interpretation may not let go of the tension between the poetic representation of God and knowledge (411:129-144).

3. That such a knowledge is not objective is equally obvious from the logic of this indirect discourse of the unconditioned as we find it in the Bible. Ricoeur calls the logic of the gospel the logic of superabundance.[8] It is a logic of extravagance, of the 'how much more' of the parables and of Paul's hymn of the grace of Christ Jesus (Rom 5:12-20). The gospel presents a logic of existence that breaks through our ordinary logic by promising an excess of sense over nonsense. In breaking apart a logic of identity and equivalence, it is not sameness that rules reality, but disruption and dislocation. Any conceptual approach seeking objective knowledge would disintegrate before this logic.

4. The self-understanding that flows out of the understanding of the religious text is, therefore, not a knowledge. It assumes the form of a theologia negativa. The human individual is 'not this' and 'not that'. But beyond this negation, Ricoeur recognizes a language about ourselves that is metaphorical: it says that we are like this and we are like that, much like the way of eminence proposed by Medieval theology (438:35). The indirect discourse of the biblical text gives us no more than a hermeneutical self-understanding. The act of faith that constitutes us is the ultimate limit of such an hermeneutics (406:32; 436:490). This faith precedes every scripture, but would remain mute without the word of the Bible. The textuality of faith must not be interpreted as a new power of control. Since it is ultimately a manifestation of the highest despoliation of the self in favour of a new self. For Ricoeur, such a self-understanding is poetic or metaphorical, inasmuch as the self of the biblical text intersects and interacts with the self that comes from the text of our own contemporary situation and experience (cf. 411:130-131). This correlation of two texts, whether fought out in conflict, as is increasingly the case today, or experienced as a mutual deepening, is an indispensible process for the religious self-understanding. As Ricoeur says,

---

8. Cf. 227:528;320(191):312;320(273); 366-368;338:57;367:70; and 404:66. "The Logic of Jesus the Logic of God." in Anglican Theological Review 62, 1980, p.87-42; "La Logique de Jésus" in Et. théol et rel. 55, 1980, p.420-425.

The ceaseless movement of interpretation begins and ends in the risk of a response which is neither engendered nor exhausted by commentary. It is in taking account of this prelinguistic or hyperlinguistic characteristic that faith could be called 'ultimate concern', which speaks of the laying hold of the necessary and unique form from which basis I orient myself in all my choices (406:32).

C. THE ETHICAL RECOVERY OF SELF IN RELIGIOUS DISCOURSE.

If a speculative recovery of the self in a conceptual onto-theology must be denied, may we shift the weight of religious discourse from the realm of knowledge to the ethical realm? Here again, Ricoeur's response is qualified. An ethical religious response at any rate would have to transcend Kantian moralism and absorb the more Spinozistic ethics based on the desire and effort to be. As we have seen above,[9] such as ethics, linked as it is with the originary affirmation, is also a hermeneutical exercise. Ricoeur's ethics, including his gospel ethics, manifests itself in symbols, parables, and myths. The gospel project for existence is not directly given but implicit. Here too, we are given only the 'figures' of our authentic existence which need to be deciphered by a hermeneutics (411:144).

The fragility of the ethical 'figure' and hence of the ethical wager is best exemplified in the notion of testimony. For Ricoeur, this notion, borrowed from J. Nabert's philosophy,[10] captures the ethical itinerary, whereby the individual comes to grips with the absolute. Philosophically, the notion of testimony provides a prolegoumenon to what theology calls revelation. The notion is necessary, because, on the one hand, the absolute or the transcendent cannot be encompassed or exhausted by either knowledge or praxis, and, on the other hand, the absolute is ultimately meaningful to human existence and, therefore, seeks a contingent, historical expression. In other words, testimony is the contingent, historical expression of the absolute.

For Nabert, testimony is indissolubly linked with the deepest constitution of myself in originary affirmation. In originary affirmation I

---

9.   See above, p.162-164.

10.   Nabert elaborated this theme in a work of research that he had not yet completed at the time of his death. The incomplete manuscript was published, with a preface of Paul Ricoeur under the title, Le désir de Dieu (Philosophie de l'esprit), Paris, Aubier, 1966. Outside of this preface, Ricoeur has meditated on testimony on two other occasions. The first article, "L'herméneutique du témoignage" in Archivio di filosofia, 42, 1972, p.35-61, deals exclusively with the notion. In the second article, "Herméneutique de l'idée de révélation" in La Révélation, Bruxelles, Facultés universitaires Saint-Louis, 1977, p.15-54, he speaks of testimony at the conclusion of his reflection on revelation.

am most myself and at the same time least a possession. Although it coincides with my real consciousness, it cannot be called an experience: it is preconscious. It is the origin from which I am separated. But this originary affirmation is at the same time an affirmation of the absolute. And it is to this generosity of the absolute of the originary affirmation that testimony bears witness. More than an example, or a symbol, testimony is an aspect of self-understanding in which the dynamism of the original affirmation enters upon its external journey towards the realization of freedom. This becoming of the self of the originary affirmation can only assume an historical and finite route (438:31).

On the philosophical level, for Ricoeur and Nabert, testimony is the point of reflection. It is the point where reflection becomes concrete, where the understanding of the absolute in the interpretation of its signs becomes self-understanding. The meditation on God becomes concrete to the extent that it signifies the self-implication of the subject (438:30-31). It is concrete to the extent that the interiority of the act of the originary affirmation obtains the exteriority of testimony by means of an intellectual and moral asceticism (380:36). Only in its concreteness can the absolute be raised to the level of a self-consciousness. Testimony is principally the external action, whereby humans attest to their interiority, their convictions and their faith (380:43).

Let us examine this in more detail. The originary affirmation of reflective philosophy, to which an ethics of the desire and effort to be seeks to return, is available not directly, but only indirectly. For that reason, reflective philosophy is a hermeneutical philosophy. Nabert proposes that the originary affirmation lets go of itself into some type of distanciation. The affirmation expresses itself in testimony, so that a plumbing of the depths of the originary affirmation is achieved only by a hermeneutics of testimony.

This hermeneutics of testimony implies two basic acts: 1. an act of the self-consciousness upon itself, and 2. an act of historical understanding exercised upon the signs of the absolute (380:53). These acts are not separable. the one implies the other: "The signs which the absolute displays of itself are at the same time the signs in which consciousness recognizes itself" (380:53).[11] This means that acts of self-consciousness can be probed only indirectly, or hermeneutically (438:32-33;245:8-9). And the signs in which self-consciousness recognizes itself are the contingent signs of historical testimony. The absolute externalizes itself only in contingency. The contingent signs are the witness of the primacy of the absolute, the primacy of the founding events (438:35).

But the attestation of the absolute in the contingent and the historical introduces simultaneously the notion of contestation. A witness testifies in a contested area. And contestation seeks out a judgment. In

---

11. "Un acte de la conscience de soi sur elle-même et un acte de la compréhension historique sur les signes que l'absolu donne de lui-même."

this context, Nabert speaks of a criteriology of the divine (245:13;380:55). By this criteriology he means two things. There is a criteriology of the divine, because the divine is a contested area of existence. For that reason testimony calls upon our judgment to judge the validity of the narrative of the witness. Thus in the struggle between Yahweh and Baal for the prophets of the Old Testament, the prophets called for a discernment between God and an idol and a decision and a commitment by the people. There is a true witness and a false witness. Because the absolute does not enforce itself upon existence incontestably, the prophets called for a decision between Yahweh and the idols. But there is also a criteriology of the divine in another sense. The taking hold of the originary affirmation means also to sort out the predicates whereby the divine might be signified. This is what the medievals undertook in their naming of God by way of negation and eminence. But Nabert adds to this that we can only take, for example, justice and goodness to their eminence to the extent that the words, deeds and lives in our history testify to that eminence by their excellence. In sifting out the true witness to the absolute, we also sift out the predicates of the divine and lay open the route towards true self-understanding. In both instances of the criteriology of the divine, interpretation alone can provide the mediation. The predicates of the divine are not immediately available. They are only delivered in an intense commitment to signs, act and events. Our finitude allows no other avenue (380:57).

Perhaps the greatest scandal of testimony is that it is dialectically attached to the historical. In testimony the historical is invested with an absolute character (438:33). Such an admission requires the renunciation of any attempt to perceive ourselves as source and ground. Our consciousness cannot arrive at the admission that the divine is dependent on the historical testimony. But without this historical initiative the absolute would remain forever Wholly Other. Through the interpretation of the historical, contingent signs, acts, and events, we gain indirect access to the absolute and to self-understanding.

As a further delimitation of this ethics of the absolute Ricoeur frequently adduces, from his earliest writings onward, the distinction introduced into ethics by Max Weber between an ethics of conviction and an ethics of responsibility. The ethics of conviction is the ethics of what is absolutely desirable. The ethics of responsibility is the ethics of the relatively possible in the political realm. Ricoeur recognizes the need in ethics for a healthy tension between the ideal and the realistically possible. In an early article, he identified it as the tension between the yogi and the commissar (see 24). The ethical quest cannot bypass the violence that comes with the political institution, and yet the political institution with its ethics of responsibility should not squelch the ethics of conviction. By retaining the tension, Ricoeur advocates a 'wounded' ethics. An ethics of the poetic of the will must co-exist with an ethics of power.[12]

---

12. Cf. the following texts, 124;234;270:251;291:243-244;367:74; 405:192.

As a final note on the notion of testimony, it must be remembered that in an evangelical ethics there is no immediate correlation between testimony in the historically contingent and our conscious experience. As we saw above, the paradoxical and the hyperbolic force themselves into our consciousness. The gospel witness is a paradoxical testimony. We wish to conclude this work with a reflection of that paradox.

D. THE SUBJECT AS GIFT.

Ricoeur has located the ultimate recovery of the self at the limit of reason and at the limit of ethical endeavour. Religious existence is boundary-existence. It is living at the limit of normal, ordinary existence, where the paradoxical invades the normalcy and intensifies existence. Faith-existence keeps, what Ricoeur has called, the schematism of hope intact (411:145). It continues to ask what is the 'perspective of the prospective' (235:140)? Faith's concern with what is and what was is only to help fuel an existence that probes what is possible. The religious self is fundamentally a prospective self. Here the non-coincidence of the self with the self is raised to its most fundamental level. If religious language infuses this non-coincidence, it is to present it with the promise of reconciliation. The self that one must lose in order to gain it is a self under the sign of hope (320(326):437).

The non-coincidence with oneself is heightened by the existence of evil. Kant's radical evil was his gate of access to the realm of hope in religion. God is, for him, the condition of the realization of human freedom. Ricoeur's approach is less transcendental. But for him too, human freedom is a threatened freedom.[13] It is a freedom that must be set free from its incapacity in the face of evil (405:189-190). The community of free human beings that is projected in the symbol Kingdom of God is a symbol of hope only to the extent that it breaks into the experience that Ricoeur has described as the amor fati, an experience filled with the sound and fury of great undertakings that seek to totalize human existence on the level of theory and praxis.

It is impossible, but also unnecessary, to retrace Ricoeur's trajectory of the historical and human stages in the symbolization of the evil that threatens human existence. The symbols of defilement, the sin and guilt of Israel's history and the myths of the theogonic creation drama, of the fall, of the exiled soul, and of tragic existence of Ricoeur's La symbolique du mal make for a fascinating and sensitive reading of the problematic of evil. Only the conclusion need detain us.

What interests us is how Ricoeur arrives at a characterization of evil that is closely related to the total project of a poetics of the will. According to this reading of the exemplary history of the confession of sin,

---

13. See G. Mainberger, "Die Freiheit und das Böse" in Freib. Z. Philos.Theol. 19, 1972, p.410-430.

sin, that is, evil in the Judeo-Christian sense, is the dialectical opposite of faith (227:528). Sin is incomprehensible without faith (320(232):342). The history of evil cannot be read and understood except in the light of its opposite: the history of faith. Only in the exemplary history of Israel and the story of the life, death, and resurrection of Jesus can we begin to understand the radicalness of sin. But the concern of the history of faith is not to explain sin, but to indicate the end of evil (320(326):439). As Ricoeur says, "We do not believe in sin, but in salvation" (83(45):93). It is in the proclamation of the death and resurrection of Jesus or in the proclamation, "The Kingdom of God has come near to you", that we can begin to understand where we ought to situate evil in the Christian sense (227:526).

The privileged symbol of the history of faith, however, remains St. Paul's doctrine to justification (cf. 320(273):359-360;372-375). Here Ricoeur has remained heir to the hermeneutical key of the Protestant Reformation, which has read the New Testament tradition through Paul's justification by faith alone. It is the experience articulated by justification by faith alone that mediates most completely the situation of the self before God (153:147).

The symbol of justification by faith is for Ricoeur the limit-expression, whereby the religious person realizes the despoliation of the conscious self as the core entity (320(294):398).[14] For the justice that we seek is not an ethical quality. It is not a virtue at our disposal. Justice is an eschatological gift, that overtakes humanity through God's initiative. Justice for St. Paul is to be justified by another. To be just is to be declared just. The future of God's justice declares us to be just even now, making the present participate in the justice that is to be imputed to humanity. The justice is eschatological, yet a present reality. It is God's justice, yet it becomes humanity's. It is other, yet mine. As mine, it creates the new creature of liberty (153:147-148). It is read to me in the history of the death and resurrection of Jesus.

It is through the symbol of justification by faith that one can begin to understand the past of existence, which Paul called sin. The supreme sin is no other than the attempt to make oneself the ground and source of justice. St. Paul read his own past history as sin in the light of the history of Jesus because of the role that the Judaic law played in his efforts to be pleasing before God. The pretense of the law to institute the reign of

---

14. In his article, "Biblical Hermeneutics", art. cit., p.137-138, the extent of his identification with Paul is accentuated when Ricoeur assumes the hypothetical thesis of E. Jüngel, who shows a similarity between the symbol of the Rule of God and the concept of God's justice. Ricoeur says, that whereas Jüngel indicates only the similarity of the two discourses, he himself would see the concept of the justice of God as a translation of the symbol of the Kingdom of God. In the justice of God Ricoeur sees then a concentration of the message of the New Testament. This relationship of the symbol of the Kingdom and its translation into the concept of the justice of God has interesting repercussions for a hermeneutics based on the Bible.

justice is shown to be an illusion and a hypocrisy in the light of the mercy of God manifested in Christ Jesus. Faith is diametrically opposed to a justice that is the work of my accomplishment: "For we hold that a man is justified by faith apart from observance of the law" (Rom 3:28).

This view of justice as a being justified, or of freedom as a being set free dominates Paul Ricoeur's recovery of the self. It might even be correct to call Ricoeur a philosopher of justification. He is Pauline in perspective not only in his reading of the history of sin in the scriptures, but also in his reading of contemporary culture. Evil is not first of all transgression or disobedience.[15] Religious evil is not immorality (320(232):347). Sin is not the opposite of virtue (202:297). It is the opposite of faith. In the contemporary context, Ricoeur translates sin into the illusion of every attempt to totalize either knowledge or existence (320(297):414). The evil of evil has its origin for Ricoeur in the search for totality and absoluteness. Today's evil is a pathology of hope because it touches the problematic of our completion. The Pauline notion of 'law' as sin is interpreted as the hubris of the subject who thinks that he or she is a self-constituting subject (186:32). It pertains to a pathology of hope for humans to perceive and act as source and ground of existence. Paul's sin, as the moment of human death, takes on a deep cultural quality in Paul Ricoeur's writings. Thus he says,

> Truly human evil concerns premature syntheses, violent syntheses, short circuits in the totality. It culminates in the sublime, with the 'presumption' of the theodicies and their numerous successors in modern politics (320(232):345; 227:526).

Ricoeur has brought the issue of evil in the religious sense right into the midst of the contemporary debates and struggles of ideology and historical existence. His most anguished warnings are directed against the great institutions of church and state, where the danger of totalitarianism is most deeply entrenched.[16] And in his own philosophy he is most wary of establishing new absolutes and new totalitarian systems. His philosophy has remained a history of philosophy, ever open to be challenged by new schools of thought, and ever willing to be transformed by them. Ricoeur viewed the last of the great philosophical systems, that of Hegel, as at once symbolic of

---

15. See his "Culpabilité tragique et culpabilité biblique", Revue d'histoire et de philosophie religieuse 33, 1953, p.285-307. "Morale sans péché ou péché sans morale?", Esprit 22, 1954, p.266-282. "Kierkegaard et le mal," in Revue de théologie et de philosophie 13, 1963, p.292-302.

16. This concern for the totalitarianism of both the church and state is expressed in a number of articles. See, for example, the articles collected in Histoire et vérité (Esprit), Paris, Seuil, 1955, Political and Social Essays, Coll. and ed. by David Steward and Joseph Bien, Athens, Ohio University Press, 1975, and Politiek en geloof, Utrecht, Ambo, 1968.

the great human thrust toward wholeness and totality, and, at the same time, as the great temptation, as the possible harbinger of the totalitarian systems of this century (227:526). For Ricoeur, human historical existence must be able to say Yes in a history that remains open. Or as he says in L'homme faillible, "Man is the Joy of Yes in the sadness of the finite" (152:215).

The joy of Yes must be sought not in the vain attempt of knowledge and will to gain totality but in the home of hope, in the passion for what is possible according to the signs of the end, which we decipher in interpretation (362:33). The reality into which these signs throw us is the reality of the possible. In scriptural language, according to Ricoeur, this reality of the possible translates "The Kingdom of God is Coming" (397:82). This home of hope invites us to live our ownmost possibilities, living the symbol of the Kingdom that does not come from us (397:82). The symbol of justification may be perceived, therefore, as both the apex of the despoliation of the self and as the reality of the self. The self is, in religious terms, the gift. In Ricoeur's words, "Our God is a God-Act, a God-Gift, who makes man a creator in his turn in the measure in which he receives and is willing to receive the gift of being free" (115:131). Faith is the invasion of the future of God into my present, the gift of self as an eschatological gift (78:397).

For Ricoeur the philosopher, Jesus, the Christ, belongs to the schema of hope. It is his witness, the narrative confession of his name, that has opened up the realm of the imagination of a new justice and new freedom (320(232):341). His death and the proclamation of his resurrection from the dead are the proclamation of hope and freedom that is, in spite of death, beyond any effort to explain it this side of death (320(297):397). In him is revealed the new meaning of existence in which freedom is my present gift. But that freedom can be lived authentically only out of that future. But it is not freedom as ordinarily understood, for it is a "capacity to live according to the paradoxical law of superabundance, of denying death and of asserting the excess of sense over non-sense in all desparate situations" (338:59).

But if there is to be a final appropriation for Ricoeur, it must be an appropriation of the subject in love (320(214):192). He has hardly developed the theme, although he acknowledges this lack as a weakness on his part (320(232):352). A theology of love is not an extension of an ethical love, for a philosophy of love is a questionable exercise (75:397). A theology of love is a suspension of ethics and the emergence of a love that has renounced desire, according to Augustine's dictum, ama et fac quod vis. For it is in the death of desire that love comes to itself and the self comes to its full measure (320(232):352). To return a final time to Ricoeur,

Charity towards the other and towards oneself is like the imagination which, through the overgrown landscape, perceives the original contours; such a loving imagination is at the same time a view of the very heart of reality (80:350).

BIBLIOGRAPHY

A Paul Ricoeur*

1935

a. "Réflections d'un étudiant protestant" in <u>Terre Nouvelle</u> II, (juin 1935), p.8-9.

1936

1. "Responsabilité de la pensée" in <u>Être</u> 1936-37, Nov. 10, p.4-5.

2. "Le risque" in <u>Être</u> 1936-37, Dec. 10, p.9-11.

1937

3. "Socialisme et christianisme" in <u>Être</u> 1936-37, March 10, p.3-4.

1938

4. "Nécessité de Karl Marx" in <u>Être</u> 1937-38, March, p.6-11.

1940

5. "L'attention. Étude phénoménologique de l'attention et de ses connexions philosophiques" in <u>Bulletin du cercle philosophique de l'ouest</u> 4, 1940, Jan.-March, p.1-28.

---

*I must gratefully acknowledge the bibliographical compilation of D. Vansina. While making use of his text, the bibliography does not follow his numeration. I have chosen to place translations with the original, in order that some type of chronological perspective might be maintained. See D. Vansina, "Bibliographie de Paul Ricoeur" in <u>Rev. Phil. de Louvain</u> 60, 1962, p.394-414; 66, 1968, p.85-101; and 72, 1974, p.156-181.

1946

6. "Le chrétien et la civilisation occidentale" in Christianisme social. Revue social et internationale pour un monde chrétien 54, 1946, p.423-436.

also in: Cité nouvelle 1959, Sept., p.1-3, Oct. 1, p.1-2, Oct. 18, p.1-4, Nov. 5, p.1-3, 56.

7. "Vérité: Jésus et Ponce Pilate" in Le semeur; Tribune libre de la fédération française des associations chrétiennes d'étudiants (XXVIIIe congrès national) 44, 1946, p.381-394.

1947

8. Dufrenne M. and Ricoeur P., Karl Jaspers et la philosophie de l'existence (Esprit). Préface by K. Jaspers, Paris, Seuil, 1947, p.399 (P. Ricoeurs' contribution: p.173-373).

9. "Le mystère mutuel ou le romancier humilié (a book review of P.A. Lesort, Les reins et les coeurs) in Esprit 15, 1947, p.691-699.

10. "La crise de la démocratie et la conscience chrétienne" in Christianisme social 55, 1947, p.320-331.

11. "Envoi" in Foi-éducation: Revue trimestrielle de la fédération protestante des membres de l'enseignement 17, 1947, p.2-3.

1948

12. Gabriel Marcel et Karl Jaspers. Philosophie du mystère et philosophie du paradoxe (artistes et écrivains du temps présent) Paris, Temps Présent, 1948, 455p.

13. Trocmé A., "Consultations fraternelles" (D'après un rapport de P. Ricoeur) in Consultations, Cahiers de réconciliation 3, 1948, October, p.3-11.

14. "Pour un christianisme prophétique" in Les chrétiens et la politique (Dialogues) Paris, Temps Présent, 1948, p.79-100.

15. "Dimensions d'une recherche commune" in Esprit 16, 1948, p.837-848.

16. "La pensée engagée. M. Merleau-Ponty. Humanisme et terreur" in Esprit 16, 1948, p.911-916.

17. "La condition du philosophe chrétien" (a book review by P. Ricoeur of R. Mehl, La condition du philosophe chrétien) in Christianisme social 56, 1948, p.551-557.

18. "Comment respecter l'enfant?" in Foi-éducation 18, 1948, p.6-11.

19. "L'expérience psychologique de la liberté" in Le semeur (Liberté) 46, 1948, p.445-451.

1949

20. "Le renouvellement de la philosophie chrétienne par les philosophies de l'existence" in Le problème de la philosophie chrétienne (Les problèmes de la pensée chrétienne) edited by J. Boisset, Paris, P.U.F., 1949, p.43-67.

21. "Possibilités ouvertes à l'évangélisation. Entendre l'évangile" in Évangile captif. Jeunesse de l'église (Cahier 10) Petit-Clamart (Seine) Jeunesse de l'église, 1949, p.69-72.

22. "Husserl et le sens de l'histoire" in Revue de métaphysique et de morale 54, 1949, p.280-316.

also as: "Husserl and the Sense of History" in Husserl. An Analysis of His Phenomenology (263) p.143-174.

23. "L'homme non violent et sa présence à l'histoire" in Esprit (Révision du pacifisme) 17, 1949, p.224-234.

also in: Histoire et vérité (83) p.230-234.

and as: "Non-violent Man and His Presence to History" in History and Truth (212) p.223-233.

24. "Le yogi, le commissaire, le prolétaire et le prophète, À propos de 'Humanisme et terreur' de Maurice Merleau-Ponty" in Christianisme social 57, 1949, p.41-45.

25. "La culpabilité allemande" (a book review by P. Ricoeur of K. Jaspers, La culpabilité allemande) in Christianisme social 57, 1949, p.150-157.

26. "Les propositions de paix scolaire de la revue Esprit" in Foi-éducation 19, 1949, p.3-8.

27. "Auto-critique et anticipation" in Foi-éducation (Rencontres et travaux de l'été 1949) 19, 1949, December, p.1-2.

28. "La violence dans l'histoire et la place de l'autre force" in Cité nouvelle: Journal bimensuel, 1949, no. 85, Nov. 10, 1 and 3.

1950

29. Philosophie de la volonté. I. Le volontaire et l'involontaire (Philosophie de l'esprit) Paris, Aubier, 1950, 464p. 2nd ed. 1963.

30. "Introduction" in Husserl E. Idées directrices pour une phénoménologie (Bibliothèque de philosophie) Paris, Gallimard, 1950, p.XI-XXXIX. 2nd ed. 1963.

31. Husserl E., La crise de l'humanité européenne et la philosophie. Prepared and presented by S. Strasser and translated by P. Ricoeur, in Revue de métaphysique et de morale 55, 1950, p. 225-258.

32. Husserl E., La philosophie comme prise de conscience de l'humanité. Presented and prepared by W. Biemel and translated by P. Ricoeur in Deucalion 3, vérité et liberté (Être et penser. Cahiers de philosophie) 1950, no. 30, p.109-127.

33. "Une philosophie personnaliste" (E. Mounier) in Esprit 18, 1950, December, p.860-887.

also as: "Emmanuel Mounier: une philosophie personnaliste" in Histoire et vérité (83) p.103-140.

and as: "Emmanuel Mounier: A Personalist Philosophy" in History and Truth (212) p.133-161.

34. "Les travaux de la Commission Philip" in Christianisme social 20, 1950, p. 9-23 and in Foi-éducation 20, 1950, Jan., p.1-12.

also as: "La querelle des écoles. Les travaux de la Commission Philip" (1944-45 in Laicité et paix scolaire (Enquête et conclusions de la fédération protestante de l'enseignement) Paris, Berger-Levrault 1957, p.219-232.

35. "Message de clôture du congrès" (de la fédération protestante de l'enseignement, Bievres 1950, consacré à 'La vie personelle de l'éducateur') in Foi-éducation 20, 1950, Nov., p.63-64.

36. "Discerner pour agir" in Le Semeur (Peut-on s'orienter dans le monde moderne?) 48, 1950, p.431-452.

1951

37. "Compte rendu de thèse" in Annales de l'Université de Paris 21, 1951, p.633-635.

38. "L'unité du volontaire et l'involontaire" (présentation des arguments et exposé suivi d'une discussion avec E. Bréhier, etc.) in Bulletin de la Société française de Philosophie 45, 1951, p.1-2, 3-22, 23-29.

A summary of this article is found under the same title in: Les études philosophiques 6, 1951, p.106-107.

also as: "The Unity of the Voluntary and Involuntary as a Limiting Idea" in Readings in Existential Phenomenology, edited by N. Lawrence and D. O'Connor, Englewood Cliffs, New Jersey, Prentice Hall, 1967, p.390-402.

and in: The Philosophy of Paul Ricoeur (452) p.3-19.

39. "Analyses et problèmes dans Ideen II de Husserl" in Revue de métaphysique et de morale 56, 1951, p.357-394.

also in: Revue de métaphysique et de morale 57, 1952, p.1-16.

and in: Phénoménologie-existence (Revue de métaphysique et de morale) Paris, A. Colin, 1953, p.23-76.

also as: "Husserl's Ideas II: Analysis and Problems" in Husserl. An Analysis of His Phenomenology (263) p.35-81.

40. "La pensée grecque": Ernest Hoffmann, Plato, and Victor Goldschmidt, La religion de Platon (two book reviews by P. Ricoeur) in Revue d'histoire et de philosophie religieuses 31, 1951, p.240-244.

41. Ricoeur P., and Domenach J.M., "Masse et personne" in Esprit 19, 1951, January, p.9-18.

also as: "Mass and Person" in Cross Currents 2, 1952, p.59-66.

42. "Pour une coexistence pacifique des civilisations" in Esprit (La paix possible) 19, 1951, March, p.408-419.

43. "Réflexions" on Le diable et le bon Dieu in Esprit 19, 1951, November, p.711-719.

also as: "Sartres's Lucifer and the Lord" in Yale French Studies, 1954-55, no. 14, p.85-93.

44. "Vérité et mensonge" in Esprit 19, 1951, p.753-778.

also in : Histoire et vérité (83) p.141-176.

and as: "Truth and Falsehood" in History and Truth (212) p.165-191.

45. "Le christianisme et le sens de l'histoire. Progrès, ambiguité, espérance" in Christianisme social 59, 1951, p.261-274.

also in: Histoire et vérité (83) p.80-102.

also as: "Christianity and the Meaning of History. Progress, Ambiguity, Hope" in The Journal of Religion 21, 1952, p.242-253.

and in: History and Truth (212) p.81-97.

46. "Tâches pour la paix" in Christianisme social 59, 1951, p.371-378.

47. "La connaissance de l'homme par la littérature du malheur" in Foi-éducation (littérature et monde moderne) 21, 1951, p.149-156.

48. "La question de l'humanisme chrétien" in Foi et vie 49, 1951, p.323-330.

49. "Nous ne pouvons nous taire. La Fédération Protestante de l'Enseignement et le problème scolaire" (The declaration of the National Committee presided over by P. Ricoeur) in Foi-éducation 21, 1951, p.234-235.

50. "L'Évangile et les intellectuels" in Le semeur (Autorité de l'Écriture) 49, 1951, p.485-490.

51. "Note sur l'Existentialisme et la Foi-Chrétienne" in La revue de l'évangélisation (Le Christianisme devant les courants de la pensée moderne) 6, 1951, p.143-152.

1952

52. "Histoire de la philosophie et sociologie de la connaissance" in L'homme et l'histoire. Actes du VIe congrès des sociétés de philosophie de langue française, Paris P.U.F., 1952, p.341-346 .

also in : Histoire et vérité (83) p.73-79.

and as: "Note on the History of Philosophy and the Sociology of Knowledge" in History and Truth (212) p.57-62.

53. "Méthodes et tâches d'une phénoménologie de la volonté" in Problèmes actuels de la phénoménologie, edited by H.L. Van Breda, Bruges-Paris, Desclée de Brouwer, 1952, p.110-140.

also as: "Methods and Tasks of a Phenomenology of the Will" in Husserl; An Analysis of His Phenomenology (263) p.213-233.

54. "Le temps de Jean-Baptiste et le temps de Galilée" (a book review by P. Ricoeur of P. Montuclard, Les événements et la foi) in Esprit 20, 1952, p.864-871.

55. "Aux frontières de la philosophie" (on A. Néher, 'Amos'; A. Béquin, 'Pascal par lui-même'; J. Roos, 'Blake Novalis, Ballanche. Aspects littéraires du mysticisme philosophique au romanticisme'; P. Burgelin, 'La philosophie de l'existence de J.J. Rousseau') in Esprit 20, 1952, Nov., p.760-775.

56. "Propositions de compromis pour l'Allemagne" in Esprit (Misère de la psychiatrie) 20, 1952, p.1006-1011.

57. "'L'homme révolté' de Camus" in Christianisme social 60, 1952, p.229-239.

58. "Urgence d'une morale" in Foi-éducation (La paix: des enfants et des hommes) 22, 1952, p.107-114.

59. "L'homme de science et l'homme de foi" in Le semeur 50, 1952, November, p.12-22.

also as: "Note sur le voeu et la tâche de l'unité" (a partial text) in Histoire et vérité (83) p.177-182.

also in: Recherche et débats 2, 1953, no. 4, p.77-88.

and as: "Note on the Wish and Endeavor for Unity" in History and Truth (212) p.192-196.

60. "Quelques conclusions du congrès" (de la Fédération Protestante de l'Enseignement, Bievres 1952, consacré à l'Université et la Nation). Notes of Ricoeur in Foi-éducation 22, 1952, p.196.

1953

61. "Geschichte der Philosophie als kontinuierliche Schöpfung der Menschheit auf dem Wege der Kommunikation" in Offener Horizont, edited by Kl. Piper, Munich, R. Piper, 1953, p.110-125.

also as: "L'histoire de la philosophie et l'unité du vrai" in Revue internationale de philosophie 8, 1954, p.266-282.

and in Histoire et vérité (83) p.53-72.

and as: "The History of Philosophy and the Unity of Truth" in History and Truth (212) p.41-56.

62. "Vraie et fausse angoisse" (a conference by P. Ricoeur followed by a debate with E. Weil, etc.) in L'angoisse du temps présent et les devoirs de l'esprit (Rencontres internationales de Genève 1953) Neuchâtel, La baconnière, 1953, p.33-53.

The conference is reprinted in: Histoire et vérité (83) p.244-266.

and as: "True and False Anguish" in History and Truth (212) p.287-304.

63. Ricoeur P., Schuman R., Calogero G. etc., "Troisième entretien public" (a discussion on the conference of Schuman, 'Les causes sociales et politiques de l'angoisse') "Troisième entretien privé" (a debate on the conference of Calogero, 'La vie morale et l'angoisse') in L'angoisse du temps présent et les devoirs de l'esprit Neuchâtel, La baconnière, 1953, p.247-277, 280-303.

64. "Culpabilité tragique et culpabilité biblique" in Revue d'histoire et la philosophie religieuse 33, 1953, p.285-307.

65. "Travail et parole" in Esprit 21, 1953, p.96-117.

also in: Histoire et vérité (83) p.183-212.

and as: "Work and the Word" in History and Truth (212) p.197-219.

66. "Aux frontières de la philosophie (suite). Sur le tragique" (on G. Nebel, 'Weltangst und Götterzorn'; H. Gouhier, 'le théâtre et l'existence'; M. Scheller, 'Le phénomème du tragique; K. Jaspers, 'Über das Tragische') in Esprit 21, 1953, March, p.449-467.

67. "Sur la phénoménologie. I" (on Tran-Duc-Thao, 'Phénoménologie et matérialisme dialectique') in Esprit 21, 1953, p.821-829.

also as: "Phenomenology" (Tran-Duc-Thao, 'Phénoménologie et matérialisme dialectique') in Southwestern Journal of Philosophy 5, 1974, p.149-168.

68. "Objectivité et subjectivité en histoire" (a report by P. Ricoeur followed by a debate with Feinberg and others) in Revue de l'enseignement philosophique. Revue de l'Association des Professeurs de Philosophie de l'Enseignement public 3, 1953, July-September, p.28-40, 41-43.

also as: "Subjectivité et objectivité en histoire" in Les Amis de Sèvres. Bulletin d'information 6, 1954, p.5-21.

and in: Histoire et vérité (83) p.25-52.

and as: "Objectivity and Subjectivity in History" in History and Truth (212) p.21-40.

69. "Les Conditions de la coexistence pacifique. Conditions de la paix" in Christianisme social 61, 1953, p.297-307.

70. "Pour la solution du problème allemande. La conférence de Berlin" in Christianisme social 61, 1953, p.625-631.

71. "La crise de la vérité et la pression du mensonage dans la civilisation actuelle" in Vie enseignante. Pour les instituteurs, 1953, November, 11p.

72. "État, Nation, École" in Foi-éducation 23, 1953, p.54-57.

1954

73. "Introduction" and "Appendix" in E. Bréhier, Histoire de la philosophie allemande (Bibliothèque d'histoire de la philosophie). Third edition, Paris, Vrin, 1954, p.181-258.

also as: "Introduction: Husserl 1859-1938" in Husserl: An Analysis of His Phenomenology (263) p.3-12.

74. "La relation à autrui. Le 'socius' et le prochain" in L'amour du prochain (Cahiers de la vie spirituelle) Paris, Cerf, 1954, p.293-310.

also as: "Sociologie et théologie. Le 'socius' et le prochain" in Christianisme social 68, 1960, p.461-471.

and as: "Associate and Neighbour" in Love of our Neighbour, London, Blackfriars Publications 8, 1955, p.149-161.

and as: "Le Socius et le prochain" in Histoire et vérité (83) p.213-229.

and as: "The Socius and the Neighbour" in History and Truth (212) p.98-109.

and as: "Medemens en naaste" in Politiek en geloof (284) p.18-31.

75. "Sympathie et respect. Phénoménologie et éthique de la seconde personne" in Revue de métaphysique et de morale 59, 1954, p.380-397.

76. "Étude sur les 'Méditations Cartésiennes' de Husserl" in Revue philosophique de Louvain 52, 1954, p.75-109.

also as: " A Study of Husserl's Cartesian Meditations" in Husserl. An Analysis of His Phenomenology (263) p.82-114.

77. "Motivation, motion et consentement" (an extract from Le volontaire et l'involontaire) in Textes choisis des auteurs philosophiques. I. Introduction générale. Psychologie, edited by A. Cuvillier, Paris, A. Colin, 1954, p.283-285.

78. "Kant et Husserl" in Kant-Studien 46, 1954-55, p.44-67.

also as: "Kant and Husserl" in Philosophy Today 10, 1966, p.147-168.

and in: Husserl. An Analysis of His Phenomenology (263) p.175-201.

79. "Philosophie de la personne. I. L'existence d'autrui" (de M. Chastaing) in Esprit 22, 1954, February, p.289-297.

80. "'Morale sans péché' ou péché sans morale?" (A. Hesnard, Morale sans péché) in Esprit 22, 1954, p.394-312.

also as: "'Morality Without Sin' or Sin Without Moralism" in Cross Currents 5, 1955, p.339-452.

81. "Le protestantisme et la question scolaire" in Foi-éducation 24, 1954, June, p.48-59.

82. "Être, essence et substance chez Platon et Aristote" (courses taught at the University of Strasbourg in 1953-54) Centre de documentation universitaire, 1960, 149p.

also as: Platon et Aristote, Centre de documentation universitaire, Paris, 1971, 147p.

1955

83. Histoire et vérité (Esprit) Paris, Seuil, 1955, 289p.

Contains the following articles:

Objectivité et subjectivité en histoire (68) p.25-52.
L'histoire de la philosophie et l'unité du vrai (61) p.53-72.
Note sur l'histoire de la philosophie et la sociologie de la connaissance (52) p.73-79.
Le christianisme et le sens de l'histoire (45) p.80-102.
Emmanuel Mounier: une philosophie personnaliste (33) p.103-140.
Vérité et mensonge (44) p.141-176.
Note sur le voeu et la tâche de l'unité (59) p.177-182.
Travail et parole (65) p.183-212.
Le socius et le prochain (74) p.213-229.
L'homme non violent et sa présence à l'histoire (23) p.230-243.
Vraie et fausse angoisse (62) p.244-266.

84. "La parole est mon royaume" in Esprit 32, 1955, p.192-205.

85. "Sur la phénoménologie. II. Le 'Problème de l'âme'" (on S. Strasser, Le problème de l'âme. Études sur l'object respectif de la psychologie métaphysique et de la psychologie empirique) in Esprit (le monde des prisons) 23, 1955, April, p.721-726.

also as: "Notes critique" in Revue de métaphysique et de morale 61, 1956 p.87-91.

86. "Philosophie et ontologie. Retour à Hegel" (on J. Hyppolite, Logique et existence. Essai sur la logique de Hegel) in Esprit 23, 1955, August, p.1378-1391.

87. "Aux frontières de la philosophie. II. Philosophie et prophétisme" (on A. Néher, L'essence du prophétisme) in Esprit 23, 1955, December, p.1928-1939.

88. "Vraie et fausse paix" in Christianisme social 63, 1955, p.467-479.

also as: Vraie et fausse paix (Questions de notre temps), Paris, Le Cep, 1955 16p.

89. "French Protestantism Today" in The Christian Century 72, 1955, p.1236-1238.

90. "Vivre 'en' adultes 'comme' des enfants" in Jeunes femmes. Bulletin des groupes 'Jeunes femmes' 4, 1955, July-August, p.61-71.

1956

91. Guardini, R., La mort de Socrate. A translation of Der Tod des Sokrates by P. Ricoeur, Paris, Seuil, 1956, 269p.

92. "Préface" in P. Thévenaz L'homme et sa raison. I. Raison et conscience de soi (Être et penser. Cahiers de philosophie) 46, Neuchâtel, La Baconnière, 1956, p.9-26.

also as: "Un philosophe protestant. Pierre Thévenaz" in Esprit 25, 1957, January, p.40-53.

93. "Négativité et affirmation originaire" in Aspects de la dialectique (Recherches de philosophie, II) Bruges-Paris, Desclée de Brouwer, 1956, p.101-124.

also in : Histoire et vérité (212) p.308-332.

also as: Zum Grundproblem der Gegenwartsphilosophie. Die Philosophie des Nichts und die Ur-Bejahung" in Sinn und Sein, edited by R. Wisser, Tübingen, Niemeyer, 1960, p.47-65.

and as: "Negativity and Primary Affirmation" in History and Truth, (212) p.305-328.

94. "Questions sur la Chine" in Christianisme social 64, 1956, p.319-335.

also in Italian.

95. "Que signifie 'humanisme'?" in Comprendre. Revue de la société européenne de culture (L'humanisme d'aujourd'hui) 1956, no. 15, March, p.84-92.

also as: "What does Humanism Mean?" in Political and Social Essays (414) p.68-87.

96. "Certitudes et incertitudes d'une révolution" in Esprit 24, 1956, January, p.5-28.

97. "Note critique sur Chine ouverte" in Esprit 24, 1956, p.897-910.

98. "Écoles de Chine" in Paris-Pekin. La revue des amitiés franco-chinoises, 1956, March, p.11-16.

also as: "Enseignement dans la Chine nouvelle" in Foi-éducation 26, 1956, Jan.-March, p.25-30.

99. "Déclaration de la Fédération Protestante de l'Enseignement" (présidée par P. Ricoeur en faveur de la laicité scolaire) in Foi-éducation 26, 1956, Jan.-March, p.4-5.

partially reproduced in: Le Monde 12, 1955, no. 3398, December 27,1956.

and under the title: "Les enseignants protestants pour la laicité" in L'express 3, 1955, no. 190, Dec. 28, p.3.

100. "Une enquête spirituelle: Quelle est pour vous la résonance actuelle de la révélation du Sinai?" (reply of P. Ricoeur) in Unir. Publication mensuelle de la communauté israélite de Strasbourg 2, 1956, no. 8, p.1.

1957

101. "Karl Jaspers" in Tableau de la philosophie contemporaine (Histoire de la philosophie contemporaine) edited by A. Weber and D. Huisman, Paris, Fischbacher, 1957, p.375-381.

102. "Appel de la Fédération Protestante de l'Enseignement" (P. Ricoeur, pres.) in Foi-éducation 27, 1957, Jan.-March, p.45.

103. "André Mandouze" in Foi-éducation 27, 1957, p.46.

104. "Les événements d'Algérie devant la conscience chrétienne" (a declaration from the office of the Protestant Teachers' Federation, P. Ricoeur pres.) in Foi-éducation 27, 1957, April-June, p.105.

105. State and Violence, Geneva, Association du foyer John Knox, 1957.

and as: <u>État et violence</u>. La troisième conférence annuelle du Foyer John Knox, Geneva, Associaton du Foyer John Knox, 1957, 16p.

also in: <u>Histoire et vérité</u> (212) p.234-247.

also as: "Le problème de la violence I. II. Guerre et violence" in <u>Foi-éducation</u> 27, 1957, July-Sept., p.7-14, and Oct.-Dec., p.15-11.

and as: "Violence. Anthologie de textes" in <u>Le semeur</u> 60, 1962, Feb., p.403-404. (abridged)

and as: "State and Violence" in <u>History and Truth</u> (212) p.234-246.

106. "Préface" in B. Sargi, <u>La participation à l'être dans la philosophie de Louis Lavelle</u> (Biliothèque des Archives de philosophie. Septième section. Philosophie contemporaine, I.) Paris, Beauchesne, 1957, p.7-9.

107. "Ecole-Nation-État" in <u>Laicité et paix scolaire</u>. (Enquête et conclusions de la Fédération Protestante de l'Enseignement) Paris, Berger-Levrault, 1957, p.280-293.

108. "Phénoménologie existentielle" in <u>Encyclopédie française</u> XIX. Philosophie et religion, Paris, Larousse, 1957 p.19.10-8 to 19.10-12.

also as: "Existential Phenomenology" in <u>Husserl. An Analysis of His Phenomenology</u> (263) p.202-212.

109. "Philosophie et religion chez Karl Jaspers" in <u>Revue d'histoire et de philosophie religieuses</u> 37, 1957, p.207-235.

also as: "The Relation of Jasper's Philosophy to Religion" in <u>The Philosophy of Karl Jaspers</u>. A Critical Analysis and Evaluation (Library of Living Philosophers) edited by P.A. Schipp, New York, Tudor, 1957, p.611-642.

also as: "Philosophie und Religion bei Karl Jaspers" in <u>Karl Jaspers</u> (Philosophen des 20. Jahrhunderts) edited by P.A. Schilipp, Stuttgart, Kolhammer, 1957, p.604-635.

110. "Analyses et comptes rendus." H. Heimsoeth, <u>Les six grands thèmes de la métaphysique occidentale</u>" in <u>Les études philosophiques</u> 12, 1957, p.408-409.

111. "Le 'Traité de Métaphysique' de Jean Wahl" in <u>Esprit</u> 25, 1957, March, p.529-540.

112. "Le paradoxe politique" in <u>Esprit</u> (Le temps de la réflexion) 25, 1957, May, p.721-745.

and in: <u>Histoire et vérité</u> (83) p.248-273.

and as: "The Political Paradox" in History and Truth (212) p.247-270.

also as: "De paradox van de macht" in Politiek en geloof (284) p.32-58.

113. "'L'essai sur le mal' de Jean Nabert" in Esprit 25, 1957, July-August, p.124-135.

114. "La 'philosophie politique' d'Eric Weil" in Esprit 25, 1957, October, p.412-429.

115. "Faith and Culture" in The Student World (the Greatness and Misery of the Intellectual) 50, 1957, p.246-251.

also in: Political and Social Essays (414) p.125-133.

116. "Place de l'oeuvre d'art dans notre culture" in Foi-éducation 27, 1957, Jan.-March, p.5-11.

117. "Réflexions finales sur le Congrès" (of the Fédération Protestante de l'Enseignement, dedicated to L'art et l'éducation) in Foi-éducation 27, 1957, Jan.-March, p.33-34.

118. "Vous êtes le sel de la terre" in Au service du maître, 1957, Nov.-Dec., p.27-35.

also as: "Ye art the Salt of the Earth" in Ecumenical Review 10, 1958, p.264-276.

and in: Political and Social Essays (414) p.105-124.

119. "Recherches d'anthropologie chrétienne sur le terrain philosophique. I. Les Grecs et le péché. II. La philosophie en face de la confession des péchés" in Supplement to La confiance. Correspondance fraternelle et privée des pasteurs de France 3, 1957, no. 1-2, p.17-32.

120. "Les théologiens, la guerre et l'objection de conscience. III. Une analyse éclairante de Paul Ricoeur" in La confiance 3, 1957, no. 4, p.8-11.

1958

121. "Perplexités sur Israel" in Esprit 26, 1958, June, p.868-876.

122. "L'aventure technique et son horizon interplanétaire" in Christianisme social 66, 1958, Jan.-Feb., p.20-33.

also as: Techniek op interplanetaire schaal" in Politiek en geloof (284) p.166-179.

also in Spanish.

123. "Le procès d'Étienne Mathiot et de Francine Rapiné" in Christianisme social 66, 1958, p.277-279.

124. "Les aventures de l'État et la tâche des chrétiens" in Christianisme social 66, 1958, p.452-463.

and as: "Adventures of the State and the Task of Christians" in Political and Social Essays (414) p.201-216.

also as: "Hoe staat de kristen in de staat?" in Politiek en geloof (284) p.77-88.

125. "Éléments de jugement constitutionnel" in Christianisme social 66, 1958, p.570-575.

126. "L'enseignant protestant en face du catholicisme d'aujourd'hui" in Foi-éducation 28, 1958, Jan.-March, p.7-13.

also in Italian.

127. "Responsabilité et culpabilité au plan communautaire" in Le Semeur 56, 1958, June, p.3-6.

128. "Formes actuelles des préoccupations morales et religieuses de la jeunesse" in L'école des parents. Organe mensuel de l'école des parents et des éducateurs, 1958, June, p.1-11.

129. "Le droit de punir" in Cahiers de Villemétrie (Groupe des Juristes) 1958, March-April, p.2-21. (polycopy)

130. "Le communisme. Une interview" in Notre chemin. Journal mensuel inter-régional des églises réformées 48, 1958, Sept., p.1-2.

also as: "Une interview de Paul Ricoeur" in Cité nouvelle, 1958, no. 284, Dec. 4, p.2.

131. "Appel" in Foi-éducation 28, 1958, Jan.-March, p.43-44.

132. "Le 'Cas' Étienne Mathiot" in Foi-éducation 28, 1958, p.45-47.

133. "Le monde de la science et le monde de la foi" (edited notes of a conference given by P. Ricoeur) in Cahiers de Villemétrie (Condition du scientifique chrétien dans le monde moderne) 1958, no. 8, p.2-21. (polycopy)

134. "Le procès d'Étienne Mathiot et de Francine Rapiné" in Cité nouvelle 1958, no. 268, March 20, 1 and 4.

also in: Christianisme social 66, 1958, p.277-279.

135. "Le jugement (suite et fin)" in <u>Bulletin du groupe d'études de philosophie</u> (The University of Paris) 1958-59, no. 8, p.27-70. (polycopy)

also as: "Le jugement" in <u>Cahiers de philosophie</u>. Published by 'Le groupe de philosophie' of the University of Paris 2, 1963-64, no. 5, 87p. (polycopy)

136. "La vision morale du monde" in <u>Bulletin du groupe d'études de philosophie</u> 1958-59, no. 10, p.1-43. (polycopy)

1959

137. "Le paradoxe de la liberté politique" in <u>La liberté</u> (Institut canadien des Affaires Publiques) 1959, p.51-55.

138. "Mémorandum pour servir à élaboration d'un statut national de l'enseignement" in <u>Foi-éducation</u> 29, 1959, July-Sept., p.121-128.

also as: "La fédération protestante de l'enseignement publie un mémorandum exposant sa position sur le problème scolaire" in <u>Le monde</u> 16, 1959, no. 4457, May 23, p.6.

139. "Le sentiment" in <u>Edmund Husserl 1859-1959</u>. Recueil commémoratif (<u>Phaenomenologica</u> 4) La Haye, Nijhoff, 1959, p.260-274.

140. "Introduction" in M. Weber, "Éthique et Politique" (conclusion of a report entitled <u>Politik als Beruf</u>) in <u>Esprit</u> 27, 1959, Feb., p.225-245.

141. "Le symbole donne à penser" in <u>Esprit</u> 27, 1959, p.60-76.

and as: "The Symbol: Food for Thought" in <u>Philosophy Today</u> 1960, Autumn, p.196-207.

142. "Du marxisme au communisme contemporain" in <u>Christianisme social</u> 67, 1959, p.151-159.

also as: "From Marxism to Contemporary Communism" in <u>Political and Social Essays</u> (414) p.217-228.

143. "Les formes nouvelles de la justice sociale" in <u>Christianisme social</u> 67, 1959, p.691-702.

144. "La crise du socialisme" in <u>Christianisme social</u> 67, 1959, p.691-702.

145. "La place des 'humanités' dans le monde moderne" in <u>Paris-Lettres. Le journal des étudiants en lettres</u> 3, 1959, août-octobre.

146. "L'enseignement des humanités dans le monde moderne" in <u>Foi-éducation</u> 29, 1959, Jan.-March, p.23-25.

147. "Conclusions du congrès" in <u>Foi-éducation</u> 29, 1959, Jan.-March, p.46-49.

148. "Le chrétien et l'État" (a copy of the notes of Pl. Morel on the conference of P. Ricoeur) in <u>La confiance</u> 5, 1959, no. 1, p.11-14.

149. "Réponse de Ricoeur à Jean Lasserre" (on conscientious objection) in <u>La confiance</u> 5, 1959, no. 4. p.2-3.

150. "Le Collège Cévenol regarde l'avenir" in <u>Nouvelles du Collège Cévenol</u> 6, 1959, March p.14-15.

also in: <u>Cité nouvelle</u>, 1959, no. 295, May 28, p.4.

151. "Les chrétiens et les besoins des hommes" in <u>Cité nouvelle</u> 1959, no. 299, July 30, p.4.

1960

152. <u>Philosophie de la volonté. Finitude et culpabilité. I. L'homme faillible.</u> (Philosophie de l'esprit) Paris, Aubier, 1960 (1963, 1968), 164p.

also as: <u>Fallible Man</u>, translated by Ch. Kelbley, Chicago, Henry Regnery, 1965, xxix-224p.

and as: <u>Die Fehlbarkeit des Menschen. Phänomenologie der Schuld.</u> II by M. Otto, Munich-Fribourg, Karl Alber, 1971, 189p.

also in Italian.

153. <u>Philosophie de la volonté. Finitude et culpabilité. II. La symbolique du mal</u> (Philosophie de l'esprit) Paris, Aubier, 1960 (1963, 1968), 323p.

also as: <u>The Symbolism of Evil</u> (Religious Perspectives) translated by E. Buchanan, New York-Evanston-London, Harper and Row, 1967 (1969), xv-357p.

also as: <u>Symbolen van het kwaad.</u> I. De primaire symbolen-smet, zonde, schuldigheid. II. De mythen van het begin en het einde. Translated by J-A. Meijers, Rotterdam, Lemniscaat, 1970, 131-162p.

and as: <u>Symbolik der Bösen. Phänomenologie der Schuld.</u> II. Translated by M. Otto, Munich-Friburg, Karl Alber, 1971, 407p.

also in Italian and Spanish.

154. "Préface" in A. Peperzak, <u>Le jeune Hegel et la vision morale du monde.</u>" La Haye, Nijhoff, 1960, 8, 1p. (no pagination)

155. "L'homme et son mystère" in <u>Le mystère</u> (Semaine des intellectuels catholiques 1959) Paris, Horay, 1960, p.119-130.

156. Ricoeur P., Simondon G., "Forme, information, potentiels" (a discussion of a report by G. Simondon) in <u>Bulletin de la Société française de Philosophie</u> 54, 1960, p.181-183.

157. "L'antinomie de la réalité humaine et le problème de l'anthropologie philosophique" in <u>Il Pensiero</u> 5, 1960, p.273-290.

also as: "The Antinomy of Human Reality and the Problem of Philosophical Anthropology" in <u>Readings in Existential Phenomenology</u>, edited by N. Lawrence and D. O'Connor, Englewood Cliffs, New Jersey, Prentice Hall, 1967, 390-402.

and in: <u>The Philosophy of Paul Ricoeur</u> (452) p.20-35.

158. "Déclaration de la Fédération Protestante de l'Enseignement" (présidée par P. Ricoeur en faveur de la laicité scolaire) in <u>Foi-éducation</u> 30, 1960, April-June, 41p.

159. "Liberté et destin" in <u>Supplement</u> to <u>La vie chrétienne</u>, 1960, April, p.1-4.

160. "La sexualité. La merveille, l'errance, l'énigma" in <u>Esprit</u> (La sexualité) 28, 1960, Nov., p.1665-1676, discussion: p.1677-1700, 1711, 1796-1808, 1820-1825, 1839-1846, 1864, 1899-1919, 1930, 1938-1946.)

also as: "The Dimensions of Sexuality " in <u>Cross Currents</u> (Sexuality in the modern world) 14, 1964, Spring, p.133-141, 142-165, 186-208, 229-255.

also as: "Wonder, Eroticism, and Enigma" in <u>Sexuality in the Modern World</u>. A symposium, West Nyack, New York, Cross Current Corporation, 1964, p.133-141.

and as: Sexualität. Wunder, Abwege, Rätsel" in <u>Sexualität</u>, Eine Deutung in Form grundsatzlicher Stellungnahmen, Umfragen und Kontroversen, Olten-München, Roven Verlag, 1963, 8.

and as: "Das Wunder, die Abwege, das Rätsel Sexualität" (with an introduction by P. Ricoeur) in <u>Sexualität</u>, 1967.

and as: "Sexualiteit. Het wonder, de dwaling, het raadsel" in <u>Sexualiteit</u>, Utrecht, 1956.

161. "Les camps d'internement" in <u>Christianisme social</u> 68, 1960, p.423-425.

162. "L'image de Dieu et l'épopée humaine" in <u>Christianisme social</u> 68, 1960, p.493-514.

also in: <u>Histoire et vérité</u> (212) p.112-131.

also as: "The Image of God and the Epic of Man" in <u>Cross Currents</u> 11, 1961, p.37-50.

and in: <u>History and Truth</u> (212) p.110-128.

and as: "Beeld van God en gang van de mensheid" in <u>Politiek en geloof</u> (284) p.180-199.

163. Ruyssen Th., and Ricoeur P., "À propos de l'insoumission" (a reply by Ricoeur to a letter from Th. Ruyssen) in <u>Christianisme social</u> 68, 1960, p.728-730.

164. "Le 'Péché Originel': étude de signification" in <u>Eglise et théologie. Bulletin trimestiel de la Faculté de Théologie Protestante de Paris</u> 23, 1960, Dec., p.11-30.

also in: <u>Le conflit des interprétations</u> (320) p.265-282.

and as: "'Original Sin'. A Study in Meaning" in <u>The Conflict of Interpretations</u> (320) p.265-282.

and as: "De 'erfzonde'" in <u>Kwaad en bevrijding</u> (353) p.88-106.

165. "Allocution prononcée à l'occasion de l'inauguration du nouvel internat des filles" (Pentecost 1959) in <u>Nouvelles du Collège Cévenol</u> 7, 1960, April-May, p.2-3.

166. "Les camps d'internement. Réponse de Ricoeur à une lettre" in <u>Cité nouvelle</u>, 1960, no. 317, May 19, p.4.

167. "L'insoumission" in <u>Cité nouvelle</u> 1960, no. 323, Sept. 22, 1 and 4.

also in: <u>Esprit</u> 28, 1960, Oct., p.1600-1604.

and in: <u>Christianisme social</u> 68, 1960, p.584-588.

168. "Les expériences du mi-temps scolaire: travailler moins pour apprendre plus" in <u>Reforme. Hebdomadaire</u>, 1960 no. 821, Dec. 10, p.4.

169. Ricoeur P., Perelman Ch., "L'idéal de rationalité et la règle de la justice" (a discussion of a report of Ch. Perelman) in <u>Bulletin de la société française de philosophie</u> 55, 1961, p.25-26.

170. "Une lettre du professeur Ricoeur" in <u>Le monde</u> 18, 1961, no. 5102, June 14, p.2.

171. "Histoire de la philosophie et historicité" (a conference of P. Ricoeur followed by a discussion with J. Taubes) in <u>L'histoire et ses interprétations</u> (Congrès et colloques III. Centre culturel international de Cerisy-la Salle, July 10-19, 1958) Paris-La Haye, Mouton, 1961, p.214-227, 227-234.

also in: <u>Histoire et vérité</u> (212) p.66-80.

and as: "The History of Philosophy and Historicity" in <u>History and Truth</u> (212) p.63-77.

172. "Les perspectives d'avenir de la civilisation occidentale. II. L'objectivité historique et les valeurs" (discussion concerning the conference of R. Aron and M. Kula) in <u>L'histoire et ses interprétations</u>. Entretiens autour de Toynbee, Congrès et Colloques III, Paris-la Haye, Mouton, 1961, p.174-178.

173. "Herméneutique des symboles et réflexion philosophique" (a paper of Ricoeur followed by a discussion with A. Caracciolo e. a.) in <u>Archivio di filosofia</u> 31 1961, p.1-2, 51-71, 291-297.

also in: <u>Le conflit des interprétations</u> (320) p.283-310.

also as: "The Hermeneutics of Symbols and Philosophical Reflection" in <u>International Philosophical Quarterly</u> 2, 1962, p.191-218.

and in: <u>The Conflict of Interpretations</u> (320) p.287-314.

and in: <u>The Philosophy of Paul Ricoeur</u> (452) p.36-58.

and as: "Hermeneutik der Symbole und philosophisches Denken" in <u>Kerygma und Mythos</u> VI-I. Entmythologisierung und existentiale Interpretation, Hamburg-Bergstedt, Herbert Reich, 1963, p.44-68.

also in Spanish.

174. "Philosophie, sentiment et poésie. La notion d'a priori selon Mikel Dufrenne" in <u>Esprit</u> 29, 1961, March, p.504-512.

also as: "Preface" in M. Dufrenne, <u>The Notion of a Priori</u> (Northwestern University Studies in Phenomenology and Existential

Philosophy) Evanston, Illinois, Northwestern University Press, 1966, IX-XVII.

175. "Civilisation universelle mondial.   Cultures nationales" in Confluent. Revue culturelle et économique de la coopération publique et privée, 1961, Jan.-Feb., p.46-56.

also as: "Civilisation universelle et cultures nationales" in Histoire et vérité (212) p.274-287; and in Esprit 29, 1961, octobre, p.439-453.

and as: "Universal Civilization and National Cultures" in History and Truth (212) p.271-287.

also as: "Universele beschaving en nationale kulturen" in Politiek en geloof (284) p.132-147.

176. "Le socialisme d'aujourd'hui" in Christianisme social 69, 1961, p.450-460.

and as: "Socialism Today" in Political and Social Essays (414) p.229-242.

also as: "Het socialisme in onze tijd" in Politick en geloof (284) p.89-98.

177. "Conclusions du congrès" in Christianisme social 69, 1961, p.461-465.

178. "Que signifie la présence des pauvres parmi nous?" in Foi-éducation 31, 1961, Jan.-March, p.9-19.

179. "Le philosophe foudroyé" in Les nouvelles littéraires. Hebdomadaire 29, 1961, no. 1758, May 11, p.4.

also in: Christianisme social 69, 1961, p.389-395.

and as: "Hommage à Merleau-Ponty" in Esprit 29, 1961, June, p.1115-1120.

180. "Pierre Nourisson. In memoriam" in Cité nouvelle 1961, no. 334, March 2, p.1.

181. "Le XXXIIIe Congrès de 'Christianisme social'.   Problèmes introductifs. Le socialisme d'aujourd'hui" in Cité nouvelle 1961, no. 338, May 11, p.3.

182. "Pour accompagner le message de Maurice Voge" in Cité nouvelle 1961, no. 334, Sept. 7, p.2.

also in: Christianisme social 69, 1961, p.594-597.

183. "Nature et liberté" in <u>Existence et nature</u>, Paris , P.U.F. 1962, p.125-137.

also as: "Nature and Freedom" in <u>Political and Social Essays</u> (414) p.23-45.

184. "Affirmation, différence et médiation" (an extract from <u>L'homme faillible</u>) in <u>Anthologie des philosophes français contemporains</u>, edited by A. Cuvillier, Paris, P.U.F., 1962, p.98-102.

185. "L'acte et le signe selon <u>Jean Nabert</u>" in <u>Les études philosophiques</u> (Jean Nabert) 17, 1962, p.339-349.

also in: <u>Le conflit des interprétations</u> (320) p.211-221.

and as: "Nabert on Act and Sign" in <u>The Conflict of Interpretations</u> (320) p.211-222.

186. "L'humanité de l'homme. Contribution de la philosophie française contemporaine" in <u>Studium generale</u> 15, 1962, p.309-323.

187. "Appel pour le mouvement" in <u>Cité nouvelle</u> 1962, no. 370, Nov. 8, p.3.

and in: <u>Cité nouvelle</u> 1962, No. 371, Nov. 22, p.3.

188. "Appel pour le mouvement" (remercîment) in <u>Cité nouvelle</u> 1962, no. 373, Dec. 29, p.3.

189. "Introduction au problème des signes et du langage" in <u>Cahiers de philosophie</u>. Publiés par le groupe d'études de philosophie, Paris, 1, 1962,-63, no. 8, p.1-76 (polycopy).

190. "Préface" in J. Nabert, <u>Éléments pour une éthique</u> (philosophie de l'esprit) Paris, Aubier, 1962, p.5-16.

and as: "Preface" in J. Nabert, <u>Elements for an Ethics</u>, Northwestern University Press, 1969, p.xvii-xxviii.

191. "Herméneutique et réflexion" (a conference of P. Ricoeur followed by a discussion with P. Filiasi Carcano e.a.) in <u>Archivio di filosofia</u>, Roma, 11-16 gennaio 1962, 32, 1962, no. 1-2, p.19-34, 35-41.

also as: "Herméneutique des symbols et réflexion philosophique" in <u>Le conflit des interprétations</u> (320) p.311-329.

and as: "The Hermeneutics of Symbols and Philosophical Reflection: II" in <u>The Conflict of Interpretations</u> (320) p.315-334.

and as: "Interpretatie van symbolen en wijsgerige reflectie II" in Kwaad en bevrijding, (354) p.107-125.

192. Ricoeur P., Fessard G., Benz, Panikkar R., Mathieu V., "Discusione" (on the conferences: G. Fessard, 'Image, symbole et historicité;' E. Benz, 'Teologia dell'icone e dell'iconoclastia;' R. Panikkar, 'Le fondement du pluralisme herméneutique dans l'Hindouisme'; V. Mathieu, 'Mito e concetto') in Archivio di filosofia 32, 1962, p.1-2, 69-79, 204-217, 260-269, 311-314.

193. "Parole de chiusura" in Archivio di filosofia 32, 1962, p.1-2, 340-342.

194. "Le procès de Michel Bourgeois" (written testimony of P. Ricoeur to the military tribunal of Paris) in Cité nouvelle 1962, no. 359, April 19, 1 and 4.

and as: "L'affaire Bourgeois" in Christianisme social 70, 1962, p.339-340.

1963

195. "Le corps dans le monde: amorce du dialogue" (an extract from "négativité et affirmation") in Nouvelle initiation philosophique. II. Phénoménologie de l'existence. Gravitations. I, edited by Fl. Gaboriau, Tournai-Paris, Casterman, 1963, p.216-217.

196. "Faith and Action: A Christian Point of View. A Christian must rely on his Jewish memory" in Criterion 2, 1963, p.3, 10-15.

197. "Morale de classe - morale universelle" in Lettre 1963, July-August, p.35-43. (polycopy)

198. "Préface" of B. Rioux, L'être et la vérité chez Heidegger et Saint Thomas d'Aquin. Montréal-Paris, Presses de l'Université de Montréal -Presses Universitaires de France, 1963, p.vii-ix.

199. "Philosophie et réalité" (a discussion of a report of E. Weil) in Bulletin de la société française de philosophie 57, 1963, p.137-139.

200. "Symbolique et temporalité" (A conference of P. Ricoeur followed by a discussion with R. Boehm e.a.) in Archivio de filosofia 33, 1963, p.1-2, 5-31, 32-41.

also as: "Herméneutique et tradition" (Bibliothèque de l'histoire de la philosophie) Actes du colloque international, Rome 1963, Rome-Paris, Instituto di studi filosofici, J. Vrin, 1963, p.5-31, 32-41.

and as: "Structure et herméneutique" (partial text) in Esprit (La pensée sauvage et le structuralisme) 31, 1963, Nov. p.596-627.

and in: Le conflit des interprétations (320) p.31-63.

and as: "Structure and Hermeneutics" in The conflict of Interpretations (320) p.27-61.

and as: "Hermeneutiek en structuralisme" in Wegen van de filosofie (334) p.59-96.

201. Ricoeur P., Boehm R., Gouhier H., Fessard G., Marlé R., Panikkar R., "Discussione" (on the conferences: Boehm, 'Progrès, arrêt et recul dans l'histoire': Gouhier, 'Tradition et développement à l'époque de modernisme': Fessard, 'Le fondement de l'herméneutique selon la XIIIe règle d'orthodoxie des exercices spirituels d'Ignace de Loyola': Marlé, 'Le problème de l'herméneutique dans les plus récents courants de la théologie allemande': Panikkar "Sur l'herméneutique de la tradition dans l'hindouisme pour un dialogue avec le Christianisme') in Archivio di filosofia 33, 196 3, p.1-2, 69-74, 100-104, 220-229, 239-224, 365-370.

also in: Herméneutique et tradition (Bibliothèque d'histoire de la philosophie) Rome-Paris, Instituto di studi filosofici, J. Vrin, 1963, p.68-74, 100-104, 220-229, 239-244, 265-370.

202. "Kierkegaard et le mal" in Revue de théologie et de philosophie 13, 1963, p.292-302.

203. "Philosopher après Kierkegaard" in Revue de théologie et de philosophie 13, 1963, p.303-316.

204. "Le conflit des herméneutiques: épistémologie des interprétations" in Cahiers internationaux de Symbolisme I, 1963, no. 1, p.152-184.

205. "Réponses à quelque questions" in Esprit (La pensée sauvage et le structuralisme) 31, 1963, Nov., p.628-653.

206. "Le symbole et le mythe" in Le semeur (Le sacré) 61, 1963, no. 2, p.47-53.

207. "Le congrès de Dijon" (of Christianisme social, Dijon 1963, on the topic, 'Le Chrétien: un citoyen responsable, où? comment?') "Les conclusions" in Cité nouvelle 1963, no. 383, May 23, p.1.

208. "Appel aux protestants de France" (by Christianisme social against nucluar armament) in Cité nouvelle 1963, no. 384, June 6, p.1.

209. "Il-y-a une autre politique que celle de la bombe" (an interview with P. Ricoeur by J. Czarnecki) in Cité nouvelle 1963, no. 394, Dec. 5, 1 and 4.

210. "Dialogue avec M. Ricoeur sur la psychanalyse" in Cahiers de philosophie. Publiés par le groupe d'étude de philosophie (de la Sorbonne), 2, 1963-64, no. 8, p.55-60. (polycopy)

211. "Entretien avec M. Ricoeur" (regarding 'le cours magistral' and the reform of the teaching of higher philosophy in France) in Philo-observateur. Publié par le Groupe d'Études de Philosophie de l'Université de Paris, 1963-64, no. 4, p.27-29. (polycopy)

212. Histoire et vérité (Esprit) Second Edition, Paris, Seuil, 1964, p.336.

In addition to the articles of the First Edition (83, 1955):

Histoire de la philosophie et historicité (171) p.66-80.
"L'image de Dieu" et l'épopée humaine (162) p.112-131.
État et violence (105) p.234-247.
Le paradoxe politique (112) p.248-273.
Civilisation universelle et cultures nationales (175) p.274-287.
Négativité et affirmation originaire (93) p.308-332.

also as: History and Truth, Essays in Phenomenology, with translation and introduction by Ch. Kelbley, Evanston Illinois, Northwestern University Press, 1965, p.xxxiv-333.

contains the following articles:

Objectivity and Subjectivity in History (68) p.21-40.
The History of Philosophy and the Unity of Truth (61) p.41-56.
Note on the History of Philosophy and Sociology of Knowledge, (52) p.57-62.
The History of Philosophy and Historicity (171) p.63-77.
Christianity and the Meaning of History (45) p.81-97.
The Socius and the Neighbour (74) p.98-109.
The Image of God and the Epic of Man (162) p.110-128.
Emmanuel Mounier: A Personalist Philosophy (33) p.122-161.
Truth and Falsehood (44) p.165-191.
Non-violent Man and His Presence to History (23) p.223-233.
State and Violence (105) p.234-246.
The Political Paradox (112) p.247-270.
Universal Civilization and National Cultures (175) p.271-284.
True and False Anguish (62) p.287-304.
Negativity and Primary Affirmation (93) p.305-328.

also as: Geschichte und Wahrheit, translated by Romain Leick, Munich, List, 1974, p.375.

213. "Message de M. Paul Ricoeur" in Hommage à Gaston Berger (Publication des annales de la Faculté des Lettres d'Aix-en-Provence) Gap, Ophrys, 1964, p.131.

214. "Technique et non-technique dans l'interprétation" (a conference of P. Ricoeur followed by a discussion with A. Vergote e.a.) in Archivio di filosofia 34, 1964, p.1-2, 23-37, 39-50.

also in: Le conflit des interprétations (320) p.177-195.

and as: "Technique and Nontechnique in Interpretation" in The Conflict of Interpretations (320) p.177-195.

215. Ricoeur P., Lacan J., De Waelhens A., Marlé R., Panikkar R., Burn J., "Discussione" (on the conferences; Lacan, 'Du Trieb de Freud et du désir du psychanaliste, (Résumé); Waelhens, 'Notes pour une épistémologie de la santé mentale': Marlé, 'Casuistique et morales modernes de situation': Panikkar, 'Technique et temps: la technocronie': Brun 'Pour une herméneutique du concept') in Archivio di filosofia 34, 1964, p.1-2, 55-60, 87-94, 117-120, 223-229, 311-318.

216. "Le symbolisme et l'explication structurale" in Cahiers internationaux de Symbolisme 2, 1964, no. 4, p.81-96.

217. "Faire l'Université" in Esprit 32, 1964, May-June, p.1162-1172.

also in Spanish.

218. "Conclusions de Congrès" (of Christianisme social, Dijon 1963, on the topic, 'Le chrétien: un responsable. Où? Comment?') in Christianisme social 72, 1964, p.193-204.

1964

219. "La critique de la religion" in Bulletin du centre protestant d'études 16, 1964, p.4-5, 5-16.

also as: "The Critique of Religion" in The Philosophy of Paul Ricoeur (452) p.213-222.

220. "Le langage de la foi" in Bulletin du centre protestant d'études 16, 1964, p.4-5, 17-31.

also as: "The Language of Faith" in The Philosophy of Paul Ricoeur (452) p.223-238. (448)

and as: "Critique of Religion and the Language of Faith" in Union Seminary Quarterly Review 28,1973, Spring, p.203-224.

221. "La prospective et le plan dans une perspective chrétienne" in Réforme 1964, no. 992, March 21, p.6.

222. "Prospective du monde et perspective chrétienne" in Cahiers de Villemétrie, 1964, no. 44, p.16-37. (polycopy) also in : <u>L'église vers l'avenir</u>, Paris, Cerf, 1969, p.127-146.

223. "Explication et commentaire des 'Ideen I'" in <u>Cahiers de philosophie.</u> Published by 'le groupe d'étude de philosophie' of the Sorbonne, 3, 1964-65, p.143 (polycopy)

224. "Reconquérir le cogito sur l'attitude naturaliste" (an extract from 'Le volontaire et l'involontaire') in <u>Nouvelle initiation philosophique.</u> IV. Les grandes étapes de la pensée. Décisions I., edited by Fl. Gaboriau, Tournai-Paris, Caterman, 1964, p.392-394.

1965

225. "Morale et métaphysique" (an extract from <u>L'homme faillible</u>) in <u>Nouvelle initiation philosophique.</u> V. Les grandes étapes de la pensée. Décisions 2, edited by Fl. Gaboriau, Tournai-Paris, Caasterman, 1965, p.662-663.

226. "Protestation contre la réforme de l'enseignement" in <u>Le monde</u> 22, 1965, no. 6357, June 23, p.10.

227. <u>De l'interprétation.</u> Essai sur Freud (L'ordre philosophique) Paris, Seuil, 1965, 234p.

also as: <u>Freud and Philosophy.</u> An Essay on Interpretation transl. by D. Savage, New Haven-London, Yale University Press, 1970, 573p.

and as: <u>Die Interpretation,</u> translated by Eva Moldenhauer, Suhrkamp, Frankfurt, 1974, 536p.

also in Spanish and Italian.

228. "La psychanalyse et le mouvement de la culture contemporaine" in <u>Traité de psychanalyse.</u> I. <u>Histoire,</u> Paris, P.U.F., 1965, p.79-109.

also in : <u>Le conflit des interprétations</u> (320) p.122-159.

also as: "Psychoanalysis and the Movement of Contemporary Culture" in <u>The Conflict of Interpretations</u> (320) p.121-159.

also as: "De psychoanalyse in de hedendaagse cultuur" in <u>Wegen van de filosofie</u> (334) p.187-234.

229. "Existence et hermémétique" in <u>Interpretation der Welt.</u> Festschrift fur Romano Guardini zum achtzigsten Geburtstag, edited by H. Kuhn, H. Kahlefeld and K. Forester, Wurzburg, Im Echter-Verlag, 1965, p.32-51.

and in: <u>Le conflit des interprétations</u> (320) p.7-28.

and as: "Existence and Hermeneutics" in The Conflict of Interpretations (320) p.3-24.

also in: The Philosophy of Paul Ricoeur (452) p.97-108.

and in: Dialogue 4, 1965, p.1-25.

and as: "Existentie en hermeneutiek" in Kwaad en bevrijding (354) p.20-40.

230. "Préface" in R. Habachi, Commencements de la créature (Le poids du jour) Paris, Centurion, 1965, p.7-12.

231. "Préface" in R. Guilead, Être et liberté. Une étude sur le dernier Heidegger (Philosophes contemporaines. Textes et études) Louvain-Paire, E. Nauwelaerts and Beatrice-Nauwelears, 1965, p.5-8.

also in Spanish.

232. "Démythiser l'accusation" (a conference of P. Ricoeur followed by a discussion with R. Mehl e.a.) in Archivio di filosofia 35, 1965, p.1-2, 49-65, 67-75.

also as: Demythisation et morale (Philosophie de l'esprit) Actes du colloque international, Rome 1965, Paris, Aubier, 1965, p.409-65, 67-75.

and in : Le conflit des interprétations (320) p.330-347.

and as: "The Demythization of Accusation" in The Conflict of Interpretations (320) p.335-353.

and as: "Demythisering van de aanklacht" in Kwaad en bevrijding (354) p.126-145.

233. Ricoeur P., Brun J., Fessard G., Vergote A., Ott H., Mehl R., Mancini I., "Discussione" (on the conferences: Brun, 'A la recherche du paradis perdu': Fessard, 'Symbole, surnaturel, dialogue'; Vergote, 'La loi morale et le péché originel à la lumière de la psychanalyse'; Ott, 'Le problème d'une éthique non-casuistique dans la pensée de Dietrich Bonhoeffer et Martin Buber'; Mehl, 'Démythisation du sérieux éthique'; Mancini, 'La morale teologica di Barth') in Archivio di filosofia 35, 1965, p.1-2, 87-89, 143-154, 205-213, 245-253, 305-310.

also in: Démythisation et morale (Philosophie de l'esprit) Paris, Aubier, 1965, p.87-89, 143-154, 205-213, 245-253, 305-310.

234. "Tâches de l'éducateur politique" in Esprit 33, 1965, July-August, p.78-93.

also as: "The Tasks of a Political Educator" in Philosophy Today 17, 1973, Summer, p.142-152.

and in: Political and Social Essays (414) p.271-293.

and as: "Vereisten voor een politieke vorming" in Politiek en geloof (284) p.56-76.

235. "Sciences humaines et conditionnements de la foi" in Recherches et débats (Dieu aujourd'hui) 14, 1965, no. 52, p.136-144.

236. "De la nation à l'humanité: tâche des chrétiens" in Christianisme social 73, 1965, p.493-512.

reprinted partially as: "Le monde et nous. Tâches des chrétiens" in Témoignage chrétien 1965, no. 1112, Nov. 11, p.13-14.

also as: "From Nation to Humanity: Tasks of Christians" in Political and Social Essays (414) p.134-159.

and in: Van natie naar mensheid: een taak voor de kristenen" in Politiek en geloof (284) p.148-165.

237. "Bilan et prospective" (the Congress of Christianisme social, Paris 1965, on the topic 'De la nation à l'humanité: tâche des chrétiens') in Christianisme social 73, 1965, p.595-600.

238. "Prospective économique et prospective éthique. Réflexions sur le rôle nouveau de l'éducation dans la société qui se fait" in Cité libre 15, 1965, March, p.7-15.

also as: "Prospective et utopie. Prévision économique et choix éthique" in Esprit 34, 1966, Feb., p.178-193.

and as: "Ekonomie en ethiek" in Politiek en geloof (284) p.99-115.

239. "Un ordre mondial: tâche des chrétiens" in Cité nouvelle 1965, no. 437, Nov. 25, p.3.

240. "Psychanalyse freudienne et foi chrétienne" (Cahiers d'orgement) 1965, no. 52, 30p. (polycopy)

241. "Notre responsabilité dans la société moderne" in Les cahiers du centre protestant de l'ouest 1965, no. 4, p.13-21.(polycopy)

242. "La recherche philosophique peut-elle s'achever?" in La philosophie: sens et limites (Cahiers Paraboles) 1965, p.1-13, 14-33. (polycopy)

also in: Orientations 1966, p.31-44.

243. "Le conscient et l'inconscient" in L'inconscient (VIe Colloque de Bonneval) (Bibliothèque Neuro-psychiatrique de langue française) under the direction of H. Ey, Paris, Desclée, de Brouwer, 1966, p.409-422.

also as: "Consciousness and the Unconscious" in The conflict of Interpretations (320) p.99-120.

and as: "Het bewuste en onbewuste" in Wegen van de filosofie (334) p.161-186.

244. "L'université nouvelle" in L'éducation dans un Québec en évolution, Québec, Presses de l'Université Laval, 1966, p.231-245.

245. "Préface" in J. Nabert, Le désir de Dieu (Philosophie de l'esprit) Paris, Aubier, 1966, p.7-15.

246. "Une interprétation philosophique de Freud" (a presentation followed by a discussion with H. Gouhier, e.a., and a response to the letter of A. Levy-Valensi) in Bulletin de la société française de philosophie 60, 1966, p.73-74, 75-102, 106-107.

also in: Le conflit des interprétations (320) p.160-176.

and as: " A Philosophical Interpretation of Freud" in The Conflict of Interpretations (320) p.160-176.

and in: The Philosophy of Paul Ricoeur (452) p.169-183.

247. "Le problème du 'double'-sens comme problème herméneutique et comme problème sémantique" in Cahiers internationaux de symbolisme 1966, no. 12, p.59-71.

also in: Le conflit des interprétations (320) p.64-79.

also as: "The Problem of the Double-Sense as Hermeneutic Problem and a Semantic Problem" in Myths and Symbols. Studies in honor of Mircea Eliade, edited by J.M. Kitagawa and Ch. H. Long, Chicago-London, University of Chicago Press, 1969, p.63-79.

and as: "The Problem of the Double Meaning as Hermeneutic Problem and as Semantic Problem" in The Conflict of Interpretations (320) p.62-78.

and as: "Het probleem van de 'dubbele' zin als hermeneutisch en semantisch probleem" in Wegen van de filosofe (334) p. 97-115.

248. "Le poétique" (on M. Dufrenne, Le poétique) in Esprit 34, 1966, Jan., p.107-116.

249. Ricoeur P., and Domenach J.M., "Invitation à la conférence de presse" in Esprit 34, 1966, March, p.527.

also in: Christianisme social 74, 1966, p.130-131.

and in: Le monde 1966, no. 6560, Feb. 15, p.6.

250. "Une lettre de Paul Ricoeur" in Critique 22, 1966, Feb., p.183-186.

251. "La parole, instauratrice de liberté" in Cahiers universitaires catholiques 1966, p.493-507.

252. "La philosophie à l'âge des sciences humaines" in Cahiers de Philosophie (Anthropologie) I, 1966, no. 1, p.93-99.

253. "Les problèmes du langage" in Cahiers de philosophie I, 1966, p.2-3, 27-41.

254. "Le projet d'une morale sociale" in Christianisme social 74, 1966, p.285-295.

also as: "The Project of a Social Ethic" in Political and Social Essays (414) p.160-175.

255. "Psychologie et philosophie" (a debate between Jean Piaget and P. Ricoeur) in Raison Présente 1966, p.51-82.

256. "L'athéisme de la psychanalyse freudienne" in Concilium. Revue internationale de théologie 2, 1966, no. 16, p.73-82.

also as: "The Atheism of Freudian Psychoanalysis " in Concilium (Is God Dead?) 2, 1966, no. 16, p.59-72.

and in: Concilium (Church and World) 2, 1966, no. 2, p.31-37.

and as: "Der Atheismus der Psychoanalyse Freuds" in Concilium (Grensfragen) 2, 1966, no. 6, p.430-435.

and as: "Het atheisme van de freudiaanse psychoanalyse" in Concilium (Grensvragen) 2, 1966, no. 6, p.68-79.

also in Spanish and Italian and Portugese.

257. Ricoeur P., and Ducros P., "À nos amis" in Cité nouvelle 34, 1966, Nov. 24, p.3.

258. "Doctrine de l'homme. Traits dominants de notre modernité. Anthropologie philosophique" in Les cahiers du Centre Protestant de l'Ouest 1966, no. 5, p.19-30. (polycopy)

259. "L'interprétation non-religieuse du christianisme chez Bonhoeffer" in Les cahiers du Centre Protestant de l'Ouest 1966, no. 7, p.3-15, 15-20.

260. "Présentation de la philosophie française contemporaine" in Bibliographie philosophique. I. Bibliographie d'histoire de la philosophie 1945-65, Paris, 1966, p.9-17.

261. "A Conversation" (with P. Ricoeur) in The Bulletin of Philosophy I, 1966, no. 1, p.7.

262. "Déclaration" (from P. Ricoeur and others on the article 'La leçon des morts' by R. Capitant) in Le monde 23, 1966, no. 6566, Feb. 22, p.7.

1967

263. Husserl. An Analysis of His Phenomenology (Studies in Phenomenology and Existential Philosophy). Translation and introduction by E.G. Ballard and L.E. Embree, Evanston, Illinois, Northwestern University Press, 1967, XXII-238p.

The book contains the following articles:

"Introduction; Husserl 1859-1938 (Appendix)" (73) p.3-12.
"Introduction to Husserl's Ideas I," (30) p.13-34.
"Husserl's Ideas II: Analysis and Problems," (39) p.35-81.
"A Study of Husserl's Cartesian Meditations I-IV," (76) p.82-114.
"Husserl's Fifth Cartesian Mediation," p.115-142.
"Husserl and the Sense of History" (22) p.143-174.
"Kant and Husserl" (78) p.175-201.
"Existential Phenomenology" (108) p.202-212.
"Methods and Tasks of a Phenomenology of the Will" (53) p.213-233.

264. "Philosophy of Will and Action" (a conference followed by a discussion with F. Kersten etc.) in Phenomonology of Will and Action (The Second Lexington Conference on Pure and Applied Phenomenology, 1964) edited by E.W. Straus and R.M. Griffith, Pittsburgh, Duquesne University Press, 1967, p.7-33, 34-60.

also in: The Philosophy of Paul Ricoeur (452) p.61-74.

265. "Husserl and Wittgenstein on Language" in Phenomenology and Existentialism, edited by E.N. Lee and M. Mandelbaum, Baltimore, The John Hopkins University Press, 1967, p.207-217.

266. "R. Bultmann" in Foi-éducation (Foi et langage) 37, 1967, no. 78, Jan.-March, p.17-35.

also as: "Foi et langage" (Bultmann-Ebeing) in Foi-éducation 37, 1967, Oct.-Dec., p.17-35.

267. "Ebeling" in Foi-éducation (Foi et langage) 37, 1967, no. 78, Jan.-March, p.36-53, 53-57.

268. "Démythologisation et herméneutique" (text transcribed from a tape) Nancy, Centre européen universitaire, 1967, 32p. (polycopy)

269. "Préface" in St. Strasser, Phénoménologie et science de l'homme. Vers un nouvel esprit scientifique (Bibliothèque philosophique de Louvain). Translated from the German by A.L. Kelkel, Louvain-Paris, Publications universitaires de Louvain et Béatrice-Nauwelaerts, 1967, p.7-10.

270. "Postscript" in J.M. Paupert, Taizé et l'église de demain (Le signe) Paris, A. Fayard, 1967, p.247-251.

271. "Langage religieux: Mythe et symbole" (a conference by P. Ricoeur followed by a discussion with M. Corbin e.a.) in Le langage. II. Langages. Actes de XIIIe Congrès des Sociétés de philosophie de langue française, Neuchâtel, La Baconnière, 1967, p.129-137, 138-145.

272. Ricoeur P., Benveniste E., Hyppolite J., Eliade M., "Discussions" (on the reports: Benveniste, 'La forme et le sens dans le langage'; Hyppolite, 'Langage et être. Langage et pensée') "Discussion générale" in Le langage. II. Langages, Neuchâtel, La Baconnière, 1967, p.41-47, 56-65, 183-199.

273. "Interprétation du mythe de la peine" (a conference by P. Ricoeur followed by a discussion with C. Bruaire) in Archivio di filosofia 37, 1967, p.2-3, 23-42, 53-62.

also in: Le mythe de la peine (Philosophie de l'esprit) Actes du colloque international, Rome, 1967, Paris, Aubier, p.23-42, 53-62.

also in: Le conflit des interprétations (320) p.348-369.

and as: "Interpretation of the Myth of Punishment" in The Conflict of Interpretations (320) p.354-377.

and as: "Interpretatie van de mythe van de straf" in Kwaad en bevrijding (354) p.146-169.

274. Ricoeur P., Lyonnet S., Scholem G., Nédoncelle M., "Discussione" (on the conferences: Lyonnet, 'La problèmatique du péché originel dans le Nouveau Testament'; Scholem, 'Quelques remarques sur le mythe de la peine dans le Judaisme'; Nédoncelle, 'Démythisation et conception eschatologique du mal') in Archivio di filosofia 37, 1967, p.2-3, 109-120, 147-164, 213-222.

also in: Le mythe de la peine (Philosophie de l'esprit) Paris, Aubier, 1967, p.109-120, 147-164, 213-222.

275. "La structure, le mot, l'événement" in Esprit (Structuralisme. Idéologie et méthode) 35, 1967, May, p.801-821.

and in: Le Conflit des interprétations (320) p.79-96.

and as: "Structure-Word-Event" in Philosophy Today 12, 1968, no. 2-4, p.114-129.

and in: The Conflict of Interpretations (320) p.79-96.

and in: The Philosophy of Paul Ricoeur (452) p.109-119.

and as: "Structuur, woord, gebeurtenis" in Wegen van de filosofie (333) p.116-136.

276. "Violence et langage" in Recherches et débats (La violence) 16, 1967, no. 59, p.86-94.

also as: "Violence and Language" in Political and Social Essays (414) p.88-101.

277. "Urbanisation et sécularisation" in Christianisme social 75, 1967, p.327-341.

also as: "Urbanization and Secularization" in Political and Social Essays (414) p.176-197.

and as: "Urbanisatie en sekularisatie" in Politiek en geloof (284) p.116-131.

278. "New Developments in Phenomenology in France: The Phenomenology of Language" in Social Research 34, 1967, p.1-30.

partially as: "La question du sujet: le défi de la sémiologie" in Le conflit des interprétations (320) p.233-262.

and in: "The question of the Subject; The Challenge of Semiology" in The Conflict of Interpretations (320) p.236-266.

279. Crespin R., "En écoutant Paul Ricoeur: l'homme à l'âge de la ville" in Cité nouvelle 1967, no. 446, p.1, 4-5.

280. "Autonomie et obéissance" in Cahiers d'Orgement (Autonomie de la personne et obéissance à un autre) 1967, no. 59, p.3-22, 23-31.

281. "Mythe et proclamation chez R. Bultmann" in Les cahiers du Centre Protestant de l'Ouest 1967, no. 8, p.21-33.

282. "L'affaire Casamayor D." (with J.M. Domenach) in <u>Esprit</u> 35, 1967, p.1-3.

1968

283. Ricoeur P., and Marcel G., <u>Entretiens Paul Ricoeur-Gabriel Marcel</u> (Présence et pensée) Paris, Aubier, 1968, 131p.

also as: "Gespräche." Translated by A. Ahlbrecht, Frankfurt-am-Main, Knecht. 1970, 110p.

284. <u>Politiek en geloof</u>. Essays van Paul Ricoeur, ingeleid door A. Peperzak, Utrecht, Ambo, 1968, 199p. (2nd edition, 1969).

contains the following articles:

Medemens en naaste (74) p.18-31.
De paradox van de macht (112) p.32-58.
Vereisten voor een politieke vorming (233) p.56-76.
Hoe staat de kristen in de staat? (124) p.77-88.
Het socialisme in onze tijd (176) p.89-98.
Ekonomie en ethiek (238) p.99-115.
Urbanisatie en sekularisatie (277) p.116-131.
Universele beschaving en nationale kulturen (175) p.132-147.
Van natie naar mensheid: een taak voor de kristenen (236) p.148-165.
Techniek op interplanetaire schaal (122) p.166-179.
Beeld van God en gang van de mensheid (162) p.180-199.

285. "Liberté: responsabilité et décision" in <u>Actes du XIVe Congrès International de Philosophie</u>, Vienne, Herder, 1968, p.155-165.

286. "L'art et la systématique freudienne" (a conference followed by a discussion with A. Green e.a.) in <u>Entretiens sur l'art et la psychanalyse</u> (Décades du centre culturel international de Céristy-la-Salle) under the direction of A. Berge, A. Clancier, P. Ricoeur, L.H. Rubenstein, Paris, The Hague, Mouton, 1968, p.24-36, 37-50.

also in: <u>Le conflit des interprétations</u> (320) p.195-207.

also as: "Art and Freudian Systematics" in <u>The Conflict of Interpretations</u> (320) p.196-208.

287. Ricoeur P., Abraham N., Elkin H., Kanter V.B., Green A., Rubinstein L.H., Aigrisse G., Flocon A., "Extraits de la discussion" (on the reports: Abraham, 'Le temps, le rythme et l'inconscient'; Elkin, 'Les bases psychiques de la créativité'; Kanter, 'La psychanalyse et le compositeur'; Green, 'Oreste et Oedipe. Essaie sur la structure comparée des mythes tragiques d'Oreste et d'Oedipe et sur la fonction de la tragédie'; Rubinstein, 'Les Oresties dans la littérature avant et après Freud'; Aigrisse, 'Hommage à Charles Baudoin Résumé de l'essai sur Racine'; Aigrisse, 'La jeune parque de Paul Valery à la lumière de la psychanalyse'; Flocon, 'Clio chez la peintre') in Entretiens sur l'art et la psychanalyse (Décades du Centre Culturel international de Cérisy-la-Salle, Paris-la Haye, Mouton, 1968, p.68-75, 151-155, 170-172, 216-223, 239-241, 244-246, 290-294, 349-356.

288. "Post-scriptum: une dernière écoute de Freud" in Entretiens sur l'art et la psychanalyse, Paris-la Haye, Mouton, 1968, p.361-368.

289. "Philosophie et communication" (a round-table discussion) in Entretiens sur l'art et la psychanalyse, Paris-la-Haye, Mouton, 1968, p.393-431.

290. "Aliénation" in Encyclopaedia universalis. I., Paris, Encyclopaedia Universalis France, 1968, p.660-664.

291. "Tâches de la communauté ecclésiale dans le monde moderne" in La théologie du renouveau. II. (Actes du congrès international de Toronto) published under the direction of L.K. Shook and G.M. Bertrand, Montréal-Paris, Fides-Cerf, 1968, p.49-58.

also as: "Tasks of the Ecclesial Community in the Modern World" in Theology of Renewal. II. Renewal of Religious Structures, edited by L.K. Shook, New York, Herder and Herder, 1968, p.242-254.

292. "The Critique of Subjectivity and Cogito in the Philosophy of Heidegger" in Heidegger and the Quest for Truth, edited by M.S. Frings, Chicago. Quadrangle Books, 1968, p.62-75.

also as: "Heidegger et la question du sujet" in Le conflit des interprétations (320) p.222-232.

and as: "Heidegger and the Question of the Subject" in The Conflict of Interpretations (320) p.223-235.

and as: "Heidegger und die Frage nach dem Subjekt" in Hermeneutik und Strukturalismus (320).

293. "Die Zukunft der Philosophie und die Frage nach dem Subjekt" in Die Zukunft der Philosophie, Olten-Fribourg-en-Brisgau, Walter-Verlag, 1968, p.128-165.

also as: "La question du sujet: le défi de la sémiologie" in Le conflit des interprétations (320) p.233-262.

and as: "The Question of the Subject: The Challenge of Semiology" in The Conflict on Interpretations (230) p.236-266.

294. "Préface" in R. Bultmann, Jésus. Mythologie et démythologisation, Paris, Seuil, 1968, p.9-27.

also as: "Préface à Bultmann" in Le conflit des interprétations (320) p.373-392.

and as: "Preface to Bultmann" in The Conflict of Interpretations (320) p.381-401.

and as: "Inleiding tot Bultmann" in Kwaad en bevrijding (354) p.41-60.

295. "Préface" in J. Drèze and J. Debelle, Conceptions de l'université, Paris, Éditions universitaires, 1968, p.8-22.

partially reprinted in: "Trois ripostes à la crise universitaire" in Le monde 26, 1969, no. 7469, Jan. 17, p.9.

296. "Préface" in J. Schwoebel. La presse, le pouvoir et l'argent, Paris, Seuil, 1968, p.7-12.

297. "Approche philosophique du concept de liberté religieuse" (a conference of P. Ricoeur followed by a discussion with C.L. Bruaire e.a.) in Archivio di filosofia 38, 1969, p.2-3, 215-234, 235-252.

also in: L'herméneutique de la liberté religieuse (Actes de colloque international, Rome 1968) Paris, Aubier, 1968, p.215-234, 235-252.

and as: "La liberté selon l'espérance" in Le conflit des interprétations (320) p.393-415.

and as: "Freedom in the Light of Hope" in The Conflict of Interpretations (320) p.402-424.

and as: "Die Freiheit im Licht der Hoffnung" in Hermeneutik und Strukturalismus (320).

and as: "Vrijheid in hoop. Filosofische benadering van het begrip godsdienstvrijheid" in Kwaad en bevrijding (354) p.170-194.

298. Ricoeur P., Pattaro G., Vergote A., Brun J., "Discussione" (on the conferences: Pattaro, 'Le kérygme et la liberté de l'écoute'; Vergote, 'La liberté religieuse comme pouvoir de symbolisation'; Brun, 'Christianisme et consommation') in Archivio di filosofia 38, 1968, p.2-3, 348-352, 378-379, 476.

also in: L'herméneutique de la liberté religieuse, Paris, Aubier, 1968, p.348-352, 378-379, 476.

299. "Contribution d'une réflexion sur le langage à une théologie de la parole" in Revue de théologie et de philosophie 18, 1968, p.5-6, 333-348.

also in: Exégèse et herméneutique (Parole de Dieu) Paris, Seuil, 1971, p.301-319.

and as: "Bijdrage van een reflexie over de taal van de theologie van het woord" in Wegen van de filosofie (334) p.137-158.

300. "Lenine et la philosophie" (P. Ricoeur and L. Althusser e.a.) in Bulletin de la Société française de Philosophie 62, 1968, p.4, 161-168.

301. "Réforme et révolution dans l'université" in Esprit 36, 1968, June-July, p.987-1002.

also as: "Rebâtir l'université" in Le monde 25, 1968, no. 7279, June 9-10, 1 and 9; no. 7280, June 11, p.9; no. 7281, June 12, p.10.

also in Portugese.

302. "Christianisme et révolution" (a communiqué co-signed by Christianisme social on behalf of the participation of Christians in the revolutionary struggle) in Christianisme social 76, 1968, p.12-2, 119.

also as: "Les chrétiens peuvent participer à la lutte révolutionnaire" in Cité nouvelle 36, 1968, no. 490, April, p.3.3

303. "À nos abonnés, à nos amis" (an appeal for support for the movement 'Christianisme social') in Christianisme social 76, 1968, no. 1-2, p.127-128.

304. "Déclaration du Congrès National du Mouvement du 'Christianisme social' (in favor of the just investigations of the students' revolutionary movement) in Christianisme social (Imagination et pouvoir. Réflections et documents, May-June 1968) 76, 1968, no. 3-4, p.221.

also in: Cité nouvelle 36, 1968, no. 492, June 13, p.3.

305. "Appel à tous les chrétiens" (on behalf of the just aspirations of the students' revolutionary movement) in Christianisme social 76, 1968, no. 3-4, p.223-224.

also as: "Appel aux chrétiens" in Cité nouvelle 36, 1968, no. 492, June 13, p.7.

306. "Faire une nouvelle société" (a communiqué of a group of catholics and protestants in favour of the transformation of society, May 22, 1968) in Christianisme social 76, 1968, no. 3-4, p.225-227.

also in: Cité nouvelle 36, 1968, no. 492, June 13, p.7.

307. "Au lecteur" (concerning the intercelebration of the eucharist) in Christianisme social 76, 1968, no. 7-10, p.385-387.

308. "Commentaire eucharistique de Paul Ricoeur" in Christianisme social 76, 1968, no. 7-10, p.400-410.

309. "The Father Image. From Phantasy to Symbol" in Criterion. A Publication of the Divinity School of the University of Chicago, 8, 1968-69, no. 1, Autumn-Winter, p.1-7.

also as: "La paternité: du fantasme au symbole" in Archivio de filosofia 39, 1969, no. 2-3, p.221-246.

and in: Le conflit des interprétations (320) p.458-486.

also as: L'analyse du langage théologique. Le nom de Dieu (Actes du colloque international, Rome, 1969) Paris, Aubier, 1969, p.222-246.

and as: "Fatherhood: From Phantasm to Symbol" in The Conflict of Interpretations (320) p.468-497.

310. "Lettre d'information des participants" in Le monde 25, 1968, no. 7274, June 4, p.4.

also in: La croix 88, 1968, no. 25980, June 5, p.7.

and in: Informations catholiques internationales 1968, no. 313-314, June, p.22-23.

and in: La documentation catholique 50, 1968, no. 1520, July 7, col. 1212.

and in: Christianisme social 76, 1968, no. 7-10, p.405-406.

and partially in: Serrou R., Dieu n'est pas conservateur. Les chrétiens dans les événements de mai, Paris, Seuil, 1968, p.58-59.

and in: Katholiek Archief 23, 1968, no. 37, Sept. 13, col. 913-914.

311. "Semaine de l'unité: un appel" (in favor of justice in the world and peace in Vietnam) in Réforme 1968, no. 1191, Jan. 13, p.11.

also in: "Pour la 'Semaine de l'unité'" in Cité nouvelle 36, 1968, no. 485, Jan. 23, p.3.

312. "La concélébration eucharistique" in Réforme 1968, no. 1212, June 8, p.2.

also in: Réforme, the supplement to no. 1212, June 8, p.4-5. (polycopy)

and as: "Le jour de la pentecôte, ils étaient tous en un même lieu" (Livre des actes) in Cité nouvelle 36, 1968, no. 492, June 13, p.2.

and as: "La concélébration eucharistique de la pentecôte" in Christianisme social 76, 1968, p.423-425.

and in: Lettre 1968, no. 11-119, p.43-44. (polycopy)

and in: La documentation catholique 50, 1968, no. 1529, July 7, col. 1216. (partial text)

and in: Le monde 25, 1968, no. 7283, June 15, p.16.

and in: "Verklaring van Prof. Paul Ricoeur naar aanleiding van de interconfessionele eucharistieviering te Parijs, 2 juni 1968" in Katholiek Archief 23, 1968, no. 37, col. 915-916.

313. "La crise des rapports hiérarchiques" in Cité nouvelle 1968, no. 495, Oct. 3, 1, 4, and 5.

314. "Être protestant aujourd'hui" in Cahiers d'études du Centre Protestant de Récherches et de Rencontres du Nord 1968, no. 26, April-June, p.1-14.

315. "Présence des églises au monde" in Cahiers d'études du Centre Protestant de Récherches et de Rencontres du Nord 1968, no. 26, April-June, p.15-37, 58-75. (mimeographed) (uncorrected notes)

316. "Sens et langage" in Cahiers d'études du Centre Protestant de Récherches et de Rencontres du Nord (sens et fonction d'une communauté ecclésiale) 1968, no. 26, April-June, p.38-57, 58-75. (mimeographed)

317. "L'événement de la parole chez Ebeling" in Les cahiers du Centre Protestant de l'Ouest 1968, no. 9, p.23-31. (mimeographed)

318. "Structure et signification dans le langage" in Pourquoi la philosophie? edited by Georges Levoux, Montréal, Les éditions de Sainte Marie, 1968, p.101-120.

319. "Interrogation philosophique et engagement" in Pourquoi la philosophie? edited by Georges Levoux, Montréal, Les éditions de Sainte Marie, 1968, p.9-22.

1969

320. Le conflit des interprétations. Essais d'herméneutique (L'ordre philosophique) Paris, Seuil, 1969, 506p.

contains the following articles:

Existence et herméneutique (220) p.7-28.
Structure et herméneutique (200) p.31-63.
Le problème de double-sens comme problème herméneutique et comme problème sémantique (247) p.64-79.

La structure, le mot, l'événement (274) p.80-97.
Le conscient et l'inconscient (243) p.101-121.
La psychanalyse et le mouvement de la culture contemporaine (228) p.122159.
Une interprétation philosophique de Freud (246) p.160-176.
Technique et non-technique dans l'interprétation (214) p.177-194.
L'art et la systématique freudienne (286) p.195-207.
L'acte et le signe selon Jean Nabert (185) p.211-221.
Heidegger et la question du sujet (292) p.222-232.
La question du sujet: le défi de la sémiologie (278-293) p.233-262.
Le "péché originel": étude de signification (164) p.265-282.
Herméneutique des symboles et réflexion philosophique I., (164) p.283-310.
Herméneutique des symboles et réflexion philosophique II., (191) p.311-329.
Démythiser l'accusation (232) p.330-347.
Interprétation du mythe de la peine (273) p.348-369.
Préface à Bultmann (294) p.373-392.
La liberté selon l'espérance (297) p.393-415.
Culpabilité, éthique et religion (297) p.416-430.
Religion, athéisme, foi (325) p.431-457.
La paternité: du fantasme au symbole (309) p.458-456.

translated as:

The Conflict of Interpretations. Essays in Hermeneutics, edited by Don Ihde, Evanston, Northwestern University Press, 1974, 512p.

contains the following articles:

Existence and Hermeneutics (220) p.3-24.
Structure and Hermeneutics (200) p.27-61.
The problem of Double Meaning as Hermeneutic Problem and as Semantic Problem (247) p.62-78.
Structure, Word, Event (275) p.79-96.
Consciousness and the Unconscious (243) p.99-120.
Psychoanalysis and the Movement of Contemporatory Culture (228) p.121-159.
A Philosophical Interpretation of Freud (246) p.1160-176.
Technique and Nontechnique in Interpretation (213) p.177-195.
Art and Freudian Systematics (286) p.196-208.
Nabert on Act and Sign (185) p.211-222.
Heidegger and the Question of the Subject (292) p.223-235.
The Question of the Subject: The Challenge of Semiology (278-291) p.236-266.
'Original Sin?' A Study in Meaning (164) p.269-286.
The Hermeneutics of Symbols and Philosophical Reflection I., (173) p.287-314.
The Hermeneutics of Symbols and Philosophical Reflection II., (191) p.315-334.
The Demythization of Accusation (232) p.335-353.

Interpretation of the Myth of Punishment (273) p.354-377.
Preface to Bultmann (294) p.381-401.
Freedom in the Light of Hope (297) p.402-424.
Guilt, Ethics and Religion (326) p.425-439.
Religion, Atheism and Faith (325) p.440-467.
Fatherhood: From Phantasm to Symbol (309) p.468-497.

and as: Der Konflikt der Interpretationen II: Hermeneutik und Psychoanalyse, translated by H. Rutsch, Kosel, Munich, 1974, 359p.

and as: Hermeneutik und Strukturalismus. Der konflikt der Interpretatonen I. Translated in part from Le conflit des interprétations by J. Rutsch, Munich, 1973, 321p.

321. "Philosophie et langage" in Contemporary philosophy. A Survey III. Metaphysics, Phenomenology, Language and Structure, La philosophie contemporaine, Chroniques III. Métaphysique, Phénoménologie, Langage et Structure edited by R. Kilbansky, Florence, La nuova Italia Editrice, 1969, p.272-295.

322. "Le philosophe et la politique devant la question de la liberté" (a conference followed by a discussion with J. Hersch e.a.) in La liberté et l'ordre social (Rencontres internationales de Genève 1969) Neuchâtel, La Baconnière, 1969, p.41-65, 185-205.

323. "Pour une prédiction au monde" in L'église vers l'avenir, Paris , Cerf, 1969, p.147-156.

324. "Croyance" in Encyclopaedia universalis V. Paris, Encyclopaedia Universalis France, 1969, p.171-176.

325. "Religion, Atheism and Faith" in The Religious Significance of Atheism, edited by A. MacIntyre, Ch. Aladair, and P. Ricoeur, New York-London, Columbia University Press, 1969, p.58-98.

and in: The Conflict of Interpretations (320) p.425-439.

also as: "Religion, athéisme, foi" in Le conflit des interprétations (320) p.431-457.

326. "Guilt, Ethics and Religion" in Talk of God (Royal Institute of Philosophy Lectures. II. 1967-68) London Melbourne-Toronto-New York, MacMillian-St. Martin's Press, 1969, p.100-117.

and in: The Conflict of Interpretations (320) p.425-439.

and in: Concilium (Moral evil under challenge) 1970, no. 56, p.11-27.

and in: Conscience. Theological and Psychological Perspectives, edited by C. Ellis Nelson, Newman Press, 1973, p.11-27.

also as: "Culpabilité, éthique et religion" in Le conflit des interprétations (320) p.416-430.

and in: Concilium (Problèmes frontières) 1970 , no. 56, p.11-23.

and as: "Schuld, Ethik und Religion" in Concilium (theologische Grenzfragen) 6, 1970, no. 6-7, p.384-393.

and as: "Schuld, ethiek en religie" in Concilium (Grensvragen) 6, 1970, no. 6, p.8-25.

also in Spanish and Italian and Portugese and Polish.

327. "Préface" in Ph. Secretan, Autorité, Pouvoir, Puissance, Principes de philosophie politique réflexive (Dialectica) (Lausanne). L'age d'homme, 1969, p.IX-XIV.

328. "La paternité: du fantasme au symbole" (a discussion on the Conferences of P. Ricoeur with K. Kerenyi e.a.) in Débats sur le langage théologique, Paris, Aubier, 1969, p.71-88.

329. Ricoeur P., De Waelhens A., Vergote A., "Débats" (on the conferences: Waelhens, 'La paternité et le complexe d'Oedipe en psychanalyse': Vergote, 'Le nom de Dieu et l'écart de la topographie symbolique') in Débats sur le langage théologique, Paris, Aubier, 1969, p.89-101, 103-122.

330. "Appel du Comité français de la Conférence chrétienne pour la paix" in Christianisme social 77, 1969, no. 1-2, p.125-126.

331. "Perspectives de la réforme universitaire" in Réforme 1969, no. 1249, Feb., no. 1250, March 1, p.4.

332. Les incidences théologiques des recherches actuelles concernant le langage, Paris, Institut d'études oecuméniques, 1969 (1972), 94p. (mimeographed).

333. "Bultmann: Une théologie sans mythologie" in Cahiers d'Orgemont (Importance de la théologie de Rudolf Bultmann) 1969, no. 72, March-April, p.21-3, 38-40. (polycopy)

1970

334. Wegen van de filosofie: Structuralisme, psychoanalyse, hermeneutiek. Essays van P. Ricoeur, selected and introduced by A. Peperzak, Bilthoven, Amboboeken, 1970, 169p.

contains the following articles:

De toekomst van de filosofie en de vraag naar het subjekt, (293) p.17-55.

Hermeneutiek en structuralisme (200), p.59-96.

Het probleem van de 'dubbele' zin als hermeneutisch en semantisch probleem (247) p.97-115.

Structuur, woord, gebeurtenis (275) p.116-136.

Bijdrage van een reflexie over de taal tot de theologie van het woord (299) p.137-158.

Het bewuste en onbewuste (243) p.161-186.

De psychoanalyse in de hedendaaagse cultuur (227) p.187-234.

Het vaderschap, (309) p.235-269.

335. "L'institution vivante est-ce que nous en faisons" in <u>Les professeurs pour quoi faire?</u> (L'histoire immédiate) edited by M. Chapel and M. Manceaux, Paris, Seuil, 1970, p.127-142.

also as: "Les professeurs de droite à gauche. Les libéraux. M. Paul Ricoeur" in <u>L'express</u> 1970, no. 975, March 16-22, p.132, 137-138, 141, 143-144, 149, 151-152.

336. "Psychanalyse et culture" in <u>Critique sociologique et critique psychanalytique</u> (Études de sociologie de la littérature) Bruxelles, Éditions de l'Institut de Sociologie. Université Libre de Bruxelles, 1970, p.179-185, 185-191.

337. "Qu'est-ce qu'un texte? Expliquer et comprendre" in <u>Hermeneutik und Dialektik. Aufsatze II. Sprache und Logik.</u> Theorie der Auslegung und Probleme der Einzelwissenschaften, edited by P. Bubner, K. Cramer, and R. Wiehl, Tubingen, J.C.B. Mohr, 1970, p.181-200.

also as: "What is a Text? Explanation and Interpretation" in <u>Mythic-Symbolic Language and Philosophical Anthropology,</u> by D.M. Rasmussen, Le Haye, M. Nijhoff, 1971, p.135-150.

338. "Hope and Structure of Philosophical Systems" in <u>Proceedings of the American Catholic Association,</u> (San Francisco 1970, Philosophy and Christian Theology), edited by G.P. McLean and P. Dougherty, Washington, The Catholic University of America, 1970, p.55-59.

339. "Lettre de protestation contre le licenciement injuste de personnel au centre de Saclay" (co-signed by P. Ricoeur) in <u>Christianisme social</u> 78, 1970, no. 1-2, p.99-101.

340. "Lettre de J. Beaumont et de P. Ricoeur, présidents du christianisme social, dénonçant l'oppression politique au Brésil" in <u>Christianisme social</u> 78, 1970, no. 3-6, p.286-287.

341. "Vers une éthique de la finitude: quelques remarques" (on the article 'Le ver dans le fruit' by R. Simon) in <u>Christianisme social</u> 78, 1970, no. 7-8, p.393-395.

342. "André Philip" in <u>Christianisme social</u> 78, 1970, no. 9-10, p.563-566.

343. "Il faut espérer pour entreprendre" in <u>Jeunes femmes</u> (Une société pour tous: aujourd'hui, demain, comment? Congrès d'Orleans, mai 1970) 1970, no. 119-120, Sept.-Oct., p.19-26.

344. Ricoeur P., Blanquart P., Schwartz B., "Table ronde" (sur la société actuelle) in <u>Jeunes femmes</u>, 12970, no. 119-120, Sept.-Nov., p.37-47.

345. "Problèmes actuels de l'interprétation" (d'après Paul Ricoeur) in <u>Centre Protestant d'Études et de Documentation.</u> (Dossier "Nouvelles Théologies"), 1970, no. 148, March, p.51, 163-170, 182.

346. "Tendenze principali della vicerca in filosofia" (a conference of P. Ricoeur followed by a discussion with F. Battaglia, e.a.) in <u>Filosofia</u> 21, 1970, p.463-471, 479-508.

347. "Une mise au point du doyen Ricoeur" in <u>Le monde</u> 27, 1970, no. 7-78, Feb. 7, p.9.

348. "Déclaration de M. Ricoeur" in <u>Le monde</u> 27, 1970, no. 7815, Feb. 27, p.10 and no. 7816, Feb. 28, p.24.

partially reprinted in: <u>Le Figaro</u> 144, 1970, no. 7918, Feb.27, p.24.

349. "Un communiqué du doyen Ricoeur" in <u>Le monde</u> 27, 1970, no. 7819, March 4, p.9.

350. "Une lettre du doyen Ricoeur" in <u>Le Monde</u> 27, 1970, no. 7820, March 5, p.32, and no. 7821, March 6, p.10.

351. "M. Ricoeur: Les étudiants ont l'Université qu'ils méritent et l'Université mérite les étudiants qu'elle a" in <u>Le monde</u> 27, 1970, no. 7827, March 13, p.9.

partially reprinted as: "Le doyen Ricoeur dénonce la fuite de la majorité silencieuse devant ses responsabilités" in <u>La Croix</u> 90, 1970, no. 26518, March 13, p.5.

352. "La lettre de M. Ricoeur" in <u>Le monde</u> 27, no. 7830, March 18, p.16.

partially reprinted in <u>France-soir</u> 1970, March 18, p.7.

also in: <u>La croix</u> 90, no. 26522, p.5.

and in: <u>Le figaro</u> 144, 1970, no. 7933, March 18, p.12.

353. "Rencontre avec le doyen Paul Ricoeur. Universités nouvelles: un périlleux apprentissage" in <u>Réforme</u> 1970, no. 1320, Feb. 28, p.16.

354. Kwaad en bevrijding. Filosofie en theologie van de hoop. Hermeneutische artikelen. Introduced by A. Peperzak, Rotterdam, Lemniscaat, 1971, 194p.

contains the following articles:

Existentie en hermeneutiek (229) p.20-40.
Inleiding tot Bultmann (294) p.41-60.
Interpretatie van symbolen en wijsgerige reflectie I., (173) p.61-87.
De 'erfzonde' (164) p.88-106.
Interpretatie van symbolen en wijsgerige reflectie II., (191) p.107-125.
Demythisering van de aanklacht (232) p.126-145.
Interpretatie van de mythe van de straf (273) p.146-169.
Vrijheid in hoop. Filosofische benadering van het begrip godsdienstvrijheid (297) p.170-195.

355. "Langage (Philosophie)" in Encyclopaedia universalis IX, Paris, Encyclopaedia Universalis France, 1971, p.771-781.

356. "Liberté" in Encyclopaedia universalis IX, Paris, Encyclopaedia Universalis France, 1971, p.979-985.

357. "Mythe 3. L'interprétation philosophique" in Encyclopaedia universalis XI, Paris, Encyclopaedia Universalis France, 1971, p.530-537.

358. "Du conflit à la convergence des méthodes en exégèse biblique" in Exégèse et herméneutique (Parole de Dieu) Paris, Seuil, 1971, p.35-53.

359. "Sur l'exégèses de Genese 1,1 - 2,4," (a conference followed by a discussion with F. Bussini e.a.) in Exégèse et herméneutique (Parole de Dieu) Paris, Seuil, 1971, p.67-84, 85-96.

360. "Esquisse de conclusion" (of the Congress, 'Exégèse et herméneutique') in Exégèse et herméneutique (Parole de Dieu) Paris, Seuil, 1971, p.285-295.

361. "Le philosophe" in Bilan de la France 1945-1970 (Colloque de l'Association de la presse étrangère) Paris, Plon, 1971, p.47-59.

362. "Événement et sens dans le discours" in Ricoeur où la liberté selon l'espérance, by M. Philibert, Paris, Seghers, 1971, p.177-187.

also as: "Événement et sens" in Archivio di filosofia 41, 1971, no. 2, p.15-34.

and in: Révélation et histoire. La théologie de l'histoire (Actes du colloque international, Rome 1971) Paris, Aubier, 1971, p.15-34.

363. "Le conflit: signe de contradiction ou d'unité?" in Contradictions et conflits: naissance d'une société? (Semaines sociales de France, Rennes, 1971), Lyon, Chronique sociale de France, 1971, p.189-204.

also in: Chronique sociale de France 80, 1972, p.77-93.

364. "Préface" in André Philip par lui-même ou les voies de la liberté. Avant-propos by L. Philip, Paris, Aubier, 1971, p.27-34.

365. "Préface" in O. Reboul, Kant et le problème du mal, Montréal, Les Presses de l'Université de Montréal, 1971, p.IX-XVI.

366. "Forword" in D. Ihde, Hermeneutic Phenomenology. The Philosophy of Paul Ricoeur (Studies in Phenomenology and Existential Philosophy) Evanston, Northwestern University Press, 1971, p.XII-XVII.

367. "La foi soupçonnée" (a conference followed by a discussion with R. Garaudy and É. Borne) in Recherches et Débats (Foi et religion. Semaine des Intellectuels Catholiques 1971) 19, 1971, no. 71, p.64-75, 76-89.

368. "D'où vient l'ambiguité de la phénoménologie"? (discussion on a conference of A. Lowit) in Bulletin de la Société française de Philosophie 65, 1971, no. 2, April-June, p.55-68.

369. "Communiqué de comité directeur du mouvement du 'Christianisme social'" (on behalf of the hunger strikes against the penitentiary system in France) in Christianisme social 79, 1971, no. 1-2, p.66-67.

370. "The Model of the Text: Meaningful Action Considered as a Text" in Social Research 38, 1971, no. 3, p.529-562.

371. "From Existentialism to the Philosophy of Language" in Criterion 10, 1971, Spring, p.14-18.

also as: "A Philosophical Journey. From Existentialism to the Philosophy of Language" in Philosophy Today 17, 1973, no. 2-4, Summer p.88-96.

and in: The Philosophy of Paul Ricoeur (452) p.86-94.

372. "'Timoléon, réflexions sur la tyrannie', d'Amédée Ponceau" in Le monde 28, 1971, no. 8165, April 14, p.10.

373. "Sémantique de l'action" (a course taught at Louvain 1970-1971) Louvain, Université Catholique de Louvain-Cercle de Philosophie, 1971, p.1-148. (polycopy)

also as: La sémantique de l'action, prepared under the direction of Dorian Tiffeneau (Centre d'histoire des sciences et des doctrines.

Phénoménologie et herméneutique, I.) Paris, Ed. du Centre National de la Recherche Scientifique, 1977, 137p.

contains the following articles:

Le discours de l'action, p.1-20.
Le réseau conceptuel de l'action, p.21-63.
L'analyse propositionelle des énoncées d'action, p.65-84.
Phénoménologie et analyse linguistique, p.113-132.

374. "Cours sur l'herméneutique" Louvain, Institut Supérieur de Philosophie, 1971-1972, 288p. (mimeographed)

375. "The Problem of the Will and Philosophical Discourse" in Patterns of the Life-World, Essays in honor of John Wild, edited by J. Edie, F. Parker, and C.O. Schray, Evanston, Northwestern University Press, 1970, p.273-289.

376. "Discours et communication: La communication problèmatique" in La communication. Montréal, Editions Montmorency, 2, 1971, p.1-25.

also as: "Diskurs und Kommunikation" in Neue H. Philos II, 1977, p.1-25.

1972

377. "Ontologie" in Encyclopaedia universalis. XII, Paris, Encyclopaedia Universalis France, p.94-102.

378. "Signe et sens in Encyclopaedia Universalis. XII, Paris, Encyclopaedia Universalis France, 1972, p.1011-1015.

379. "Remarques sur la communication de Karl Lowith" in Truth and Historicity. Vérité et historicité (Entretiens de Heidelberg 1969) edited by H.-G. Gadamer, La Haye, M. Nijhoff, 1972, p.22-28.

380. "L'herméneutique du témoignage" in Archivio di filosofia 42, 1972, no. 1-2, p.35-61.

also in: Le témoignage (Actes du colloque international, Rome 1972) Parls, Aubier, 1972, p.35-61.

also as: "The Hermeneutics of Testimony" in Anglican Theological Revue 51, 1979, p.435-461.

381. "La métaphore et le problème central de l'herméneutique" in Revue philosophique de Louvain 70, 1972, Feb., p.93-112 (Resumé and Summary, p.115).

also as: "Metaphor and the Central Problem of Hermeneutics" translated by Jeff L. Close, in Philosophy Journal 3, 1973-1974, p.42-58.

and as: "Metaphor and the Main Problem of Hermeneutics" in New Literary History 6, 1974-75, p.95-110.

and in: The Philosophy of Paul Ricoeur (452) p.134-148.

382. "Les aspirations de la jeunesse" in La foi et le temps 2, 1972, no. 5, Sept.-Oct., p.539-554.

383. "Foi et philosophie aujourd'hui" in Foi-éducation 42, 1972, no. 100, July-Sept., p.1-12, 12-13.

384. "Sprachwissenschaftliche Analyse und Phänomenologie des Handeln" in Wissenschaft und Weltbild 25, 1972, no. 4, p.254-260.

1973

385. "Volonté" in Encyclopaedia Universalis XVI, Paris, Encyclopaedia Universalis, France, 1973, p.943-948.

386. "Herméneutique et critique des idéologies" in Archivio di filosofia 43, 1973, no. 2-4, p.25-61.

also in: Démythisation et idéologie (Actes du colloque international, Rome 1973) Paris, Aubier, 1973, p.25-61.

387. "Creativity in Language. Word. Polysemy. Metaphor" in Philosophy Today 17, 1973, no. 2-4, Summer, p.97-111.

also in: Language and Language Disturbances (the 5th Lexington Conference on Pure and Applied Phenomenology 1972) edited by Erwin W. Straus, Pittsburg, Duquesne University Press, 1974, p.49-71.

388. "The Task of Hermeneutics" in Philosophy Today 17, 1973, no. 2-4, Summer, p.112-128.

also in: Heidegger and Modern Philosophy (critical essays) edited by Michael Murray, New Haven, Yale University Press, 1978, p.141-160.

also as: "La tâche de l'herméneutique" in Exégèsis, Neuchâtel, Paris, 1975, p.179-200.

389. "The Hermeneutical Function of Distanciation" in Philosophy Today 17, 1973, no. 2-4, Summer, p.129-141.

also as: "La fonction herméneutique de la distanciation" in Exégèsis, Neuchâtel, Paris, 1975, p.201-215.

390. "Ethics and Culture. Habermas and Gadamer in Dialogue" in Philosophy Today 17, 1973, no. 2-4, Summer, p.166-175.

also in: Political and Social Essays (414) p.243-270.

391. "A Critique of B.F. Skinner's Beyond Freedom and Dignity" in Philosophy Today 17, 1973, no. 2-4, Summer, p.166-175.

also in: Political and Social Essays (414) p.46-67.

392. Marcel G. and Ricoeur P., Tragic Wisdom and Beyond, translated by St. Jolin and P. McCormick, Evanston, Illinois, Northwestern University Press, 1973, 256p.

393. Ricoeur P., and Levinas E., "In memoriam: H.L. van Breda" in Bulletin de la Société française de Philosophie 67, 1973, p.179-183, Paris, Armand Colin, p.149-187.

394. "Préface" in G.B. Madison, La phénoménologie de Merleau-Ponty, Klincksieck, Paris, Publications de l'Université de Paris X Nanterre, Lettres et sciences humaines, 1973, p.9-14.

395. "Le 'lieu' de la dialectique" in Dialectics/Dialectiques, International Institute of Philosophy, edited by Ch. Perelman, the Hague, Nijhoff, p.92-108.

1974

396. "Science et idéologie" in Revue Philosophique de Louvain 72, 1974, p.328-356.

also as: "Can There be a Scientific Concept of Ideology"? in Phenomenology and the Social Sciences: A Dialogue, edited by Joseph Bien, The Hague, Boston, London, Nijhoff, 1978, p.44-59.

397. "Philosophy and Religious Language" in Journal of Religion 54, 1974, p.71-85.

also as: "La philosophie et la specificité du langage réligieux" in Revue d'histoire et de philosophie religieuse 55, 1975, p.13-26.

398. "Phénoménologie et herméneutique" in Man and World 7, 1974, p.223-253.

also in Phänomenologie heute. Grundlagen-und Methodenprobleme. Redaktionelle Vorbemerkung, Freiburg, Verlag Karl Alber, 1975, p.31-75.

399. "Hegel aujourd'hui" in Études théologiques et religieuses 49, 1974, p.335-355.

400. "Stellung und Funktion der Metapher in der biblischer Sprache" in Metapher. Zur Hermeneutik religiöser Sprache, a Special Issue of Evangelische Theologie, edited by P. Ricoeur and E. Jüngel, Münster, Kaiser, 1974. (See nos 405 and 406).

401. "Recherches phénoménologiques sur l'imaginaire: Séminaire 1973-1974" Paris, Centre de Recherches Phénoménologiques 1974, p.1-8.

402. "L'itinéraire husserlien de la phénoménologie pure à la phénoménologie transcendentale, Exposé: Père Herman Leo van Breda" in In Memoriam H.L. van Breda, E. Levinas and P. Ricoeur, Paris, Armand Colin, 1974, p.149-187.

403. "Conclusions" in Vérité et vérification (Wahrheit und Verifikation) Actes du quatrième colloque international de phénoménologie, Schwabisch Hall, 1969, edited by H.L. van Breda, Den Haag, Martinus Nijhoff, 1974, p.190-209.

404. "Manifestation et proclamation" in Le Sacré. Études et recherches. Actes du colloque organisé par le centre international d'études humanistes et par l'institut d'études philosophiques de Rome, edited by E. Castelli, Paris, Aubier, 1974, p.57-76.

1975

405. "Le problème du fondement de la morale" in Sapienza 28, 1975, p.313-337.

and as: "The Problem of the Foundation of Moral Philosophy" (adapted and enlarged version) in Philosophy Today 22, 1978, p.175-192.

406. "Philosophical Hermeneutics and Theological Hermeneutics" in Studies in Religion/ Sciences Religieuses 5, 1975-1976, p.14-33.

also as: "Herméneutique philosophique et herméneutique biblique" in Exégèsis. Problèmes de méthode et exercices de lecture. Ed. F. Bovon and G. Rouiller, Neuchâtel, Paris, Delachaux et Niestlé, 1975, p.216-228.

407. "The Metaphorical Process" in Semeia 4, 1975, p.75-106.

408. "Puissance de la parole: science et poésie" in La philosophie et les savoirs (Coll: L'univers de la philosophie 4) Montréal, Bellarmin, 1975, p.159-177.

409. "Phenomenology of Freedom" in Phenomenology and Philosophical Understanding, edited by E. Pivevic, London, Cambridge University Press, 1975, p.173-194.

410. "Listening to the Parables of Jesus" in Criterion 13, 1974, p.18-22.

also in: The Philosophy of Paul Ricoeur (448) p.239-245.

and in: Christianity and Crisis 34, 1975, p.304-308.

411. "Biblical Hermeneutics" in Semeia 13, 1975, p.29-148.

also in Spanish.

412. "Phänomenologie des Wollens und Ordinary Language Approach". Authorized translation by Alexandre Métraus, in Die Münchener Phänomenologie. (Vorträge des Internationalen Kongresses in München 1971) edited by H. Kuhn, Eberhard Avé-Lallemant, und Reinhold Gladiator, Den Haag, Martinus Nijhoff, 1975, p.105-124.

413. "Objectivation et aliénation dans l'expérience historique" in Temporalité et aliénation. Actes du colloque organisé par centre international d'études humanistes et par l'institut d'études philosophiques de Rome, edited by Enrico Castelli, Paris Aubier-Montaigne, 1975, p.27-38.

also as: "Objektivierung und Entfremdung in der geschichtlichen Erfahrung" in Philosophisches Jahrbuch 84, 1977, p.1-12.

414. Political and Social Essays, collected and edited by David Stewart and Joseph Bien, Athens, Ohio University Press, 1975, 293p.

contains the following articles:

Nature and Freedom (183) p.23-45.
A critique of B.F. Skinner's Beyond Freedom and Dignity (390) p.46-67.
What does Humanism Mean? (95) p.68-87.
Violence and Language (276) p.88-101.
Ye are the Salt of the Earth (118) p.105-124.
Faith and Culture (115) p.125-133.
From Nation to Humanity: Tasks of Christians (236) p.134-159.
The Project of a Social Ethic (254) p.160-175.
Urbanization and Secularization (277) p.176-197.
Adventures of the State and Tasks of Christians (124) p.201-216.
From Marxism to Contemporary Communism (142) p.217-228.
Socialism Today (176) p.229-242.
Ethics and Culture. Habermas and Gadamer in Dialogue (390) p.243-270.
The Tasks of the Political Educator (234) p.271-293.

415. "Au Carrefour des cultures" in Les cultures et le temps. Studies prepared for Unesco, Payot, Paris, Unesco Press, 1975, p.19-41.

also in Spanish.

416. "Parole et symbole" in Le symbole (Coll. international, held from Feb. 4-8, 1974) edited by Jacques E. Menard, Strasbourg, Palais Universitaire, 1975, p.142-161.

also in: Revue des sciences religieuses 49, 1975, p.142-161.

417. La métaphore vive (L'ordre philosophie) Paris, Seuil, 1975, 414p.

also as: The Rule of Metaphor. Multidisciplinary Studies of the Creation of Meaning in Language, translated by Robert Czerny and Kathleen McLaughlin and John Costello, Toronto, University of Toronto Press, 1977, VIII-384p.

418. "Le Dieu Crucifié de Jurgen Moltmann" in Les quatres fleuves. Cahiers de recherches et de réflection religieuses (Le Christ visage de Dieu) 4, 1974, p.109-114.

1976

419. "Correspondance Paul Ricoeur, Peter Kemp" in Bulletin de la société française de philosophie 70, 1976, p.77-79.

420. "Gabriel Marcel et la phénoménologie" in Entretiens autour de Gabriel Marcel. Published with the co-operation of the Fondation Européene de la Culture, Neuchâtel, et de La Baconnière, 1976, p.53-72, (Discussion: p.20-52, 73-94, 103-114, 123-130, 139-148, 163-186, 202-210, 220-228).

also as: "Gabriel Marcel and phenomenology" in The Philosophy of Gabriel Marcel, by Paul A. Schilpp. Vol. XV of The Library of Living Philosophers, La Salle III, The Open Court Publishing Company, 1978, p.

421. Translation of E. Husserl, La crise de l'humanité européenne et la philosophie, Paris, Aubier Montaigne, 1976, 176p.

422. "History and Hermeneutics" in The Journal of Philosophy, tr. by D. Pellauer, 1976, p.683-695.

also in: Philosophy of History and Action (Papers presented at the First Jerusalem Philosophical Encounter, December 1975), edited by Yirmiahu Yovel, Dordrecht, Boston, London, D. Reidel, 1979.

423. Interpretation Theory: Discourse and the Surplus of Meaning. (Four essays comprising the centennial lectures delivered at Texas Christian University, Nov.27-30, 1973) Fort Worth, Texas, The Texas Christian University Press, 1976, 107p.

424. "L'imagination dans le discours et dans l'action" in Savoir, faire, espérer: les limites de la raison I-II volume, published on the occasion of the 50th anniversary of L'école des Sciences philosophiques et religieuses, and in honor of Mrg. Henri van Camp, Bruxelles (Publications des facultés universitaires Saint-Louis 5) Facultés universitaires Saint-Louis, 1976, p.207-228.

also as: "Ideology and Utopia as Cultural Imagination" in Philosophical Exchange 2, 1976, p.16-28.

and as "Imagination in Discourse and in Action" in Analecta Husserliana 7, 1978, p.3-22.

425. Gadamer H. Georg, Vérité et méthode. Les grandes lignes d'une herméneutique philosophique, translated from the second German edition by Étienne Sacré and Paul Ricoeur, Paris, Seuil, 1976, 346p.

426. "Entre Gabriel Marcel et Jean Wahl" in Jean Wahl et Gabriel Marcel, edited by J. Hersch, Paris, Beauchesne, 1976, p.58-59.

427. "Le 'Royaume' dans la parabole de Jésus" in Études théologiques et religieuses 51, 1976, p.15-20.

428. "Interview," in La philosophie d'aujourd'hui 84, (Bibliothèque Laffont des grands thèmes) R. Laffont, Paris, 1976, p.

429. "What is Dialectical," in Freedom and Morality by Richard B. Brandt and others, edited with an introduction by John Bricke, Lawrence, University of Kansas, 1976, p.173-189.

430. "L'herméneutique de la sécularisation: Foi, idéologie, utopie" in Archivio di filosofia 1976, p.49-68.

also in: L'herméneutique de la sécularisation. Actes du colloque organisé par le centre international d'études humanistes et par l'institut d'études philosophiques de Rome, Rome, Jan. 3-6, 1976, edited by Enrico Castelli, Paris, Aubier-Montaigne, 1976, p.49-68, 333-334.

and in: "Die Hermeneutik der Säkularisierung. Glaube, Ideologie, Utopie" in Kerygma und Mythos VI, 9, edited by Theunis F. Hamburg, Bengstedt, Evangelischer Verlag, 1977, p.33-46.

431. "Philosophical Hermeneutics and Theology" in Theology Digest, vol. 24, 1976, p.154-164.

432. "Préface" in A. Lacocque, Le livre de Daniel (Commentaire de l'ancien testament 15b) Neuchâtel, Delachaux et Niestlé, 1976, p.XVII-XXVI.

433. "Schleiermacher's Hermeneutics" in The Monist 60, 1977, p.181-197.

434. "Expliquer et comprendre" (Sur quelques connexions remarquables entre la théorie du texte, la théorie de l'action et la théorie de l'histoire) in Revue philosophique de Louvain 75, 1977, p.126-147.

also as: "Explanation and Understanding" in The Philosophy of Paul Ricoeur (448) p.149-166.

435. "Préface" in Jocelyn Dunphy, Paul Tillich et le symbole religieux, Paris, Jean-Pierre Delarge, Ed. Encyclopaedia universitaire, 1977, p.11-14.

436. "Nommer Dieu" in Études théologiques et religieuses 52, 1977, p.489-508.

437. "The Rule of Metaphor" in Philosophy Today 21, 1977, p.409-467.

438. "Herméneutique et l'idée de révélation" in La révélation, Bruxelles, Facultés universitaires Saint-Louis, 1977, p.15-54.

a condensed version in: "Toward a Hermeneutic of the Idea of Revelation" in Harvard Theological Review 70, 1977, p.1-38.

439. "Jan Patocka, Le philosophe-résistant" in Istina 22, 1977, p.128-131.

also in: Liberté religieuse et défense des droits de l'homme. Vol. II: En Tchecoslovaquie. Hommage à Jan Patocka, Paris, Centre d'études Istina, 1977, p.128-131.

440. "Préface" in Raphael Celis, L'oeuvre et l'imaginaire. Les origines de pouvoir-être créateur. Bruxelles, Facultés universitaires Saint-Louis, 1977, p.7-13.

441. "Foreword" in Stephen Strasser, Phenomenology of Feeling. An Essay on the Phenomena of the Heart, translated by Robert E. Wood, (Philosophical Series 34) Pittsburg, Duquesne University Press, 1977, p.XI-XIV.

442. "Ideologie und Ideologiekritik" in Phänomenologie und Marxismus, Bd. I: Konzept und Methoden, edited by Bernard Waldenfels, Jan M. Broekman and A. Pazanin; Foreword by B. Waldenfels, Frankfurt a. M. Suhrkamp Verlag, 1977, p.197-233.

443. "Foreword" in E. Husserl, Expositions and Appraisals, translated by Peter Pellauer, edited by F.A. Ellison and P. McCormick, Notre Dame, Ind., University of Notre Dame Press, 1977, p.IX-XI.

444. "The Question of Proof in Freud's Psychoanalytical Writings" in Journal of the American Psychoanalytical Association 24, International University Press, 1977, p.

also in: The Philosophy of Paul Ricoeur (448) p.184-210.

445. "Writing as a Problem for Literary Criticism and Philosophical Hermeneutics" in Philosophical Exchange 2, 1977, p.3-15.

446. "Toward a Theory of Narrative Discourse" The Brick Lectures, the University of Missouri, 1977. (mimeographed)

446a. "Phenomenology and the Social Sciences" (Conference: Phenomenology and the Liberal Arts) in: When is Phenomenology Sociological?, Ann. Phenomenol. Sociol. 2, 1977, p.145-159.

1978

447. "Culture, Truth and Hermeneutics" in America 138, Jan. 28, 1978, p.54-57.

448. "Response to Karl Rahner's Lecture: On the Incomprehensibility of God" in Celebrating the Medieval Heritage. A Special Supplement to the Journal of Religion, 1978, p.126-131.

449. "The Problem of the Foundation of Moral Philosophy" in Philosophy Today 22, 1978, p.175-192.

450. "The Metaphorical Process as Cognition, Imagination and Feeling" in Critical Inquiry 5, 1978, p.143-159.

451. "My Relation to the History of Philosophy" in The Iliff Review 35, 1978, p.5-12.

452. The Philosophy of Paul Ricoeur. An Anthology of His Work, edited by Charles E. Reagan and David Steward, Boston, Beacon Press, 1978, VIII-262p.

contains the following articles:

The Unity of the Voluntary and the Involuntary as a Limiting Idea (38) p.3-19.
The Antinomy of Human Reality and the Problem of Philosophical Anthropology (157) p.20-35.
The Hermeneutics of Symbols and the Philosophical Reflection (173) p.36-58.

Philosophy of Will and Action (264) p.61-74.
Existential Phenomenology (108) p.75-85.
From Existentialism to the Philosophy of Language (371) p.86-94.
Existence and Hermeneutics (229) p.97-108.
Structure, Word, Event (275) p.109-119.
Creativity in Language: Word, Polysemy Metaphor (387) p.120-133.
Metaphor and the Problem of Hermeneutics (381) p.134-148.
A Philosophical Interpretation of Freud (246) p.169-183.
The Question of Proof in Freud's Psychoanalytical Writings (444) p.184-210).
The Critique of Religion (219) p.213-222.
The Language of Faith (220) p.223-238.
Listening to the Parables of Jesus (410) p.239-245.

453. "The Narrative Function" in Semeia 13, 1978, p.177-202.

also as: "La fonction narrative" in Etudes théologiques et religieuses 54, 1979, p.209-230.

454. "Le 'Marx' de Michel Henry" in Esprit 22, Oct. 1978, p.124-139.

455. Knapp, V. and Ricoeur, P., Tendences principales de la recherche dans les sciences sociales et humaines. Vol. II, 2: Science juridique, philosophie, under the direction of Jacques Havet, Paris, The Hague, New York, Mouton; Paris, Unesco, 1978, XI, 868-1645.

Also as: Main Trends of Research in the Social and Human Sciences. Vol. II, part 2: Legal Science/Philosophy, preface by Amadou-Mahtar M'Bow, foreword by Jacques Havet, Paris, The Hague, New York, Mouton; Paris, Unesco, 1978, p.1071-1567.

456. "Imagination in Discourse and in Action" in Analecta Husserliana 7, 1978, p.3-22.

457. "Rückfrage und Reduktion der Idealitäten in Husserls 'Krisis' und Marx' 'Deutschen Ideologie'" in Phänomenologie und Marxismus. Vol. III: Sozialphilosophie (Suhrkamp Taschenbucher Wissenschaft, 232), edited by B. Waldenfels e.a., translation by B. Waldenfels, Frankfurt a.M., Suhrkamp, 1978, p.207-239.

458. "Philosophie et langage" in Rev. phil. France Etrang. 103, 1978, p.449-463.

459. "Introduction" in Honorat Agiesay e.a., Le temps et les philosophies, Presses the l'Unesco, 1978.

460. "Image and Language in Psychoanalysis" in Psychoanalysis and Language, edited by Joseph H. Smith, Gloria H. Parloff, and Katherine S. Henry, published under the auspices of the Forum on Psychiatry and the Humanities 3) New Haven, Conn., Yale University Press, 1978, p.293-324.

460a. Histoire et vérité, (Collection "Esprit": La condition humaine) 3e éd., Paris, Seuil, 1978, 363p.

1979

461. "The function of Fiction in Shaping Reality" in Man and World 12, 1979, p.123-141.

462. Main Trends in Philosophy, New York, London, Holmes and Meier Publishers, Inc., 1979, 469p. (a reprint of no. 455)

463. "Preface: Response to My Friends and Critics" in Studies in the Philosophy of Paul Ricoeur, Athens, Ohio, Ohio University Press, 1979, (11 pages, no pagination).

464. "La raison pratique" in Rationality Today/La rationalité aujourd'hui, Actes du colloque international sur "La rationalité aujour'hui" tenu à l'Université d'Ottawa du 27 au 30 octobre 1977, edited by Theodore F. Geraets, Ottawa, The University of Ottawa Press, 1979, p.225-241, 241-248.

465. "Hegel and Husserl on Intersubjectivity" in Reason, Action and Experience, translated by David Pellauer, edited by Helmut Kohlenberger, (Essays in Honour of Raymond Klibansky) Hamburg, Meiner, 1979, p.13-29.

466. "Foreword" in A. Larocque, The Book of Daniel, translated by D. Pellauer, London, S.P.C.K.; Atlanta, J. Knox Press, 1979, p.XVII-XXVI.

467. "The 'Sacred Text' and the Community" in The Critical Study of Sacred Texts, edited by W.D. O'Flaherty (Berkely Religious Studies Series), Berkely, Graduate Theological Union, 1979, p.271-276.

468. "Conclusion Arezzo" in The Teleologies in Husserlian Phenomenology. The Irreducible Element in Man. III: "Telos" as the pivotal factor of contextual phenomenology. Papers read at the VIth International Phenomenological Conference, University of Arezzo/Siena, July 1-6, 1976. Edited by Anna-Teresa Tymieniecka Anal. Husserl., 1976, Vol. 9) Dordrecht, Boston, London, D. Reidel, 1979, p.415-426.

469. "Narrative Time" (Unpublished lecture, given at the University of Chicago, 1979) 39p. (mimeographed).

470. "The Logic of Jesus: the Logic of God" in <u>Anglican Theological Review</u> 62, 1980, p.37-41.

471. "La logique de Jésus" in <u>Études théologiques et religieuses</u> 55, 1980, p.420-425.

472. <u>The French Historiographical Tradition</u>, London, Toronto, Oxford Press, 1980, 65p.

473. "La critique de l'événement dans l'historiographie contemporaine" (Lecture given at the International Bilingual Conference 'Philosophie de l'histoire et practique historienne d'aujourd'hui' held at the University of Ottawa, April 18-20, 1980.

474. "La fonction narrative et l'expérience humaine du temps" in <u>Archivio de filosofia</u> (Esistenze mito ermeneutica), Vol. I, Padua, Cedam, 1980, p.343-369.

Also as: "The Human Experience of Time and Narrative" in: <u>Studies in Phenomenology and the Human Sciences.</u> Edited with an Introduction by John Sallis, <u>Res. Phenomenol.</u>, 9, 1979, p.17-34.

475. "Herméneutique et sémiotique" in "Supplement" of the <u>Bulletin de Centre Protestant d'Études et de Documentation</u>, no. 255, Nov. 1980, p.I-XIII.

476. "A Response" in <u>Biblical Research</u> 24-24, 1979-1980, p.70-80.

477. "Prefazione" in Giuseppe Grampa, <u>Ideologia e poetica. Marxismo e ermeneutica par il languaggio religioso</u> (Scienze filosofiche, 25) Milano, Vita e Pensiero, 1980.

478. "Note introductive" in <u>Heidegger et la question de Dieu</u> with articles by J. Beaufret, F. Fédier, E. Levinas, J.-L. Marion e.a. Edited by Richard Kearney and Joseph O'Leary (Figures), Paris, B. Grasset, 1980, p.17.

479. "L'originaire de la question-en-retour dans le <u>Krisis</u> de Husserl" in <u>Textes pour E. Levinas</u>, Edited by François Laruelle (Collection Surfaces, 2) Paris, Éditions Jean-Michel Place, 1980, p.167-177.

480. "Reply to Lewis S. Mudge" in <u>Essays on Biblical Interpretation.</u> Edited with an introduction by Lewis S. Mudge, Philadelphia, Fortress Press, 1980, p.41-45.

481. <u>Essays on Biblical Interpretation.</u> Edited with an introduction by Lewis S. Mudge, Philadelphia, Fortress Press, 1980, ix-182p.

contains the following articles:

Preface to Bultmann (294) p.49-72.
Toward a Hermeneutic of the Idea of Revelation (438) p.73-118.
The Hermeneutics of Testimony (380) p.119-154.
Freedom in the Light of Hope (297) p.155-182.

1981

482. "A Response by Paul Ricoeur" in <u>Hermeneutics and the Human Sciences.</u> Edited and translated by J.B. Thompson, Cambridge, London, New York, New Rochelle, Melbourne, Sydney, Cambridge University Press, Paris, Éditions de la Maison des Sciences de l'homme, 1980, p.32-40.

483. <u>Hermeneutics and the Human Sciences.</u> Edited and translated by J.B.
Sydney,
Cambridge University Press, Paris, Éditions de la Maison des Sciences de l'Homme, 1981, viii-314p.

Contains the following articles:

The Task of Hermeneutics (388) p.43-62.
Hermeneutics and the Critique of Ideology (386) p.63-100.
Phenomenology and Hermeneutics (398) p.101-130.
The Hermeneutical Function of Distanciation (389) p.131-144.
What is a Text? Explanation and Understanding (337) p.145-164.
Metaphor and the Central Problem of Hermeneutics (381) p.165-181.
Appropriation p.182-196.
The Model of the Text: Meaningful Action Considered as a Text (370) p.197-221.
Science and Ideology (396) p.22-246.
The Question of Proof in Freud's Psychoanalytic Writings (444) p.247-273.
The Narrative Function (453) p.274-296.

B. Other texts.*

Alexandre, J. "Notes sur l'esprit des paraboles en réponse à P. Ricoeur" in Études théologiques et religieuses 51, 1976, p.367-372.

Austin, An Essay in the Philosophy of Language, Cambridge, Cambridge University Press, 1969.

Bachelard, G. La poétique de l'espace, Paris, P.U.F., 1957.

---------- La poétique de la rêverie, Paris, P.U.F., 1960.

Barthes, R. "Introduction à l'analyse structurale des récits" in Communications 8, 1966, p.1-27.

---------- "L'analyse structurale du récit. À propos d'Actes X-XI" in Recherches de sciences religieuses 58, 1970, p.17-37.

Beardsley, M. Aesthetics, New York, Harcourt, Brace and World, 1958.

Beardsley, W. Literary Criticism of the New Testament, Philadelphia, Fortress Press, 1970.

---------- "Uses of the Proverbs in the Synoptic Gospels" in Interpretation 24, 1970, p.61-76.

Benveniste, E. Problèmes de linguistique générale, Paris, Gallimard, 1966.

---------- "La forme et le sens dans le langage" in Le langage II, Actes des xiiie Congrès des Sociétés de Philosophie de Langue Française, Neuchâtel, Baconnière, 1967, p.29-40.

Bergeron, R. La vocation de la liberté dans la philosophie de Paul Ricoeur, Montréal, Les éditions Bellarmin, Freiburg, Éditions universitaires, 1974.

Berggren, D. "The Use and Abuse of Metaphor" in Rev. of Metaphysics 16, 1962-1963, p.227-258.

Black, M. "Metaphor" in Models and Metaphors, Ithica, Cornell University Press, 1962.

---------- "Models and Archetypes" Idem p.219-243.

---

* This bibliography contains only those titles which have been quoted in the text and in the footnotes or which have otherwise been consulted.

Bollnow, O. "Paul Ricoeur und die Probleme der Hermeneutik" in Z. philos.Forsch. 30, 1976, p.167-189 and p.389-412.

Bouchard, G. "Sémiologie, sémantique et herméneutique selon Paul Ricoeur" in Laval théol.philos. 36, 1980, p.255-284.

Bourgeois, P. Extension of Ricoeur's Hermeneutic, The Hague, Nijhoff, 1975.

---------- "Paul Ricoeur's Hermeneutical Phenomenology" in Phil. Today 16, 1972, p.20-27.

---------- "From Hermeneutics of Symbols to the Interpretation of Texts" in Studies in the Philosophy of Paul Ricoeur, ed. Charles E. Reagan, Athens, Ohio University Press, 1979, p.84-95.

---------- "Hermeneutics of Symbols and Philosophical Reflection: Paul Ricoeur" in Phil. Today 15, 1971, p.232-235.

Braunsweiger, H. "Auf dem Weg zu einer poetischen Homiletik. Einige Aspekte der Hermeneutik Ricoeurs als Impuls für die Homiletik" in Ev. Th. 39, 1979, p.127-143.

Brémont, Cl. "Le message narratif" in Communications 4, 1964, p.4-32.

---------- "La logique des possibles narratifs" in Communications 8, 1966, p.69-76.

Charles, D. "Dire, entendre, parler. L'herméneutique et le langage selon P. Ricoeur" in Algemeen Nederlands Tijdschrift voor Wijsbegeerte 68, 1976, p.74-98.

Cipollone, A. "Religious Language and Ricoeur's Theory of Metaphor" in Phil. Today 21, 1977, p.458-467.

---------- "Symbol in the Philosophy of Paul Ricoeur" in The New Scholasticism 52, 1978, p.149-167.

Crossan, D. In Parables, New York, Harper and Row, 1973.

---------- "Paradox Gives Rise to Metaphor: Paul Ricoeur's Hermeneutics and the Parables of Jesus" in Biblical Research 24-25, 1979-1980, p.38-69.

Dagognet, F. Écriture et Iconographie, Paris, Vrin, 1973.

Depoortere, Chr. "Mal et libération. Une étude de l'oeuvre de Paul Ricoeur" in Studia Moralia 14, 1976, p.337-385.

Derrida, J. "Mythologie blanche (La métaphore dans le texte philosophique)" in Poétique 5, 1971, p.1-52.

---------- La voix et le phénomène, Paris, Presses Universitaires de France, 1967.

---------- L'écriture et la différence, Paris, Seuil, 1967.

---------- De la grammatologie, Paris, Ed. de minuit, 1967.

Dornisch, L. "Symbolic Systems and the Interpretation of Scripture: An Introduction to the Work of Paul Ricoeur" in Semeia 4, 1975, p.1-19.

Dumas, A. "Savoir objectif, croyance projective, foi interpellée" in Sens et existence; en hommage à Paul Ricoeur G. Madison (ed), Paris, Seuil, 1975, p.160-169.

Eliade, M. Le mythe de l'éternel retour, Paris, 1943.

---------- Traité d'histoire des religions, Paris, 1949.

---------- Aspects du mythe, Paris, 1963.

---------- La nostalgie des origines. Méthodologie et histoire des religions, Paris, 1971.

Frege, G. "Über Sinn und Bedeutung" in Zeitschrift fur Philosophie und philosophische Kritik 100, 1892.

Gadamer, H. G. Wahrheit und Methode, Tübingen, J.C.B. Mohr, 1960.

---------- Kleine Schriften, Tübingen, J.C.B. Mohr, 1967.

---------- "Rhetorik, Hermeneutik und Ideologiekritik, Metakritische Erörterungen zu 'Wahrheit und Methode'" in Hermeneutik und Ideologiekritik, Frankfurt a.M., Suhrkamp Verlag (Theorie-Diskussion), 1971, p.57-82.

Gallie, W.D. Philosophy and Historical Understanding, New York, Schocken, 1964.

Geerts, A. "Het fundament van de ethiek en de opbouw van de ethische intentie volgens Paul Ricoeur" in Tijdschr. Filos 40, 1978, p.270-305.

Gerhart, M. "La métaphore vive" in Religious Studies Review 2, 1976, p.23-30.

---------- "Imagination and History in Ricoeur's Interpretation Theory" in Phil. Today 23, 1979, p.51-68.

---------- "Paul Ricoeur's Notion of 'Diagnostic': Its Function in Literary Interpretation" in Journal of Religion 56, 1976, p.137-156.

---------- "Paul Ricoeur's Hermeneutical Theory as Resource for Theological Reflection" in The Thomist 39, 1975, p.496-527.

---------- The Question of Belief in Literary Criticism. An Introduction to the Hermeneutical Theory of Paul Ricoeur (Stuttgarter Arbeiten zur Germanistik, 54) Stuttgart, Heinz, 1979, 408p.

Gisel, P. "Paul Ricoeur" in Etudes théologiques et religieuses 49, 1974, p.31-50.

Goodman, N. An Approach to a Theory of Symbols, Indianapolis, The Bobbs-Merrill Co., 1968.

Granger, G.-G. Essai d'une philosophie de style, Paris, A. Colin, 1968.

Greimas, A-J. Sémantique structurale, Paris, Larousse, 1966.

Greisch, J. "Bulletin de philosophie. La tradition herméneutique aujourd'hui: H.G. Gadamer, P. Ricoeur, G. Steiner" in Rev. Sc. ph. th. 61, 1977, p.296.

Habermas, J. Erkenntnis und Interesse, Frankfurt a.M., Suhrkamp Verlag, 1968.

---------- "Erkenntnis und Interesse" in Technik und Wissenschaft als Ideologie, Frankfurt a.M., Suhrkamp Verlag, 1969, p.146-167.

---------- "Zu Gadamers 'Wahrheit und Methode" in Hermeneutik und Ideologiekritik, Frankfurt a.M., Suhrkamp Verlag (Theorie-Diskussion), 1971, p.45-56.

---------- "Der Universalitätsanspruch der Hermeneutik" in Idem., p.120-159.

Heering, H.J. "Paul Ricoeur als Godsdienstwijsgeer" in Nederl. Theol. Tijdschr. 25, 1971, p.437-453.

Heidegger, M. Sein und Zeit, Tübingen, Max Niemayer Verlag, 1926.

Hempel, K. "The Function of General Laws in History" in Aspects of Scientific Explanation and Other Essays in the Philosophy of Science, New York, Free Press, 1965 (1942), p.231-245.

Hegel, G. Philosophie des Rechts, Stuttgard-Bad Cannstatt, Fremman-Holzboog, 1974.

---------- Phänomenologie des Geistes, (Ed. by Eva Moldenhauer and Karl Markus Michel) Frankfurt a.M., Suhrkamp, 1970.

Henle, P. "Metaphor" in Language, Thought and Culture, Ann Arbor, University of Michigan Press, 1958.

Hesse, M. "The Explanatory Function of Metaphor" in Logic, Methodology and Philosophy of Science, ed. by Bar-Hiddel, Amsterdam, North Holland Publ. Co., 1965.

Hester, M. The Meaning of Poetic Metaphor, The Hague, Mouton, 1967.

Husserl, E. I Die Idee der Phänomenologie: funf Vorlesungen Ed. and introduced by Walter Biemel, 2nd ed., The Hague, M. Nyhoff, 1958.

---------- Cartesianische Meditationen und pariser Vorträge, 2nd ed., The Hague, M. Nijhoff, 1963.

---------- Logische Untersuchungen ed. by E. Holenstein, The Hague, M. Nijhoff, 1975.

Ihde, D. Hermeneutic Phenomenology. The Philosophy of Paul Ricoeur, Evanston, Northwestern University Press, 1971.

Jakobson, R. "Two Aspects of Language and Two Types of Aphasic Disturbances" in Fundamentals of Language, The Hague, 1956.

---------- Essais de linguistique générale, Paris, Ed. de Minuit, 1963.

Kemp, P. "Phänomenologie und Hermeneutik in der Philosophie Paul Ricoeurs" in Z. Theol. Kirche 67, 1970, p.335-347.

Kirkland, F. "Gadamer and Ricoeur. The Paradigm of the Text." in Graduate Faculty Philosophy Journal 6, 1977, p.131-144.

King, E., Interpretation of Pastoral Experience. A Study in Hermeneutical Theory and Practice, Unpublished Dissertation defended at the University of Notre Dame, November 1980), Notre Dame, Department of Theology, 1980.

Ladrière, J. "Discours théologique et symbole" Rev. Sc. relig. 49, 1975, p.116-141.

Lacroix, J. "Un philosophe du sens: P. Ricoeur" In Panorama de la philosophie française contemporaine, Paris, Presses Universitaires de France, 1966.

Laplanche, J. "Interpréter (avec) Freud" in L'Arc 34, 1968, p.37-46.

Lavers, A. "Man, Meaning and Subject. A Current Reappraisal" in J. Brit. Soc. Phenomenol. 1, 1970, p.44-49.

Lapointe, F. "A Bibliography on Paul Ricoeur" in Phil. Today 16, 1972, p.28-33; 17, 1973, p.176-182.

---------- "Paul Ricoeur and His Critics: A Bibliographical Essay" in Studies in the Philosophy of Paul Ricoeur, Athens, Ohio University Press, 1979, p.164-177.

Lévi-Strauss, Cl. Anthropologie structurale, Paris, Plon, 1963. (Structural Anthropology, New York, Doubleday, 1969.)

---------- La pensée sauvage, Paris, Plon, 1963.

Lowe, W. Mystery and the Unconscious. A Study in the Thought of Paul Ricoeur, Metuchen N.J., The Sacrecrow Press and the American Theological Library Association, 1977.

Mainburger, G., "Die Freiheit und das Böse" in Freib. A. Philos. Theol. 19, 1972, p.410-430.

Mannheim, K. Ideology and Utopia; an introduction to the Sociology of Knowledge. Pref. by Louis Wirth, London, K. Paul, Trench, Trubner, 1936.

Marcel, G. Journal métaphysique in Être et avoir, Paris, Aubier, (c. 1935), p.7-222.

---------- Le monde cassé, Paris, Desclée de Brouwer, 1933.

Merleau-Ponty, M. Le visible et l'invisible, Paris, Gallimard, 1963.

---------- Signes, Paris, Gallimard, 1960.

---------- L'oeil et l'esprit, Paris, Gallimard, 1964.

Mink, L.O. "Interpretation and Narrative Understanding" in The Journal of Philosophy 69, 1972, p.735-737.

Moltmann, J. Theologie des Hoffnung, München, Chr. Kaiser Verlag, 1965.

Mudge, L.S. "Paul Ricoeur on Biblical Interpretation" in Biblical Research, 24-25, 1979-1980, p.38-69.

Nabert, J. L'expérience intérieure de la liberté, Paris, P.U.F., 1924.

---------- Éléments pour une éthique, Paris, P.U.F., 1943.

---------- Essai sur le mal, Paris, P.U.F. (Collection Épiméthée), 1955.

---------- Le désir de Dieu, Paris, Aubier, 1966.

Nkeramihigo, Th. "La problématique de la transcendence chez Ricoeur" in Rev. Africaine de Théologie 5, 1981, p.7-18.

Otto, R. Das Heilige; über das Irrationale in der Idee des Göttlichen und sein Verhältnis zum Rationalen, München, C.H. Beck, 1917.

Pannenberg, W. "Hermeneutik und Universalgeschichte" in Grundfragen systematischer Theologie, Göttingen, VandenHoeck und Ruprecht, 1967, p.91-121.

Pellauer, D. "The Significance of the Text in Paul Ricoeur's Hermeneutical Theory" in Studies in the Philosophy of Paul Ricoeur, Charles E. Reagan (ed.), Athens, Ohio University Press, 1979, p.98-114.

Perelman, C. and L. Olbrechts-Typeca, Traité de l'argumentation, Paris, 1958.

Perin, N. "The Parables of Jesus as Parables and Metaphors, and as Aesthetic Objects: A Review Article in The Journal of Religion 47, 1967, p.340-347.

Philibert, M. Paul Ricoeur ou la liberté selon l'espérance. Présentation, choix de textes. (Philosophes de tous les temps, 72) Paris, Sehers, 1971.

Piscitelli, E. "Paul Ricoeur's Philosophy of Religious Symbol. A Critique and Dialectical Transposition" in Ult. Real.Mean. 3, 1980, p.275-313.

Propp, Vl. Morphology of the Folktale, Austin, University of Texas Press, second rev. ed., 1968.

Rad, G. von Theologie des Alten Testaments, Munchen, Chr. Kaiser Verlag, 1960, 2 Vol.

Ramsey, I. Christian Discourse; Some Logical Explorations, London, Oxford University Press, 1965.

Rasmussen, D. Mythic-Symbolic Language and Philosophical Anthropology. A Constructive Interpretation of the Thought of Paul Ricoeur. The Hague, Nijhoff, 1971.

Reagan, Ch. (ed.) Studies in the Philosophy of Paul Ricoeur, Athens, Ohio University Press, 1979.

Robert, M. "Remarque sur l'exégèse de Freud" in Les Temps Modernes 20, 1965, p.664-681.

Richards, I.A. The Philosophy of Rhetoric, London, Oxford University Press, 1936 (1971).

Russell, B. Principia mathematica, London, Allen and Unwin, 1964.

Saussure, F. de Cours de linguistique générale, Paris, Payot, 1971 (1916).

Schaldenbrand, M. "Metaphoric Imagination: Kinship Through Conflict" in Studies in the Philosophy of Paul Ricoeur, Athens, Ohio University Press, 1979, p.57-81.

Schillebeeckx, E., "Le philosophe Paul Ricoeur, docteur en théologie" in Christianisme Social 76, 1968, p.639-645.

Scholes, R.E. and R. Kellogg The Nature of Narrative, New York, Oxford University Press, 1966.

Searle, J. Speech-Acts. An Essay in the Philosophy of Language, London, 1958.

Seeburger, F. "Ricoeur on Heidegger" in The Iliff Review 35, 1978, p.49-57.

Skousgaard, St. Language and the Existence of Freedom. A Study in Paul Ricoeur's Philosophy of Will. Washington, D.C., University Press of America, 1979.

Smitherans, V. "Man, Mediation and Conflict in Ricoeur's Fallible Man" Phil. Today 25, 1981, p.357-369.

Spiegelberg, H. The Phenomenological Movement, The Hague, Martinus Nijhoff, 1960, Vol. II, p.563-579.

Strawson, P.F. "On Referring" in Mind 59, 1950.

Individuals; An Essay in Descriptive Metaphysics, London, Methuen, 1959.

Tort, M. "De l'interprétation ou la machine herméneutique" in Les Temps Modernes 21, 1966, p.1461-1493 and p.1629-1652.

Turbayne, C. The Myth of Metaphor, New Haven, Yale University Press, 1962.

Ullmann, St. The Principle of Semantics, Glasgow, Glasgow University Publication,

--------- Précis de sémantique française, Berne, A. Francke, 1952.

--------- Semantics. An Introduction to the Science of Meaning. Oxford, Blackwell, 1962 (1967).

Vansina, D. "Schets, orientatie en betekenis van Paul Ricoeurs wijsgerige onderneming" in Tijdschr. Filos. 25, 1963, p.109-178 (Summary p.178-182).

--------- "Het heil in de filosofie van Paul Ricoeur" in Bijdragen 27, 1966, p.484-510.

--------- "Bibliographie de Paul Ricoeur" in Rev. Phil. de Louvain 60, 1962, p.394-414; 66, 1968, p.85-101; 72, 1974, p.156-181.

Vincent, G. "'La métaphore vive' de P. Ricoeur" in Rev. Hist. Philos. relig. 56, 1976, p.567-582.

Vuillemin, J. De la force du langage à la théologie. Cinq études sur Aristote, Paris, Flammarion, 1967.

Waelens, A. de "La force du langage et le langage de la force" in Revue philosophique de Louvain 63, 1965, p.591-612.

Weber, M. Politik als Beruf: "Éthique et politique" in Esprit 27, 1959, p.225-230.

Wells, H. "Theology and Christian Philosophy: Their Relation in the Thought of Paul Ricoeur" in Studies in Religion/Sciences religieuses 5, 1976, p.45-62.

Wheelwright, Ph. The Burning Fountain, Bloomington, Indiana University Press, 1968, rev.ed.

---------- Metaphor and Reality, Bloomington, Indiana University Press, 1962, 1968.

Wilder, A. The Language of the Gospel, New York, Harper and Row, 1964.

Wimsatt, W.K. and M. Beardsley, The Verbal Icon, Lexington, University of Kentucky Press, 1954.

Wittgenstein, L. Tractatus logico-philosophicus, 2nd ed. Tr. by C.K. Ogden, introd. by B. Russell, London, Kegan Paul, Trench Trubner & Co., 1933.

---------- Philosophical Investigations, New York, MacMillan, 1953.

Author Index.

331

The author: John Van Den Hengel S.C.J. is assistant professor of systematic theology at St. Paul University in Ottawa, Ontario. He obtained his Doctorandus degree in theology at the Katholieke Universiteit of Nijmegen in 1969 as a member of the "Werkgroep Gezag" with a thesis entitled, In diskussie met G.E. Lessing. Het conflict van de menselijke autonomie en het religieuze gezag.